WEST OF EDEN

WEST OF EDEN
Essays on Canadian
Prairie Literature

Sue Sorensen, editor

CMU Press
Winnipeg, Manitoba
2008

West of Eden : essays on
Canadian Prairie writing
2008.

2009 03 05

CMU Press
500 Shaftesbury Blvd.
Winnipeg, Manitoba R3P 2N2

CMU Press is an academic publisher of scholarly, reference, and general
interest books at Canadian Mennonite University. Books from CMU Press
address and inform interests and issues vital to the university, its constituency,
and society. Areas of specialization include Mennonite studies, and works that
are church-oriented or theologically engaged.
For more information about CMU Press contact cmupress@cmu.ca
or tel. 204.487.3300 or visit www.cmu.ca/publications.

Design and layout: Karen Allen and Tammy Sawatzky
Index: T.S. Christianson
Cover painting: *Speedway Service* by David Thauberger
Photograph by Kathleen Brady
With thanks to Nouveau Gallery, Regina, Saskatchewan

Library and Archives Canada Cataloguing in Publication

West of Eden : essays on Canadian Prairie literature / edited by Sue Sorensen.
Includes bibliographical references and index.

ISBN 978-0-920718-81-0

1. Canadian literature (English)--Prairie Provinces--History and criticism.
2. Prairie Provinces in literature. I. Sorensen, Sue
PS8131.P7W48 2008   C810.9'9712   C2008-905927-1

Printed in Canada by
Friesens Corporation, Altona, Manitoba

— • —

Dedicated to Robert Kroetsch,
such a good companion to be alongside
during the writing of the prairies
that if you had not existed
we would have had to invent you.

— • —

Contents

Cultural Studies "But I was going to tell you a story, and perhaps I am telling you a story"

Teaching The Prairies "Now we're getting somewhere"

Note:
The maxim-like proclamations for each section are all quotations from Robert Kroetsch, as follows:
"The moment of the discovery of the prairies continues" adapts the title "The Moment of the Discovery of America Continues," an essay in *The Lovely Treachery of Words*. "Not bad for / a start" is from "Sonnet #1" in *Sounding the Name*, found in *Completed Field Notes*. "We must take care of our stories" is from "The Winnipeg Zoo," a poem in *Completed Field Notes*. "But I was going to tell you a story, and perhaps I am telling you a story" is from "The Cow in the Quicksand and How I(t) Got Out: Responding to Stegner's *Wolf Willow*," an essay in *A Likely Story: The Writing Life*. "Now we're getting somewhere" is from "Don't Give Me No More of Your Lip; or, the Prairie Horizon as Allowed Mouth," an essay in *Toward Defining the Prairies*, ed. Robert Wardhaugh.

Acknowledgements

―――――――― • ――――――――

M y thanks first of all to the authors of these essays, who were a pleasure to work with, and to all the prairie writers, past and present, who made our endeavours possible.

A grant from the Faculty Research Fund of Canadian Mennonite University supported some of this work. Two of these essays were previously published. Pamela Banting's "Deconstructing the Politics of Location" appeared in an earlier version in *The International Journal of Canadian Studies*. Alison Calder's "Why Shoot the Gopher" appeared in a slightly different form in *The American Review of Canadian Studies*.

Thanks to Warren Cariou, who agreed to let his address "Occasions for Feathers, Or, The Invention of Prairie Literature" stand as the Foreword to this collection. This presentation was first made at St. John's College, University of Manitoba on 22 February 2007, at a panel (with Dennis Cooley and Robert Kroetsch) entitled *The Invention of Prairie Literature*.

I am grateful to Karen Allen and Tammy Sawatzky, who were involved with all aspects of design and production, inside and out, and to Harry Huebner, chair of CMU Press and stalwart colleague. My affectionate thanks to all the students, faculty, and staff of Canadian Mennonite University, who are a joy to work with. Thanks also to Jonathan Dyck, Sandra Sorensen, Paul Dyck, and Michael Kurtz, who offered helpful comments on my own writing. Loving thanks to my mother, Phyllis Sorensen, who instilled in me a love of literature. And a huge thank you to my extraordinary research assistant, Stephan Christianson, for his intelligence and companionship.

Finally, warm thanks to someone not directly involved in the project, but who became a kind of guide to Stephan and myself, although he never knew it. Prairie literature would be nothing like it is without the great poet, novelist, teacher, and critic Robert Kroetsch, and we are so happy you are who you are.

Sue Sorensen, Winnipeg, September 2008

Introduction

Sue Sorensen

•

West of Eden

The fear of

      paradise

haunts all our
dreams.

I'm sorry,
I said, I thought

I wanted
      (you)

to be happy.

Robert Kroetsch, "After Paradise"

A bout Eden there is too much to say. It was a place of perfect and innocent fertility, of naming, of close communion with the creator. Then it became a place of temptation and fallibility, of dangerous but surely necessary knowledge, of desire. It was a place where woman and man were punished so differently for disobedience. For centuries, humans have been perversely proud of the Fall—well, we say, we are what we are—and have simultaneously, contrarily longed for the perfection of the garden now denied to us. The whole complex of ideas was more or less established by 1667, when Milton finished *Paradise Lost*. Adam's "amorous intent well understood / Of Eve, whose Eye darted contagious Fire" leads them to a new kind of delectation after the couple has eaten the forbidden Fruit:

Flow'rs were the Couch,
Pansies, and Violets, and Asphodel,
And Hyacinth, Earth's freshest softest lap.
There they their fill of Love and Love's disport
Took largely (9.1035-1943)

The lust, the sensual beauties of creation, and the irresistible mistake: they are all there. Many have never regretted Eve's curiosity and Adam's willingness to trespass, and indeed have celebrated it. As Robert Pogue Harrison says in his recent study *Gardens: An Essay on the Human Condition*:

> Eve's transgression was the first true instance of human action, properly understood. It was in itself already an act of motherhood, for through it she gave birth to the mortal human self, which realizes its potential in the unfolding of time, be it through work, procreation, art, or the contemplation of things divine. (15)

Is it true that Eden was no place for us, that Eden did not require human ingenuity? Are we better off west of Eden?

What does it mean to be "west of Eden"? I first came across the phrase in Dennis Cooley's 2006 book *The Bentleys*, a long poem improvising on Sinclair Ross's influential prairie novel *As For Me and My House*. Early in the book, playfully recasting Ross's mostly-grim novel as an entertaining melodrama, Cooley lays out the playbill of:

WIND AND HORSES

a puritan tale of romance and intrigue

set in the dirty thirties

a stirring drama that dares
to ask the question
can a woman find happiness
as the wife of a small-town minister
as keeper of journal & lover
in:

> full black & white
> full view
> full frontal (3)

After listing the *dramatis personae* (including "Philip: torn between wish and refusal," "Judith: pale figure, a voice like the wind," and Cooley himself), Cooley adds a note at the bottom of the page: "copyright by Sinclair Ross / West of Eden Productions / 1947." Reading this, I could see "West of Eden" in my mind's eye. A place not Eden, but nearby. A place here on the prairies.

In the book of Genesis there are two references to "east of Eden." In the first, it is reported that when God drives Adam and Eve out of the garden for overreaching themselves, "at the east of the garden of Eden he placed the cherubim, and a sword flaming and turning to guard the way to the tree of life" (3:24). In the next chapter, Cain, after murdering his brother Abel, is likewise banished, this time to the land of Nod "east of Eden" (4:16). In each case, "east of Eden" would seem to signify a place for those who disappoint God. They are not utterly cast away from God—it is clear that God continues to care for Adam and Eve, and for Cain, despite their disobedience. But still, it must be preferable to be west of Eden, a Biblically undocumented location we are free to imagine.

To be west of Eden is to be in a space both apart from the main action and yet inherently attached to it. It is somewhat apart from wickedness, but still not far from it. After all, those banished to the east of the garden are close relations. To be west of Eden is certainly not ideal: it is not the garden itself. It cannot be and never will be paradise. Yet (and how we love that "yet" here on the prairies, here in "next year country"), surely this western spot is not so distant from the glory of the garden. We can almost see its ideal beauty, almost smell the singular scent—Wallace Stegner would probably say it is the "tantalizing and ambiguous and wholly native smell" of the shrub that would give his famous prairie memoir its name, *Wolf Willow* (18). The idea of being west of Eden is an idea only, and mostly a mischievous one, but it is, I think, an improvement on the full-fledged garden myth that was once in earnest play here.

Time and again, writers about the Canadian prairies have pondered and exploited the ambiguous sanctity of the place, its alleged resemblance to the first garden. For government and railway magnates aiming to recruit settlers for the west, an Edenic image was useful on posters boasting of "Free Land" and "The Last Best West," advertisements "rendered in clear, radiant colours. . . .The horizon was often set high so as to diminish the immensity of the prairies and everywhere the vegetation was lush" (Murray, "Printed Advertisements"). Beginning in 1897, the government even sent abroad thousands of immigration atlases of the Canadian west, the text of which used, as archivist Jeffrey S. Murray notes, "such superlative terms as 'unexcelled,' 'prosperity' and 'inexhaustible' throughout every edition" ("Sell, Sell, Sell"). One has only to open any honest homesteading memoir for a sharply conflicting view. For example, look at the photograph of Monitor, Alberta in Arthur Kroeger's 2007 *Hard Passage*. What appears to be acres of dirt is, instead, a nearly empty main street, with one vehicle, one or two spindly trees, and some desolate storefronts, one with an incongruously bold sign that proclaims "TED'S" (107).

For early preachers of the Social Gospel, like J. S. Woodsworth and T. C. Douglas, the prairies were identified with an ethico-religious Kingdom of God on earth. The League for Social Reconstruction (1930) and, later, the

Cooperative Commonwealth Federation (1933) crusaded for reforms with rhetoric well fortified with the Promised Land and the New Jerusalem. And it worked. Douglas's CCF party, elected in Saskatchewan in 1944, was the first socialist government in North America. Ralph Connor, one of Canada's most popular novelists in the early twentieth century, was also a crusading Christian reformer (he was Presbyterian minister Charles William Gordon), and in novels like *Sky Pilot* (1899) he invoked a similar romance of landscape. This connection between Christianity, prairie politics, and allegedly Edenic location is still surprisingly robust: it was only in 2007 that Lorne Calvert was unseated as leader of the Saskatchewan NDP government, a post he had held since 2001. Calvert is ordained in the United Church, the denomination in Canada that remains closest to Social Gospel precepts. It could be said about prairie Christians that they countered tough times with dreams of a Genesis garden, and subsequently that prelapsarian vision became a treacherously solidified component of their identity.

In his 1977 literary study *Unnamed Country*, Dick Harrison was one of the first to tackle the dangers of the Eden myth. (The term "myth," by the way, should not be seen as pejorative; the word as I use it denotes "sacred story.") To hint that the prairies are Edenic is, for one thing, to claim that they have "no past" (80), a claim surely not pleasing to aboriginal peoples who have lived here for thousands of years. The Eden myth also gives an undeservedly high status to a settler-invader; as Harrison puts it, a pioneer in "Eden" can claim to be taking his place in "a divine natural order" (76). Being in Eden also requires the writer or reader to think in terms of "moral simplicity and optimism" (84), which is fine if one wants sentiment and romance in literature, but fatal for realism or experimentation.

> The Garden Myth was not merely too sunlit and superficial for good fiction. It encouraged a dangerous cultural tendency. For the settlers, the assumption of a land contained within familiar cultural patterns which were ultimately divinely sanctioned obscured the fact that their relationship to environment had changed or needed to change from what it had been in Britain or Ontario. The attractions of the myth could make them forget that it was only precariously in touch with the realities of the new environment, which had still to be reckoned with. (97)

The Eden myth, therefore, is one element separating many prairie dwellers from the reality of the environment, and that estrangement from the land, or that misreading of it, is a subject that many writers have taken up. Rather wonderfully, I think, Dick Harrison allows us to applaud the ejection from the garden, because it is the *felix culpa* which brings forward the realism of Sinclair Ross and Margaret Laurence. Without the Fall we do not achieve *As For Me and My House* or *The Stone Angel*, novels important not merely for the west, but for all of Canada. According to George Woodcock, "[I]t was in the prairies, and in the west in general, that the most important developments in the Canadian novel took place from the 1920s onward" ("The Meeting of Time and Space" 38).

Frank Davey, in his 1988 essay "A Young Boy's Eden: Notes on Recent 'Prairie' Poetry," does not explicitly examine the Eden myth, but he worries that idealized notions of prairie are creating a nostalgic, simplistic, idealized style of poetry that does not adequately serve either the region's people or Can Lit more generally. Alison Calder, in her recent essay "Who's From the Prairie? Some Prairie Self-Representations in Popular Culture" points us toward the extremely popular 1998 coffee table/children's book *if you're not from the prairie . . .* by David Bouchard and Henry Ripplinger, with its cute photo-realism and overwhelmingly rural sensibility, and warns: "In describing only one kind of prairie experience, Bouchard evokes a sense of nostalgia for a prairie that never really existed" (94). She continues: "[I]f the region is a lost Eden, already vanishing in the imagination, then the economic and cultural deprivations it suffers can be easily naturalized" (95).

All of this is to say that the Edenic qualities, imagined or not, of the Canadian prairies are still very much under discussion, and thus, I decided, a worthy title for this collection. Eden, or someplace west of Eden, while too extravagant and idyllic to be true, can at least serve for a while as a functional counterpoint to the jokes about the prairies that continue to be as prevalent as, well, grasshoppers. When presenting the Macmillan anthology *Stories from Western Canada* in 1975, Rudy Wiebe stated dryly in his introduction that "everybody knows the Canadian West . . . consists of equal parts of Puritanism, Monotony, Farmers, and Depression" (xi). One of my favourite Canadian literary jokes, one that I should probably not admit to liking, is the title of a 1959 Hugh MacLennan essay: "Boy Meets Girl in Winnipeg and Who Cares?" (23). And we all know about those dismal contests where the first prize is one week in Moose Jaw / Medicine Hat / Brandon, and the second prize is two weeks in Moose Jaw / Medicine Hat / Brandon. Guy Vanderhaeghe once noted, in an essay, that merely naming Regina as a site of high culture in Paul Hiebert's 1947 satire *Sarah Binks* is all that is needed for hilarity to ensue (121).

As I am writing, Guy Maddin's very funny and strange film *My Winnipeg*, which he calls a docu-fantasia, is playing in his hometown. The repetitive, trance-like narration by Maddin offers the expected—"We're in the coldest city in the world" and "I must get out of here"—as well as the unexpected—"Winnipeg has 10 times the sleepwalking rate of any other city in the world." Could it be true that the Happyland amusement park was flattened by bison, or that there was once a night club on the top floor of The Bay which featured lurid "man pageants"? The film opens with the heavily loaded irony of an old jingle called "Wonderful Winnipeg." Its lyrics? "It's no Eden that you would see / But it's home sweet home to me." The tune is so jaunty that it almost reinscribes Eden as soon as the image is undercut. Maddin's work delights critics, but the Winnipeg cineplex audience I sat with this July seemed semi-bewildered, and I think about the other audiences in other places, perhaps even more bewildered about Winnipeg. I also worry a little about the readers of John le Carré's 2001 novel *The Constant Gardener*, which allegedly uses the Canadian prairies as a setting. The main character visits a university town in eastern Saskatchewan, "three hours' rail ride out of Winnipeg in the middle of a thousand-mile snowfield" (408). A prairie reader might say: *what could this possibly mean?* A reader from elsewhere might say: *what could possibly possess me to want to go there?*

———————————— • ————————————

These extremes in popular perception—here is Eden, or "I must get out of here"—can create a certain amount of defensiveness in the western cultural community. Reading through the introductions to various prairie literature anthologies published over the last few decades, I was struck by two tendencies: to patiently explain the unique qualities of the prairies, or to refuse to acknowledge that the prairies are much different than anywhere else, thank you very much. In the former camp is Ken Mitchell, who in *Horizon* (1977) patiently lists key prairie subjects as "the conquest of the land; survival; human endurance and frailty; nostalgia for the secure family circle that was a bulwark against lonely, bleak surroundings; the beauties that unfolded when nature turned benign" (xi). Also in this camp is Dennis Gruending, who says in his introduction to the anthology *The Middle of Nowhere: Rediscovering Saskatchewan* (1996) that Saskatchewan is "defined by the intensity and intelligence of our politics" (4). The manner in which David Arnason and Mhari Mackintosh, in *The Imagined City: A Literary History of Winnipeg* (2005), use The Weakerthans song "One Great City" is an example of the latter inclination, insisting that prairie people are rather urbane and chic: "When John Samson can write a love song to the city with the refrain 'I hate Winnipeg,' we have arrived at a level of sophistication that few cities can dare" (xii). In

Post-Prairie: An Anthology of New Poetry, edited by Jon Paul Fiorentino and Robert Kroetsch in 2005 (and intriguingly published by the non-prairie publisher Talonbooks), there is a strong sense that the prairie has gone missing, that the region's rural bias has been successfully challenged, and that it is language, discourse, aesthetics which will be the ground of operations for the next generation. A surprising number of prairie anthologists refuse to define or defend their projects in any detail. Geoffrey Ursell's anthologies for Saskatchewan's Coteau Books insist on being read for their excellence only, as do some of Dennis Cooley's for Manitoba's Turnstone. Perhaps this is to avoid being betrayed into using unfortunate old formulas, or anthropomorphism or mysticism. "Saskatchewan is shaped like a big empty page" is the opening sentence of Barbara Klar and Paul Wilson's introduction to *Fast Forward: New Saskatchewan Poets* (2007). Ah, emptiness.

Lately, no one seems satisfied with the manner in which the prairie is being represented. George Melnyk says, in his essay "The Five City-States of the West" that he is "disappointed with the limited role that the cities of the West play in the dominant mythology of the region. Compared to the Métis buffalo hunter or the sun-burnt farmer on his tractor, the images of the prairie city are almost an afterthought" (136). Yet this rural bias is not only a regional issue. Robertson Davies, in an interview on *Adrienne Clarkson Presents* in 1992, once offered this irreverent overview of the prairie classic *Wild Geese*:

> *Wild Geese* by Martha Ostenso was thought of at one time as the true Canadian novel. . . .The heroine was a strong, vivid girl. . . .I was very much startled as a boy of about 12 or 14 to read that it was her way to associate herself with the soil to go out into the meadow, and take off her blouse, and root with her breasts in the good soil and get the feel of it. And I thought—God, I don't know any girls like that! And I've never met them since. That was thought to be a real Canadian heroine.

Note that Davies does not remember (and mock) *Wild Geese* for its prairie qualities, but for its apparent reputation as an emblematic Canadian book. One opens Jane Urquhart's essay in her new *Penguin Book of Canadian Short Stories* (2007) and reads that she embarked on her role as editor with the curiosity of "the canoeist (to use a Canadian metaphor) about to journey beyond the lakes and rivers she knew well and into unfamiliar waters bordered by beautiful and oddly shaped shores" (ix). Should it be any more Canadian to embark on a ride in a canoe than in an elevator in a downtown Calgary skyscraper? Or, to accommodate the explorative aspect of her metaphor, why not propose an internal medicine specialist using endoscopy to assess our human organs? My point is that these limited tropes—the lonely canoeist, the woman as earth goddess—are a Canada-wide problem.

Or are they a problem? The loneliness of the prairies is a fact that Moose Jaw poet Gary Hyland embraces:

> It is not the stimulus of the metropolitan writing/publishing scene that is important to me. It's the environment here in Moose Jaw. It's almost the *absence of stimulus* here, if you like. I need a certain stability at the core in order to write. I don't work well when I'm in a foreign place and surrounded by sensory input. When I'm in Toronto or in a strange city, I record a lot of experience, but I'm too stimulated, too agitated to write. I need peace, space, time to meditate. (Hillis, *Plainspeaking* 239)

———————— • ————————

What are the prairies? What, if anything, can we safely say about the cultural identity of Canadian regions more generally? These questions have been circulating restlessly in the past few years, in scholarly collections like Christian Riegel and Herb Wyile's *A Sense of Place: Re-evaluating Regionalism in Canadian and American Writing* (1998), Robert Wardhaugh's *Toward Defining the Prairies: Region, Culture, and History* (2001), and Alison Calder and Robert Wardhaugh's *History, Literature, and the Writing of the Canadian Prairies* (2005). These collections strive to topple some of the key concepts about prairie literature that arose from the first flurry of critical activity in the region, which took place in the 1960s and 1970s. Laurie Ricou's 1973 *Vertical Man/Horizontal World* is possibly the clearest example of seventies style. Ricou's study drew welcome attention to the region's writers, and his thesis that they were using a difficult landscape to describe existential dilemmas left an impression of modish nightmarishness that allowed prairie literature to be taken seriously in the era. But ultimately Ricou's description of the prairies was a little too tidy and has become dated. Note his introduction to the 1976 anthology *Twelve Prairie Poets*:

> Indeed there is a nice harmony between the preference, in modern poetry, for spare language and open rhythms, and the prairie poet's most immediate subjects. An unadorned style, a simple landscape and the tradition of an honest, direct laconic people are neatly linked. (17)

Distancing himself at least in part from land-based critics, Eli Mandel a few years later would state: "It is not place but attitude, state of mind, that defines the western writer" ("Writing West: On the Road to Wood Mountain" 40). And then there's Robert Kroetsch, who has done the most to catapult prairie lit crit from its land-locked status, emphasizing instead gaps, contradictions, paradoxes, misquotation, and unspeakability. He has destabilized myths, and stated that the strategies of prairie writers are necessarily "strategies of evasion" ("The Cow in the Quicksand" 72).

The terms "space" and "place" recur in these discussions, and it is Kroetsch who puts most plainly the difference between the two terms. Our constant fear is that this place will dissolve back into "mere space" ("No Name is My Name" 46), always doubting that we even know where or what space is. Place is humanly defined or constructed space, space transformed by human presence. The anxiety about space has been taken by some critics to be an all-purpose Canadian dilemma; Cynthia Sugars for example writes in *Unhomely States* of the prevalence of "the notion of the unhomeliness of the Canadian locale" (xix). Deborah Keahey in *Making it Home: Place in Canadian Prairie Literature* cautions that "Rather than discard the notion of place entirely and replace it with the notion of culture . . . place must instead be reimagined as a creation of the social, psychological, and cultural relationships that people have to particular landscapes or physical spaces" (7). For Keahey, ultimately place has to be put in its place: "of all the factors influencing the creation of home and its success or failure, land and landscape in themselves have relatively little effect or importance" (12). Alison Calder splendidly sums up the stereotype of prairie that Keahey is arguing against:

> The land and climate are everything. The prairies exist in a permanent, drought-produced dust storm, the tedium of which is broken only by the occasional blizzard. It is always circa 1935. There are no colours and no animals, unless you count the domestic livestock that freeze or smother. Human beings die natural deaths only in that their deaths are caused by nature: they freeze, suffocate, drown, burn, or are driven to suicide. There are no urban centres; the ones that do exist are immeasurably far away from the isolated farm houses where the works are set. Even when there is a town, no one speaks to another; no one has any friends. There are vicious rivalries but no politics. Sex, when it occurs, is frequently adulterous, and usually followed by death. ("Reassessing Prairie Realism" 55)

Calder and Wardhaugh in *History, Literature, and the Writing of the Ca-*

nadian Prairies recognize two competing drives in prairie creative and criti-cal work: the desire to deconstruct, de-centre and break down conventional assumptions of prairie, and a countering reactionary drive to construct and reinforce traditional boundaries and definitions—the latter being a move-ment significantly driven by market forces that require prairie writing to be identifiable, static, and therefore appropriately controlled and commodified (10). They suggest that one way forward is to cultivate a stronger awareness that the Canadian prairies exist in time as well as space (3). Jason Wiens, in a provocative recent essay, insists, among other things, that we allow the word "cosmopolitan" to expand to include the prairies (153). In addition, Wiens is one of several critics who realize that if we abandon "local difference" we may not have much to offer as a "defence against a homogenizing global culture" (152). Although Daniel Coleman's *White Civility: The Literary Project of Eng-lish Canada* is not explicitly about prairie literature, Coleman's aim to encour-age a "self-conscious critical positioning, an immersion in our melancholic national history" (45)—in other words, his project of "wry civility," to uncover and counter the stories of white anglo-Canadian civility—sounds rather like prairie critics calling for a self-conscious reassessment of those interpretive strategies that seem to have been germinated in grain elevators and small-town pool halls.

But note how the grain elevator still lurks, as in the David Thauberger painting on the cover of this book. We can locate ourselves on the "Speedway," but can we really get anywhere until we come to better terms with the past? All this critical positioning and troubling of consensus is the postmodern prairie academy clearing its throat, and the more one reads, the more it looks rather like we have barely begun to articulate what the region's literature is. There has not been nearly enough response to Indigenous scholars like Daniel Heath Justice, who has declared emphatically that "Colonization has given Aborigi-nal peoples and their literatures two ultimately untenable options: assimila-tion, or tokenism. Neither choice acknowledges Native humanity and agency" (156). Similarly, Terry Goldie warned back in 1989 that the reified images of Indigenous peoples in our nation are such that actual people are barely signi-fied at all by the representations in use; alarmingly, "the referent has little pur-pose in the equation" (4). Or has there been enough consideration of George Melnyk's assertion that since the 1970s Alberta has stood apart from the other two prairie provinces? At that time, he says in Volume Two of *The Literary History of Alberta* (1999), it became "rich, populous, urbane, and powerful compared to its prairie sisters. The province tended not only to lead but to stand alone. From the new leadership and independence arose the possibility of conceiving a distinctly Alberta canon" (xvi-xvii). Melynk also declares that Alberta language is undergoing a dramatic transformation:

> Rather than being purely English (either British or American), Alberta literature is now becoming an internationalized english. English, as a global language, now has a multitude of important dialects that draw on the indigenous languages and cultures of postcolonial societies to modify and transform the language. (225-6).

Lest anyone go charging off into an overly rosy postcolonial future, Gerald Friesen is one who reminds us to look back at our history. He declares that "regionalism implies protest" (170), that the prairie west has been known in the past for its vigorous sense of "economic grievance" (173). If we go looking for exciting new conceptual strategies, if we eagerly seek to survey a prospect beyond regional borders, what will we gain and what will we lose? What are the intellectual, economic, artistic, and indeed spiritual and moral tasks that we have not nearly yet completed in this unique prairie locale?

•

I am in a good position to survey some of this discussion, having lived in all three prairie provinces, in cities, towns, and on a farm. Yet, to an extent which I hope is helpful, I am an outsider. I am neither a Canadianist nor a specialist in prairie literature, although I have always had a keen interest. In my twenties, I managed for a while the Saskatchewan publisher Coteau Books and have reviewed prairie books for many years. But my doctoral research centered on British fiction, and as a child growing up on a farm near the shores of Last Mountain Lake in Saskatchewan, my great pleasure was not to contemplate the prairies but to dream of a place without wind and dust. I became an anglophile, dreaming early of Camelot and Anne Boleyn, reading Narnia, later devouring the absurdly-necked women of Pre-Raphaelite paintings and reading Sherlock Holmes mysteries. We had W. Earl Godfrey's magisterial *Birds of Canada* but I preferred Grolier's old *Books of Knowledge*, which imparted little useful knowledge, at least about my surroundings, and instead offered me fables from other places, with unlikely and beautiful drawings. Although I must have read W. O. Mitchell's *Who Has Seen the Wind* when young, I cannot recall the impact it made on me, while L. M. Montgomery's Anne books, set in the exotic locale of PEI (red roads!) enraptured me, and I remember well one of my first profound bouts of weeping over a literary character when, at about the age of 12, I read of the death of Anne's son Walter, in *Rilla of Ingleside* (1921).

The closest village to our farm at Sorensen Beach was Silton, seven miles away. I was aware, as a child, that there was an author living in Silton, the novelist, naturalist, and amateur historian R. D. Symons; his books (*The Hours and the Birds, The Broken Snare, Still the Wind Blows*) were on sale in the General Store, where the Burrows family still took orders and served people from behind a long counter and tied up meat with brown paper from a hugely imposing roll. Or so it seems in my memory. I was more interested in the spinning rack of comics and getting back home to my project of typing out all the progeny of the god Zeus in my personal encyclopedia of Greek mythology. Nearly 20 years later, at the Banff Publishing Workshop, I met Douglas Gibson, who had been Bob Symons's editor at Macmillan. He discovered that I came from Silton and exclaimed over that fact: he admired and had such affection for Symons.

Only recently have I finally read Symons, in particular his natural history memoir *Silton Seasons* (1975). Now I find Symons's descriptions of the land around his cottage at Pelican Point, just down the road from Sorensen Beach, fascinating, familiar, and rather guilt-inducing. I am surprised to see what an environmental activist he is, but not surprised by his vigorous annoyance aimed at what he calls "city folk," and we called "beach people." My mother says he was considered an eccentric and the locals were abashed by his desire for a funeral cortege that included horses. I say guilt-inducing, above, because Bob Symons, born in Sussex, appears to know everything about the prairie while I, born on the prairie, know nothing. He knows there are many colours in snow if you look carefully enough; the way to cut wood in winter and load it in a bobsleigh just so; that if you ruffle the fur on a bush rabbit, there is a bluish tinge below the surface; what a pipit nest looks like; that a red crossbill looks the way it does because it apparently attempted to "remove the nails from the crucified Christ" (78); that the first leaves always appear around May 12; that there is always a last storm of winter, after initial thaw, and it is called the Storm of Crows; that the "weeds" around his cottage include yellow prairie parsley, beardtongue, sage, willow herb, and wild roses, only the last of which would I be able to identify. I cannot tell you how to spot a pipit.

I recently read, in the introduction to Riegel and Wyile's *A Sense of Place*, that the word "regional" has over the years become associated with the word "provincial," with the latter's traditional suggestion of "second-rate" (xi). I cannot recall how old I was when I realized, surely reading something from Europe, that the word "provincial" could have an uncomplimentary meaning. As a very young child I had pride in my province and my region, but it was not long before I decided that this pride must be, in worldly and civilized terms, naïve. It must be abandoned.

In fleeing the farm for the university and the glamour of British literature, I have forgotten, if I ever knew, what buffalo berries are or what thrashers look like. In defiance of the never-ending dust, my father's rages, and the summer boredom because the bookmobile arrived in Silton only once a week, I turned away from the prairie and toward, eventually, George Eliot and A. S. Byatt. Cautiously, this year I decided to read more key prairie books: first Sharon Butala's *The Perfection of the Morning* and Trevor Herriot's *River in a Dry Land*. Butala's belief that returning to nature includes embracing primitive and essentialist notions that "women are the soul of the world" (188) irritates me, but Herriot's explorations of the Qu'Appelle Valley—the territory I grew up in—stimulate in me Proustian moments of distinctly prairie sensation. I had not, of course, forgotten the restrained beauty of the coulees around our farm, but I had lost sight of the conspicuous pleasure of pumping purple gas by hand from barrels in our old stone oil house into our farm vehicles. I could feel again the liberating ride to town to take a load of grain to the elevator and get the mail, could smell the upholstery of the old truck. I experienced again the itchiness of the wheat's choking dust, so strangely evocative of my family's "living." I could feel the bump of the cattle gate as we rode over to visit our "rich" neighbour who had cattle and a pristine farmyard that contrasted sadly with my father's own lackadaisical approach to farming. And for some reason, a mention in Herriot of roll-your-own cigarettes prompted in me the most vivid lost sensation: helping my father make cigarettes on a machine he had for the purpose. It used long papers, which he licked shut around the tobacco—strange envelopes to mail to the land of bronchitis or emphysema—and at intervals he taught me to cut the irregular little cigarettes with a razor blade. I suppose people elsewhere roll their own, but my father's cigarette-making machine, in its thrift, its disregard for health, and its rusticity, seems absolutely "prairie" to me.

Trevor Herriot treats the Qu'Appelle as if it were the Nile, storied and valued. He seems aware of all the factors in the past 12,000 years or so since the glaciers receded that have made the Qu'Appelle what it is. But I am more akin to the woman he tells of who "lives in the valley north of Regina [and] once told me that she never realized that her parents' cabin at Buffalo Pound Lake is in the same valley" (114). For Herriot this river that I grew up with "appears to the traveller as a wandering line of returnings, a shelter you leave and rejoin and leave again" (6), and he asserts that to aboriginal people the Qu'Appelle Valley is "God's country" (5).

The book that haunts works like *The Perfection of the Morning* and *River in* a Dry Land is Wallace Stegner's *Wolf Willow* (1962). It is a curious book to have such a powerful reputation in prairie literature. *Wolf Willow* is an odd amalgam of memoir, history, fiction, and treatise. Stegner is an American explaining Saskatchewan to itself, someone who lived there for a few years at the beginning of the twentieth century, who both hates and loves Eastend / Whitemud, who can no longer (in the fifties) see the point of its existence. Stegner's insights are independent and eloquent; his assessments tough, usually unsentimental, his metaphors idiosyncratic. When a cactus spine becomes permanently imbedded in his finger, it is "a needle of calcified Saskatchewan, as much a part of me as the bones between which it wedged itself" (275). Any writer who takes him as a model struggles to keep up with his ingenuity and resourcefulness, his keen recall and fearless disputatiousness:

> I may not know who I am, but I know where I am from. I can say to myself that a good part of my private and social character, the kinds of scenery and weather and people and humor I respond to, the prejudices I wear like dishonorable scars, the affections that sometimes waken me from middle-aged sleep with a rush of undiminished love, the virtues I respect and the weaknesses I condemn, the code I try to live by, the special ways I fail at it and the kinds of shame I feel when I do, the models and heroes I follow, the colors and shapes that evoke my deepest pleasure, the way I adjudicate between personal desire and personal responsibility, have been in good part scored into me by that little womb-village and the lovely, lonely, exposed prairie of the homestead. (23)

My mother is one of many prairie people who love this book. I opened up her copy recently and out tumbled her pressed wolf willow blooms, picked on a trip to Stegner country a few years ago. Why should a prairie woman love a book that claims: "By most estimates, including most of the estimates of memory, Saskatchewan can be a pretty depressing country" (5)? Possibly because the author of that book also wrote: "I feel how the world still reduces me to a point and then measures itself from me" (19). In that sentence is a peculiar prairie sensation of simultaneous insignificance and worth, an assertion that we have value, but not so much that we should go getting ourselves all wound up about it. What I appreciate is Stegner's honest evaluation of his heritage of ignorance. "Living in the Cypress Hills, I did not even know I lived there, and hadn't the faintest notion of who had lived there before me," he says (27). Whereas Bob Symons in *Silton Seasons* would speculate affably about the lives of the Cree who once hunted on the acres that became Sorensen Beach and Pelican Point, it never occurred to me to wonder about the missing original peoples, and as a child I rarely met any. I also admire Stegner for the way he blows the whistle on prairie people for their "folklore of hope" (281). This unrealistic hope, he says, victimized those trying to homestead, particularly in the arid Palliser Triangle. "[T]he fact is, failure was woven into the very web of Whitemud" (255) is his blunt judgement. In reading his list of all the accoutrements of civilization (art galleries, bookstores, "stimulating instruction") denied to him as he grew up "in this dung-heeled sagebrush town on the disappearing edge of nowhere" (24), I almost leapt out of my chair in recognition. And in Stegner's statement of impoverishment and then, importantly, in his rejection of any further self-pity, I experienced a catharsis as important for me as for any spectator at *Oedipus Rex*. For years whenever I had heard the scriptures about Jesus exclaiming bitterly that he could get no respect in his own hometown, or when I read "Wherever they do not welcome you, as you are leaving that town shake the dust off your feet as a testimony against them" (Luke 9:5), I had secretly decided that these messages were about people like me, estranged from the prairie that didn't understand or nurture them. But I have put these scriptures back where they belong, and admit that maybe the bitterness I put in Christ's mouth did not really belong to him.

——————————— • ———————————

But why all this about rural existence, when, as we all know, the majority of prairie people are now urban? The direct ties to agriculture in Manitoba and Alberta, in particular, are loosened year by year, although Saskatchewan, as Gerald Friesen says, "actually conforms to the stereotype that outsiders apply to all the western provinces. Its major exports are the products of farms, on the one hand, and of resource extraction—oil and potash and uranium—on the other." People in Saskatchewan still talk about the weather obsessively, because it really matters for the crops, he says (99-100). Still, where are the novels and films about the Regina Riot, about the downtown Calgary oil dramas that must rival those in Dallas or New York, about the rise of the Guess Who? Guy Vanderhaeghe has said that there are few representations of urban life in prairie fiction before the 1960s, and even now there are not enough. He admits his own embarrassment about refusing in his novel *My Present Age* to name Saskatoon as the obvious (and noteworthy) site of action:

> What seemed an insignificant matter then, does not, with
> hindsight, seem so insignificant now, but rather a retreat

into evasion, a failure of artistic nerve, and a refusal to assert the validity of a place and a voice. It seems that for artists on the margins, autonomy can only be bought at the
price of vigilant self-awareness. (129)

Vanderhaeghe has been one of the great chroniclers of the prairie city. Saskatoon, in *My Present Age* and in some of the stories in *Man Descending,* insists
on its own (I almost wrote, *her* own) authenticity, persistently making itself
felt on every page. Yet Vanderhaeghe's most recent novels, *The Englishman's
Boy* and *The Last Crossing* are, for the most part, forays back into prairie history and into the countryside.

Perhaps the suspicion is that a city is a city, and there isn't much to distinguish an Edmonton schoolteacher or cop from one in Chicago or Edinburgh.
Although Regina mystery writer Gail Bowen overtly stages her plots in Regina, on her website the reviews for her books say nothing about place, with
the exception of one quotation, from the *Halifax Chronicle-Herald*: "Bowen
can confidently place her series beside any other being produced in North
America." So, is she a prairie mystery writer, or just a mystery writer?

One can locate the urban prairie experience more readily in poetry or
song lyrics. Moose Jaw is a memorable presence in the poems of Gary Hyland,
for whom its Home Street is the "equator of my youth": "I still gauge distance
/ from your boulevards" ("Home Street"). And here is multimedia artist Clive
Holden (now living in Toronto) in his poem "Trains of Winnipeg":

i am a train of winnipeg
we lie on gravel beds
i cross and cross your river arms
your legs, your dreams, your head

. . .

i am a train of winnipeg
i'm wintering in you
i'm embers in your winter glove
(each day your skin is new)

Holden's playful poem shuttles up to and away from the presence of his
lover, which is also the presence of the city, a particular city that pulsates with
the sounds of trains, the sensations of leaving and returning. One receives
a similar impression about the way Winnipeg pushes and pulls in John K.
Samson's lyric for the song "Left and Leaving" by The Weakerthans: "I'm back
with scars to show. Back with the streets I know. They never take me anywhere
but here." Samson's protagonist is as resentful of the city as if it were a traitor-
ous parent or lover (or perhaps that is who he *is* addressing):

> Memory will rust and erode into lists of all that you gave
> me: some matches, a blanket, this pain in my chest, the best
> parts of Lonely, duct-tape and soldered wires, new words
> for old desires, and every birthday card I threw away.

The weedy protestors enlisting "the cat in the impending class war" in the Samson lyric "Confessions of a Futon-Revolutionist" are the leftover left, scrabbling for a toehold on a monument to the glory years when Winnipeg was a centre of the labour movement. There is hardly a song on the four Weakerthans albums released since 1997 that does not somehow feature Winnipeg—wounded, wounding, beloved, failing to live up to its potential, but, I assert, never really boring, despite strong hints to the contrary.

Yet Holden and Samson are somewhat unusual among young poets, if one judges by the contents of the *Post-Prairie* anthology. Instead of setting poems in a recognizable urban environment to counter the elevators-and-weathered-barns of the rural past, most young poets are resolutely living inside language, inside an intense privacy that is often hard to fathom or share. A poem in that anthology like Catherine Hunter's "Two Thousand and Two," with its insistence on the shared aches and blizzards and joys of a very recognizable Winnipeg, shimmers in contrast. The bridges of the city are named in a painful and tender litany, markers of distance and desire between the houses of the speaker and her lover: "Love is a kind of counting / or counting down: Norwood, Provencher, / Louise, Disraeli, Redwood. The rungs of a river as long / as winter." The streets as well enact a difficult and angry love, they explicate and embody:

> You followed me from Ellice to Portage from Portage to Graham
> from Graham to St. Mary, and on the corner of York and Garry,
>
> > I stopped
>
> and let you reach me. Love is elementary.
> A peeling down to the square root.

George Woodcock once wrote that regionalism "is the sense of locality which is indispensable to a consciousness of regional identity, but which is not all of that consciousness" (22). One of the things which has been difficult for people in Alberta, Saskatchewan, and Manitoba to decide is just what style of locality—and how much of it—to embrace in their explicit prairie "consciousness." If we embrace the cities, what does it mean when the architecture of those cities is imploded and carted away? When Winnipeg lost its Eaton's Building, Regina its McCallum-Hill Building, and Edmonton its 1911 Court House, should citizens have been as saddened as they were? For what does it mean to lose buildings derivative of the Chicago Style or faced with Ionic columns? According to Janice Fiamengo, in current Canadian literature

> two narratives of city life seem to dominate: one explores
> how the bourgeois dream of consumer affluence and cul-
> tural vitality becomes a nightmare of overconsumption,
> shallow trendiness, and middle-class despair; the other ex-
> plores the city from the perspective of those for whom the
> bourgeois dream has never been achievable. (257-8)

The former examination is currently a crucial one, but a prairie perspective is not necessary to the investigation. The latter is more indicative of the prairie experience, but both approaches are reactive and bound rather strictly by the times. It is hard to imagine such fictions (especially those in the first category), with their loaded and distinctive economic framework, lasting into the next century.

———————————— • ————————————

To get the wheels of your snazzy new SUV stuck in the ruts of the old dirt track of rural versus urban is to demonstrate that you haven't been reading your Kroetsch. Eli Mandel said of Robert Kroetsch that he "focussed the attention of cultural critics on the distinction between region *as place* and region *as voice*, between setting and language, between environment and story" ("Strange Loops" 21, emphasis in original). As Kroetsch himself wrote in "Don't Give Me No More of Your Lip; or, the Prairie Horizon as Allowed Mouth," prairie "is as much performance as it is either place or answer" (210). This essay, apparently occasioned by a late night phone call from Dennis Cooley, states its objective with a comic prairie modesty I can only describe as characteristic, and more complicated than you think:

> [So] that I might get back to sleep, [I] agreed to say a few
> words at a meeting in St. John's College on a subject he an-
> nounced as prairie. 'What do you mean?' I asked him. 'Ah,
> you know,' he said. And hung up." (209-210)

One of the suppositions (never conclusions) that Kroetsch approaches in this essay is that "prairie is people," although Kroetsch would never allow that to sit too simplistically. But he might say (and does): "Now we're getting somewhere" (210 ff). Also, the prairie is more usefully seen as something active, in movement, which is possibly the exact opposite of its reputation. "This is a landscape not as something fixed and static, but as motion, as gesture, as event, as turmoil" (213).

When Kroetsch edited the Coteau Books fiction anthology *Sundogs* in 1980, he praised prairie writers who could combine "personal vision with the sense of talk as something shared....both the public and the private dimensions of story" (i). He himself does that in, using just one well-known example, "Stone Hammer Poem," in which the stone maul on the poet's desk provokes the appearances of the Blackfoot or Cree boy who might have lost it, the woman who might have left it in the skull of a buffalo, the Kroetsch grandfather and father who thought the Alberta field where the stone resided belonged only to them. These people, the smell of wheat, the blood of the long-gone buffalo, and the colours of saskatoons emanate from and around the stone, instilling it with a meaning that the poet's open parentheses and short, often inconclusive stanzas then short-circuit. When Kroetsch states, in this deceptively simple poem: "Sometimes I write / my poems for that // stone hammer" he is also writing for all the bodies, known and unknown, who surround him and inhabit his past.

Within the rough and tumble of prairie story Kroetsch found his own accent. In a conversation with Rudy Wiebe at Canadian Mennonite University in 2007, he noted that

> one place that my story was being told was in the oral tradition, people sitting around the kitchen table bullshitting, talking to each other, so that we created each other, created ourselves. That was about the only place where we had authenticity.

Gerald Friesen says we are quickly losing that short-lived sense of authenticity: "Both Manitoba and the Canadian Prairies, two important communities in my life, are under siege. . . .This state of affairs exists because popular understanding of the communities themselves—their boundaries, their histories, their place in the wider world—has diminished" (ix). George Woodcock might say that as soon as Canadians turned their backs on enigmatic historic failures (such as Riel) that served so well to toughen our sensitive hides, and instead began to look for mythical models of success, as other nations have done, we began to be diminished (cited in New, *History* 241). R. D. Symons would not say that we must embrace our enigmatic failures but instead would insist that history's liberators have often arisen "from the deserts, from the solitude of waste places" (174): i.e. *here*. Symons would remind us that the word "waste" originates from a meaning of wilderness—sparsely populated and uncultivated land—and that even that reverberant modernist term "wasteland" in the OED just means "land in its natural, uncultivated state." These enigmatic failures or liberators might be the "unassuming people in an assuming landscape" that Kroetsch locates in Friesen's influential readings of prairie history, in which, as Kroetsch reads it, we find "our epic and the communality of that epic not in what rises but, rather, in what falls" ("Don't Give Me No More of Your Lip" 213).

The sense of community has been unusually strong in the prairie past, but, as Dennis Gruending points out, our perception of this community is becoming sentimentalized, in community history books, for example: "The central message in most of these histories is that the past was a much more comfortable place than the present. The future rarely intrudes, perhaps because many people fear there is no future for their communities" (4). Yet in the essays in the present volume, and in the literary works of the region, I continue to find a living and particular characteristic that I identify with the prairies: a guarded, tough, even cantankerous personal humility, often (but not always) intersected with a principled commitment to the well-being of others.

I referred earlier to Dick Harrison's study *Unnamed Country* but did not draw attention to the key term in his subtitle, *The Struggle for a Canadian Prairie Fiction*: "struggle." If there were not problems with prairie literature, we would have to invent them, because once we flatly accept the literature of this place we stop struggling for it, and the life goes out of the discussion. The opening of Frederick Philip Grove's *Settlers of the Marsh* is representative here: "On the road leading north from the little prairie town of Minor two men were fighting their way through the gathering dusk" (15). All sorts of (mostly gloomy) points insist on being noticed here—that any town called Minor doesn't want to be remembered, that the novel starts not in a hopeful dewy morning but at dusk, that there are no walkers in Manitoba but instead fighters—but I draw your attention to one of the hopeful points. There is not one solitary figure, but two figures together. Yet companionship or community, in prairie literature, is not wholly an advantage. It does improve the probability of survival, but Kroetsch has noted that "exceptional pressure" is placed on individuals by communities: "The small town remains the ruling paradigm, with its laws of familiarity and conformity" ("No Name is My Name" 51). Small towns, like Horizon in *As For Me and My House*, suggest the oppositions of invisibility and visibility, namelessness and articulation. These mixed messages about prairie community refute nostalgia and easy affection, yet there are still positive notes to be heard.

—————————— • ——————————

In conceiving *West of Eden*, I had no particular argument to which I expected the essays to adhere. In the past few years, collections of analytical essays have narrowed in focus, and I have often wondered what this insistent specialization means to undergraduates, or high school students or members of the general public, trying to do research or find out a little more about literature. Thus the decision to make a general call for papers on prairie literature, and wait and see what was happening out there, among writers and teachers and thinkers. I particularly hoped to see some work in popular culture, and I additionally hoped for essays with a pedagogical bent. Other than that, I wanted my colleagues in Canadian universities to commandeer such arguments as they saw fit. If what resulted was a miscellany, I would be content; many wonderful ideas can tumble out of miscellanies. But the result was less miscellaneous than I expected.

The major and exciting argument that recurs in this collection is that, although we have been told in the last few years that the environmental basis of prairie literature is dead, this thesis is, in fact, not dead yet, as Monty Python would say. Nor are the discussions of realism and the importance of vernacular language done. Prairie people and prairie writers are still enormously engaged with the specific realities of land and climate, and the literary academy is being called to turn again toward these subjects. However much we are tired of hearing about droughts and blizzards and what they do to the human psyche, we must still hear it. This will be an unexpected realization for many academics, although I suspect it is not news for the ordinary reader of prairie literature. Henry Kreisel infamously said in 1968, "All discussion of the literature produced in the Canadian west must of necessity begin with the impact of the landscape upon the mind" (44), and other scholars of that generation agreed. Scholars of the current generation, in concentrating on language and theory and in examining, more abstractly, notions of "place" and "home," abandoned a scarred and wounded landscape that still sustains us and demands our attention, affection, and care. This volume prompts readers and critics to take seriously again the precise location where prairie literature is situated.

Everyone in this collection is aware of and interested in feminism, postcolonialism, deconstruction, queer studies, and other critical manifestations of the past 30 years or so, and no one wants to return to the time when it was acceptable to ignore (for example) female and aboriginal presences, as in Dick Harrison's admirable but limited *Unnamed Country*:

> The land was a challenge not only physically but psychologically; like all unsettled territory it had no human associations, no ghosts, none of the significance imagination gives to the expressionless face of the earth after men have lived and died there. The prairie, in effect, lacked the fictions which make a place entirely real. (ix)

Yet, as Pamela Banting says in her spirited polemical essay in this volume, "I would argue that rather than scrapping that scholarly work of the 1960s and 1970s it is time for a thorough reconsideration and critical, theoretical update of notions of region and regionalism." For Banting, the land demands our respect—even our love—more urgently than ever. One of the things that Debra Dudek realizes, with some reluctance, in her essay, involves this issue: "Here . . . for me, is one of the conundrums of teaching Canadian prairie literature in Australia: I realize that the landscape and the weather *are* primary differences that characterize life on the prairie and the writing that emerges from those lives."

This is not to say that the scholars in this volume are not arguing, vigorously, for heavily revised models of environmental criticism, mimesis, the role of settlement myths, the shape of vernacular poetry, and the like. Dennis Cooley, in providing here a valuable overview of the key critical statements about the region's literature, reminds us how much critical work is still to be done, for example on the role of comedy. He writes:

> Realism, it turns out, is not the final answer, certainly not the only answer, for . . . as a practice it would dictate a tragic view and eliminate comic structures more in keeping with a sense of constant renewal, a crazy and ineradicable faith in next year country that has long informed prairie people.

Brian Johnson, in examining Martha Ostenso's *Wild Geese*, a novel usually identified as a key early realist text, instead emphasizes its Gothic tones, which "may be read as symptoms of the bad conscience that accompanies the novel's substantial investment in settler-invader narratives of indigenization." Diane Beattie aims to place *As for Me and My House* more firmly in its age, pointing out that Sinclair Ross not only conveys the personal aridity of the Bentleys but also is very conscious of the need to situate the couple within the artistic and psychological debates of their time. Jenny Kerber strives to open up the discussion of just who "prairie poetry" might now belong to:

> For prairie poetry to remain vibrant, it must be given the room to creatively anticipate and respond to these changes in ways that acknowledge that the prairies are neither fixed, nor "over," but rather exist in a perpetual state of becoming, the outcome of which we may only glimpse through refraction from our present vantage.
>
> Further, any attempt to extricate the term "prairie" too tidily from its connections with the countryside—whether that countryside is located in rural Manitoba or southwest Trinidad—risks suppressing acknowledgement of the ma-

terial bases of production upon which so much of urban life depends. In short, geography may be reconfigured through processes of globalization, but it still *matters*.

The essays on film, music, and popular culture uncover issues that have rarely been broached in books about prairie literature, although there is a growing body of this research in periodicals. Alison Calder's pleasurable "Why Shoot the Gopher" examines, among other things, the strange contradiction that a region could both want to exterminate a particular prairie animal and exploit it as a symbol of the region: "My own suspicions are that the draw of gopher tourism is independent of the existence of the real animal, much as the existence of Mickey Mouse has not rendered mousetraps obsolete." Elspeth Tulloch offers a careful analysis of four NFB films based on prairie short stories and the ways in which the key figure of the outsider is rendered, these adaptations serving as a barometer of the NFB's ideological engagement with an often hurtful social reality. Michael J. Gilmour provides a thoughtful discussion of the symbolic prairie that singer Neil Young creates in the album *Prairie Wind*, "a kind of self-reflexive space . . . permitting Young to 'reconstitute' himself through the idealization of prairie space."

Two essays about Margaret Laurence testify to this author's continuing importance in the field. Brenda Beckman-Long investigates the ways in which *The Diviners* was "positioned such that it coincided with political and critical debates about both a developing national literature and gender equality." Nora Foster Stovel directs our attention back toward Laurence's neglected African books, in particular noting the ways in which *The Stone Angel* can be read not only as her first Canadian novel but her last African fiction. Another writer who attracts the attention of multiple scholars is Frederick Philip Grove. Archivist Gaby Divay has a tremendous knowledge of Grove's extremely complicated personal and literary history, and provides a fascinating summary of the rapidly changing estimations of Grove in recent times. Cristina Artenie's article focuses exclusively on Grove's *Settlers of the Marsh* as an immigrant novel which discusses "in depth the immigrant experience, with its implicit processes of deterritorialization and subsequent reterritorialization."

Wolfram R. Keller's essay is unusual (in this collection) both in its linguistic conception and in the way it provides an example of what a European academic is doing with a Canadian prairie text. Keller approaches Rudy Wiebe's *A Discovery of Strangers* as a novel able to generate "an important conversation about alternative ways of negotiating and discovering cultural difference, advancing an epistemology that ultimately promotes allegory as a trope of difference over metaphor as a trope of identity—a kind of allegorical mapping that I refer to as conceptual allegory." And in their essay, Tina Trigg and Philip Mingay take us through the planning of a Canadian Literature course with a prairie focus, with the added specification that the course takes place in a Christian college. This absorbing essay is helpful not only in revealing the ever more decent resources and difficult decisions that Can Lit instructors now have, but also in providing a glimpse into the surprising attitudes that students bring to the classroom.

Each of these highly varied essays helps us come to grips with what Robert Kroetsch, in his address "The Cow in the Quicksand and How I(t) Got Out: Responding to Stegner's *Wolf Willow*," once hypothesized in this way: "Surely one of the intentions of literature is just this: to acquaint us with the dangers of and to coax us into intimacies with the landscapes we wear" (81).

——————————— • ———————————

Although I have no desire to revivify the damaging and foolish Eden myth of the prairies, there is an insistent spiritual strain in prairie literature that asks to be heeded. Here is Sharon Butala, in her recent bestseller, *The Perfection of the Morning* (1994):

> Now when I looked out over the rolling hills and grassy plains I began to see, in the place of emptiness, presence; I began to see not only the visible landscape but the invisible one, a landscape in which history, unrecorded and unremembered as it is, had transmuted itself into an always present spiritual dimension. (113)

Even naturalist Trevor Herriot, a writer usually less inclined to the mystical than Butala, succumbs, in *River in a Dry Land* (2000):

> As we walked out of the woods where we had spent the afternoon, Brian [Hoxha, painter] told me he sometimes wished he could "breathe this all in without exhaling." *This*, I understood, is the whole of the eastern Qu'Appelle: the valleys, the river, the skies, the big bluestem, the light and shade, the farms, the elk, the sharp-shinned hawk, and all that unites them here in life. His wish is the shaman's wish, the "dream of congruency" to which every dweller worthy of his place in the land aspires. In such a wish, I thought, there is hope for renewal. (329)

Our small book of essays will not settle any questions about the inherent qualities of this region's literature, nor should it. But if it can provoke some new responses about the place of landscape, solitude, divinity, work, nostalgia, cultivation, and a host of other key issues, I will be satisfied. The prairies are not the first region to feel the pressure both of Edenic delight and consternation. While Shakespeare wrote in *Richard II* of England as "this other Eden, demi-paradise," (2.1.42) and Wordsworth, Dickens, George Eliot, and Yeats also invoked Edenic ideals, British literature eventually found the idealism thwarting and stultifying, and modernists rejected it unambiguously. But the paradise notion, in the Lake District of England or the Interlake District of Manitoba, is far from spent, whether we would like it gone or not. There will always be someone who, reading *Paradise Lost*, comes to the line "A Heaven on Earth: for blissful Paradise / of God the Garden was" (4.208-9), and thinks of Melfort. And there will always be others who read of Adam and Eve, expelled into reality and mortality, walking "hand in hand with wandr'ing steps and slow," and finding "The World was all before them" (12.646-9) an utterly right conclusion.

West of Eden, human activity and ingenuity have definitely been required, and cultivation of all kinds, including artistic, just as definitely continues. Art does not happen unless we bump up against the facts of mortality—living and dying—in our own distinct places. And if that prairie living and dying happens to include a desire to circle back to paradise—well, we are what we are.

Warren Cariou

●

Occasions for Feathers, Or, The Invention of Prairie Literature

What is prairie literature, and why does it matter? I find I have plenty to say about the invention of prairie literature, very little of which is original. I fear that any ideas I come up with have already been said, better, by people like Robert Kroetsch and Rudy Wiebe and Aritha van Herk, and by the entire generation of other writers and critics who have worked with them on the project of creating a prairie literature. That generation has made it their artistic business to define the place, and I think they have done a good job of it much of the time. So I wonder sometimes if there is anything more to say. However, being an heir to a long line of raconteurs, I still can't resist the opportunity to make a case for the value of the unoriginal.

I have never studied prairie literature systematically. I have only dipped into it whenever and wherever I found something that caught my fancy. Magpie methodology, you might call it. A horde of borrowed things: this is my nest of prairie literary knowledge. But perhaps that is not so entirely shameful. Maybe a horde of borrowed things is in fact an appropriate enough metaphor for a certain idea of prairie literature, one that I would like to argue in favour of.

When I was growing up, the magpie's identity was not something to aspire to. The snowy owl, maybe, or the robin, or the bald eagle, each of which were mysterious or cheery or magnificent enough to inspire a kind of respect, if not outright imitation. But we were taught to despise the magpie with the same kind of intensity that my Grandpa reserved for the potato beetle, and my Grandma saved for the weasel. Alison Calder writes, "We hate the animals / who live among us / as we hate our own reflections gone to seed," and certainly that was true in my upbringing. The most ubiquitous creatures were almost always the most despised. That was, I suppose, what a particular strand of "prairie" culture thought at the time—the strand that was tied to agriculture and that emphasized use-value in our relationships with the environment. Those animals that had no visible use-value—mice, rats, skunks, coyotes, gophers, magpies—were to be rooted out, to be purged.

Dad had an ongoing battle with the magpies that nested in the willows south of our farmhouse, their nests hanging like inverted crowns of thorns. The magpies stole robins' eggs, he said. They badgered the other birds at the bird feeder and at the bird bath. They even tormented our pets, squawking and swooping whenever one of our resident dogs or cats tried to take a nap in the sun. The magpies were surely collecting our lost jewelry, our dropped coins, our missing tools from the shop. They liked shiny things, after all. And the racket they made in the springtime was unbearable: at sunrise, 3:45 AM, it sounded like a thousand screen doors were being opened and slammed, opened and slammed.

One summer, just after the young magpies had left the nests, Dad marched over to the willows with a stepladder over his shoulder and an old curling broom in his hand. He stood there at the top rung of the ladder for several minutes, sweeping maniacally with that broom as if there was a bonspiel in the sky, as if those colossal nests were stones that must be hurried hard all the way to the edge of our back forty. The magpies squawked and wheeled around his head. When he finally fell—I remember the red blur of that "RinkMaster" label sweeping down through the underbrush—the birds said nothing at all. Several of them simply landed immediately in their nests, which were entirely undamaged.

We were given pellet guns that year, my brother and I, and we were told that it was open season on magpies. We sat on the corral fence and fired shot after shot, breaking our guns open on our knees between rounds. We shot until our arms ached, until our eyes were bleary from squinting down the barrels, but never once did we hit a magpie. In fact, we shot at them for years without ever inflicting so much as a flesh wound. The birds even seemed to enjoy the game, swishing toward us, alighting on the fenceposts, presenting their Alfred Hitchcock profiles. All to no avail, as far as we were concerned. Finally we were so frustrated that we told Dad about our failure, admitted that we had done absolutely nothing to reduce the numbers of these pests in our midst.

He looked thoughtful for a while.

"Well I guess that proves it," he said then. "A magpie has no body at all. It's only an occasion for feathers."

For some reason we accepted this wisdom without question, and eventually it helped us to tolerate the magpies. We came to accept the screen-door sounds, the missing coins, the harassed tomcats. And I think in a way our dad's lesson in magpie anatomy was a good thing for us all, because we came to believe that the magpie was going to be there whether we wanted it or not.

On the other hand, I also still wonder why we couldn't ever get at the magpies, why they remained for us disembodied things, always in our periphery, never fully present. They were like ghosts, haunting us. Ghosts in tuxedos.

I wonder: who invented the magpie? Was it here all along, or did it only become a magpie when it was labeled as such, when it was assigned a place in a particular narrative of agricultural settlement, a narrative of use? I don't know any Cree or Métis stories about magpies, though I'm sure there must be some. I know plenty of stories about Wesakejack, and perhaps those stories are as much about the magpie as they are about the whiskeyjack, the Canada Jay. But perhaps this is merely an issue of nomenclature, of the particular brackets we put around a thing in order to give it some reality in our human worlds. An issue of feathers, in other words.

Did the prairie falcon exist before Audubon? Did the gopher exist before Henry Youle Hind?

We might say, "of course they did," but I'm not entirely sure that the concepts existed in the same way, the same context, that they have now. Were those animals different animals—were they companions rather than pests, for example? And do they *continue to be* different animals to people who speak other languages, and who have a different experience of the place?

This makes me wonder: who invented the prairie? We know it is a European concept, not an indigenous one. If we agree with Robert Kroetsch's essays and poems, we will also have a strong suspicion that Prairie Literature in a certain sense invented the prairie. "The fiction makes us real," as he said. Prairie Literature was begun largely by writers working in the English language, and a few in French: writers educated in basically European traditions. But when we look at the field of literature produced in the prairie region these days, it is obvious that there are other kinds of writers working now, too, ones who have different cultural backgrounds than the European, ones who can bring to their work an alternative set of parameters and paradigms that derive, for example, from indigenous stories and ways of knowing. I am thinking of writers like Louise Bernice Halfe, Thomas King, Gregory Scofield and Marilyn Dumont. To my mind these writers are writing about something that *might* be encapsulated within the term Prairie Literature, but they do not often place their work under that particular rubric. Similarly, writers like Hiromi Goto and Suzette Mayr and Sally Ito may not consider their work to be "prairie literature," even though they live in the prairie region. Can the term remain useful, given this reality, given the multicultural differences and the decolonizing imperatives of much contemporary literature that emanates from this region? Are we living now in a world that is "post-prairie," to quote from the title of a poetry anthology recently co-edited by none other than Robert Kroetsch?

There it is again, my magpie methodology, always returning to the words and ideas of others. Unoriginal. But maybe that magpie mentality has a kind of appropriateness to this time, this place. Perhaps it represents, after all, a kind of invention, or at least re-invention. Because it seems to me that the idea of prairie literature and the idea of the prairie itself both need to be re-invented, continually—and that this has always been the case. I think about Jules Tonnerre in the Nuisance Grounds. I remember John Fraser, the proprietor of Fraser's Museum in Beauval, Saskatchewan, who presided over the most motley collection of wonderful and quirky local artifacts, both Native and European. These are a couple of my favourite cultural magpies, and they inspire me to think that maybe we need something more of that border-crossing and eclectic sensibility. I believe that a concept like prairie literature is elastic enough to provide a venue for continued re-evaluation, for the kind of re-invention that is necessary to a vibrant, living and changing reality.

We are presented here with what my dad might call an occasion. The shape of the feathers is yet to be determined.

Notes

This essay is based on a presentation made at St. John's College, University of Manitoba, February 22, 2007, for a panel entitled *The Invention of Prairie Literature.*

---•---

In the end, we are
defeated by gardens.
They know too much.

Robert Kroetsch, "Hornbook #19"
The Hornbooks of Rita K. (2001)

And I love this place, the enormous sky,
and the faces, hands that I'm haunted by,
so why can't I forgive these buildings,
these frameworks labeled "Home"?

John K. Samson, "This is a Fire Door Never Leave Open"
The Weakerthans, *Left and Leaving* (2000)

---•---

Dennis Cooley

•

The Critical Reception of Prairie Literature, from Grove to Keahey

It's 1925 and prairie literature begins. People have been writing for quite a while actually, but nobody takes their stuff seriously. It's 1925 and Frederick Philip Grove, reconstituted German, writes *Settlers of the Marsh* and Martha Ostenso returns to the interlake region of Manitoba to write at high speed *Wild Geese*. And that's where it starts, prairie literature, with these two books of "realist" fiction.

The first criticism of the literature isn't far behind, though for a long stretch there is very little of it. Grove contributes a set of essays, *It Needs to be Said* (1926), and establishes a continuing principle of prairie literature—the central role writers will play in assessing, sorting, and explaining the "fiction" they and others produce. In that respect they act in a larger Canadian tradition, though criticism of prairie literature still is dominated by writers to degrees that writing in the rest of Canada perhaps no longer is.

I want to isolate the handful of statements which we can receive as crucial to definitions and to a lesser extent evaluations of what has been written "out of" or "about" the prairies. That means I will be invoking those texts that go out of their way to speculate on prairie writing or to explain it as a phenomenon, and there certainly have been several attempts to identify central or recurring features, to analyze prairie aspirations and visions. That means I will not be looking at material that primarily concerns itself with single authors and with evaluating or interpreting only one or two texts.

One part of this story is very simple. Once we step past the first generation of writers and the various manifestos they wrote (Grove, Arthur Stringer, Robert Stead, Frederick Niven)—mostly apologies for increasing realism—we run into the first substantial efforts to survey the territory, and we're off and running.

Edward A. McCourt, himself a novelist of repute, published in 1949 *The Canadian West in Fiction*, which in 1970 he followed with a revised and enlarged text that covered subsequent developments. McCourt, emphasizing geography and climate, wittily extends and refines the story writers such as Grove had begun to tell. McCourt comes down heavily

on the side of "life." "[S]ymbols," he tells us, "no matter how ingeniously created, are in the end lifeless things." This worry proves especially acute when
Grove "is impelled to see man not as an individual but as a symbol" (65).
Symbols, McCourt supposes, too readily serve "the work of fly-by-night travellers, journalists, and romantic novelists whose knowledge of the prairies was
at best seldom more than second- or third-hand" (12). Those writers, whose
commitment to the place is as dubious as their knowledge of it, suffer from
a "tendency of the average Literary Society to derive its stimulus from traditional rather than native sources" (13). They are more apt to prefer "slavish
imitation of existing models rather than the creation of a vigorous and authentic regional literature."

McCourt, scrupulous and illuminating in his research, lays before us the
situation of romantic novels so bent on hair-raising adventure that they fail to
develop atmosphere and characterization (19). McCourt tries and finds wanting a series of early novelists on the grounds that they fail to select telling
details and, partly as a result, fall short in creating dramatic interest. What
prairie writers need, he tells us, is "to understand people in relation to their
surroundings" (56-7).

McCourt sets out his criteria in a sustained passage:

> The writer who seeks to inform his readers of the peculiar
> quality of a region such as the prairie provinces should be a
> pictorial artist able to describe accurately the physical fea-
> tures of a characteristic prairie landscape; he should be a
> poet with power to feel and to re-create imaginatively the
> particular atmosphere which invests the prairie scene; and
> lastly, he should be a psychologist with sufficient knowledge
> of human nature to be able to understand and describe the
> influence of the region upon the people who live within its
> confines. True regional literature is above all distinctive in
> that it illustrates the effect of particular, rather than gen-
> eral, physical, economic and racial features upon the lives
> of ordinary men and women. It should and usually does do
> many other things besides, but if it does not illustrate the
> influence of a limited and peculiar environment it is not
> true regional literature. (56)

What this means is that conversation must be reproduced with accuracy (66),
the problems of prairie settlement must be acknowledged (77), endings must
be "probable," incidents must be in keeping with ordinary notions of reality.
McCourt says much more, but for our purposes his book stands as the first

sustained statement on behalf of prairie realism as it derives from, and gives expression to, physical setting. A conspicuous sense of that connection appears in several other subsequent statements.

In what has become one of the most invoked statements on prairie literature, "The Prairie: A State of Mind" (1968), Henry Kreisel tells us: "All discussion of the literature . . . must of necessity begin with the impact of the landscape upon the mind" (*Trace* 6). Kreisel identifies two figures who, he proposes, derive from the force of that impact: "Man, the giant-conqueror, and man, the insignificant dwarf always threatened by defeat, form the two polarities of the state of mind produced by the sheer physical fact of the prairie" (6). In either case, the topography and the climate of the prairies would be formidably inhospitable. We learn from Kreisel that "The prairie, like the sea . . . often produces an extraordinary sensation of confinement within a vast and seemingly unlimited space" (9) and that the prairies often induce certain states of mind (10). Faced with this land—colossal, intractable—the first settlers reacted with a desire to put their imprint upon it (10). They sought to dominate it and to contain it. In Kreisel's distinctly sexual language, they tried to "pour an awesome, concentrated passion" into the land (11). Such single-mindedness is necessary if pioneers were to survive, Kreisel realizes, but in an inspired comment he goes on to say it led to a crippling puritanism:

> It can be argued that in order to tame the land and begin the building, however tentatively, of something approaching a civilization, the men and women who settled on the prairie had to tame themselves, had to curb their passions and contain them within a tight neo-Calvinist framework. (13)

Kreisel takes care to enunciate the consequences of that ethos:

> But it is not surprising that there should be sudden eruptions and that the passions, long suppressed, should burst violently into the open and threaten the framework that was meant to contain them . . . . It is natural that novelists should exploit the tensions which invariably arise when a rigid moral code attempts to set strict limits on the instinctual life, if not indeed to suppress it altogether. Thus illicit love affairs, conducted furtively, without much joy, quickly begun and quickly ended, and sometimes complicated by the birth of illegitimate children [begin to figure in the novels]. (13-4)

Kreisel's is a deciding statement, one which, like McCourt's, projects literary origins upon the physical environment and locates them in a direct experience of that world.

McCourt's and Kreisel's leads shape the next major statement, Laurie Ricou's *Vertical Man/Horizontal World* (1973). McCourt had identified a gap between "place" and expectations about "place" that got in the way of an indigenous literature, one that in its most dramatic formulations figured in places such as Cannington Manor, where young men played at being English gentlemen in the middle of the prairie. (The discrepancy would perhaps be mainly, if not entirely, ludicrous if the cultural snobbery attendant upon it did not infect views of prairie literature to this day).

Ricou picks up McCourt's points and, even as he refines them in crucial ways, accedes to them. He too calls for a new language which would be in keeping with a new place. For the most part Ricou thinks of the struggle toward an emerging literature as located in accurate describing and naming— that is in some referential measure of language that largely extends the earlier statements by McCourt and Kreisel.

Ricou is careful to establish that McCourt's terms are themselves dependent upon literary precedents and by no means confined to naked observation. Still, it becomes Ricou's task, too, to invoke some criterion of authenticity by which he can measure the language with which writers speak of the prairies. Even as Ricou shows awareness of literature as a made thing in a world which because of unavoidable cultural mediations is inhospitable to naked contact, even as he establishes the power of genre in depicting landscape, and even as he attaches literary modes to contemporary history, he still makes a decisive claim for a gap between the prairies as they "are" or "really are" and the prairies as they are rendered through inappropriate models. He finds, for example, in Ethel Kirk Grayson's *Willow Smoke* "A gap [that] yawns between the author's sense of the importance of the land and the distinctly false and affected tone of her description" (67). Extravagant and remote formulae often lead to the neglect of "a local and recognizable setting," Ricou warns us, so much so that idealized and romantic clichés "leave the actual prairie" unperceived and unappreciated (65). "Such reliance on conventional literary formulas is clearly inadequate to the evocation of a new land; it stands as a measure of the challenge which the prairie writer faced in articulating his sense of place" (11), Ricou reminds us. What is needed is "a new language suitable to a new, and what was felt to be a distinctive land" (14). Prairie writers need to interpret "their own time and place with less slavish adherence to a vocabulary and a formula created to fit circumstances far removed in time and space" (15). In Ricou's book a crucial distinction emerges between the realities of prairie landscape (and its consequences), and a sensibility that is exotic, out-dated, and out of place, and as a result insufficient as literary means.

The literary form we might name as popular romance had been impeding the development of prairie fiction, for "agriculture did not easily fit itself to the formulas of romantic adventure" (15) and "The vocabulary [of romance] inevitably seems inconsistent with the country being described" (14). The story Ricou tells, then, is one of aesthetic progression (these are his words) "from the romantic to the realistic" (16). According to this understanding, it is within the terms of a literary enterprise known loosely as "realism," that narrative in general and details in particular would more properly align with a place called the prairies. Allowing for subtle adjustments and qualifications to the argument, one could suppose that his thesis remains within the ambit of McCourt's and Kreisel's—which is to say within the conventions of description and reference. A domain of verifiable and understated truth which we know roughly as "realism" has traditionally instituted it. Ricou's vocabulary of disapproval marks those measures: sentimental (128); glib, excessive, exaggerated, and "crudely exaggerated" (112); melodramatic and improbable (111). In unsuitable fiction some things are "idealized" (73) or a life is seen "not as it is, but as the author wishes it could be"; as a result "Actual details of land and climate are neglected" (73). In Laura Goodman Salverson's books, for example, "melodramatic incidents proliferate endlessly" and we regret the "lack of authenticity" and the prominence of "standard descriptions" (69).

The diagnosis is clear: in practicing realism we avoid the false, eschew the inaccurate, renounce the exaggerated, refuse the inappropriate, abandon the imported, and attend to the local. What's needed is precise detail: writers should "delineate or describe in detail specific aspects of the prairie" which show "attention to man's interaction with landscape" (71); they should observe "fidelity to details" (69), "small, delicate details of nature" (98). Such care for detail, Ricou's story of realist improvement reassures us, demonstrates reverence for the prairies (103), even a discovery of nationhood or selfhood (70).

Dick Harrison in *Unnamed Country: The Struggle for a Canadian Prairie Fiction* (1977) picks up a number of the points that McCourt, Kreisel, and Ricou have made, notably their finding of discrepancy between the prairies as a place with its special phenomena and the imported linguistic and literary models to cope with it. The prairies are unattainable to those bringing conventions of what has been already written or painted elsewhere. But Harrison takes pains to emphasize that the writing is a search for apt forms and that its vision derives from complex and multiple causes. His statement comes four years after Ricou, nine years after Kreisel, and a full 28 years after McCourt.

Harrison's contribution is an account of the search for appropriate strategies and for forms that would free prairie writers into a more adequate writing of their world and is, therefore, more oriented towards issues of invention and construction. His book lays out the history of prairie fiction and the difficulties it has faced. At every turn there have been large and harmful precedents which, taken together, have obscured the prairies. Old conventions of landscape poetry; the consequences of imported technology (the land surveyors' instruments, the railroad, the plough); outdated European practices in landscape painting that informed Paul Kane's versions of prairie and the illustrations which artists like Charles Comfort developed for Eaton's catalogues—all these had deep effects in misrecognizing and misappreciating the prairies. So did the Puritan ethic (this is more my term than Harrison's) and the impact of the Old Testament. So too did colonial definitions of the prairies as an extension of Ontario and Britain; the role of the Mountie as emblem of a world already defined, elsewhere; and the proprietorship that British audiences for years held over the fiction. And so did—perhaps most profoundly of all—the myth of the garden, transposed—blindly, damagingly—to the often arid Canadian prairies.

Although Harrison extends his story to encompass a wider sense of cultural formation, he too retells the story of a new land and an old culture brought into collision. He recounts the attempts, many of them unsatisfactory, to develop an indigenous prose fiction. (Why prose fiction? we might ask. Why not poetry? Drama?) New arrivals "could not see clearly what was around them: (1), partly because the "imagination is always more at home with what has already been rendered imaginatively" (6). Harrison's story, as his title implies, is in part lexical and residually Adamic—concerned with finding the right word and the indigenous name. Once more the task is to bring land and language into harmony. But Harrison stresses forms or structures more than he promotes a particular vocabulary of perceiving. Pioneers "had no ready paradigms for describing" the land and "must have had difficulty even observing it very carefully" (3-4). This line of understanding runs through his book, even as he traces stages in the fiction and develops generalizations about its forms. Here is what he says in summary of prairie realism:

> The dominant culture of the new land seems to be represented, paradoxically, by a cluster of domestic images suggestive of ruin: the derelict house, the failing patriarch [who becomes what Harrison later identifies as the "disappearing father"], the stifling mother, the frustrated artist, the culturally starved child. . . .(137)

We can detect a recurring disparity in Harrison's account. On the one hand he wants to argue that early writers fail accurately to depict the prairies. (The point does not emerge quite so overtly nor so centrally as it does in Ricou, but it is there nonetheless). We are asked to note "the realities" of the settlers' lives (137), to appreciate that the prairies have been "misrepresented" (183) and that we need "significant detail" (28), as well as "particular, and realistic" descriptions (58) if we are going to arrive at anyone "treating realistically the problems of the place" (84), or able to uncover the "indigenous" (212). The myth of the garden, we read, was probably "a dangerous illusion" (94). Familiar forms got in the way of the imagination which, freed, could "see the new country as it was" (50), could remove "the disparity between what they [the settlers] brought with them and what they found there" (17). It is evident that Harrison is invoking, within the complexities of his argument, a principle of verifiable truth that depends on the referential use of language—language, that is, as it informs what we roughly think of as underwriting realist fiction.

But that's not the whole story. Harrison again and again speaks of literature as culturally derived. This understanding enables him to escape earlier stories critics have told. Realism, it turns out, is not the final answer, certainly not the only answer, for, Harrison is careful to argue, as a practice it would dictate a tragic view and eliminate comic structures more in keeping with a sense of constant renewal, a crazy and ineradicable faith in next year country that has long informed prairie people.

That dissatisfaction with old forms and the enthusiastic search for new structures Harrison centers for obvious reasons in Robert Kroetsch's lead as writer and critic. Kroetsch may feel uncomfortable being enlisted in this argument but there he is, in essay after essay, interview after interview, himself advancing claims about how the fiction makes us real and how we need, flagrantly, to pull down the old apparatus of demotion and neglect. Kroetsch is hoping that change will allow something more in keeping with the prairies. We make books out of books, he instructs us (42). Jack Hodgins' character Strabo "invents the world by an extravagant telling of its story" (59). Kroetsch, in response to the long tradition of representational writing, which he thinks of as the tyranny of realism, opens up the territory. We don't *describe* what's there, we *make* what is there, he assures us.

Or almost make, for there is in Kroetsch another streak, one in accord with McCourt, with Kreisel, with Ricou, and with Harrison, and one at odds with the widespread perception of Kroetsch as through-and-through international postmodernist. This Kroetsch, the local and referential Kroetsch, says: all those old stories and the imported language—know what?—they've been screwing us, keeping us from ourselves. They are forever coming between us and the place, jealous lovers, villains hoping to break up our affairs or keep us from ourselves. And so the same guy who tells us fiction makes us real, also tells us "The act of perceiving what is actually there is possibly the most difficult act of all" (and why is it so many readers simply ignore these entries?) because we come to it with memories and expectations that don't fit (40). Actually *there*? Yes, in a way, for Kroetsch, that is the case—true to our sense of being wronged and overrun by somebody else's stories of what we ought to be and are, and what our world is or ought to be: "Our genealogies are the narratives of a discontent with a history that lied to us, violated us, erased us even" (84).

If I make more than seems warranted of the point it is only because Kroetsch is so frequently identified—this holds especially true for critics and theorists from outside the prairies—as unreserved champion for reflexive writing and scourge of referential writing. But there is another message he tells us, buried beneath that line: a story of denied aspirations and distorted identity. And it is precisely in this narrative that Kroetsch aligns himself with the recurring story of prairie criticism: the need for an authentic, indigenous writing that, freed from the dictates of foreign and inappropriate models, reflects our place to ourselves.

In one strategy Kroetsch looks to orality: "Our endless talk is the ultimate poem of the prairies. In a culture besieged by foreign television and paperbacks and movies, the oral tradition is the means of survival. The bastards can't keep us from talking" (30). This is one of the reasons, surely, Kroetsch writes so warily of British sources. He joins with others in this—Ricou to a degree, Harrison certainly. Even McCourt, who supposes it is virtually impossible as an immigrant to speak authentically out of the prairies, is not far away. Kroetsch, along with most of the native-born critics and critics who have lived much of their lives on the prairies, shows a suspicion, if not a resentment, of foreign precepts located in Britain, seeing them as bane to indigenous writing. Those who come from elsewhere, or who have developed allegiances to elsewhere (again chiefly Britain), continue in various guises to advocate the need for some form of British authority. (More recently we get, among Canadian critics from places other than the prairies, another line of dismissal, in their case as it derives from poststructuralist theory.)

That note gets sounded a number of times in *RePlacing* (1980), the first collection of essays on prairie poetry, edited by Dennis Cooley. Cooley complains that in the past the cachet of old or British forms had impeded the development of prairie poetry, and that orality in part had released it. We are invited to see a disparity between ear and place, whereas in the first critical surveys we were asked to see a gap between eye and place. *RePlacing*, however, is harder to summarize for the purposes of this essay because it includes a range of subjects and contributors, though it does represent the first book-length gathering of material on prairie poetry.

In its mixture of material, at least, it sets a pattern for the next three books, which appear soon after: *Trace* (1986), edited by Birk Sproxton; *Essays on Saskatchewan Writing* (1986), edited by E. F. Dyck; and *Writing Saskatchewan: 20 Critical Essays* (1989), edited by Kenneth G. Probert. *Trace* contains the greatest reach of pieces, ranging from a set of older selections—Kreisel's among them—to a batch of commissioned pieces written by newer readers and writers. In *Trace* some of the old issues are revisited, but in it too the new contributions diverge along postmodern and anti-postmodern lines, the post-modernists promoting what to them are the virtues of the oral, the formally adventurous, the inventive, the playful and the joyful; those in opposition preferring what they see as artistic control, accurate or satisfying representation, accessibility, ethical responsibility, and appreciation for standards and tradition. The oppositions rotate in some versions around suspicion toward, or sympathy for, formally conservative examples.

The other two collections, *Essays on Saskatchewan Writing* and *Writing Saskatchewan*, are related in strategy and structure. Dyck's collection in particular combines older statements with newer contributions. Probert's includes entirely new material, all of it prepared for a literary conference held in the summer of 1987 and sponsored by the Saskatchewan Writers' Guild. For the most part the essays from the conference seek to find overviews of their subjects, that being their commission. Again, the statements are disparate, as one would expect.

One new feature begins to emerge in the four new collections of the 1980s. Quite a few contributions abandon the judicious tone of the first retrospective and scholarly studies. In varying degrees the newer essays take on more interventionist, contentious, and promotional overtones. They begin to migrate from the third-person of the book-length studies to the first- and second-person talk of more immediate engagement. They tend to mark out territories, to advance particular causes (gender, form, voice, etc.) and to solicit assent, if not allegiance. They are, in short, more combative. They are not always so, and they are not certainly without their own thoughtfulness (particularly the pieces written by scholars from outside Saskatchewan). But the newer entries come more often from those who are immediately embattled in the making and appraising of prairie literature and on occasion from those who are not practised as scholars.

There is in many of these essays a growing awareness of how the letter institutes the world and a furthering of the movement from earlier expressive and realist precepts to formal and pragmatic practices. One of the ironies is that some of the most determinedly "prairie" of the critics tend also to look to contemporary theory as it derives ultimately from elsewhere.

The emphasis upon language and literature as systems of invention is one that we saw as early as Ricou, saw in further development in Harrison, and found too and more fully in its most renowned proponent, Kroetsch. That line of thinking finds perhaps its purest champion in Eli Mandel. Mandel harboured a life-time belief in the efficacy of the written word and a respect for the word as impetus to a larger life. In several essays of the 1970s and after, he develops those views powerfully. In "Images of Prairie Man" he confronts what at that point certainly would still have been the prominent view of prairie writing—the notion that the literature derives from the place: "The temptation is to believe that 'accurate description' really means the imitation of certain clichés and stereotypes about landscape and environment" (47). No, says Mandel, that argument is dangerous and mistaken. In his view the claim is too easy and ultimately misleading. Mandel opens a counter claim: "It is difficult to keep steadily in mind that 'prairie' means nothing more than this, that it is a mental construct, a region of the human mind" (47). The move is bold to say the least. Where McCourt and Ricou and Kreisel, and to a lesser extent, Harrison and even Kroetsch have argued for some principle of adequate representation, Mandel irrevocably strikes out in a contrary direction. And then, at his most eloquent, Mandel promotes a story of mythic innocence. Prairie literature, he tells us, speaks of a lost Eden, an eroded home, seeks in magic realism the first place, the first vision of things. That first site reappears as preternaturally clear in the memories we dream. (Frank Davey will pick up this line of analysis a bit later and less sympathetically.)

In "Romance and Realism in Western Canadian Fiction" Mandel supplements this position and argues that "it is no longer the historical and social, or even the geographical West, so much as the literary one, that concerns us" (56). And so we go in search of folklore, look inward to find ourselves, create more than discover the West, or ourselves. And so we seek to locate ourselves—these terms are not so explicit as I have made them—as characters in literature, *our* literature. As we've seen, this version of prairie writing finds antecedents at least as early as Ricou, but it never finds quite so pure expression anywhere else, not even in Kroetsch. Little wonder, for Mandel, long exiled from the prairies, steadfastly held that writing at its best can and perhaps should include "artifice, contrivance, and self-consciousness" (60). We may be tempted to discern in these words evidence of a residual modernism and the emerging of a certain kind of postmodernism in Mandel, and to assign to such inscription his search for writing that has pulled back from the world.

And yet, wait (wouldn't you know it?) Mandel, himself, also tells another story. To be sure, "the fiction dreams us" (66), but in "Writing West: On the Road to Wood Mountain" Mandel speaks in quite different terms of what he finds in the poetry of Andy Suknaski. Mandel was by this time intimately informed by his personal return to the prairies in the 1970s (as re-visitor but also as contributor to the famous writers' colonies at Fort Qu'Appelle, by his growing friendship with Robert Kroetsch, and by his term as writer-in-residence at the Regina Public Library). Standing as tourist on the shores of Spain, he finds himself leaning homeward, his imagination drawn to Estevan, Saskatchewan, where he grew up. In the Suknaski essay we learn there is "a tension between place and culture, a doubleness or duplicity" (69). We do find here the central Mandel belief in writing ourselves into existence, true, and a continued faith in the fact that books lay claims upon us, but we find also a surprising enthusiasm for Andy Suknaski's poetry as "something I should have written, its terrible authenticity, its powerful directness" (69). The appreciation finds comparable expression in another essay of that decade in which Mandel seeks the "realization of the object" and an "acceptance of what is there" (88). And we then see that Mandel, too, in these moments of turning outwardly to the phenomenal world—time of his return to the prairies perhaps, seeking to rejoin—enlists in that long line of representational apologists, however buried it may have been for him. In these more recent prairie talks, he says that in the deepest sense we must find fitting words for the prairies, and that those words must emerge, somehow, out of the place, or at least embody the place. In these passages his is a call for adequate language, true words. That line of thought means that whatever other tales these critics tell, every single one of them, every one of them who cares about prairie identity, whatever their sophistication or theoretical derivation, whatever their differences—every one of them affirms some version of directness and immediacy. Every one of them, that is to say, deeply concerned about how their worlds have been mediated, acknowledges the pull of reference, tugs at the shirt-tails of realism.

Dennis Cooley, during the early 1980s—"The Vernacular Muse in Prairie Poetry" and "Placing the Vernacular: The Eye and the Ear in Saskatchewan Poetry," both included in *The Vernacular Muse* (1987)—picking up on Kroetsch's interest in the oral, named a new version of prairie poetry as based in part at least on social class, pragmatic situations, and oral styles; and as operating in opposition to a long and honoured tradition of the lyric which was written for the eye and the page, and given to inwardness. Cooley's pieces, even as they offered minute and extended analyses of texts, were polemical in manner and interventionist by design.

Two years later, in *The Great Prairie Fact and Literary Imagination* (1989), Robert Thacker argued along the line which had been first established in statements about Canadian prairie writing: Early Europeans, ill equipped by virtue of their cultural baggage, perennially misread the place, often as not as the picturesque or the sublime, as garden or desert. Their response to the place is a history of "the collision between inculcated esthetics and literary convention, on the one hand, and prairie landscape, on the other" (3). Thacker's consideration of Canadian literature takes only a fraction of his space (the book mainly examining American literature and the writing of early visitors to the grasslands) but his arguments are important and in keeping with Kreisel in particular.

In a gadfly essay, "A Young Boy's Eden: Notes on Recent 'Prairie' Poetry," which appeared in 1988, Frank Davey interrogates what it is that the word "prairie" might mean and mounts a daunting attack on arguments for regionalism in prairie poetry. Davey proposes that debates about what might constitute "prairie" poetry are ultimately "ones of politics" (214) and are often confused and self-contradictory. Davey reads a series of prairie poets as naïvely aligning themselves with nature and failing to perceive, or refusing to admit, that their own writing is an act of cultural construction in an urban and literate world. "A literate present pretends to efface itself in deference to an oral past, the industrial and technological pretend to bow to the pastoral" (220). Davey finds behind Cooley's appeal to the vernacular "binaries that lock human culture into overly simplistic choices" "by asserting the culturally despised alternative against the privileged other" (224). What is needed, Davey contends, are not deluded acts of supposed recovery in memory, not nostalgic callings up of an edenic past, nor beliefs in an unproblematic connection to the world, but writing that investigates the processes of memory and the "fabrication of history" (227). Davey, perhaps more than any other critic of prairie writing, raises doubts about regional aspirations to find any characteristics that might inform the literature. Davey tacitly assumes that prairie writing simply is what is written by its residents and in a sense, then—hence his use of quotation marks: "prairie poetry"—is beyond definition.

What Deborah Keahey has to say in *Making it Home: Place in Canadian Prairie Literature* (1998) constitutes the last major statement on prairie writing. In that book she seeks with a generous and searching intelligence to expand the terms and to redefine the approaches by which we might read prairie literature. Her book is the first to look at a rich mix of texts as they embody distinctions by region, gender, genre, ethnicity, urban and rural experience, etc., as does Jason Wiens in "The Prairies as Cosmopolitan Space: Recent 'Prairie' Poetry," a statement originally presented in that same year (1998) and raising doubts about regionalism in prairie writing. "What is needed for the Canadian Prairies," Keahey writes, "is a more flexible concept of the relationship between home and place" (6). Dissatisfied by arguments that would make inordinate claims either for landscape or culture, she proposes that "place must instead be reimagined as a creation of the social, psychological, and cultural relationships that people have to particular landscapes or physical spaces" (7), seeing in the literature a dynamic process that both responds to place and inscribes place. In fact, of the various "causes" of the literature, at least of the literature she is considering, Keahey considers landscape to be the least important (12). Against the body of environmentalist criticism, and its frequent sense of maladapted residents, Keahey muses about the "many prairie dwellers (both literary and otherwise) [who] are in fact quite firmly 'settled' and at home in their places" (148). She also loosens the canon by carefully reading a large number of relatively unknown or unexalted writers, including playwrights and aboriginals, that are entirely in keeping with her reading of prairie literature as oppositional (a position, I would argue, that had its first push with Robert Kroetsch) and as very much a part of the tugs and pulls that are so much a part of contemporary writing all over the world. She brilliantly distills the advantages and the dangers of arguing for an environmentalist position (159) and goes on to say that

> the prairies have neither a single shared landscape nor a single shared culture, and all attempts to define such are necessarily exclusionary or reductive. The environmentalist view also tends to essentialize a land and/or culture, resulting in the restrictive assumption that there is a single appropriate culture in each place, or a single appropriate way to place home, and thus misjudging the broad, eclectic, resourceful, and pragmatic range of strategies used by prairie writers. (159)

In thinking past those earlier "'naturalized' versions of the regional that attempt to define it on the basis of 'intrinsic' qualities," we come, Keahey proposes, to "more overtly political, 'extrinsic' definitions of regionality—versions that, as W. H. New says, are 'not simply a descriptive posture but a political gesture'" (152). One of these is "oppositional" and emerges in a "liberatory regionalism" and "thus reversing the usual flow of influence and power. In this way regional literatures may be seen as centres of vitality, and the energy sources driving national and global cultures" (160). Where others have argued for a relatively untroubled relationship between word and world, and still others for an impossible relationship between word and world, Keahey opts for reciprocity, a notion that we both observe and create the worlds we inhabit.

In that same year Wiens, drawing perhaps on Frank Davey's "A Young Boy's Eden: Notes on Recent 'Prairie' Poetry," argued that prairie writing suffers from a lack of cosmopolitanism. Wiens's essay appeared in the collection *Toward Defining the Prairies* (2001), which gathered papers from a conference held in 1998. In that same collection Alison Calder opened a related line of enquiry. Invoking a few major examples, Calder proposes that "In situating prairie identity only in the past, only in an idealized rural landscape that may not ever have existed, these books deny regional identity a future" (95). The nostalgia is understandable, she says, in view of a felt sense of inconsequence in a colonized world. But it often removes from attention a substantial range of prairie existence. It limits options when "the only true prairie person is a rancher or a farmer," when "no real prairie person has any sort of intellectual curiosity," and when "'prairie' is an ossified definition with strict and impermeable boundaries" (97). Calder joins other recent critics of prairie literature in raising great reservations about finding or enforcing fixed identities.

George Melnyk published in 1998 and 1999 a two-volume study of Alberta writing. Strictly speaking it does not look at "prairie" writing if by that term we mean writing from the region that has formed the three "prairie" provinces. It is worth mentioning here, however, inasmuch as it is an ambitious and courageous look at a large reach of writing, that many of his examples include figures who as explorers or travellers would have traversed large parts of the prairies. Melnyk offers in his historical survey a luminously informative account of the writing as it evolved within the histories of the place, from aboriginal times to the most recent years. Melnyk's account is fascinating in its linking of the writing to larger patterns of history, particularly as they involved local responses to European imperialism, technological developments such as the steam engine, and significant changes in economics and communications as the writing derived from, or responded to, forces directed from elsewhere. The kinds of issues—in effect and in response—that Melnyk identifies could inform studies of writing from the other prairie provinces and frame them, too, within imperialist and colonial narratives. His concluding statement, which might well be adapted in looking at writing from across the prairies, indicates ways in which contemporary forms of Alberta writing exist within the pull of the local and the global:

> Alberta writing has benefitted from the postmodernist emphasis on new narratives, particular localities, small cultures, the mixing of styles and genres, the revelling in contradiction, the embracing of fragmentation and occasionally even the chaotic, the everchanging pastiche of electronic technology and the spirit of the World Wide Web. . . . Alberta literary trends are in step with continentalism and globalism. (Vol. Two 230)

And what tale then have I been telling? It says our first critics sought realism and promoted the referent. It says that though that preference has been profoundly challenged as part of a postmodern take on the world, and as reading the material has brought us to fuller consideration of race and gender, genre and region, it has never disappeared, at least not among authors deeply connected to the prairies, and that most of the critics who have looked for some kind of "prairie" writing have at some time or other argued for the need of models that would enable writers to write from and of the prairies, and those critics have been tempted by a representational understanding of its literature. Even as critics have lamented the inadequacy of old forms and forms that are alien to the prairies, they have sought remedies in description, in voicing, or in formal play. My account implies that until recently there has been little criticism meant to define or to develop an overview of prairie writing in its manifold creations, and that what there is has been written overwhelmingly by men. It says that beginning in the 1970s and increasing in the 1980s more and more of those who have written about the literature have been drawn to linguistically-inspired readings and that in that same period, finally, poetry got some attention.

There was a surge of statements from 1973 to 1989. One wonders: where now are the new statements?

Pamela Banting

•

Deconstructing the Politics of Location:
The Problem of Setting in Prairie Fiction and Non-Fiction

Unfortunately my family has had a very hard summer. Most of our crops were destroyed in a tornado. We had a few small fields left. And these crops were good, very good, thanks to more rain than anyone has ever seen. So not all was lost, or so we thought. But on Monday my Dad was down at that farm, literally sitting out in the field at 3:00 in the afternoon, enjoying the warm sun while admiring his prize crop when this tiny hail cloud comes over and rains HUGE hail balls down on it. Totally unbelievable. But it gets worse. The crop was destroyed, but he swathed it hoping to sell the remains for feed. But now it has been raining for 4 days straight so the swaths will rot and are ruined. Anyway, I guess you roll with the punches.

Kendra Mulatz, Maple Creek, Saskatchewan,
email correspondence, Sept. 7, 2002

The West doesn't need to wish for good writers. It has them. It could use a little more confidence in itself, and one way to generate that is to breed up some critics capable, by experience or intuition, of evaluating western literature in terms of western life.

Wallace Stegner, *Where the Bluebird Sings to the Lemonade Springs: Living and Writing in the West*

During a dust storm in the Dirty Thirties two farmers are looking up at the blackened sky. One of them says, "Geez, there must be at least a quarter section swirling around up there." The other farmer replies, "Yeah, but where're you gonna set 'er down?" This anecdote, attributed to novelist W. O. Mitchell but possibly apocryphal, encapsulates a farmer's complex notion of location and setting, one more nuanced than that with which some Canadian critics of prairie literature have been working for the past couple of decades. In much current critical practice, though not in the literary texts themselves, the prairie earth is simply ignored.

While race, class, and gender theory and criticism have blown a necessary, just, healthful, and invigorating breeze into the academy, ironically the variable which scholarship on the so-called "politics of location" has ignored almost completely is that of physical, geographical location. The connections between spatial coordinates, topography, landscape, terrain, soil conditions, weather, bioregion, watershed, the environment, rural or urban setting, and identity have received short shrift from identity critics. The global soul, to borrow travel writer Pico Iyer's term, is more conscious now of its historical privilege or oppression, its gender, its skin colour, the skin of the Other, the sexual proclivities skin may arouse, and occasionally of its own class allegiances (although more often or more poignantly of its class aspirations), but in much recent critical discourse the global soul's multiple "locations" seldom extend to its position on the ground under its highly mobile and busy feet. Now that our fossil-fueled global souls get to see so much more of the planet, we seem to have become less rather than more interested in geography. This shrinkage of the physical, material world to bodies, on the one hand, and, on the other, its expansion to the global not only bypass the nation state and tired, outworn questions as to what constitutes *the* Canadian national character (which is almost entirely a good thing) but also, more dangerously, bypass the local and regional as sources of grounding, nurturance, significance, and identity. However, as Wendell Berry, Wallace Stegner, and many other theorists of place maintain, "If you don't know where you are, . . . you don't know who you are" (Berry, paraphrased in Stegner 199). In other words, in the absence of a sense of place, all theorizing of identity is rendered partial.

Although novelists and poets continue to write out of place, many literary texts which reflect upon and interrogate place have been ignored or even strongly denigrated by critics whose tacit assumption is that the teleological mission of criticism has marched on beyond the place-based studies of the 1960s and 1970s to the politics of location, also known as identity politics. It is helpful to remind ourselves of key statements of the recent past that did not omit the variable of place from identity theory. To take one important example, in her highly influential 1984 essay "Notes Toward a Politics of Location," Adrienne Rich, far from overlooking geography, refers to it several times in conjunction with race, gender, class, and the body: "I need to understand how a place on the map is also a place in history within which as a woman, a Jew, a lesbian, a feminist I am created and trying to create" (212). Two pages later she writes "let us get back to earth—not as paradigm for 'women,' but as place of location" (214). Moreover, the unexamined assumptions that theory in general—by definition and as opposed to practice—is placeless or global (that is, that theory is not written by embodied individuals from particular cultures, histories and languages) are strangely Platonic notions. This is strikingly contradictory, given that it is literary theorists who exhort us to rethink precisely those subjective facets of texts. As Robert Thacker succinctly states, "So like all writers, literary critics are 'never completely shed' of their place—whether it has to do with locale, interests, assumptions, intellectual debts, or the sheer expediency of shaping a piece of writing to an editor's demand for a given length" (180).

In a previous article, "The Angel in the Glacier: Geography as Intertext in Thomas Wharton's *Icefields*," I theorized that the physical setting of that novel can be read intertextually with other signs therein. The present paper is also part of a larger project of rethinking the literary notion of setting from an ecocritical perspective. In the first section of this paper, I briefly survey literary criticism of selected texts, noting significant instances of critical neglect of fiction and creative non-fiction texts which portray the arid Canadian prairies. As I surveyed criticism of prairie literature, I began to realize both how persistent the subject of aridity and drought is in prairie literature and how comparatively little attention the topic has garnered in our criticism. Not only has aridity attracted little note beyond articles on such classic prairie texts as *Who Has Seen the Wind* and *As for Me and My House,* but concerns about aridity and drought *since* the Depression—conditions associated with global warming, accelerated melting of glaciers, agricultural irrigation, the oil industry's rampant consumption and pollution of our water resources, and our rivers' diminution—seem not to have reached many literary critics. Together with the centrist biases built into Canadian cultural industries and their critical reception, the prevailing focus on and privileging of the urban in contemporary sociopolitical, media, and intellectual circles is resulting not only in the neglect of rural literature—a serious omission but one which could be addressed and rectified by those of us who value the literature of rural places—but also in the cavalier and vociferous denigration of the rural both at home and abroad.[1]

In the second part of the article, in a detailed case study, I analyze and deconstruct two sustained and, in my opinion, unwarranted critical attacks upon the fiction and creative non-fiction of one prominent rural Canadian writer, Sharon Butala, in order to highlight the need to reconsider setting from an ecocritical standpoint, that is, as something much more complex than simply the stage upon which a human drama plays itself out, more than just a horizon upon which writers "set 'er down." My purpose is not to analyze or critique Butala's work myself on this occasion. Moreover, it is emphatically *not* to oppose ecocriticism to identity politics, post-structuralism, globalization studies, or any other critical approaches.[2] To the contrary, what I shall argue is that as literary critics we need to add the supplement of place or geography to the other variables which constitute the politics of location. Otherwise, as I shall show through my two examples, we risk ignoring or writing off an entire body of literature, specifically the literature which examines the local, regional, national, and global problems associated with drought, planetary warming, and globalized agricultural economics, and more broadly the literature of the rural prairies, the writers who produce it and the lives and experiences of all of those people who live outside Canada's urban perimeter highways.

•

The Literature of Aridity and Drought

A contradictory thread runs through Canadian history and literature with regard to deserts, watersheds, and the prairie landscape in general. On the one hand, there is a tendency set into play by early European explorers and surveyors of the country to describe many different kinds of North American landscapes metaphorically as deserts or wastelands.[3] In fact, Canada has no true deserts, just a few very localized sandy places. Neither the Carberry Desert in Spruce Woods Provincial Park in southern Manitoba nor the Athabasca Sand Dunes in northern Saskatchewan is a true desert but rather glacially deposited sand dunes. But we do have arid and semi-arid zones, the Palliser Triangle in southern Saskatchewan and Alberta being one. These days average annual precipitation in the Palliser Triangle is fourteen inches, with eighteen inches lost to evaporation. Due to the recent drought cycle and global warming, most of Alberta all the way up to and including the Peace River country in the north has experienced severe drought, and some places in Saskatchewan are undergoing progressive sand dune activity and desertification, with corresponding economic, social, and psychological consequences. Wild cacti, the botanical emblem of aridity, are not uncommon in southern Alberta and Saskatchewan.

For all its apparent dryness, and although many writers have written about them, however, the semi-desert regions of the prairies and aridity in general have been given scant attention in our literary criticism since the heyday of national and regional identity and place studies of the late 1960s and the 1970s, the decades when such thematic studies as Laurie Ricou's *Vertical Man / Horizontal World: Man and Landscape in Canadian Prairie Fiction*, Dick Harrison's *Unnamed Country: The Struggle for a Canadian Prairie Fic-*

tion, Margaret Atwood's *Survival: A Thematic Guide to Canadian Literature*, John Moss's *Patterns of Isolation in English-Canadian Fiction*, D. G. Jones's *Butterfly on Rock: A Study of Themes and Images in Canadian Literature*, and others were published.[4] It is not as if the dryness of southern Saskatchewan and Alberta has escaped detection historically. In his 1869 report based on his 1857 survey of what is now southern Saskatchewan and southern Alberta, John Palliser summed up the area as an extension of the Great American Desert and recommended against future agricultural settlement. As they traversed the southern prairies from Red River to Fort Macleod in 1874 to establish law and order, the Northwest Mounted Police certainly noticed that it was an extremely thirsty zone, many of them succumbing to dysentery and some to typhoid from drinking the bad water in the few places they could find any water at all. In western Canadian literature, prose writers as various as W. O. Mitchell, Sinclair Ross, Andreas Schroeder, Sharon Butala, Robert Kroetsch, Sid Marty, Andy Russell, and Thomas King (to name just a few) have written about aridity and its natural, historical, agricultural, cultural, political, and psychological effects.

However, despite the lived, scientific, and literary evidence, Canadians historically have been in denial about the relative lack of precipitation in the southern prairies since before settlement—for instance, the Northwest Mounted Police were not even issued canteens for their westward trek through territory previously uncharted by white people and unknown to them. The famous settlement propaganda that "rain follows the plow" is merely the most quotable emblem of this historical refusal to acknowledge the terms and conditions of climate and geography, a refusal co-signed by some of our literary critics. This is in direct contrast to the critical tradition in the western United States where aridity is taken to be, in Stegner's terms, the defining feature of the west (60).

In other words, the aridity of the southern Canadian prairies is not a secret and never has been. Even today we continue to live in a strange condition of denial of aridity on the one hand —from, in Alberta where I live, our extensive irrigation agriculture and the use of billions of litres annually in the oil industry to our daily running of the tap—and, on the other hand, an ill-defined fear of some kind of arid apocalypse in a country which, to most non-aboriginals, is still so new to us that we do not know quite what to make of it. In addition, the rural parts of the country are getting less familiar to us all the time, with the ongoing shift of population from rural to urban and little movement in the other direction. As novelist Fred Stenson says, "What we need is an urban equivalent to Sinclair Ross's 'The Lamp at Noon.' We need an urban novel or short story about drought."[5]

Strangely, a couple of writers from generally much moister and more heavily urbanized provinces, Ontario and Quebec, have each set a novel in a true desert, and these two books are much better known nationally and internationally, but they are about deserts elsewhere in the world. The desert of Michael Ondaatje's *The English Patient* is in Libya, and that of Nicole Brossard's experimental, lesbian feminist novel *Mauve Desert* is in Arizona and New Mexico. Both of these novels, by writers from central Canada, have received considerable critical attention to date, and I will not be discussing them here because they are outside the geographical parameters of this essay, though it is worth noting that, with the exception of a conference paper by Bev Curran, "Against the Grain: The Canadian Desert," most articles on these two books pay less attention to the actual desert terrain than to its symbolic resonances.

The most obvious way in which critics have ignored the portrayal of aridity in western Canadian fiction and non-fiction is by ignoring not all but many of the books which have been written about it and their authors. Even the books which *have* attracted considerable critical discussion—partly because they have been around longer and became canonized, if precariously so, during the 1970s—have largely attracted notice for other reasons. Articles on Sinclair Ross's classic novel *As For Me and My House* (1941), set during the dustbowl of the Depression, have been devoted, in the main, to deftly analyzing the "hypocrisies" of small-town life (as if cities were hypocrisy-free zones), the personality and housekeeping skills of the narrator Mrs. Bentley, narrative technique, sexual imagery, paternity of the child, realism, and modernism, but the aridity of the setting is usually handled as mere historical fact or pathetic fallacy, the symbolic backdrop mirroring the strained marriage of the two central characters. Only a few articles and books, most of them from the same decade in which Laurie Ricou's *Vertical Man, Horizontal World* (1973) and Dick Harrison's *Unnamed Country* (1977) were published, actually deal with the terrain and climate as literal manifestations.[6]

Robert Kroetsch's fiction and poetry have fared somewhat better. The majority of the critical articles on Kroetsch's books are devoted to his frequent use of postmodern literary devices and theory. However, the sheer profusion of criticism devoted to Kroetsch's important body of work in several genres—fiction, poetry, literary, and cultural criticism—coupled with an interest in his work internationally (critics from other countries sometimes being more intrigued by the western Canadian landscape than many of their Canadian counterparts) has meant that a modest but respectable number of articles acknowledge the important role of place in his work. Kroetsch himself never fails to remember his roots and has always written and spoken in interviews out of a profound attachment to place.[7]

For a novel which I am including in this brief overview of prairie literature pertaining to aridity, Thomas King's *Green Grass, Running Water* is surprisingly damp. Water leaks everywhere. The first two sentences read "So. In the beginning, there was nothing. Just the water" (1), and the novel contains many puddles, seeps and drips, and concludes with inundation. *Green Grass, Running Water* is based on native protests against construction of a dam, and I include it here because dams represent the political side of aridity. Although lack of moisture is a fact, albeit a relative one, dams are as political as the treaty language and broken promises alluded to in the book's title, and moreover despite their role in irrigation they are not necessarily a panacea for low annual rainfall. The plenitude of water throughout *Green Grass, Running Water* both continually foreshadows the next plot development and the book's ending and suggests that the dam will only wreak mischief and havoc with the landscape, culture, and lives of the people of southern Alberta, not turn the area into a moister version of a capitalist paradise.

However, most articles about *Green Grass, Running Water* deal, variously and productively, with King's Biblical revisionism, subversion of mainstream paradigms through magic realism, construction of the novel as a post colonial puzzle, trickster discourse, ridicule of written authority, and intertextuality. Those which do allude to the fictional dam of the novel connect it exclusively with a major hydroelectric project in northern Quebec. For instance, Florence Stratton's essay, "Cartographic Lessons: Susanna Moodie's *Roughing It in the Bush* and Thomas King's *Green Grass, Running Water*," contains a section which discusses the politics of dams, though she does not mention the Oldman River Dam of southern Alberta where King lived for ten years, a time spanning the dam controversy, protests, and construction. The Oldman River runs through the city of Lethbridge, and Thomas King taught at the University of Lethbridge from 1980-1990, so it is surprising that the Oldman River Dam has not been explored in relation to the novel. Irrigation issues, native land rights, government corruption, and law-breaking in the building of the Oldman River Dam, and the Great Whale Hydroelectric Project, upon all of which the Grand Baleen Dam in the novel is based, are not the topic of any scholarly articles I have been able to find so far.[8]

Andy Russell's creative non-fiction narrative *The Life of a River* (1987) was written out of his activist involvement in trying to halt construction of the Oldman River Dam,[9] and one of the author's stated purposes of the book is to "make us look again at the conventional wisdom of using a river as a resource, not treating it as a living thing" (28). The book is not about aridity *per se* but about the natural and cultural history of the river, including the imminent building of the dam and the multiple kinds of damage it would cause. Nevertheless, it is noteworthy that the jacket copy provided by McClelland & Stewart dismisses the landscape which is the book's subject: "The Oldman River runs through all of these stories. To be swept along, you don't need to know the Oldman, which bursts out of the Rockies in Southern Alberta to become the South Saskatchewan and head for Hudson's Bay. You don't even need to know this foothills area, so well described elsewhere by Sid Marty and here by Andy Russell." Though it must be acknowledged that the author, in the final paragraph of his Introduction, states that the story he is about to tell about the geology and history of the Oldman "can be transposed to any river" (29), I think that, given the content and the timing of the book, Russell's objective in making this claim is to stir readers to action against the political machinations behind and the environmental consequences of dams, and to inspire solidarity. It is not to posit that the Oldman, to which he has devoted his entire book, is merely a representative case. Although there have been many reviews of his work, there are no academic articles yet published on any of Russell's dozen books.[10]

Andreas Schroeder's novel *Dustship Glory* (1986), based on a true story, is about a Finnish immigrant named Tom Sukanen in Manybones, Saskatchewan, a thousand miles from any ocean, who, during the drought of the Great Depression, begins building an ocean-going ship, a project which he continues with increasing obsession over a period of many years, causing his community to question his sanity. It is as if his mind takes literally the metaphor of the prairies as resembling the ocean. It is not that he is desperate to leave Manybones, since for the cost of his materials he could have purchased a ticket home to Finland or most anywhere else in the world, or simply walked away. Rather the novel sympathetically presents his actions as making about as much sense as breaking the land for farming in southern Saskatchewan before and during the Dirty Thirties. As the town elevator operator muses, "Oh, it all looked pretty good when the rain fell and the wind didn't blow your summerfallow clean into Manitoba, but underneath that thin layer of sweetgrass and crocuses, of wolfwillow and wild roses, it was really nothing more than a great goddamn desert just waiting for the chance to resurface" (15). I could not find any critical articles on this book in any of the relevant article indexes.[11]

Of course, as the son of failed farmers in southern Saskatchewan, Wallace Stegner, devoted several books and essays to the topic of aridity in both the Canadian and the American Wests, but his American citizenship and the way we typically demarcate our courses according to national boundaries has deterred many critics from taking up his work in the context of Canadian literature.[12]

In *Leaning on the Wind: Under the Spell of the Great Chinook* (1995), Sid Marty writes extensively about his ancestors being dehydrated out of the area around Medicine Hat and the preoccupation with weather and climate he inherited from them. Chapter 6, "Rain Follows the Plow," opens this way: "I was raised in a desert among the Philistines where there were no poets to people the landscape with heroes, where history waited to be discovered in a land where few people valued what had happened before their own arrival" (80). There are two critical articles on Marty's poetry, one by poet and critic Tom Wayman, published in 1993, two years before *Leaning on the Wind*, which also discusses Dale Zieroth, and a more recent one by W. H. New on the poetry of Marty, Peter Christensen and Jon Whyte.[13] Wayman explores a number of historical, institutional, and political reasons for the critical and academic neglect of Marty and Zieroth, two writers whose work he considers to be as fine as that of many canonized Canadian writers (41). Wayman posits that due to the increasing corporate commodification and homogenization of experience and the preponderance of urban and indoor experiences in our daily lives,

> it probably follows that a preference would be generated for
> art that is unspecific as to place, concentrating instead on
> the constituents of the art itself (forms, language, et cetera),
> or on magical or other non-geographic experiences. Writ-
> ers like Marty and Zieroth, whose writing is planted firmly
> in identifiable locales, will perhaps seem out of step with, or
> even in opposition to, such present trends. (43)

Sharon Butala, who with her late husband Peter Butala ranched for many years near Stegner's hometown of Eastend, has, like Stegner, taken on the issues of aridity, drought and the crisis in agriculture. She has done this most notably in the non-fiction account of her first eighteen years in that country, *The Perfection of the Morning: An Apprenticeship in Nature* (1994), and her novels *The Fourth Archangel* (1992) and *The Garden of Eden* (1998), the latter of which is set in both the Saskatchewan prairies and drought- and famine-stricken Ethiopia, but also in her short stories, essays, radio interviews, and talks. What relatively skimpy published scholarly attention Sharon Butala's work has garnered to date tends to focus more on psychological matters than on the landscape about which she writes. A recent search of the MLA bibliography for "Sharon Butala" yielded six scholarly articles on the work of a writer who has published more than a dozen books and been nominated for and won many writing awards.

———————————— • ————————————

Sharon Butala Criticism: A Case Study and Deconstruction

One article on Butala—Cheryl Lousley's "Home on the Prairie? A Feminist and Postcolonial Reading of Sharon Butala, Di Brandt, and Joy Kogawa"— deals centrally with place but only through a reading which, regrettably, pits race, class, and gender *against* place. The narrowness of Lousley's interpretation of identity theory either proceeds from or results in a formulaic reading of the three authors by which Lousley posits that the more officially "Other" is the writer's biography, the better her work. As such her article illustrates well the pitfalls of applying theories of the "politics of location" to a text without incorporating geographical location into the mix and merits close examination both on those grounds and in order to attempt to repair some of the damage that may have been done to the writer's reputation by such unfair criticism.

In several places throughout her article Lousley first distorts and then dismisses Butala's texts for not reading like standard fictional and creative non-fictional applications of current identity theory. Indeed her agenda to discredit Butala becomes plain when Lousley first quotes Butala's statement, in *The Perfection of the Morning*, that "I was in a position few people, especially women, are ever fortunate enough to be in . . . . It was the first time since childhood I had experienced such freedom" and then, on the same page, criticizes her for neglecting to consider class, and how her freedom to go for walks is a mark of privilege (Lousley 76). Immediately after quoting Butala on her difficulties in finding a social footing in her newly adopted rural, agricultural community, a painful struggle which Butala describes at considerable length in the book, Lousley accuses her of failing to consider her privilege to observe the community free of any sense of responsibility and accountability to it. What Lousley calls Butala's "privilege" is the psychologically painful condition of anomie from which Butala strives to free herself, ultimately effectively, during her first several years on the ranch.

Similarly, Lousley charges that Butala fails to consider the power which her representations of the rural carry due to her authority and status as writer. Lousley puts "writer" into quotation marks, as if placing Butala's artistry and status as a writer in doubt, even while accusing Butala herself of ignoring her position as such and the power and authority that come with it. First of all, *The Perfection of the Morning* is largely about the time before Butala had begun to write, the period when she was engaged in the process of finding a suitable identity within her new family and community, and moving from being a visual artist to a writer. The book is not about the time following the publication of *The Perfection of the Morning* which garnered Butala national attention and a far wider audience than she had enjoyed for her first several books. Secondly, if Butala is unaware of the power of her representations of the rural, then how are we to account for her outspoken activism—for writing and publishing books and newspaper articles and giving speeches about the agricultural crisis in the rural west? Lousley mistakes the stated purpose of her own article, which is to problematize the concept of rural, for its proof. Her claim that a prairie woman writer who writes about rural life and rural people has performed an illegitimate action is illogical. She claims that "Butala takes the geographical referent of 'rural' . . . and essentializes it into an identity" (78) and that "Butala claims not only to be able to accurately know and depict these other lives, but also to understand the underlying principle which shapes them . . ." While this is often what writers do (attempt to understand and write about the lives of the people around them), and while writing about one's own community (rather than those about which one knows significantly less) is what most advocates of identity politics and the non-appropriation of voices recommend, Lousley censures Butala for writing about the community in which she has lived for more than twenty-five years.

For Lousley only the always already sanctioned categories of identity politics—race, class, gender, sexual preference, ethnicity, and physical ability—qualify as legitimate categories of difference. She makes the bold statement that Butala has no regard for cultural appropriation and then immediately afterward quotes a passage where Butala clearly states "If I were Native, I would follow the dream's instructions, but I am not Native" (quoted in Lousley 79).[14] Having dismissed the category of place and ridiculed Butala's statement that her husband Peter, who lived his whole life on the ranch, is a true rural man, she berates the writer, claiming that her idea of the rural person is not inclusive, that she "neglects, indeed actively excludes, the possibility of Others, such as gays and lesbians, people of colour, and people with disabilities, within the rural as she creates her idyllic 'home'" (77-78). Her supporting evidence for this generalization is that in her novel *Luna* Butala writes that a woman with mental disabilities lives in a group home in the city "full of people like herself who couldn't manage on their own" (quoted in Lousley 79). In order to illustrate how Lousley decontextualizes the foregoing phrase, it is necessary to read the paragraph of the novel in which the phrase appears:

> Across the table, Sandy, a fifty-year-old woman who didn't look more than thirty-five, served herself from the bowl of carrots and peas that Selena had canned in the fall. Sandy, whose home was a big house in the city, full of people like herself who couldn't manage on their own in the world. Taken by her parents when she was fifteen to an institution and left there, then moved out of it into a group home. Allowed to go home only for the occasional holiday. She felt sorry for Sandy, who would never have her own house or children. She had been sterilized when she was a teenager. It's better that way, they had all agreed. (202)

I quote this passage in full not for its mention of Selena's sympathy for Sandy, as if it might stand in for Butala's own, but instead to question on the basis of the passage itself whether Butala is dismissing the character of Sandy and advocating segregation (and sterilization), as Lousley implies she does, or whether, conversely, Butala is criticizing practices which render "home" no more than a holiday and deploying a pointedly critical irony in the sentence "It's better that way, they had all agreed." Nevertheless, on the basis of a single abstracted phrase—and as if there were not people who benefit from or even need assisted living—Lousley dismisses *Luna,* a novel which is devoted almost entirely to an examination of the lives of three generations of rural women and girls in a prairie community, and ignores the other two novels, *The Gates of the Sun* and *The Fourth Archangel,* which together with *Luna* form Butala's trilogy about rural life in the arid west.

Lousley accuses Butala of essentializing and universalizing "home," "prairie" and "rural": in short, for not providing us with the socio-economic statistics for Eastend and district. Ironically, however, it is Lousley who fails to take into account that information, which is contained both in the preface to *The Perfection of the Morning* and throughout the main body of that text, and in several other published articles and radio interviews Butala has done precisely about the drought and the associated socio-economic situation of southwestern Saskatchewan.[15] In yet another contradiction, while taking Butala to task for not supplying economic specifics, Lousley fails to explain on what basis she herself formed her own notion of Butala's "idyllic" home (78) and privilege. Judging by Lousley's own comments, it seems to be because Sharon Butala frequently goes for a long walk at some point in the day between the hours of nine and five, that is, during the workday of the typical urban office employee.[16] Lousley proclaims that she wishes to undo the essentializing of the notion of place, but her method of achieving that objective is to essentialize the writer—as white, wealthy, a privileged housewife with time to go for walks on what Lousley refers to as Butala's husband's ranch. She overlooks the possibility that, like gays and lesbians, people of colour, and others whom she herself champions (77-78 and throughout her article), "rural" might also be a marginalized category Lousley's article would seem to constitute what Wendell Berry has referred to as "the prejudice against country people" because the inescapable implication of her article is that it is permissible for urban professors like Lousley to lobby on behalf of race, class, gender, sexuality, and differential abilities, but a rural non-academic is not to be permitted to speak on behalf of *her* community and locale, the often denigrated and sometimes ridiculed rural prairies.[17]

This type of critical approach to texts, at least in the context of Canadian criticism and cultural history, is, in part, a latter-day version of the colonial cringe, a type of national inferiority complex denoted by, among other symptoms, the repeated appeal to the overseas expert and the derogation of local, regional, and even national culture, initiative, and achievement. Prior to and even during the 1960s and 1970s critical apparatus and support used to be drawn routinely from foreign sources, primarily Britain and the United States, yet now the voice of authority is that of the (usually class-privileged) Continental philosopher or postcolonial theorist originally from a developing country (Jacques Derrida, Julia Kristeva, Hélène Cixous, Trinh T. Minh-ha, Gayatri Chakravorty Spivak), most of whom have made their deservedly major careers in one of two imperial nations, France and the United States.[18]

A second article on Butala's work which also traffics in the colonial cringe and gives her work short shrift is Smaro Kamboureli's "The Culture of Nature and the Logic of Modernity: Sharon Butala's *The Perfection of the Morning: An Apprenticeship in Nature.*" A thorough point-by-point deconstruction of Kamboureli's argument would occupy more space than would be permissible here, so I will confine myself to demonstrating why it is crucial to adduce the notion of geographical location not just to identity-based criticism but also to literary criticism which takes globalization as its central preoccupation.

In her introduction Kamboureli reflects on the popularity and Canadian bestseller status of *The Perfection of the Morning*, deciding that because the book has been read widely by non-academic readers it must be ideologically conservative. She writes: "the popular success of a literary title often says more about the social and political climate of the culture in general, and cultural and literary institutions in particular, than about a title's inherent merits

. . . .[Such a book] must surely communicate a message that strikes a chord in many readers" (38). While the book has sold well in Canada, citing this literary text as a bestseller, along with formula romances and genre fiction, is misleading. Over the course of her article, Kamboureli attributes its Canadian bestseller status to the book's anti-intellectualism, its undoing of the values of the European Enlightenment, and its author's failure or stubborn refusal to deconstruct binary oppositions. In her introduction she quotes two descriptions from book reviews which refer to Butala as "one of this country's true visionaries" and "a wonderful guide." Then through a sleight-of-hand manoeuvre she tries to buffalo her reader into thinking that it is Butala—not the reviewers—who proffers herself as a "visionary," "guide," and "advocate" for a decidedly pre- or anti-Modern "return" to nature and the rural life, and her book as a kind of spiritual instruction manual. That is, on the one hand, following Michel Foucault and Roland Barthes, Kamboureli purports to separate author intentionality from the text: "Contrary to Butala's authorial intentions, *the text's own intentionality*, as I hope to show, announces an uneasy alliance between nature and subjecthood" (40, emphasis added). Paradoxically, while removing author intentionality with one hand, Kamboureli returns it with the other, attributing the words of reviewers to the author herself, and implying that Butala claims some kind of self-assigned cult-leader status. Although Kamboureli writes that the text's intentions differ from those of the author— "*The Perfection* does not want to be read as a single individual's life story,"—it is the author who bears the brunt of her condemnation.

Kamboureli premises her argument on the logical fallacy of the straw adversary, the technique whereby one ignores another's actual position and substitutes instead a distorted version of it. On the opening page of her article, she contends that on page 12 of the hardcover edition of *The Perfection of the Morning*, "Butala advocates a 'return to Nature.'" Here is the passage from page 12:

> By the time I was twenty I had developed contempt for those who wanted to return to Nature, believing they were all romantic dreamers, nitwits from the city, people raised in the lap of luxury who did not know about Nature's nasty side, who had never done a day's real work in their lives and thus had no idea of the grinding labor a life in Nature demanded for mere survival. I liked to look at Impressionist paintings of Nature, having once harbored the dream of becoming a painter, and I was not averse to sunsets or moonlight on water, but I was just as happy to look at pic-

tures of them while seated on a soft couch, with my feet on
a thick rug and a well-insulated wall between me and the
thing itself. (12)

While the above passage might well be irritating to some, I cannot find in
it evidence of what Kamboureli describes as "the passion and conviction with
which she advocates a 'return to Nature'" (Kamboureli 38). No such sentiment
is expressed on that page or, allowing for possible errors in her works cited, on
page 12 of the paperback edition either. She claims that Butala "promotes" a
particular vision with "fervor" (39, 45). In fact, Butala subtitles her book "An
Apprenticeship in Nature," figuring herself not as the visionary guide who will
lead others into some simple, utopian reunification with a natural paradise
but as an apprentice or novice. (It is worth noting that Butala begins her book
with a brief history of the Palliser Triangle in which her ranch is located, its
semi-desert aridity and non-paradisiacal climate.) If anything, one might fault
Butala for excessive scrupulousness about her own lack of previous knowledge and expertise in matters natural and spiritual. Despite this, throughout
her article Kamboureli freights Butala's autobiography with grandiose, even
megalomaniac, intentions and ambitions:

> Rather than celebrate her book as "brave" [as Helen Buss
> does], it would be more pertinent to wonder aloud whether
> the terms in which Butala's project intends to curtail, if not
> transform, the emerging world order of globalism are at all
> feasible, or just a mere re-dressing of "the local/global fig-
> ure," which, as Paul Bové, among others, has argued, "is in
> some ways a figure of neocolonial struggle." . . . . This may
> account for the anti-intellectualism that marks Butala's text,
> a point I will return to below, but also begs the question
> as to what master narratives she seeks to unravel by relo-
> cating from the city to a rural area. That this movement is
> validated by the appearance of supernatural signs, by her
> promulgation of conceptual and mystical distinctions she
> offers as alternatives to what troubles urban subjectivities
> today, would imply that her project is intent, at least in part,
> on reversing the course of modernity. . . .The progress that
> her 'dream' promises is not tantamount to creating an alter-
> native course of human development. (41)

To suggest that with a single book the author "intends to curtail, if not transform, the emerging world order of globalism," or that her move to the country
is motivated not by marriage but by a desire to "unravel" master narratives

from some rural bunker is a striking misreading of the text. Is Butala offering her autobiography as a kind of chicken soup for the urban soul? When Butala offers three or four significant dreams and her interpretation of them, she does so not to validate her move to the country but, more often, to call attention to her uncertainties, fears, and initial spiritual ennui in her new home.

Another of Kamboureli's fundamental premises is that what she calls the "localism" of *The Perfection of the Morning* marks it as allied with the outdated Canadian regionalism of the 1970s. She writes: "Since that movement has ceased to be the determining force behind the recognition of western authors in the last fifteen years or so, the fact that her narrative is firmly located in one particular area, 'the extreme southwest corner of Saskatchewan, just north of the Montana border,' would suggest an instance of residual regionalism" (38). She claims that the book has emerged from a movement which is passé—superseded by post-structuralism, most specifically deconstruction, and globalist critique. I would argue that rather than scrapping that scholarly work of the 1960s and 1970s it is time for a thorough reconsideration and critical, theoretical update of notions of region and regionalism. However, I differ with Kamboureli's unquestioned assumption about the teleological completion both of history and literary criticism. In the first instance, while the regionalism of those two decades has indeed served its term as a vibrant critical paradigm and needs extensive retooling in the light of subsequent theories, including feminist theory, identity theory, post-structuralism, and ecocriticism, what I would question is the underpinning of a belief that regionalism is a *fait accompli* while deconstruction is still living on, especially given that, interestingly, both movements commenced at approximately the same time in the late 1960s. Of course, it could be said that deconstruction is a globalist project and, tautologically, that Canadian regionalist criticism, North American regionalism, or any kind of regionalism is, well, merely regional. I am not opposed to deconstruction: the present article *is* a deconstruction. Nevertheless, there are risks in a totalizing and reductive application of this theory as with any other.

I would question whether literary works are or ever were regional. To what exactly does the term "regional" apply—to texts, author intentionality or critical apparatus? Are literary works regional in their intention or their composition? Are they regional only by virtue of being placed under the lens of the critical microscope? What or who dictates that a novel by a writer based in Toronto is of national and even international significance whereas one by a writer based in, say, Medicine Hat, Saskatoon, or Edmonton is a regional text? What makes Armin Wiebe's novel *The Salvation of Yasch Siemens*, about a hired man in southern Manitoba, any more "regional" than Michael Ondaatje's novel about the working-class builders of the Toronto waterworks *In the Skin of a Lion*? Authorial ambition? Authorial address (the geographical kind)? The larger population of Toronto as compared to that of Winnipeg?[19]

As one works through Kamboureli's extended argument and experiences the full measure of her umbrage at Butala's reasons for leaving her low-paid, exploitative sessional appointment at a university to go and live with her new husband, whose ranch is not within commuting distance of the University of Saskatchewan, one begins to feel as if some of Kamboureli's discontent with Butala may be of a personal nature. On page one of her narrative, Butala writes that she experienced a great deal of suspicion and misunderstanding about leaving the university for a country life: "Such is the prestige of a university job, the sense of those who make a life there as being the anointed, that my fellow graduate students and lecturers must have found my abdication from it very hard to understand" (1). While the choice of the word "anointed" may rankle for seeming to erase all those years of hard work and poverty that often go hand-in-hand with acquiring a doctorate, nevertheless Butala's friends and former colleagues at the University of Saskatchewan are not alone in their sentiments about the prestige of the ivory tower. Although Kamboureli as-sumes an unequivocally elitist stance in pointing out in her article's intro-duction her suspicions about the literary tastes of those readers who made *The Perfection of the Morning* a Canadian bestseller, nevertheless she bristles at Butala's statement that her friends and university colleagues believed that university positions are privileged ones. Without considering the privileges of a university professor, especially relative to those of a rancher/writer who lived the first few years of her new life on the ranch without indoor plumb-ing (*Perfection* 54), Kamboureli counters what she views as Butala's assault on the academy by chastising her for her privileged life as a rancher (without substantiation as to the average annual income of ranchers, acreage figures, number of cattle sold in a given year, or the like).[20] In any event, Kamboureli devotes much more space in her 21-page article to taking Butala to task for her views about the university than Butala herself devotes to the topic in her 221-page book. Kamboureli's suspicion of what she perceives to be a rural woman writer's dangerous naïveté in writing within an aesthetic purported to be outdated, failure to deconstruct binary oppositions, and failure to keep up with the latest books about the university as institution—actual charges she levels against Butala in her article—is the obverse of her own correspond-ing faith in the necessity, power, authority, and efficacy of deconstruction, the university, and globalism.[21] For her, the regional and the rural alike are *a priori* literary, historical, epistemological, and theoretical backwaters.[22]

Even while mounting such a strenuous case against *The Perfection of the Morning* as to, in effect, discredit Butala as a writer and intellectual, like Lousley, Kamboureli also accuses her of the serious charge of cultural appropriation. Here is one of Kamboureli's accusatory passages:

> Instead, though she decidedly follows an itinerary which reverses modernity's progress by taking her back to a "primal" state of being, recurring statements like "This land makes Crees of us all" demonstrate Butala's intention to extract from them a universal natural law which at once annuls the Crees' specificity and discloses the complicity of her project with modernity, and colonialism as its civilizing mission. (41-2)

There is no question that a statement like "This land makes Crees of us all" could be fairly construed as problematic. However, in her next sentence Butala explains what she meant by this spontaneous utterance to a friend, an explanation which is not taken up by either Lousley or Kamboureli. Butala describes going for a walk on the ranch with a visiting friend, rambling together wherever the land suggested itself to them:

> In this is [sic] semiarid country where rain is rare and precious, walking in it is exhilarating, imbued even with a touch of magic. . . .
>
>   . . . .
>
> I thought, then said, "This land makes Crees of us all." By this, I meant that it appeared to me that the Crees, for example, developed the culture they developed because it was the best fit between themselves and the land. And it was the *land* that taught them that. They adapted to the land, and not the other way around as we Europeans so stupidly did, trying to force this arid western land to be, as government propaganda had for seventy-five years and more put it, "the breadbasket of the world." (99-100)

In his article "The Terrible Truth about 'Appropriation of Voice'" on the often unexamined complexities of the politics surrounding the issue of appropriation, Stephen Henighan concisely flags many of the issues pertinent to both the Lousley and Kamboureli articles. He writes:

> Broadcasting concern for minority issues to the point of promising sanctions against "appropriators," while actually

diverting attention from their own positions of authority, established cultural figures have found in "appropriation of voice" the ideal mechanism of co-optation. . . . "Appropriation of voice" depends for its legitimacy on the assumption that there exists an undiluted, "authentic" core to each culture, reflected in its traditional art. Yet most of this century's literary criticism, from Bakhtinian polyglossia to New Criticism to Derridean deconstructionism to Cixous's efforts to "write the body" to Bloom's descriptions of the "anxiety of influence" to Marxist and Lacanian approaches, has developed, in different ways, from the notion that literary language is a hybrid, impure conglomeration of coded assumptions and shadows of half-absorbed past systems of writing. One of the most bizarre spectacles induced by the "appropriation of voice" carnival has been the sight of trendy fellow-travellers of literary fashion simultaneously proclaiming their allegiance to the mutually exclusive assumptions of contemporary literary theory and "appropriation of voice" (65 -67).

The risks of silencing minority writers are a genuine danger associated with voice appropriation. However, if the sanctions delineated in Lousley's and Kamboureli's arguments were imposed they would largely foreclose on the possibility that anyone other than a First Nations person, including minority writers, could ever be or become at home here in Canada or North America.[23] In their terms, any implication that living for decades or even generations in a locale might lead to a non-aboriginal person's becoming intimate with the plants, animals, climate, terrain, and people of that place may only be met with censure. In any case, it would certainly not seem productive of future understanding and genuinely healthy inter-relations between First Nations and other Canadians to forbid development of knowledge of and intimacy with place and the natural world. It would also seem pointless to worry about appropriation issues around First Nations' storytelling and other artistic and cultural productions if non-aboriginal Canadians are prohibited from learning from them, and if aboriginal literature and other artistic productions and performances are nothing more than an occasion for the rest of us to show off our newly-acquired listening skills, sensitivities and manners. Moreover, I am not sure that the kind of respect First Nations' artists and cultural workers want and deserve is the kind which must be withdrawn from some other group (for example, rural Canadians) in order to be bestowed upon them.

That seems more like investment than genuine respect.

Kamboureli not only levels the charge of "appropriationism" against Butala, a serious and potentially career-damaging charge against which it is extremely difficult to defend oneself once it has been made in a public forum, but over the course of her article she also accuses Butala of a number of other "isms" as well. Including appropriationism, I count at least twenty-two: Kamboureli charges Butala with regionalism (38), fundamentalism (39), personalism (39), voluntarism (40), anti-Modernism (41), pro-Modernism (54), anti-globalism (41), anti-rationalism and anti-intellectualism (41 and throughout), reductionism (45), mysticism (51), visionaryism (39), ethnographism (53-54), ignoring or failing at deconstructionism (throughout), pedagogicalism (44), romanticism (46), individualism (52), localism (52+), ideological adventurism (42, 53), detailism (53), and having a Christopher Columbus complex (i.e., neocolonialism) (54). While Kamboureli may very well have no good reason to appreciate *The Perfection of the Morning*, the sustained vindictiveness of her attack upon its author is cause for serious concern.

Kamboureli's derision builds to a climax near the end of her article where she mocks Butala's knowledge of her own locality. Earlier in the article she criticizes her, as a newcomer to the Eastend / Cypress Hills area, for carrying a notebook and gathering information and knowledge about her new surroundings. While conceding that through walking, concentration, and careful observation, "Butala constructs an astounding archive of local detail" which offers a "faithful record of the phenomenal world in the midst of which she lives" (52), nevertheless Kamboureli concludes that the collection of these details is "not meant so much to engage with that landscape in its own terms, but rather to facilitate Butala's release from the immediacy of that locality, to open the road, as it were, toward the grand abstractions of Nature and Self" (52-3). The writer's common practice of keeping a notebook incurs at least three charges: localism, detailism, and ethnographism. Ironically, Kamboureli blames "globalism-as-neocolonialism" on "localists" like Butala. She writes: "Perhaps the popular success of *The Perfection*, what has prompted me to write about this book in the first place, is an example of the phenomenon that, as a number of intellectuals have observed, it is a certain kind of localists that prevail over globalization arguments today" (55). In his essay "Writer and Region," Wendell Berry suggests the opposite, that in the national or the global point of view "one does not pay attention to anything in particular" (81). Once she has dismissed both Butala's details and her right to make larger observations about nature, landscape, and her own sense of place, Kamboureli concludes that "It is a good thing, then, at least according to this reader, that

Butala's locality is just a dream" (56).

Both by implication and by overt claim, Kamboureli elevates her own views, as a professor of English and a literary critic, on the farm and ranch crises of Saskatchewan over those of a rancher. Although she concedes in her final footnote that, even as she is writing, farmers in Saskatchewan are organizing mass demonstrations to publicize the cycles of economic disasters they have been facing over the past few years, Kamboureli makes no mention in the rest of her article of aridity, drought, BSE, corporate agri-business, or economic problems in the west. She writes: "The problem with her project lies not so much in that she has no 'clear vision' of how we should go about it, but in the fundamental inability of her vision to perceive that a return to the land, let alone to Nature, that is not accompanied by a radical questioning of 'the foundation of our nation' will only further solidify what is wrong with this nation's foundation in the first place" (55). She ridicules Butala's tentative suggestion of a guaranteed annual income for small farmers in order to preserve Canada's food production systems and to keep some of the struggling rural communities alive in western Canada, calling it a "welfare system introduced and managed by the state" (55) which "could materialize only through docile subjects or through subjects that would have to be disciplined" (56). Why rural people would have to be disciplined is not clear. Moreover, reading this startling conclusion made me question the difference between a guaranteed annual income for small farmers and salaried university teaching positions. In Canada, where universities are largely state-supported institutions, a more-or-less guaranteed annual salary is paid by the state to a subject (the professor) who has been disciplined at various post-secondary institutions and taught to produce in the classroom and on paper "food for thought."

The flipside of examining the reasons for the popularity of *The Perfection of the Morning*, as Kamboureli purports to do, would be to question why this particular text brings out such animosity and intolerance in these two female academics who have allied themselves with so-called "international" theorists, theorists, that is, whose work is widely believed to transcend their own regional and national boundaries. Why does this text unsettle Lousley and Kamboureli to such an extent? My argument that the absent supplement in the politics of location is geography or sense of place cannot account for the degree of their hostility. However, in the course of untangling just some of the points raised by these two fraught articles I have been drawn to the observation that one of the things which *The Perfection of the Morning* upsets is the traditional division separating non-aboriginal and aboriginal views of the natural world. Though the words which ostensibly make Lousley and

Kamboureli see red are the ones like "Nature" which are capitalized in the book, an easy target for charges of essentialism, it is at root, I think, the slight blurring of European and First Nations world views in some rural people's perspectives which truly exercises them. SueEllen Campbell observes that one of the critical tactics common to both post-structuralism and deep ecology is "to question the concepts on which the old hierarchies are built" (128). Some nature writing also questions the same hierarchies, among the most cherished of which are urban versus rural and European versus First Nations. Cultures often live on, surviving individuals' uprooting and transplantation, surviving even so-called "conquest," and what is often forgotten (perhaps because of that very resilience and tenacity) is that what constitutes the distinctive cultures of many groups are the languages, beliefs, and practices which emerged during the time when groups were connected to and almost entirely dependent upon the land—that is, when they were nomadic or rural. Culture is at root and in many important respects ecologically based. Though there may be exceptions, First Nations cultures are not among them. Place or geographical location is the missing supplement which lurks within and, unacknowledged and untheorized, confounds the arguments of both Lousley and Kamboureli. Place—physical location, the lived world—is the supplement in the Derridean sense of "an inessential extra, added to something complete in itself, but the supplement is added in order to complete, to compensate for a lack in what was supposed to be complete in itself" (Culler 103) to what is supposed by Lousley, Kamboureli and others to be already complete in identity politics.

———————————— • ————————————

In their 1997 essay "Firing the Regional Can(n)on: Liberal Pluralism, Social Agency, and David Adams Richards's Miramichi Trilogy," Herb Wyile and Christopher Armstrong write that during the past few decades of critique along race, class and gender lines, "The politics of spatial divisions and cultural differences within nations . . . has received less emphasis, even in a country as preoccupied with geography and space as Canada, but the situation is starting to change" (1).[24] While the point of the valuable work in the field of "the politics of location" has been to assert and analyze differences which had previously been ignored, suppressed, or repressed, and the notion that people who live within a given district or region may have things in common was, in many respects, rightly suspect for its potential and actual investment in the hegemony of liberal or conservative humanism and neo colonialism, the time has come when the variable of place can play a role in supplementing and further developing notions of agency and solidarity within and among differences, and when "the politics of location" may be and, as I have argued here, must be opened up to include geographical location.

The literature and politics of immigration and displacement is the literature and politics of entering the new country, the new landscape. Contemporary immigrant literature is the new literature of settlement, the new settler literature. It is, to put it another way, the "pioneer" or "sodbuster" literature of the urban milieu (perhaps we could call it "pavement pounder" literature to acknowledge the urban setting of most of this literature and to avoid assimilating it to the hegemony of the previous literary tradition which was almost completely dominated by Euro-Canadians). A number of pioneering critics today seem to feel that, in order to advocate on behalf of First Nations or immigrant literature, or to undo the effects of colonization or marginalization, they must first clear the land of the literature of the rural—both the older wave of settler literature as well as any recent literature which is agriculturally rooted or rurally based. This kind of thinking presupposes that immigrants to Canada who choose to live in cities are not settlers, and that city dwellers and city life are diverse whereas country dwellers and rural towns and villages are all the same.

However, like Canadian geography itself, the field of Canadian literature is large and commodious and can contain multitudes, especially if one includes rather than excludes readers from outside the universities, those not confined to the narrowness of the canon and the limitations of the thirteen- or even the twenty-six week syllabus. That is, there is room within Canadian literature not only for the literature of displacement but also for that of coming to terms with and acceptance—even love—of place, climate, geography, landscape, nature, the local and regional, including the urban. While the language of inclusiveness I am using in this paragraph could be easily assailed as nothing but liberal pluralism, alternatively to posit an economy of scarcity—that there is no need and no room for literature from the prairies or other rural parts of Canada—where there is none, is equally problematic. Moreover, what I am advocating is more than inclusiveness; it is the pressing need to incorporate into our thinking and critical practices some recognition of the environmental conditions and crises we all face, urban and rural alike, in the many diverse places we inhabit here in Canada. As ecocritic Harold Fromm reminds us, "A thought may have no weight and take up no space, but it exists as part of a stream of consciousness that is made possible by food, air, and water" (38). Whether as an academic discourse regionalism is or is not a dead horse, and whether thinking about rural places and rural literature can only be carried out within the discourse of regionalism and no other, are worthy topics for further debate. However, whether the purported death of regionalism as a critical discourse means that prairie writers should cease writing about rural places or be silenced through neglect, censure, or our own lack of adequate critical tools and local knowledge, and whether rural people deserve as much respect as city people, are questions I hope to have resolved here. What we need is a politics of location and a revisioning of literary criticism which includes rather than excludes a place to "set 'er down."

Notes

The first draft of this paper was presented in the Sonora Desert at the 2002 Western Literature Association Conference in Tucson, Arizona. I wish to thank Christine Wiesenthal for reading and commenting on the penultimate draft of the full version of this paper, Fred Stenson for talking over with me several of the ideas presented here, and the editors of *IJCS* for publishing an earlier version of this article in *International Journal of Canadian Studies* 32 (2005): 237 - 67.

1. In addition to the Lousley and Kamboureli articles which I analyze closely in this article, see also Alan Hepburn's "Urban Kink: Canadian Fiction Shakes Off Its Rural Roots."
2. I myself research and publish in the fields of identity politics, post-structuralist theory, and ecocriticism.
3. William Cronon writes that "As late as the eighteenth century, the most common usage of the word 'wilderness' in the English language referred to landscapes that generally carried adjectives far different from the ones they attract today. To be a wilderness then was to be 'deserted,' 'savage,' 'desolate,' 'barren'—in short, a 'waste,' the word's nearest synonym" (70).
4. This flowering of criticism was fertilized to a significant degree by the nationalist sentiments and granting programs surrounding Canada's 1967 Centennial celebrations.
5. Conversation with Fred Stenson, August 2005.
6. Many articles and book chapters have been published on Ross's novel. I refer the reader to the relevant webpage of the Canadian Literature Archive at http://www.umanitoba.ca/canlit/bibliographies.
7. See the Canadian Literature Archive at http://www.umanitoba.ca/canlit/ bibliographies for a list of critical sources pertaining to Kroetsch's work. See also the four chapters on Kroetsch's long poems in my book *Body Inc.: A Theory of Translation Poetics*.
8. One exception is Laurie Ricou's roundup review of a number of books,

"Other Edens," in which he refers to *Green Grass, Running Water* as "Canada's finest dam novel" and notes its connection with the Oldman River Dam (n.p.). Another is the published version of Cheryl Lousley's article on the book which, by chance, came to me to vet for publication. I added to my reader's report notes about the Oldman River Dam, the Piegan Lonefighters and Milton Born With a Tooth and urged the then-anonymous author to use those leads to research the novel's setting in southern Alberta.

9. The Alberta government changed the name from the Three Rivers Dam to the Oldman River Dam to make the project appear less comprehensive and therefore less controversial.

10. Generally speaking, historically Canadian literary critics have concentrated far more on poetry, fiction, criticism and theory, and drama than on creative non-fiction.

11. Editor's note: Nor has Ken Mitchell's play *The Shipbuilder*, first performed in 1978 and published in 1990, received much notice from the academy. It is also based on Sukanen's story. A film about Sukanen, *Sisu*, is currently in production, directed by Chrystene Ells. The Sukanen ship can be viewed just outside of Moose Jaw.

12. Writers such as Kroetsch and Butala and critics such as Ricou, Harrison, and Thacker consider Stegner's work important to the western Canadian literary tradition. In addition to viewing him as an influential literary predecessor, Butala was also instrumental in having the Stegner house in Eastend, Saskatchewan, restored and converted to a writers' and artists' retreat.

13. I discuss Marty's creative non-fiction along with that of Don Gayton and Sharon Butala and the novel *Icefields* by Thomas Wharton in my article "The Land Writes Back: Notes on Four Western Canadian Writers."

14. Lousley often makes a claim and then attempts to support it with textual evidence which, to my reading, directly contradicts her claim.

15. See Butala's essay "Field of Broken Dreams" and her interview with Allan Casey. See also Krista Foss's account of how the Butalas donated one third of their land and sold the rest to the Nature Conservancy of Canada, in order to turn the former ranch into a buffalo commons. Swift foxes, a nearly extinct species, have also been released into their former natural grass prairie habitat on the Old Man On His Back Prairie and Heritage Conservation Area, as the Butala ranch is now called.

16. Lousley characterizes Butala as having lived "on her husband's ranch . . . for almost twenty years" (76). While the ranch was in Peter's hands

before his marriage, I find this anti-feminist attitude regarding marital property surprising and offensive. Moreover, Lousley's claim that Butala's walks betray her privilege is confusing. Would a similarly long walk in the city (whether for shopping, exercise, sheer *flâneurie*, or to catch the subway train) be marked as privileged? Interestingly, Smaro Kamboureli also objects to Butala's walks, though Lousley sees walking in nature writing as a humanist activity (77) whereas Kamboureli finds fault with it because the walks partake of the "romanticism of detail" and valorize "the minute, the partial, and the marginal" (53).

17. Compare Richard Lewontin's attack on Vandana Shiva as summarized by Berry in "The Prejudice Against Country People." Lewontin, Berry writes, criticizes Shiva for being under the influence of and appealing to "a false nostalgia for an idyllic life never experienced." Berry observes that industrial capitalists and their allies typically deploy anti-rural rhetoric. Lousley uses the same phrase "idyllic life" to find fault with Butala. Berry's essay is widely available on the internet.

18. It would be worth interrogating the assumption that it is acceptable to earn a good income from theory but not from agriculture.

19. Stephen Henighan, among others, has taken on the politics of literary reception in his provocative book *When Words Deny the World.*

20. Even if the Butalas were prosperous ranchers, in order to be fair and consistent one would have to attack her for her ranch income rather than her writing. It is rare to see a writer attacked in print solely on the basis of his or her livelihood or income.

21. Kamboureli is not alone in subscribing to the view that deconstruction can only happen at universities, although as an operation of logic I would contend that it can happen anywhere at any time.

22. See Eric Zencey on "The Rootless Professors" and the work of Stan Rowe, Wendell Berry, David W. Orr, Wes Jackson, and others on the relationship between the rural and the university.

23. I would distinguish between being and becoming native to a place. For an informed overview of the complexities and ironies surrounding the question as to who is and is not an Indian, see Chapter 5 of Thomas King's *The Truth About Stories.*

24. Things have begun to change. In 1998 the journal *Studies in Canadian Literature* published a special issue on "Writing Canadian Space," in 2000 *Essays on Canadian Writing* did a special issue on "Where is Here Now?" and a 2001 issue of *Canadian Literature* was devoted to nature writing and ecocriticism. Newer voices such as those of Herb Wyile, Lisa

Chalykoff, and David M. Jordan are beginning to rethink regionalism, and familiar voices such as those of W. H. New and Arnold Davidson have also reconsidered these matters. See W. H. New's *Land Sliding: Imagining Space, Presence, and Power in Canadian Writing* and Dallas Harrison's remarkable essay "Where is (the) Horizon? Placing As for Me and My House" in which he sets out to discover on which Saskatchewan town Ross may have based the fictional town of Horizon. There is also a growing interest in environmental literature and ecocriticism. See the website of the Association for Literature, the Environment and Culture in Canada at http://www.alecc.ca.

Jenny Kerber

•

Displacing the "Home Place": Madeline Coopsammy's "Post-Prairie" Poetry

"How do you write in a new country?" This question, posed by Robert Kroetsch in his 1983 essay "The Moment of the Discovery of America Continues," became a clarion call for prairie poets to inscribe a set of previously neglected regional voices and landscapes into the national literature. In works by writers such as Dennis Cooley, Aritha van Herk, Eli Mandel, Andy Suknaski, and Kroetsch himself, prairie poetry became a powerful new presence on the national stage, and a legitimate site for the articulation of what Cooley termed "vernacular" expression. In Kroetsch's long poem *Seed Catalogue*, for example, readers encounter a persona who not only wrestles with how to write "in a new country," but who also experiments with different ways to claim the prairies as a "home place": "the home place: N.E. 17-42-16-W4th Meridian"; "the home place: one and a half miles west of Heisler, Alberta, / on the correction line road / and three miles south"; "The home place: / a terrible symmetry" (8).

The central questions and desires underlying Kroetsch's regional poetics remain important today, but some writers and critics argue that the particular vision of the "home place" his work offers—one centred on the rural, agricultural prairie of the mid-twentieth century—looks familiar to fewer and fewer contemporary prairie residents. Consequently, in a recent anthology co-edited with Kroetsch, Jon Paul Fiorentino proposes a new critical term—the "post-prairie"—to describe works that reflect an increasingly urban, fragmented, cosmopolitan prairie identity, rather than one rooted in predominantly rural or historical settings. As Fiorentino remarks, "There is an anxiety of geography at work in the post-prairie poem. It longs for its home only to 'trouble' the very articulation of home" (11).

In what follows, I will consider the critical possibilities and limits of Fiorentino's term by examining how one prairie poet, Winnipeg's Madeline Coopsammy, expands the meaning of the "home place" by situating regional experience within a larger diasporic context. By exploring the limits of the vernacular's conception of prairie identity and geography, Coopsammy's 2004 volume *Prairie Journey* ends up raising important questions about how to fit within an established tradition of writing prairie environments when, as Lauret E. Savoy puts it, "one's primary experience of landscape and place is indigenous or urban or indentured or exiled or degraded or toxic" (Deming and Savoy 8). While Coopsammy's work resonates with Fiorentino's mission to expand the category of prairie poetry beyond exclusively local or rural concerns, I will suggest that it ultimately rejects the idea of *temporal* progress implied by the "post-prairie" in favour of a *spatial* orientation that understands the region through its relationships with other geographical scales and spaces. Her approach thus encourages readers, writers, and critics of prairie literature to think about how "writing the local" can contribute to a transnational ethics of place.

As a writer of South Asian descent born in Trinidad, educated in India, and then relocated to the urban terrain of Winnipeg in the 1960s, Coopsammy does not easily fit into the mould of prairie immigrant experience mythologized in the works of the regional poets mentioned above. Coopsammy thus begins her series of poems gathered under the heading "Seasons on the Prairies" with a poem that contests the image of the prairie immigrant as a version of Clifford Sifton's "stalwart peasant in a sheepskin coat" (Hall 77).[1] In "Immigrant" the reader is introduced to a "black anomaly within a land of snow" who has come to Canada neither as "ayah nor domestic," but as a member of the professional class who is "wistfully seeking a better life" (26). While her membership in a class of immigrants that official Canadian immigration policy favours helps guard her against poverty, it does not insulate her from "hostile looks / that stop the blood more than the blizzards and the frosts / of barren Prairie winters" (26). The prairie winter will demand some adjustment, but ultimately it proves more flexible than the social environment that regards the dark-skinned person as perpetual outsider.

One of the paradoxes of visible minority experience is that even as one is made to stand out from the fabric of the surrounding social and physical landscape, one is also compelled to merge into it without leaving a trace. Coopsammy proceeds to explore this dynamic of exceptionality and assimilation in the poem "Invisible Woman," wherein the title character encounters the barriers erected by an unseen hierarchy that systemically prioritizes some varieties of immigrant experience over others. Against a backdrop of Canadian immigration policy historically propelled by labour needs, the title character is asked, "Invisible woman / can you type?" and "[p]arlez-vous Français?" (38), suggesting that her value to society will be gauged by her capacity to fill certain labour sectors and to conform to the linguistic codes of official bilingualism. Although the woman has been trained by a colonial British system of education that allows her to assert a shared knowledge of the English literary canon, once she reaches Manitoba this kind of cultural capital is devalued as impractical and anachronistic:

> Invisible woman
> you must forget
>> the sweat and tears
> that filled the Urn
> once called
>> a classical education
>
> that was in
> another country
>> prestigious symbols
> of the old world
> mean nothing in the new. (37)

The colonial education that might have given her a competitive edge is now deemed ill-suited to a prairie economy that prides itself on a form of egalitarianism that keeps outsiders in their places. Instead of functioning as a carrier of cultural prestige, then, Keats's ode serves as a metaphor for the very forms of imported, smothering ideas of "high" culture from which the prairie vernacular sought to free itself in favour of a more populist ethos dealing with local history, people, and places.

Coopsammy's poem then moves on to challenge some of the assumptions underlying constructions of prairie identity championed by literary regionalists in the 1970s and 1980s. After her labour and language skills have been assessed according to how well they suit the needs of the Canadian market, the invisible woman is asked a series of rhetorical questions designed to place her within a hierarchy of prairie immigrant experience:

> did your people homestead here?
> eat the red dust of
> Depression years?
> flee from ravaged
> Europe?
> Discard the 'Skis" [sic]
> and anglicise their names? (38)

These questions reveal a particular set of assumptions about what immigrant identity means on the prairies, assumptions that attempt to render universal what are in fact very specific kinds of historical and geographical experience. The forms of exclusion practiced here thus illustrate how regionalism's claim to the margin can ironically lead to the hegemonic enforcement of homogeneity (Dainotto 488). In this case, the invisible woman's inclusion in or access to regional identity ultimately depends on her relationship to whiteness," a condition that places her in an impossible bind as a *visible* minority: in the end, she is told, "though you cannot buy / a change of skin / You have to serve / your time" (38).[2] One imagines that even after years of living in the region, the woman may still not be able to claim the status of prairie dweller with the same ease as someone who passes as white. The language of "serving time" further suggests that prairie dwelling can be a form of incarceration in which one's status as a Canadian is continually determined by the power of others.[3] The reality of racial discrimination means that the invisible woman's difference cannot simply be neutralized by a politically palatable rhetoric of diversity that seeks to mute differences within prairie immigrant experience based on factors such as race, class, and gender.

The ways in which differences in race, gender, sexuality, and economic opportunity influence a person's experience of a physical environment suggest that perceptions and descriptions of the prairie may vary a great deal depending not only on the dimensions of the prairie on which one focuses, but also according to whom one consults. Though both can be categorized as prairie immigrant experiences, for example, Coopsammy's perspective of the prairie will almost certainly be different from the experience of a child of European immigrants who settled on a homestead near Brandon in the 1920s. At the same time, I do not want to suggest that the most appropriate or most natural place for the visible minority immigrant on the prairies is in the city, for such an assumption risks essentializing certain kinds of relationships between people and landscapes, and presumes that the countryside cannot become a place of deep social as well as natural diversity.[4] Indeed, it was precisely the assumption of an essentialized relationship between people and environment that discouraged African American immigration to the prairies in the early twentieth century, despite the fact that most of the immigrants who wanted to settle in the region were African Americans from Oklahoma who had abundant agricultural experience. The attempt to exclude them was based on a presumed correspondence between race and physical climate (Shepard 100; Waiser 75). Further, it is also necessary to keep in mind that not all immigrants of colour necessarily come from urban environments in their home countries; for those from locations that could best be described as rural, the comfort of finding oneself amidst others who "look the same" in a larger city may come at the cost of distancing oneself from the type of rural or small-town geographies one had previously known.

In the poem "The Second Migration," Coopsammy further complicates the relationship between immigration and regionalism by introducing the reader to an interpretation of the prairie from the perspective of one who is not only an immigrant but also a diasporic subject. Here the speaker of the poem challenges three common assumptions about the newcomer's transition to the Canadian prairies: first, that the immigrant's relocation to this region is always one of upward mobility on the social ladder; second, that it necessarily entails a move from cramped to expansive physical surroundings; and third, that it involves a temporal shift from past to present and future. In the poem the narrator challenges the idea of immigration as upward mobility by making clear that she arrived in Canada as a member of the professional class, one of those who immigrated during the 1960s, "a time of joy and greening" (28). During this period, Canadian legislation started to address the overt racial discrimination in its immigration policy, and began to open its doors to well-educated, skilled, middle- and upper-class immigrants from a wider variety of countries than it had in previous decades (Whitaker 18). Such immigration was deemed necessary to meet the labour needs of the postwar economic boom. But the poem suggests that the demand that immigrants be of the well-educated, privileged classes in their home countries was also self-interested, motivated in part by a desire to avoid the kinds of internal strife that had recently erupted in other Northern countries who were accepting large numbers of immigrants.[5] The poem alludes, for example, to Canada's desire to avoid the kinds of racial and ethnic tensions that had flared in England in the 1950s, as the Notting Hill riots were sparked by British anxieties about the increased competition for lower-wage jobs presented by Caribbean immigrants during a period of high unemployment (Pilkington 96-97). The narrator recalls the official rhetoric of the time:

> "We want your best,
> No Notting Hills for us," you warned.
> So once again we crossed an ocean
> convinced that little Notting Hills we'd never be. (29)

The narrator's people have already crossed one ocean, moving from the "green wastes of the Indo-Gangetic / to the sweet swards of the Caroni" (28) in the first "voluntary" migration of South Asian people to Trinidad and Guyana after the official abolition of slavery in the Caribbean in 1838 created a need for indentured labourers to work in the sugar plantations (Mehta 2). The second migration of the title then points to this same group's transition "to Manitoba's alien corn" where they "angled and trimmed" themselves to fit into the Canadian mosaic (28).[6] The "greening" of this second migration, while initially suggestive of the wholesome growth of the nation, might also refer to a less idealistic form of economic "greening" in which the colour of botanic growth becomes the colour of money.

Instead of encountering an open door of social opportunity, the speaker and her diasporic fellows are met with mere tolerance upon their arrival in Canada (28), and the way in which their cultural identity must be tailored to fit into the Canadian idea of multiculturalism is paralleled by their similarly regulated experience of prairie space. While the speaker's family has arrived in a geographical region lauded for its apparent spaciousness, their personal experience of space is one of "bite-sized backyards" (29) overwhelmed by smoke from neighbours' backyard barbeques. The poem concludes with the narrator and her family asking themselves "how far we are / from San Juan, Belmont and St James" (29). By invoking the Caribbean environment as a means of comprehending her present surroundings in Winnipeg, the narrator resists the idea that adopting a Canadian identity means forgetting her pre-Canadian identity, and challenges the notion that a journey from the global South to the global North must necessarily be interpreted as "progress." Instead, she chooses to traffic back and forth between the Canadian prairie and the Caribbean in order to better understand each place through its relation to the other.

By providing space for the co-existence of Trinidadian and Manitoban environments within the boundaries of the same poem, Coopsammy sidesteps the critical double-bind that otherwise restricts how writing about place by Canadian minority writers of colour is interpreted. Where the category of Canadian writing has not outright excluded minority writers of colour, as it often did in the past, Arun Mukherjee argues that it has tended to divide this writing into two categories: "if it deals with subject matter that alludes to where the writer came from, it is perceived as nostalgic. If, on the other hand, it has Canadian content, it is automatically considered to be about an immigrant's struggle to adjust to new realities" (431-432). These kinds of critical categories are premised on the idea that "home" can only ever be located in one place; for Coopsammy, however, home is Manitoba, home is Trinidad, and home is even, to some extent, India. The vision of prairie place and space her poetry generates is thus contingent upon an understanding of other spaces and times. This leads to two possible interpretations of the diasporic subject in these poems: on one hand, one might see the subject as "unhomed," an exilic figure wandering the liminal space between places but never truly at home anywhere; on the other, however, one might consider how the diasporic subject opens up the space for a hybrid vision of place to emerge, one is at once local *and* transnational. The latter option is explored in the poem "Prairie Journey," wherein the past landscape of the Caribbean becomes a living presence within the inland sea of the prairie:

> Sometimes
> through the windows of the bus
> those shimmering fields of white
> assume a new dimension
> and deceive me into thinking
> that I am once more
> on the verandah of my uncle's house
> dreaming hourly
> as I gaze upon the sea
> and the flickering beacons of the distant farms
> are really only
> twinkling lights
> of ships on the horizon
> stars which beckoned us
> in all their wonder and their beauty
> to the worlds beyond the seas. (48)

The narrator insists that what she sees is a "new dimension"; neither wholly prairie nor wholly Caribbean, the "place" it produces is in motion, situated somewhere between points of arrival and return. The speaker's double vision emerges out of what Janice Kulyk Keefer has described as the "middle distance" that inflects immigrant life in Canada (103).

One might initially interpret the first section of "Prairie Journey" as a nostalgic allegory in which the narrator retreats to an idealized Caribbean landscape as a means of escaping the unpleasant effects of change in her present environment. Seeing the Caribbean landscape in the winter prairie could thus be interpreted as a form of imaginative flight from the reality of the "new west" in which the narrator finds herself, wherein "decaying inner-cities" and "suburban ghettoes" form her daily experience of place (48). However, if we think of each of the "homes" Coopsammy's narrator traffics between as a dynamic entity, we soon see that the Trinidadian environment is one that has undergone change as well. She may experience nostalgia in its original sense as a "longing for home," but also recognizes that a return to the homeland she once knew will always necessarily be a return with a difference, altered by time, experience, and shifting material circumstance. Upon returning to her home in Trinidad, Coopsammy's narrator thus engages in the following reflection:

this residential neighbourhood
once coveted and sought by
those who wished to climb
the ladder of respectability
has now become
a marketplace
grotesque and utilitarian
its edifices soar relentlessly
while we strain futilely to glimpse the
shoreline
to revel in the blue light of the waves
to be soothed by their eternal wash. (49)

The disdain for the appearance of vertical architecture that mars the cultural and physical landscape —in this case, hotels and condominiums serving the foreign tourist trade—provides an interesting contrast with a prairie lament for the disappearance of similarly vertical structures from the landscape: those small-town grain elevators that have largely been dismantled as farmers are now required to transport their grain to more distant, concrete inland terminals. One might argue that the vertical structure of the elevator has undergone a kind of migration, finding itself transported and reconstituted into the edifice of an urban condominium tower designed to fill the needs of a new global economy where investment is redirected away from primary production towards the retail and service sectors. Whether in a state of construction or dismantlement, however, both of these environments experience the effects of decisions based on the needs of transnational capital, rather than the long-term sustainability of local communities. In "Prairie Journey," the persona attributes this phenomenon to the ceaseless pursuit of "the Yankee dollar," which "only leaves us decrying / the loss of our heritage / for all that once had nurtured us" (49).[7] In her concern about the ramifications of Trinidad's increasing reliance on foreign capital, and the way this leads the government to bow to the pressures of the tourist trade in spite of its negative effects on local environments, Coopsammy shares the attitude of a number of other diasporic Caribbean writers, including Jamaica Kincaid and Olive Senior.[8] In Senior's poem, "Rejected Text for a Tourist Brochure," for example, the persona bitterly refers to the hidden ecological costs of development in Jamaica:

Truckers steal sand from beaches,
from riverbeds, to build another ganja palace,
another shopping centre, another hotel
(My shares in cement are soaring). The rivers, angry,

are sliding underground, leaving pure rockstone
and hungry belly. (53)

The natural environment is treated as a free source of aggregates to be appropriated for the production of wealth, but it is wealth only for the few, and
Senior's poem implies that there will eventually be a price to be paid for the
ecological devastation wrought in order to serve the tourist industry.[9]

While neither Senior nor Coopsammy hesitates to condemn the negative
effects of indiscriminate development on their respective Caribbean islands,
both of these authors also acknowledge their own complicity in the systems of
power they speak against; Senior, for example, wryly notes that her shares in
the cement company are "soaring" (53). Coopsammy also acknowledges that
she is neither exclusively on the receiving nor the administering end of globalization and the time-space compression it involves. While her own mobility is
restricted by the politics of race, the poems in *Prairie Journey* also make clear
that it has also been to some extent enabled by the politics of class.[10] The title
poem of her collection concludes with a consideration of these issues, as the
persona acknowledges how her own pursuit of opportunity in Canada left her
native Trinidad vulnerable to foreign exploitation:

To mourn the loss
is futile now
we only have ourselves to blame
for while our children pursued
the North American dream
we left our borders
undefended
the stranger at the Gate has entered
and raped and pillaged
leaving us once more
hewers of wood and drawers of water

we are the new colonials. (49-50)[11]

These lines suggest a high degree of ambivalence about the price of individual
success, and also exhibit a conflicted attitude about crossing the boundaries
of the nation-state. In particular, Coopsammy's use of the phrase "stranger
at the Gate" suggests two complex and contradictory readings. On one level,
the "stranger at the Gate" is simply the colonial master in a new guise, one
who seeks to enter and ultimately control the Caribbean using the carrot and
stick of foreign capital. The postcolonial Trinidad may now be a site of capital
investment rather than resource extraction, but many of the profits of that

investment continue to be funnelled out of the country while local people remain trapped in low-wage jobs with little opportunity for advancement.

At another level, however, the "stranger at the Gate" can be interpreted as a challenge to empire rather than a mechanism of it. The stranger in this context is one who threatens to storm the barricades of civilization. Coopsammy's use of the term in this latter sense ironically redeploys the title of fellow Manitoban J. S. Woodsworth's *Strangers Within Our Gates, or Coming Canadians* (1909), a text which sought to reduce the anxiety of people alarmed by the flood of non-British immigrants into the Canadian prairies in the early twentieth century, focusing on how best to assimilate (and if possible, Christianize) them into the existing social fabric of prairie society. Although Woodsworth's text can ultimately conceive of no form of prairie identity other than one based on "Britishness," it is also remarkable for its acknowledgement of the prairie immigrant's ambivalent position as at once newcomer and resident, colonizer and colonized. Speaking of the incoming tide of immigrants, Woodsworth remarks: "'Strangers within our gates'—perhaps, in one sense, we are the strangers. Throughout the long years before the coming of the white man the Indian possessed the land" (14). Woodsworth proceeds to acknowledge the negative impacts of colonization upon the region's Aboriginal population, but also refuses to see the First Peoples as a vanishing race; instead, he states that their descendants will "have a place in *our* new nation" (14, emphasis added). The possessive adjective used here, however, leaves it ambiguous as to whether or not the First peoples will be considered co-creators of the new nation or merely invited residents of it.[12]

The last line of the poem similarly exploits the ambiguity of collective terms as the speaker positions herself in a fraught dual role, voicing solidarity with those in the global South under siege by Northern capital even as she acknowledges her alignment with the forces of neocolonialism. The declaration that "we are the new colonials" capitalizes on two different meanings of the term *colonial*—one of which designates someone whose native country is a colony, and the other which designates someone who lives in a colony but who is a national of the colonizing country. As a diasporic Canadian writer, Coopsammy straddles and challenges these categories, living in a colonizing country that also happens to be a former colony. The collective "we" with whom Coopsammy aligns herself is therefore deliberately ambiguous, a flexible term that acknowledges the speed with which an economically prosperous group or region can become impoverished when capital investment is pulled out and directed elsewhere, justified by claims about shifting markets, uncooperative climates for investment, or the need to stay globally competitive. The freedom with which global capital travels from one region to another means that, barring more intensive government and social regulation over the activities of transnational corporations, certain groups of people on the Canadian prairies and in the Caribbean islands alike find themselves in danger of becoming "the new colonials."

In asserting a shared plight I certainly do not want to downplay the differences among various groups' experiences of neocolonialism, which are dependent on the particularities of geography and political history in addition to factors such as gender, race, and class. What I want to assert instead is the potential *commonality*—rather than the universality—of experience that a poem like "Prairie Journey" asserts. Coopsammy's work encourages us to consider how experiences of living with the negative effects of neoliberal development schemes and environmental precarity in both the Canadian Prairies and the Caribbean might form a basis for what Chandra Mohanty has termed shared "cartographies of struggle" (Mohanty 43). Instead of conceptualizing placedness in a way that risks a reactionary return to ideas of permanence and rootedness in the local, Coopsammy's work encourages readers to understand the local by branching outward. The mapping of global capital's negative environmental effects might then lead to alliances based not on essentialist notions of colour or sex, nor on presumptions of an undivided natural space, but on shared political interests that traverse national boundaries. What then emerges is a "transnational ethics of place" (Nixon 239) that constellates the concerns of environmentalists and postcolonialists, keeping in mind how decisions about the physical environment are often structured in and through assumptions about race, gender, economics, and history. Coopsammy's poems clearly demonstrate that local environments—whether in Manitoba or in Trinidad—cannot be conceptualized in isolation from transnational and global ones; to think meaningfully about prairie landscapes and the environmentally degrading effects on them caused by resource extraction and corporate agribusiness then involves the connection of these issues to similar struggles in other countries and countrysides. As Doreen Massey puts it:

> [instead] of thinking of places as areas with boundaries around, they can be imagined as articulated moments in networks of social relations and understandings, but where a large proportion of those relations, experiences and understandings are constructed on a far larger scale than what we happen to define for that moment as the place itself, whether that be a street, a region or even a continent. And this in turn allows a sense of place which is extroverted,

which includes a consciousness of its links with the wider
world, which integrates in a positive way the global and the
local. (154-155)

In Massey's conception, the idea of community does not necessarily need
to be coterminous with bounded physical place (146). Instead, our ability
to develop "a global sense of place" depends upon the imaginative capacity
to make connections across culture, space, and time. This approach to community avoids the danger of making ungrounded universal claims by basing
its observations in the local, and also averts the risks of eco-parochialism by
situating the region within a broader context.

What emerges from the establishment of these connections is the possibility of forming transnational environmental solidarities, for example,
between communities in the Caribbean that suffer the social and ecological
costs of opening their lands to resort developments so there will be employment (better low-paying work than no work at all), and small towns and rural
municipalities across the prairies who open their doors to industrial agricultural operations in order to stem the tide of rural depopulation and bring
much-needed capital investment into the community.[13] Thinking about environmental solidarity in a transnational context might further prompt one
to consider the possible connections between the Manitoba grain farmer's
lament about low grain prices and the low price of bananas in a Winkler gro-
cery store, for example. It may mean thinking about regulations concerning
the use of agricultural herbicides and pesticides and how these so often stop
at the national level, even though many of our foods are imported.[14] And, it
means contemplating the disproportionately large influence corporate devel-
opers have over what shape downtown communities will take—concerning
issues such as how much green space will be preserved, what kind of housing
will be available, and what balance of residential and commercial space will
be achieved—whether that downtown is located in Winnipeg or St. James.
This is not to ignore or diminish the particularities of the local, but to extend the personal and the local to a transnational, "hybridized community
of political awareness" (Mehta 11), one that makes connections between the
"sweet swards of the Caroni" and "Manitoba's alien corn" while seeing "the
green wastes of the Indo-Gangetic" in both (Coopsammy 28). As Winnipeg
writer and critic Uma Parameswaran explains, this imaginative process is not
one of simple assimilation, transference, or substitution; rather, it is a process
whereby the immigrant comes to figuratively see his or her native river in the
river that runs through his or her adopted place: in Parameswaran's case, this
confluence occurs when she comes to see Ganga *in* the Assiniboine. Ideally,

this process transforms not only the immigrant, but the citizens of his or her adopted land as well. Parameswaran's riverine metaphor thus becomes a way of imaginatively calling into being a future time when not only will "those from India see their holy river in the Canadian landscape but when the average literate Canadian would recognize as a matter of course the literary connotations of the word 'Ganga' and thereby the emotional configurations of his [or her] East Indian neighbours" (120).

To return to the concerns with which this essay began, what can we conclude about Coopsammy's relationship to a category such as the "post-prairie"? First, it is clear that her work shares many of the concerns voiced by Fiorentino about ways in which the regionalist vernacular tradition tended to define prairie culture and prairie landscape: as rural, as agricultural, as white, and, very often, as male. While the vernacular as a regional form of poetics did much to help build a distinctly prairie culture in the 1970s and 80s, it also performed its own acts of exclusion, both in the kinds of writing it privileged and in the kinds of readers it assumed. Consequently, many writers and critics now argue for a more flexible conception of prairie writing that includes and accounts for the complex contradictions, hybrid identities, and multiple allegiances of the writers themselves.[15] If the vernacular, as Cooley defined it, is the "common, everyday language of ordinary people in a particular locality" (175), who are these "ordinary" prairie people today, what spaces and places do they claim as home, and what are their relationships to the prairie landscapes in which they find themselves? Responses to these questions cannot remain static: just as the prairie environment has undergone massive change over the past one hundred and fifty years, so too have the compositional demographics of those who call this region home undergone significant shifts. For prairie poetry to remain vibrant, it must be given the room to creatively anticipate and respond to these changes in ways that acknowledge that the prairies are neither fixed, nor "over," but rather exist in a perpetual state of becoming, the outcome of which we may only glimpse through refraction from our present vantage.

Second, for Coopsammy the question of how to write in a new country is always inflected by the experience of diaspora. The ways in which her poems traffic between Manitoba and the Caribbean illustrate that the idea of community does not necessarily end with one's physical departure from a particular region. The fact of travel unsettles fixed notions of the regional "home place" and allows the contemporary prairie dweller to see him or herself as part of a community of contingency that encompasses different regional places and times; it also opens up new channels of solidarity and resistance to the expanding forces of globalization and the impoverishment of local communities by corporate capital. The spatial orientation of "the prairie" that results understands the transnational and the global in complex relation—rather than strict opposition—to the local. As Iain Chambers has remarked:

> Any narrative, any accounting of the world, willing to receive and offer hospitality to a disturbance that uproots the *domus* and that invites us not to feel at home at home (Adorno) renders the universal story many of us think we are living more localized, particular. In the poetical power of language to reconfigure space in a diverse understanding of location and identity, home is made a more open-ended and vulnerable habitat. (28)[16]

To think about the "home place" in this way does not mean that prairie poets and critics should abandon concern for the particularities of local environments in order to participate in a homogenous, jet-setting global culture. Indeed, one of the reasons I am cautious about Fiorentino's category of the "post-prairie" is the apparent ease with which it relegates a whole series of environments and ways of relating to them to the past. Further, any attempt to extricate the term "prairie" too tidily from its connections with the countryside—whether that countryside is located in rural Manitoba or southwest Trinidad—risks neglecting the material bases of production upon which so much of urban life depends.[17] In short, geography may be reconfigured by processes of globalization, but it still *matters*. Arguably few issues illustrate the interdependencies of people and places as persuasively as environmental ones; to see the prairies as a set of places profoundly interconnected with the well-being of other places therefore has profound implications not only for how prairie poetry will be defined in the future, but also for the kinds of environmental solidarities that might be formed in the here and now.

Notes

1. Sifton was Canada's Minister of the Interior from 1897-1905, and was responsible for the promotion of immigration and settlement in the Canadian West. He particularly focused his energies on attracting large numbers of settlers with agricultural experience from the United States, Britain, and Europe. The flip side of this endeavour was the discouragement of immigration of other groups, including Jews, Italians, Asians, and Blacks, whom he believed were ill-suited to farming and would not stay long on the land before migrating to cities (Waiser 63-64).

2. For more extended discussion of how Canadian identity is premised on

a racialized discourse of "whiteness," see Dionne Brand 187-188, and Himani Bannerji 108.

3. For further discussion of tropes of incarceration in writing by racial minority women in Canada, see Mukherjee 424.

4. For more on this point, see Nourbese Philip, who notes that while most recent immigrants to Canada reside in urban areas because they usually feel more comfortable in the ethnically- and racially-diverse space of the city, she also hopefully looks ahead to a time of "being able to share in the land—in all aspects of the land and not only in the urban areas with which we are identified. Moreover, we must be able to share the land [not only] in the recreational sense, but in a sense of the land as a source of strength and support, as it has been for First Nations people" (274).

5. As Will Kymlicka points out, the debate continues today about what kinds of immigrants Canada should be seeking. He notes, for example, that recent evidence suggests highly skilled immigrants are having more difficulty in the current labour market than family-class immigrants and refugees. This is likely due to factors such as discrimination and the fact that the information economy requires high levels of professional linguistic proficiency that are difficult to access and costly to fund (D22). Kymlicka suggests that "[r]ather than cherry picking the most talented immigrants—and thereby contributing to a brain-drain from develop-ing countries—perhaps we should accept a broader range of immigrants and refugees. A one-track obsession with skilled immigrants is, arguably, both short-sighted and a betrayal of our international responsibilities" (D22).

6. For today's reader, the designation of Manitoba's corn as alien points not only to its visual foreignness to one who has not seen it grown before, but may also refer to its altered status as a genetically-modified organ-ism. Interestingly, alien status might equally be applied to Trinidad's sugarcane, which is a colonial transplant to the Caribbean. In both cases, the planting of foreign species as agricultural crops became a means of colonization justified by the Roman legal principle of *res nullius*, wherein "all empty things," including lands not occupied by humans, remained the common property of all until they were put to some "useful," gener-ally agricultural, purpose (Casid 7).

7. The narrator's characterization of economic globalization as simply the pursuit of the "Yankee dollar" is admittedly reductive, since the United States is just one of several countries that profit from investment in the Caribbean. However, there is no denying the immense influence of

American capital in the region when it comes to economic and environmental decision-making. Recently, protests erupted in southwest Trinidad over a governmental memorandum of understanding with the US-based aluminum giant Alcoa to build a 340,000 tonne smelter. Although Alcoa and the government promised that the smelter's construction would bring jobs to Trinidadians, many local residents protested that it would result in massive land clearance, displacement of residents with meager compensation, traffic congestion on narrow island roads, and pollution of air, soil, and water. As a result of these protests, the Trinidad and Tobago government turned down the proposal in early 2007, but Alcoa remains committed to finding an alternative site in the region for its smelter construction. The presence of large natural gas reserves off the Trinidadian coast is the main incentive behind the Alcoa proposal. I thank Madeline Coopsammy for notifying me of these recent environmental struggles. For two different perspectives on the proposed project, see www.nosmeltertnt.com/trinidad_master_plan.html, and Alcoa's official site: http://www.alcoa.com/trinidad_tobago/en/home.asp. Accessed 19 December 2007.

8. See, for example, Kincaid's book about Antigua, *A Small Place*, as well as Stephanie Black's documentary *Life and Debt*, which lifts the curtain of benign Caribbean tourist imagery to expose Jamaica's struggles for financial and social security in the face of strict World Bank and IMF policies of lending and structural adjustment.

9. M. Nourbese Philip similarly speaks about the pressures the tourist industry places on people's relationships to nature in her own ancestral country of Tobago: "In Tobago, all beaches are free and open to the public, which runs counter to the capitalist approach; so you can see very clearly these new colonizers trying to find ways of making a commodity of this land, this resource, which has served the people for so long" ("Fortress" 23).

10. The phrase "time-space compression" is Doreen Massey's. See her essay, "A Global Sense of Place" (146-156). As David Harvey points out, class is a major influence on one's experience of placedness within the time-space compression of globalization, since it helps determine whether one is in a position of control or vulnerability in relation to these processes (295). Massey concurs that class is an important factor in one's relationship to the "power-geometry" of globalization, but cautions against viewing class as the main influence on one's experience of place at the expense of other factors such as gender, race, or sexuality.

11. See also the poems "Re-Colonization" and "The Mango Tree," which also express concern for the way indiscriminate development has altered the Trinidadian landscape (Coopsammy 89-91; 104-105).

12. In 1989 this ambiguity was eventually challenged by Manitoba MP Elijah Harper, who opposed the Meech Lake Accord because it did not adequately acknowledge the First Peoples as a founding nation of Canada on par with the English and the French.

13. The possibilities for building such enviro-political alliances are expanded even further when one considers that many of those working in these industries on the Canadian prairies are themselves recent immigrants of colour. For example, at the Lakeside Packers facility in Brooks, Alberta, which processes forty percent of the country's beef, sixty percent of the workers are immigrants, mostly from Sudan, while a large portion of the domestic workers are from Newfoundland. A 2005 strike at the plant illuminated the possibility for building enviro-political alliances across cultures and regions, but in the end this process was hindered by factors such as anxiety related to lost employment, anti-union sentiment, racism, and regional discrimination. See "Lakeside" n.p.

14. According to data cited in a recent lecture by environmental journalist Andrew Nikiforuk, Saskatchewan currently imports seventy percent of its vegetables (Nikiforuk, "Pandemonium"). This statistic would seem to challenge the myth of self-sufficiency promoted by traditional characterizations of the prairie provinces as the breadbasket of the world.

15. See Calder 7. For a collection that attempts to take a more expansive view of the connections between poetry and prairie place, see Robert Stamp's anthology of Alberta poetry, *Writing the Terrain*.

16. The reference to Adorno is found in "Refuge for the Homeless" in *Minima Moralia* 39.

17. The systemic denial of the interdependency of urban and rural life in literary depictions of country and city is pointed out most memorably by Raymond Williams in *The Country and the City* (1973).

Cristina Artenie

•

Re-reading Grove's *Settlers of the Marsh* as an Immigrant Novel

In more than eight decades since its publication in 1925, *Settlers of the Marsh* has never been squarely read as an immigrant novel. Canadian critics have acknowledged that the characters are immigrants but viewed their experience of the West as an example of settler experience. This article focuses exclusively on what makes this novel an immigrant one, discussing in depth the immigrant experience, with its implicit processes of deterritorialization and subsequent reterritorialization. In *Settlers of the Marsh* Frederick Philip Grove adapts the conventions of immigrant fiction to portray the immigrant experience of a young Swede, Niels Lindstedt, in a specific time and place: Northern Manitoba in the first decades of the twentieth century. According to Canadian critic Jonathan Kertzer, the narrative pattern of immigrant fiction begins with a conflict—usually a generational conflict—within the family that is trying to adapt to a new life. This conflict among the family members is a source of great pain; conventionally, "this pain is therapeutic: it expresses a loss of self necessary to create a new and stronger identity" (135). Instead of choosing a conflict between first- and second-generation immigrants as the novel's main theme, Grove focuses on Niels's inner conflict, generated by his newly acquired status as immigrant and member of an ethnic minority. However, later in the novel, the conflict between Niels and his wife, Clara Vogel, adds another dimension to the idea of family conflict which, eventually, will prove beneficial to the formation of Niels's new identity. The novel thus broaches a double conflict: the inner struggle, resulting from the effect of dislocation upon the uprooted individual; and the external conflict, suggested by the growing animosity between Niels and his German wife, metonymically signalling the political, social, and economic climate encountered by immigrants in Canada, before and during the First World War. As Homi Bhabha would say, Grove "locates" this hostile climate by "redrawing the domestic space" and by showing how "the personal-*is*-the political; the world-*in*-home" (15; emphasis in original).

From the novel's first pages, which find Niels unable to articulate himself on the prairie, through the long years of hard work and painful relationships that eventually displace his Swedish identity in favour of a Canadian one, Grove concentrates on conveying the immigrant experience. The motifs specific to the genre as outlined by Kertzer, such as uprooting, travel, entry, and dispersal, are all explored in *Settlers of the Marsh*. So are the main themes: exile, betrayal, metamorphosis. The only major exception in Grove's novel is that the story does not follow three generations (heroic ancestors, degenerate offspring, rootless grandchildren), as is usually the case in more recent immigrant fiction (Kertzer 135). Grove concentrates all these themes and motifs specific to immigrant fiction in Niels's story. He portrays a young man's heroic attempt to re-root in a new country, his descent into hell, his metamorphosis in a Canadian prison, and his final rebirth into a newly-forged identity. Indeed, Grove runs the gamut of the immigrant's struggle, revealing the intensity of the conflicts that the immigrant experiences before he can adjust to his new life.

Recent studies of immigrant fiction show how each author adopts some of the narrative patterns of the genre, while adapting some of its features. Daniel Cowart has identified ten such features in contemporary immigrant fiction and although his analysis draws on novels written since the 1950s, most of these traits can be found—if in a less developed form—in *Settlers of the Marsh*. Cowart notes that the immigrant novel is often fragmented and that sections have often been previously published as freestanding stories, with the same "set of characters and experiences" (7). While this is not exactly the case with Grove's first novel, the characteristic becomes pertinent when one takes into account *Settlers of the Marsh* alongside his second novel *A Search for America*. Published separately, the novels boast similar characters (both protagonists are young Swedes) and similar events (both heroes travel within the North American continent and both find their home in Canada after long years of hardship). These two novels could be read as a reflection of the author's own fragmented narrative, stemming from his personal experience.

Among the characteristics of immigrant novels Cowart identifies the interpolation of "[o]ld-country folktales or other material" (7). Such tales are alluded to in the novel. For example, although Grove does not tell us which folktale Niels recalls when he sees Amundsen's house and yard, the place nonetheless reminds him of "wood-cutters' houses in fairy tales" (Grove 24).[1] Since Niels could not have learned such tales in Canada, he is thinking of Swedish fairy tales. Another element of immigrant fiction is "travail in school, especially in learning English" (Cowart 7). Again, while Grove does not actually describe a classroom or a lesson, he writes that during the winters, Niels goes to night-school to learn English while working and living in Minor. Several times in the novel the narrator mentions Niels's progress in learning the language of his new country.

One of Cowart's characteristics refers to authors/narrators, who, having immigrated themselves and having experienced a "smoother" transition than their characters, "make wry, quasi-anthropological observations regarding the diffidence vis-à-vis the self-assurance of the native-born" (7). Often, the narrator in *Settlers of the Marsh* conveys directly to the reader Niels's feelings of alienation, his questions and doubts about the new country and about ways to fit in, to belong: "He himself might be forever a stranger in this country. . . .But if he had children, they would be rooted here. . . .He might become rooted himself, through them" (45). According to Cowart, always present in immigrant fiction are memories and images "of what makes the homeland unlivable" (7). Niels vividly remembers his childhood, and especially recalls that his mother worked as a cleaning woman in the houses of the rich. The sad eyes of his mother seem to follow him in his Canadian life as a constant reminder of the poverty and unhappiness of his past life.

Another characteristic of immigrant novels is showing the "immigrant's struggle with a sense of psychological and cultural doubleness" (7); Cowart notes that the narrator conflates the protagonist's past and present, showing how he is simultaneously "a maladroit immigrant and a child or young man in the motherland" (7). This same motif is employed by Grove, who consistently shows Niels's incapacity to understand the people around him and to integrate into the new community, always feeling a stranger among those who should be his newly-found friends, and—episodically—recollecting scenes from his childhood. According to Cowart, immigrant fiction also concerns "immigrants exploit[ing] immigrants" (7). Such an example is briefly sketched in the novel: prosperous farmer Amundsen, Ellen's father, charges Niels's friend Lars for the cartridge that Lars uses to shoot the rabbit that "contributed to the [Amundsen] family larder" (Grove 37). Lars has to pay for the cartridge with the little money he earned while working for Amundsen. He tries to protest: "not that it matters; but I turned the rabbit in." And Amundsen replies: "you shot the rabbit on my place. You will remember I asked about that" (37).

An immigrant novel, argues Cowart, shows the experience of "prejudice and homesickness" in the beginning of the story and the way he or she "eventually becomes empowered by a new identity" (7). In the beginning of *Settlers of the Marsh* Niels often compares Sweden to Canada, feels a stranger in the community, and does not seem to connect with anyone. After having spent almost seven years in jail, Niels comes back to his farm reformed and reborn; he is by now a Canadian. Cowart notes that even though the new identity is the ultimate aim of the narrative, it can be read as actually referring to the author-narrator's "real assimilation"(7).

Another way of suggesting the immigrant's experience of prejudice and homesickness is through the cultural contrasts between the Old and the New World, for example through the trope of generational conflict. In *Settlers of the Marsh*, this is suggested through Niels's disapproval of the Lunds, who are considerably older than him. Mrs. Lund, a mother figure in the community, is in her late forties and her husband is about ten years older than her. Swedish immigrants like Niels, the Lunds have had the longest experience in the fledgling community, and their economic failure is the reason Niels does not want to be associated with them. He finds fault with Mrs. Lund, who, allegedly in a European fashion, is more concerned with keeping up appearances than working hard and proving up. He sees Mr. Lund as lazy and hypochondriac and blames him for his poverty.

A different way to suggest the cultural conflict between the Old and the New World is through sexual tropes. Just as other writers of immigrant fiction (starting with Nabokov, in Cowart's analysis) will do subsequently, Grove makes use of Niels's virginity as a "trope for ethnic integrity" (Cowart 8). Cowart notes that virginity is often rendered through a sort of "exotic puberty," and Niels is just such an exotic pubescent character, still virgin at the age of 29. Grove suggests that both Niels and Ellen, as Swedes living in Canada, are displaced human beings who do not feel part of the community or the nation in which they live. In this context, the fact that one parent is absent becomes important. Cowart argues that this absence symbolizes the missing homeland. Niels does not remember his father, who died when he was very young, suggesting he has lost his fatherland.

The last characteristic of immigrant fiction, according to Cowart, is the portrayal of the immigrant protagonist as an adult who has regressed into childhood. This feature is probably the most substantial one in *Settlers of the Marsh* and, ironically, it has given critics fodder for constant attacks on the novel. It is through Niels's inability to speak English, which often renders him child-like, that the "symbolic regression to infancy" (Cowart 8) is suggested. Niels's naïveté has been called into question from the time of the novel's publication to this day, and because of this alleged flaw Grove is often seen as a less artful writer. Nevertheless, understood as a key feature of immigrant fiction, Niels's naïveté, his childlike behaviour, as well as his sexual innocence take on a completely different connotation and illuminate for us Grove's ability in rendering the immigrant experience. As Cowart observes, the "old theoretical paradigms, at any rate, do little justice to the literary practice of writers with a personal belief and investment" (8) in the new country. Accordingly, new theoretical approaches are needed to understand the full extent to which authors like Grove subscribed to and/or undermined the conventions of this genre. As I will show, Frederick Philip Grove's ability to render the immigrant experience in Canada does not stop at following the conventions of the genre. Instead, he appropriated a number of anthropological tools to expose and explain Niels's experience inside the immigrant community in Northern Manitoba.

——————————— • ———————————

Immigrant Fiction and Ethnoscape

Among the many readings of Frederick Philip Grove's *Settlers of the Marsh* at least one is missing: an anthropological one. Re-read through the lens of (trans)cultural anthropology this novel gains a new and significant importance as it is the only novel by a non-British immigrant in the 1920s focussing on the processes involved in the uprooting and re-rooting of the individual who does not belong to the main ethnic group. This new reading is an important step toward liberating the novel from the critical straitjacket in which it has been held—as a dark, realist text. As a consequence, this reading of Grove's first Canadian novel will challenge the main currents of Canadian literary criticism, showing that, although often unheard, the voice of the Other has always been present in Canadian literature.

I suggest that the anthropological concept which can help elucidate the place and role of Grove's first novel in Canadian literature is Arjun Appadurai's notion of the ethnoscape. As defined in Appadurai's essay "Global Ethnoscapes: Notes and Queries for a Transnational Anthropology," the term designates "the landscape of group identity" while acknowledging "dilemmas of perspective and representation" (191). As I will explain presently, Grove's novel portrays just such an ethnoscape and shows the group of characters, each with their own individual identities, sharing with one another the same physical space and a group identity. The notion of ethnoscape is useful in understanding how the immigrant author recreates his own experience of Canada through these characters, namely how his socially-constructed view as an immigrant alters his perception of the new country. The ethnoscape, Appadurai writes, "admits that . . . traditions of perception and perspective, as well as variations in the situation of the observer, may affect the process and product of representation" (191). It is thus important to bear in mind that *Settlers of the Marsh* is a novel by an immigrant about immigrants.

Appadurai emphasizes that, in contemporary society, the changes involved in "social, territorial, and cultural reproduction of group identity" are central to understanding such migrant communities in general and the individual in particular: "As groups migrate, regroup in new locations, reconstruct their histories, and reconfigure their ethnic 'projects', the *ethno* in ethnography takes on a slippery, nonlocalized quality" (191). Arguably, the dislocations and relocations of global reach that Appadurai identifies today were just as real more than a century ago, during the late-nineteenth- and early-twentieth-century migrations from Europe to North America, interrupted only by the world wars. It was just as possible for an early-twentieth-century immigrant to lose his or her sense of place as it is today. In light of Appadurai's concept of ethnoscape, both Grove's own ethnicity, and that of his novel's main character, acquire a non-localized quality, which explains, on the one hand, why Grove is *not* viewed as an "ethnic writer" and, on the other, why Niels's ethnicity does not seem to define him. For example, Smaro Kamboureli notes that although "Grove is neither German nor Canadian, it is hardly surprising that he cannot be German Canadian either: i.e. ethnic" (36). Furthermore, she writes that Niels "has to negotiate many differences between himself and those he encounters, but those differences are not ethnic-specific, nor do they relegate him to a position of an object" (40). Her goal is to show that these types of situations are common for people who find themselves in a "perpetual exilic condition," which she calls "diasporic bodies." Appadurai's concept enables us to understand the importance of the immigrant community in Northern Manitoba, as its members reconstruct their ethnicity while taking into consideration their new location. Grove's community of Scandinavians and Germans, although heterogeneous, has a distinct ethnicity that is no longer the same as the one these people had in their countries of origin. Rather, they have acquired a new one, specific only to them as a minority group in Canada. It is through this new, communal, identity that one ought to study their representation of their new country.

As Appadurai explains, these ethnoscapes from around the world, these landscapes of group identity, "are no longer familiar anthropological objects, insofar as groups are no longer tightly territorialized, spatially bounded, historically unselfconscious, or culturally homogenous" (191). The group of immigrants in Grove's novel cannot be analyzed as an ethnic group (or even a mélange of ethnic groups) with a long common history, since this ethnic community is no longer similar to those in Europe. The Northern Manitoban community in Grove's novel is absolutely new, and its traditions are just beginning to take shape. The newcomers no longer belong to a specific place, language, or culture. Their identity is not made up of their—former—histories, but by their lack of a common one. Therefore, any master analytical narrative or all-inclusive theoretical framework applied to an individual text that is both the product and reflection of a particular ethnoscape, will fail to recognize the uniqueness of the new world being forged.

To understand the interior dynamics of such groups of migrant communities, Appadurai calls for a "focus on the cultural dynamics of what is now called deterritorialization" (192). This process affects loyalties within groups, culminating in the "loosening of the bonds between people, wealth, and territories [which] fundamentally alters the basis for cultural reproduction" (192-3). *Settlers of the Marsh* is a compelling example of literature produced by an immigrant and reflecting the immigrant experience. All the aspects of the volatile deterritorialization process can be analyzed from this perspective, starting with the immigrant's social relationships and affecting his understanding of life, culture, history, and politics. Niels's story is not just one of a young man who makes mistakes because he has little life experience. It is the story of a young immigrant, whose limited knowledge of the new country affects his actions to a greater degree than his age or his intelligence. As a deterritorialized person, Niels does not belong to a stable community that, through tradition and innate moral codes, survives many challenges. His sense of right and wrong is altered to such a degree that his actions are not understandable to an old, traditional community, one that neither shares nor understands his sense of alienation.

Rereading *Settlers of the Marsh* through the concepts of ethnoscape and deterritorialization will illuminate Niels Lindstedt's attitude toward the prairie. A brief look at the characters at the novel's beginning will show that Grove was concerned about non-British immigrants only:

Niels Lindstedt: Swedish; speaks very little English; communicates mainly in Swedish; 23 years old; has been in Canada for "only three months" (15).

Lars Nelson: Swedish; Speaks English and Swedish; young, exact age unknown; recent immigrant; came to Canada three years before Niels.

Sigurdsen: Icelandic; speaks Icelandic and English, understands Swedish; old, exact age unknown; has been in Canada for a long time.

Amundsen: Swedish; speaks Swedish; no indication he speaks another language; around 50 years old; has been in Canada for 9 years; came to Canada with wife and daughter.

Ellen Amundsen: Swedish; speaks Swedish; no indication she speaks another language; young, exact age unknown; immigrated to Canada with her parents, Mr. and Mrs. Amundsen.

Carl Lund: Swedish; speaks more English than Swedish, even a little German between fifty-five and sixty years old; has been in Canada longer than everyone else; came over with his wife.

Anna Lund: Swedish; speaks English well; ten years younger than her husband; came over after her marriage.

Olga Lund: Canadian? most likely born in Canada; speaks English and Swedish; sixteen years old; later in the novel she will marry Lars Nelson; daughter of Carl and Anna Lund.

Bobby Lund: Canadian? probably born in Canada; speaks English and Swedish; eleven or twelve years old; adopted son of Carl and Anna Lund.

Clara Vogel: German; speaks English; considerably older than Niels; exact age unknown; owns land close to the Lunds.

Hahn: German; lives close to Lars Nelson.

Dahlbeck (and his wife): Germans; new in the community.

As the list of characters shows, with the exception of Olga (sixteen) and Bobby Lund (eleven), they are not even born in Canada but came over in their early adulthood. The ethnic origin is important as it indicates that these people are not yet Canadians, no matter how well they speak English or how long they have been in the country. Grove identifies each one's ethnic origin to emphasize that what binds these people together is the same as what makes them different from the wider Canadian society. They function as human markers to a place in which they feel at home only because they are close to each other.

Besides being a novel about non-British immigrants, *Settlers of the Marsh* describes their particular physical world. The representation of the place (northern Manitoba) supports Appadurai's idea of a landscape based on group identity. A close look at the descriptive geography of Grove's novel shows that these characters inhabit a physical place that makes their community both ethnographically distinct and geographically bound. Group identity, with its implicit resonance of family and home, is an important element in Grove's novel, as the following passage will show. In the beginning of the novel, Niels and Lars are headed into that part of northern Manitoba that is populated by group settlements based on ethnicity, and they function as landmarks for the two young men:

About five miles from town they reached, on the north road, the point where the continuous settlement ran out

> into the wild, sandy land, which, forming the margin of the
> Big Marsh, intervened between the territory of the towns
> and the next Russo-German settlement to the north, some
> twenty miles or so straight ahead. (15)

There is no other reference to this other community, nor is there any explanation given about why such settlements exist in that part of the province. Perhaps Grove is suggesting that this immigrant community is representative of all the other non-British communities, or that Niels's story could be that of any other immigrant. Whatever the case, the two newcomers are aware that people like them, immigrants from European countries other than Britain, live on the margins of the Big Marsh. The town of Minor, with its implicit connotation of law, government, and English language, is safely separated from these settlements of strangers by some twenty miles of sandy land.

Throughout the novel, Niels travels from one place to another, always passing one farm or another. These farms belong to German, Icelandic, or Swedish immigrants. There is no reference to farms outside the immigrant community, not even when Niels goes to town. Throughout the novel, there is little interaction between Niels's community and the outside world. Whereas Kamboureli sees this fact as a reflection of the benevolence of Canadian society, which lets these people work and prosper in peace (52), I suggest that it reflects the real-political environment at the time when non-British immigrants, desired or not by the federal government, were not to be seen or heard. It shows that the mainstream English-speaking society, at best, ignored them[2].

A compelling example of how essential the peculiar, socially-constructed view of the "relative location" (i.e. the place in relation to other, surrounding, places) is for the immigrant community, is provided by Clara Vogel. Ironically, she is the character who is the least connected to the land but who is more than aware of its landmarks. When she first talks to Niels after not seeing him for several years, she is very precise in giving him the directions to her place:

> Go north from your corner, across the bridge; then, instead
> of continuing north, along the trail which would lead to
> Amundsen's, turn to the east, along the first logging trail.
> Three miles from the bridge you will find me. Apart from
> Sigurdsen who does not count I am your nearest neighbour
> now. . . (52)

Clara Vogel's geography takes into account bridges, trails, and immigrant farms. Although she lives most of the time in the city and speaks English, once she is back among the immigrants she resorts to the communal vocabulary. Her understanding of the place has not changed and this is in part due to the fact that the community itself does not seem to have acquired a new identity. She speaks to Niels in terms Niels understands, in the terms used only by those who make up the community. Deborah Keahey argues that such a symbolic geography of a given space shows one's familiarization with the place. "Landmarks that are overwhelmingly of human origin," says Keahey, function "as minor centres of gravity, pulling [one] along from point to point" (75). The landmarks suggest that these immigrants share a familiar space, some sort of home to which they belong. Besides bridges and trails, which are landmarks in any community, the names of Amundsen and Sigurdsen have meaning only for the members of this particular immigrant community, which is exactly how an ethnoscape functions.

Not surprisingly, since all the important characters in the novel are, without exception, immigrants of non-British background, the persistence of the ethnoscape is ensured not only through their presence in the same place, but also through the use of their native languages instead of English. Indeed, Grove draws attention to the languages these immigrants speak among themselves. Early in the novel, when Niels and his friend and countryman, Lars, arrive at the old Icelander Sigurdsen's place, Lars tries to win him over by speaking to him in Swedish and thus identifying himself as non-English speaking, hoping that the old man will help them if he knows they are of the same ethnicity.

> "You Swedish?" asked Nelson in his native tongue.
>
> The old man hesitated as if taken off his guard by the personal question. "Naw," he said at last, still in English. "Icelandic. Get on."
>
> "Listen here," Nelson reasoned, persisting in his use of Swedish, "you aren't going to turn us out into a night like this, are you?"
>
> "No can," the old man repeated. "Get on."
>
> "Say," Nelson insisted. "We're going to Amundsen's to dig a well for him. We come from Minor. We don't know where we are or how to get there."
>
> "One mile east and four mile nor," the old man said without relenting. (17-18)

Lars Nelson's persistence in continuing the conversation in Swedish even after Sigurdsen has told him that he is Icelandic and not Swedish shows that he is aware that for Sigurdsen, as for himself, English is not the defining language. In this way he hopes to build a connection with the stranger based on their non-Canadian identity. He also counts on the fact that Swedish is a language the old man understands, which shows some intrinsic connection between the representatives of the two different nations. In this particular case, the implicit complicity between people sharing both an immigrant status and a minority status does not immediately bring the men closer, although it will later. What is important is Lars's own stratagem to win Sigurdsen's sympathy by appealing to his otherness. As Grove shows, Sigurdsen is "taken off his guard" by Lars's approach, since he has just been revealed to be one of them, an immigrant.

This incident shows that the dynamic inside the new community is changing and that each individual experiences the community through personal history. As an immigrant who has been in Canada longer than Lars and Niels, Sigurdsen does not feel compelled to behave as expected by his fellow immigrants. It is through Sigurdsen's unfriendliness that Grove signals the changes that occur in the psyche of the immigrant, who in the beginning feels tied to his fellow newcomers and in time grows apart from them. Just as Niels's later feelings of estrangement will reflect his changing status from immigrant to Canadian, Sigurdsen's refusal to accommodate Lars shows that he does not feel he is a member of the immigrant community anymore. Furthermore, his stubbornness to pursue the conversation in English asserts his place among Canadians and not among the others, the non-Canadians.

When Niels first addresses Ellen, he does so in his native tongue: "[he] sang out, in Swedish, 'A penny for your thoughts, miss'" (22). Since Grove mentions that Niels's first words to Ellen are spoken in Swedish but does not do so later, one may infer that their subsequent conversations are carried out in Swedish. Grove carefully mentions any change in terms of languages spoken. When, for the first time, Niels meets the people who come to visit Mrs. Amundsen, he is struck by the fact that very few of them spoke English:

> Some of the callers were Germans, some Swedes, some Ice-
> landers, two or three English or Canadian. . . .Many spoke
> German which Amundsen seemed to understand though he
> spoke it only in a broken way. Apart from the Canadians, one
> single couple—elderly Swede—used English exclusively. (25)

The elderly Swedes, who have been in Canada for at least twenty years, are Mr. and Mrs. Lund, but even the Lunds speak Swedish with those who cannot understand English. Mrs. Lund, "[t]urning to Niels and changing back into Swedish" (28), tells him why she has so many callers at her house every Sunday. In another instance, when Mrs. Lund tells Niels about her plans for Bobby, she does so in Swedish. Grove is drawing attention to this fact because her conversation has a significant effect on Niels: "Since she had spoken in Swedish, he had understood" (33). Conversely, the first time Niels meets the people, mostly Germans, who live close by the Lunds, he has difficulty communicating with them, "partly on account of his inability to speak either English or German" (31).

As an immigrant and, as such, a deterritorialized person, Niels is on the margins of society, both in a geographical and a social sense. Although space and land are key elements in Canadian literature, as Chelva Kanaganayakam writes, the marginal position that Niels occupies has little in common with the marginal position of the British settlers (primarily in Ontario) explored, for instance, by Atwood in *Survival*. The margins between which Niels tries to function are different from the margins that threatened the British colonizer, who, according to Atwood, needed to protect the border between his house and the hostile wilderness. Niels finds himself on the margins of the Big Marsh, which separates people into majority and minority subjects; he is on the margins of a country with a different language from his own, a country with different policies and laws that he does not yet know, and because of that he feels outside of the nation. Kanaganayakam correctly notes that in *Survival* Atwood sees the experience of the Canadian landscape as spatial rather than temporal. If she had taken into consideration the historical developments inside the landscape she writes about, she would have been forced to abandon her thematic approach. Niels's hardships are defined not by the geography of the place but by its political reality. The wilderness he has to survive in is well regulated and controlled by the Canadian government.

Niels's experience of Canada is furthermore complicated by his traumatic marriage with Clara Vogel. Sophie Levy states that in immigrant fiction "[b]oth home and narratives can be described as war zones, refugee camps, and sites of resistance" (865). Although Levy focuses her study on texts that deal with sexually abused daughters, her observations can be extended to Niels, whose youth and sexual innocence are shattered by Clara Vogel. His newly built house, which should be the sign of his success in Canada, becomes a site of ongoing cruelty, with sordid sexual implications. The house becomes for Niels a real war zone, and his body seeks refuge outside of it. As Levy argues, "writing *home* is performed *within* these narratives by a family dynamic that is modelled on the larger political order" (865, emphasis in original), suggesting the immigrant's feeling of being abused in the new country. The war between husband and wife that takes place in his newly built home in Canada signals the hostility that Niels as an immigrant faces in the social and political realm of Canadian society. The fact that he kills his German wife suggests the violence of the anti-German feelings expressed by Canadians in general as well as by the government[3]. Kertzer claims that "[i]mmigrant stories often depict a hellish scene in the midst of mundane reality, a scene revealing the cruelty that underlies official claims of tolerance and liberty" (128-9). Such a "hellish scene" shows Niels shooting his wife, a gesture echoing those of the soldiers on the European battlefront and, perhaps, suggesting that Niels is breaking away from his European past.

It comes as no surprise that for many years, while attempting to feel at home in this new place, Niels is torn between two countries. Grove signals that there is "a disjunction between an actual experienced home and the abstract idealized home" (Keahey 11), between the poor home that Niels has left and the warm, prosperous one in his imagination. In the context of the First World War, which shattered long-standing relationships between the British and German people, Niels, and through Niels, Grove himself, have to confront the new political environment and sever the ties to their pasts in order to adapt to the new world order. It is through the constant comparison of Canada to Sweden, or of Sweden to Canada, that Grove shows Niels's inner struggle towards complete social adaptation. Although the inevitable comparisons between the old and the new country in *Settlers of the Marsh* generally pertain to the physical similarities and differences of Sweden and Canada, they actually serve as a pretext for a deeper and more complex psychological process. Writing about the immigrant experience in post-World War Two American fiction, Gilbert H. Muller remarks that immigrants take on the task of inventing their new country (7).

Grove illustrates this process through Niels's recurrent dream-image of a house of his own, warmed by a fireplace, and, later, with a wife waiting for him. Niels invents a story for the lonesome prairie, populating the place with fairy-tale characters. Naïve as it may seem, Niels's invention of a magic country on the Canadian plains shows his desire to feel enchanted, to believe in the happiness that in real life eludes him. This projection is violently contrasted by the image of Amundsen's dying wife.

> The [Amundsen] place was so utterly lonesome that it reminded Niels of the wood-cutters' houses in fairy tales. . . . Whenever Nelson and Niels were alone, the latter asked questions. Once he enquired after Amundsen's wife. Somehow she reminded him of his own mother; and like his mother she aroused in him a feeling of resentment against something that seemed to be wrong with the world. (24)

His ties to Sweden, the place that he used to look upon as his home, are slowly replaced by his connection to Canada, and he thinks that no matter how hard it may be for him to be accepted, he will keep on trying:

> He himself might be forever a stranger in this country; so far he saw it against the background of Sweden. But if he had children, they would be rooted here. . . .He might become rooted himself, through them. (45)

This passage is a compelling example of how Niels is experiencing his loss of roots (deterritorialization), and his search for new ones (reterritorialization). Gilles Deleuze and Félix Guattari explain this process through the analogy of "a stick, [which] is in turn, a deterritorialized branch" (67). This analogy echoes Grove's description of Niels as "a leaf borne along the wind, a prey to things beyond control, a fragment swept away by torrents. That made him cling to the landscape as something abiding, something to steady him" (55). Niels has to decide if he wants to belong or be "forever a stranger."

In this novel, Frederick Philip Grove shows in great detail the immigrant's struggle to feel at home in Canada. This long and agonistic process involves more than learning to speak English and proving up. It is, first of all, a psychological struggle, and each individual, whether or not a member of a community, has to go through it alone. Grove successfully portrays Niels's homelessness, by showing him simultaneously outside the nation and outside the immigrant community. Niels's feelings fit Georg Simmel's definition of the "stranger," homeless among his peers, a "potential wanderer . . . who, although he has gone further, has not quite got over the freedom of coming and going. . . .[H]is position within [the group] is fundamentally affected by the fact that he does not belong in it initially and that he brings qualities into it that are not, and cannot be, indigenous to it" (276-277). Therefore, he does not feel as attached to this community of immigrants as the others, who organize their lives around the same ideals. He wants something different for himself, not just his own house and his own family, but to feel at home. By placing Niels in a non-British immigrant community Grove shows both the individual's and the group's immigrant experience. The persistence of the ethnoscape enables him to elaborate on the particularities of these communities in Northern Manitoba. He shows both how such immigrant settlements function and what role they fulfil. Reading *Settlers of the Marsh* as an immigrant novel might just be the solution to Grove's complaint that *Settlers of the Marsh* does not "convey to others what it conveys to [him]. If it does, nobody has ever said so" (qtd. in Pacey 76).

Notes

1. All quotations from *Settlers of the Marsh* refer to the New Canadian Library edition (1966).
2. As James Gray says, the anti-foreigner discourse in Western Canada in the 1920s "never really subsided completely during the decade" (246). There was constant pressure on the government to stop foreigners coming to Canada and allow only British immigrants to come in.
3. Once again, Gray gives a detailed account of the part anti-German feelings played in Canadian society during and immediately after the First World War.

Gaby Divay

•

FPG (Greve/Grove) Criticism since 1973 and Mutual Reflections in Else von Freytag-Loringhoven's and FPG's Writings

Grove, Greve, and Else: Criticism and Documents in the University of Manitoba Archives' Collections

Frederick Philip Grove (1879-1948) hardly needs an elaborate introduction in a collection of essays on prairie literature.[1] To recapitulate briefly the Canadian career of this pioneer author: he arrived in Manitoba in 1912, and taught school in remote rural areas for ten years, before he emerged as an author of nature sketches in 1922 (*Over Prairie Trails*) and 1923 (*The Turn of the Year*). Among the twelve books published during his lifetime are the covertly confessional novel *Settlers of the Marsh* (1925), and the autobiographies *A Search for America* (*ASA*, 1927) and *In Search of Myself* (*ISM*, 1946).[2] In 1929, Grove left Manitoba to spend the second half of his life in Canada on his Simcoe estate in Ontario. Though he felt perpetually underestimated, he received many honours, such as the Lorne Pierce Medal in 1934, Honorary Doctorates from the University of Manitoba (D.Litt.) and Mount Allison University (LLD) in 1946, and the Governor-General's Award in 1947. The University of Manitoba acquired Grove's papers from his widow, Catherine Wiens Grove, in the early 1960s,[3] and Leonard Grove donated his father's personal library of some 500 volumes in 1992.[4] In 1997, a substantial collection of letters by Grove to A. L. Phelps was added, providing documentation about FPG's still tentative self-representation in the early 1920s.[5] Several related research collections were added over the years, making the UM Archives the single most important repository of primary and secondary FPG materials. Since the mid-1990s, an endowment and the establishment of a website have assured online visibility and easy access to these truly special collections.

Twenty-five years after Frederick Philip Grove's death in 1948, Douglas O. Spettigue dropped a bombshell at the 1973 Ottawa Grove Symposium, when he announced that Grove had lived his first thirty years as Felix Paul Greve in Germany. The sensational discovery, fully described in *FPG: the*

European Years (1973), made Grove a German-Canadian author after the fact, and widened the scope of Grove criticism considerably. Greve's contacts with renowned poets like Stefan George and Karl Wolfskehl, archaeologists like Adolf Furtwängler, but most of all, with contemporary authors Thomas Mann, André Gide, and H. G. Wells (and likely also Meredith, Swinburne, Knut Hamsun, Hermann Hesse, and Karl Kraus) place him at the center of European literary relations and reception history. His many translations include the *Arabian Nights*, Cervantes, Swift, Balzac, Flaubert, Dickens, Browning, Pater, Dowson, and Oscar Wilde. With this new background information, the intellectual lineage of Grove's books could be evaluated in a different light. The debate about his "realism" or "naturalism," for instance, can be laid to rest with the demonstrable fact that Grove adopted Flaubert's technique of symbolic realism as a life-long model for his own writing while in prison in 1903-4. Young Greve even esteemed this author so highly that he claimed he wanted to *be* Flaubert (Freytag-Loringhoven, *AB* 34).[6]

FPG's switch from a decadent lifestyle in imitation of his pre-prison model, Oscar Wilde, to the austere, hard-working Greve/Grove identifying with Flaubert is documented in Gide's "Conversation avec un allemand." In a reversal of the decadent "Art" and "Life" poles, Greve declares that "Life" now has priority for him, and that "Art" is demoted to a means of making a living.[7] Grove's poetry, which remained largely unpublished until 1993, shows that he continued to apply the so-called "George-Mache," or the crafting of poems as practiced by Stefan George, which he had absorbed as Greve around 1900. However, the precious and neo-romantic aspects of both form and content are toned down with time, resulting in a more becoming realism reminiscent of Goethe and Heine. Both these authors' lyrics are heavily annotated in Grove's bilingual American editions found in his library.[8]

Spettigue's research papers were acquired by the University of Manitoba Archives in 1986, and carefully curated by 1990. Apart from describing how the scholar, while researching in the British Museum in 1971, found that the German Gide translator "FPG" was the Canadian author "FPG" who flaunted his former acquaintance with the French author in his autobiographies, the Spettigue collection contains documents about Greve's parents from the area near Schwerin, Mecklenburg, his schooling at the famous Hamburg *Gymnasium* Johanneum, archaeological and classical studies at Bonn University, his arrest for defrauding a friend Herman Kilian of Dresden (whose maternal Rutherford family background Grove made his own) in May 1903, as well as some letters to Insel Publishers obtained in Weimar, East Germany, and a good record of Greve's few publications and many translations. Only the identity of Greve's Else, the subject of his two German novels, and the compelling reasons for why he would have faked his "suicide" in 1909, still eluded Spettigue. The Canadian scholar was still groping at unlikely leads, like Paul Ernst's wife whose first name she shared, by the time Desmond Pacey had accurately identified her as Else Greve, born Ploetz, and divorced Endell. Pacey, in his magisterial edition of the *Letters of Frederick Philip Grove* (1976), also exposed her successful attempts at extorting money from Insel Publisher A. Kippenberg for her allegedly dead husband's work (550ff). In 1995, a second instalment of the Spettigue Collection was added to the UM Archives. It included valuable manuscript clusters like the Gide, O. A. H. Schmitz, and Wolfskehl correspondence (in French or German), a number of Greve's translations, and biographical materials by and about Else.

Margaret Stobie, Professor in the English Department at the University of Manitoba, published her quite different Grove book for the Twayne *World Authors* series also in 1973. Her investigation does not take Spettigue's spectacular findings into consideration, but confirms independently that former pupils from the German-speaking area near Winkler, Manitoba, and his wife Catherine's Mennonite family had never doubted Grove's German origins. Stobie's research papers contain, among taped interviews and information about Grove's early publishers, the author's very first Canadian publication. The sprawling Nietzsche-like essay "Rousseau als Erzieher" by the teacher "Fred Grove" appeared in the German-Canadian newspaper *Der Nordwesten* in four parts from November to December 1914. One can draw a link from this text to Greve's first-known publication, a review of the influential philosopher's posthumous works in Munich's *Allgemeine Zeitung* in 1901, which neatly bridges the two separate FPG identities. Nietzsche's "Dritte unzeitgemäße Betrachtung" ("Third Untimely Meditation," 1873) bore the title "Schopenhauer als Erzieher," an imitation of that philosopher's "Goethe als Erzieher." Thus, Grove's first public manifestation in Canada is of great interest, not only because it is in German, but also because it provides an excellent example of Grove's habit of applying multi-layered referencing to himself and the vast knowledge he had acquired in pre-Canadian times.[9] The only other conclusive proof of a literary kind that Grove had indeed been Greve is more direct: one of the six German manuscript poems extant in the Grove collections echoes Greve's poem "Erster Sturm" which was published in *Die Schaubühne* in 1907. Ironically, Spettigue, who had secured a copy of the latter in 1972, was unaware of the former until his FPG book was in print. This is why this crucial connection is only mentioned there in passing.[10]

Another seminal discovery by Professor Spettigue[11] has introduced further interdisciplinary and international dimensions into FPG studies: in the late 1980s it became apparent that the Else von Freytag-Loringhoven Collection at the University of Maryland, College Park, contains writings by the New York dadaist (1874-1927) in which the decade she spent with FPG in Europe and America looms large. Here finally was the previously lacking documentary proof that Greve had not perished by means of suicide, but had started a new life in America instead. Doubts about his demise were raised by Insel publisher Kippenberg in his September 1909 refutation of Else's impertinent accusations that his establishment had overworked, underpaid, and unfairly criticized her husband. After distancing himself from any responsibility in the alleged suicide, Kippenberg delicately provides the real and rather urgent motive for Greve's disappearance: a never-decreasing mountain of debts, and, more to the point, the recent double-selling of one of his latest translations. This key document has been published in Pacey's 1976 edition of Grove's *Letters* in the German original and in English translation (548-552). Greve's objectionable transaction, which might well have resulted in another and likely less lenient fraud conviction, probably concerned Swift's *Prosawerke*. Three of its four volumes appeared "posthumously" in 1910. Note that all twelve volumes of Temple Scott's Swift edition which Greve used for his translation are extant in the UM's Grove Library Collection. The famous satire "A modest proposal . . ." in the first volume bears many of Grove's pencil annotations. Greve's translation of how to resolve rampant poverty by marketing small children for human consumption was especially successful, and it is still in print today.

In 1987, in *A Stranger to My Time: Essays by & about Frederick Philip Grove*, editor Paul Hjartarson was the first to reveal details of Freytag-Loringhoven's reminiscences of her life with Greve, from the time they "eloped" to Palermo in early 1903, to when he left her in Kentucky in 1911. That they operated a small farm near Sparta, Kentucky, is known from a single German Freytag-Loringhoven poem dedicated to "FPG" which was not discovered until 1991. That the two were actually married in Berlin in August 1907, and that therefore both became bigamists when they remarried respectively Baron Leo in New York (November 19, 1913) and teacher Catherine Wiens in Canada (September 1, 1914), was not documented until 2002 when Irene Gammel published her comprehensive Freytag-Loringhoven biography.

Else's autobiography (*AB*) was composed in the early 1920s in Berlin, and provides an expressive social commentary on three decades covering the Wilhelmine Empire, the Weimar Republic, World War I America, and the 1920s in Berlin and Paris. Its importance goes well beyond the confines of FPG studies. Freytag-Loringhoven describes how she, like many women of her generation, had always defined herself through her relationships with men, and how she only attached value to her considerable creative talent when ardent advances towards William Carlos Williams or Marcel Duchamp, for example, remained unrequited at best, or resulted in decidedly negative attention. She is mentioned in most art history books, and recently, exhibitions in New York, Berlin and Zürich were exclusively devoted to her.

D. O. Spettigue and Paul Hjartarson published this autobiography, along with a selection of letters, in 1994 as *Baroness Elsa*. The astonishing text throws a special spotlight on: her marital problems with Endell, whose impotence earned her a "womb-squeeze excursion" at Dr. Gmelin's sanatorium on the North Sea island Föhr (built in 1898 by her husband); her infatuation with dashing young Greve, Endell's friend, who sent her one of his Oscar Wilde comedies; the affair they started at Christmas 1902; their unusual "elopement" to Palermo, taking the distraught Endell along as far as Naples; Greve's first, involuntary, abandonment when he was lured back to Bonn and arrested for defrauding his friend Herman Kilian; her reunion with Greve in June 1904, their exile in Switzerland and France, and their return to Berlin where he abandoned her for the second time to become "a potato king" in America in 1909. His final abandonment, within a year of their Pittsburgh reunion in 1910, is more scantily documented in her autobiographical writings. Else's autobiography also confirms that Greve's novels *Fanny Essler* (1905, eng. 1984) and *Maurermeister Ihles Haus* (1907, *The Master Mason's House* 1976) were about her life. Though she abstains from directly accusing him of it, he clearly appropriated her own written "story of my childhood" for "his" second novel. The situation is more complicated for the earlier "Fanny Essler" complex in poetry and prose, which will be addressed in more detail below.

In their 1994 introduction to *Baroness Elsa*, the editors share the information Else gave New York immigration officials on June 29, 1910: she had travelled from Rotterdam to New York on the *Rijndam*, she had $50, she was a 35-year-old author from Swinemünde; five-foot seven inches tall, with copper hair and grey eyes. Her next of kin was her father-in-law Eduard Greve, and she was on her way to meet her brother-in-law, T. R. Greve, at 57, 4th Ave in Pittsburgh. The editors' laconic comment: Greve must have "doctored his passport" by cleverly rearranging the initials "F" and "P" into "T" and "R" (*Baroness Elsa* 24). Details of Greve's own 1909 passage, which would have to await discovery until October 1998, were still unknown, though Else states that he came "via Canada" (*AB* 33). Already in 1991, the University of Manitoba had arranged an exchange with the University of Maryland, trading both the manuscript version of Else's autobiography, which the editors had chosen for their publication, and the more complete typescript Djuna Barnes had prepared in the 1930s for a microfilm copy of the *Fanny Essler* novel, because the latter provides a particularly striking mirror-image of Else's recollections. Indeed, her close relations with members of Stefan George's illustrious circle, like the artist Melchior Lechter, the writers Karl Wolfskehl, Ernst Hardt, and O. A. H. Schmitz, the sculptor Richard Schmitz, the architect August Endell whom she married, and finally Greve make the novel a *roman-à-clef* of this prominent group, while her memoirs provide the clear-text version of her experiences in Berlin and Munich.

———————————— • ————————————

My own involvement in FPG studies dates back to the time when I catalogued the galley-proofs of Spettigue's and Tony Riley's introduction to Greve's *The Master Mason's House* (1976), and a rare copy of his self-published poetry collection *Wanderungen* (1902) around 1980. As soon as I had obtained a doctorate in French Renaissance literature from l'Université Laval in 1984, I embarked on an M.A. program in German philology at the University of Manitoba, which culminated in a comprehensive edition of Greve/Grove's poetry in 1993.[12] During these years, I also curated the Spettigue research papers, and catalogued the Grove library Collection. Both of these labour-intensive projects, and countless hunting expeditions in European and American libraries, archives, and antiquarian bookstores have helped me make a certain number of contributions to FPG scholarship. Discovering important new materials and connecting them to known sources was made possible by a facility in Greve/Grove's three primary languages.

Spettigue had addressed Gide's "Conversation" in his 1973 FPG book, but he had used an English translation of the version published in 1919 in which Greve's name was camouflaged with the initials "B. R." In Claude Martin's excellent edition, from the original 1904 manuscript sources, in the October 1976 *Bulletin des amis d'André Gide* (*BAAG*), I found not only a far more explicit text, but also two highly revealing letters by Greve.[13] These led me straight to the 1990 discovery of the 1904-5 "Fanny Essler" poetry cycle in the Deutsche Literaturarchiv, Marbach (DLA): under this joint pseudonym, Greve and Else had published seven poems in the *Freistatt*, with a clear division of labour reflecting *her* content and *his* form.[14]

The two *BAAG* letters are lacking in the Gide correspondence in the UM's Spettigue collection, and also from the scholar's detailed discussion about unpublished correspondence by Greve and Else in a 1992 article in *Canadian*

Literature. In particular Greve's long account to Gide of October 1904 has confessional character and provides an interesting perspective on his post-prison situation, his titanic translation and creative efforts, and his "Fanny Essler" plans: what became Greve's 1905 novel was at this stage projected as an anonymous autobiography by a gifted poetess. In a truly manic twist, which lends credence to Karl Wolfskehl's concerns about Greve's mental state two years earlier,[15] he assumes, in addition to his own, the two public identities of "Mme Else Greve" (for Flaubert translations) and "Fanny Essler" (for her poems and biography), and declares "I am three . . . ".[16] In this way, he entirely negates Else's essential contribution, and denies her role in their collaborative partnership.

Also in May 1990, I obtained poems Greve had submitted for publication in Stefan George's exclusive *Blätter für die Kunst* in 1902,[17] and similar manuscript treasures[18] in the Stefan-George Archiv in Stuttgart, and secured Greve's entire extant correspondence with Insel Publishers in Weimar. A year later, the University of Maryland Freytag-Loringhoven collection allowed me to link two of her many German poems dedicated to "FPG/Greve"—notably, "Herbst" and "Du"—to their 1904-5 "Fanny Essler" poetry cycle. In "Herbst" Freytag-Loringhoven artfully combines elements of Fanny Essler's central three sonnets about Greve's brutal hands, cold eyes, and lying mouth[19] with his favourite Fall poem "Erster Sturm" (1907 & UMA mss, ca. 1914).[20]

Most critics have concentrated on Grove's supposedly "true" autobiography *In Search of Myself.* However, it was a close and literal reading of his supposedly "fictional" book *A Search for America* which allowed me to make the following discoveries, listed in order of importance: FPG's 1909 passage from Liverpool to Montreal on the White Star Liner *Megantic* (October 1998), the Bonanza Farm in "the Dakotas" as the Amenia & Sharon Land Company near Fargo (in March 1996), and a two-line listing for "F. P. Greve, manager" at a 4th Avenue business address in the Pittsburgh directory for 1910 (in April 1995). In 2000, I found that the same directory showed in its classified section that Greve was the local book agent for National Alumni, the New York publisher for whom naïve Phil Branden/Greve sold over-priced deluxe copies of a multi-volume history set to gullible Pittsburgh industrialists.[21]

With increasing ease of online searching, routine explorations have resulted in lucky findings like a September 1910 note in the *New York Times* reporting "Elsie Greve's" arrest in Pittsburgh for cross-dressing and smoking in public (she had barely been in the country for three months, and she and Greve, who was supposedly dead, threatened to complain to the German Embassy in Washington),[22] another *NYT* article about Freytag-Loringhoven posing for New York artists in December 1915 (at the end, there is reference to "certain records with regards to a previous marriage" which are investigated by the German Consulate),[23] and two photographs of Else in exotic costume, one showing her with the Jamaican poet Claude Mackay.[24] Lately, a closer reading of Grove's *Travelogue*-selling adventures in New York in *A Search for America* has convinced me that his gifted young colleague "Mr. Ray" who "has since left his mark in American art" (197), is Man Ray, who was 19 at the time. This means that Freytag-Loringhoven's contact with this great artist may have been indirectly mediated by Greve. Else collaborated with Man Ray and Marcel Duchamp on their single *New York Dada* issue in 1921, and she was the subject of an early nude film experiment of which only a still photo has survived in a Man Ray letter to Tristan Tzara.[25]

These and other texts or documents have been deposited in the University of Manitoba Archives' collections since the late 1980s, and many are freely available at the UMA's FPG & Freytag-Loringhoven website today. Major e-editions are Grove's *A Search for America* (2001), his unpublished novel *Jane Atkinson* (2000),[26] *In Search of Myself* (2007), Grove's letters to A. L. Phelps (Dec. 2006), and Greve/Grove's poetry edition (2007). Important key documents include Gide's 1904 "Conversation," Greve's 1907 autobiographical sketch for Brümmer's *Lexikon*, and Thomas Mann's letters to Grove in 1939,[27] as well as FPG's and Freytag-Loringhoven's 1904-5 "Fanny Essler" poems, and her satirical poems about Ernst Hardt and August Endell. The online annotated bibliography of the Grove Library Collection, a detailed description of the Greve Translation Collection, and materials related to the "In Memoriam FPG: 1879-1948-1998" anniversary symposium[28] provide further opportunity for researchers and educators to explore FPG and Freytag-Loringhoven sources.

———————————— • ————————————

Mutual Reflections in Else von Freytag-Loringhoven's and FPG's Writings

Grove's importance for prairie literature is obvious, but why should the eccentric Baroness, who never set foot into Canada, be considered in this context? Though Else did not know what became of FPG after he left her in 1911 near Sparta, Kentucky, and her reminiscences dwell mostly on their common European past, she provides several informative comments about Greve's reasons for starting a new life, their rather brief American reunion, his ultimate abandonment, and his conservative aesthetics.

FPG's and Freytag-Loringhoven's autobiographical techniques stand in stark contrast. Grove's, not surprisingly, is one of clever dissimulation, while Else's frank recollections hide nothing. Grove applies a distorted time frame to his narrative, Else gives an exact chronological account despite her associative method and total disregard for dating events. Grove abstains from ever referring to her directly, whereas Greve occupies centre-stage in her memoirs. Their Kentucky year, which Else addresses in her autobiography, letters, poems, and notes, is carefully omitted from Grove's otherwise fairly accurate description of the three years he spent in the United States in *A Search for America*.

There can be no doubt that Grove had an eye on Else's whereabouts from his Canadian retreat. While she flourished in the New York art world, he kept a low profile in rural Manitoba. His first two books in 1922 and 1923 were landscape descriptions devoid of biographical content. No sooner had she returned to Berlin in 1924, than he published his first Canadian novel, which is based on their rocky marriage (*Settlers of the Marsh*, 1925), and not two months before her suicide in Paris in December 1927, he came out with his quite openly autobiographical *A Search for America*. Family anecdotes furthermore assert that Grove moved his wife and small daughter to an isolated teacherage near Waldersee in 1917, because he feared that a woman might find them. And even years after her death, in a fever delirium, he was terrified that she would appear to confront him.[29]

One of Grove's earliest Canadian poems is dated 1913 and specifies the "Pembina Hills" near Grove's first teaching assignment in Kronsfeld as the setting. Aptly entitled "Dejection," it reflects a depressed mood, which could well be related to a guilty conscience about his cowardly separation from Else. In a February 1914 letter, Grove states that a marriage he had "been working for the last five years" had "gone to smash," and that he had spent Christmas 1913 with a "raging fever" in a hospital.[30] This sounds like Grove had tried to negotiate an ill-timed reconciliation with the recently titled Baroness in New York. An Insel Publishers' employee reports in 1972 that Kippenberg had questioned Greve's alleged suicide in 1909, because the grieving widow was seen in bright summer dress and in good spirits, and that Greve had later contacted him from a New York hospital.[31] No time frame is given, nor does any documentation support this intriguing anecdote. The five years Grove refers to point to 1908, when Greve announced to Gide that he would soon be "divorced" (*Letters* 547), and when O. A. H. Schmitz similarly noted in his diaries that this marriage was troubled.[32] When Greve left Berlin in late July 1909 to cross the Atlantic from Liverpool to Montreal on the White Star Liner *Megantic* (just as later described in *A Search for America*), Else likely was left in the dark about his plans. But when she sent her accusatory note about her husband's "suicide" to Kippenberg some eight weeks later,[33] she must have known that Greve was alive and well in New York. This makes her approach a highly successful attempt to extract money from Greve's former employer. She probably raised further funds from other publishers in similar ways, until, within a year of his disappearance, she could finance her own crossing and follow his summons to join him (*AB* 72).[34]

In the same 1914 letter, Grove confesses that he was seduced by a much older married woman at age fifteen. This is echoed in the *In Search of Myself* episode, where Mrs. Broegler, the wife of FPG's chemistry teacher, seduces him on his seventeenth birthday. While this woman may bear some resemblance to Else, she was twenty-nine and Greve almost twenty-four when they became lovers in 1902, and the seduction went both ways. Palermo, well-covered in Else's memoirs, is also mentioned several times in Grove's autobiographies, but the only reference to a woman he admired there clearly does not apply to Else (*ISM* 164).[35]

What appears as a resentful omission in *A Search for America* is paradoxically an indication of the very special treatment Grove reserved for Else in *Settlers of the Marsh*. Couched in Manitoban disguise, Else appears as the depraved older woman Clara Vogel, who manages, despite Niels' platonic attachment to his virginal neighbour Ellen, to trick the virtuous protagonist into a disastrous marriage, from which he can only free himself by shooting her. This rather mean monument to Else in which she is cast all in black while Grove paints himself in flattering shades of white, represents a therapeutic piece of writing, in which he comes to terms with the ending of his first marriage in Sparta, Kentucky. Grove took great care to transpose the infrastructure, distances, and the country/city dichotomy into the novel's Manitoba Interlake region, so that Sparta/Cincinnati becomes "Odensee" (Waldersee)/Winnipeg. Even the mansion Niels builds "on a bluff" near a meandering creek (the Grassy River) resembles the Sparta location on the winding Eagle Creek.

No one in 1925, or for the next fifty years for that matter, ever suspected such confessional undercurrents in this "pioneer novel." Today, it can be understood furthermore as a direct filiation of Greve's *Fanny Essler* novel. Not only are both books about Else, both also draw on Flaubert's *Madame Bovary*. Greve's 1905 book ends with Fanny's death from malaria in 1903, which spares her "the biggest disappointment of her life," namely, her lover's impending conviction for fraud in May 1903. The detailed death-scene is an homage to Flaubert's famous novel, in which his heroine Emma dies from swallowing arsenic to escape her own social disgrace.

Grove himself drew attention to similarities between *Madame Bovary* and *Settlers* on at least two occasions: once privately, in December 1924, when he said in a letter to A. L. Phelps that he tried to put "the corrupt, sexually hypertrophied woman of French upper-class novels on the soil,"[36] and a second time, when he thought in retrospect that his novel's perceived censorship was the controversy surrounding Flaubert's 1853 book all "over again" (*ISM* 381).[37] The lopsided comparison is reminiscent of Freytag-Loringhoven's report about Greve's disappointment over *Fanny Essler*'s lack of success: he believed it to be at least as good as Thomas Mann's *Buddenbooks* (*AB* 35). Sadly for FPG, neither book by Greve (1905) nor Grove (1925) ever came even close to the acclaim of his admired models.

———————— • ————————

Else von Freytag-Loringhoven's recollections of the entire 1904-5 "Fanny Essler" complex reveal that she contributed more than just her biographical material. While Greve was in prison, she composed poems about their relationship which Greve then expertly polished into the Petrarchan "Fanny Essler" cycle. Its structure resembles a medieval wing-altar, in which two dynamic, historical scenes (here, "Tunis"/Palermo in early 1903 and "Husum"/Wyk in October 1902) flank the centre-piece usually depicting God in His static, timeless, and universal attributes (here, the woman's absent lover FPG in a three-sonnet "portrait").

In her own bitter squaring of accounts, Else later used her poem "Schalk" (entitled "Herbst" in some variants) to expand the central "Fanny Essler" sonnets into an even less flattering portrait of FPG: his cold eyes, brutal hands, and lying mouth are now topped with further attributes emphasizing his cruelty, and culminating in his "dagger-rigid heart." FPG's more destructive and ruthless tendencies are illustrated with elements from Greve's favourite poem "Erster Sturm." To make these connections quite clear, she states next to the title "Sparta, Kentucky, am Eagle Creek,"[38] and, at the bottom of the page, "Der Herbst ist - als Bild - ein Porträt Felix Paul Greves" ("The Fall is - as a metaphor - a portrait of FPG").[39] Else's assessment of his characteristics can be found throughout her autobiography: he was rigid, restless, ambitious, infertile as an artist, conceited; he only loved himself, he had a sinister will-power, he was calculating (*AB* 96). About his likely success she knows nothing: "He might be very successful now in America, if he is not dead. I do not know. I became separated from him by his suddenly leaving me, alone and helpless without even knowing much English in the midst of . . . Kentucky" (*AB* 36).

On a detailed note under her Palermo-inspired poem "Wolkzug" she adds that she didn't know how to work, was haughty and considered insane ("für verrückt gehalten"), and that Greve had sent her a token amount of $20 "verborgen von da" ("hidden from there"), which seems to indicate that he was still somewhere in the vicinity.[40]

Else blames two factors for the failing of her marriage. One was that Greve's ideal had always been that of a "ladylike" (*AB* 96) and "Junoesque" woman, after the model of his mother. Here is how Grove refers to the most important woman in his life on the very first page of *A Search for America*: "my mother, whom I adored and whom I remember as a Junoesque lady." Else was lacking both these qualities. She describes herself as decidedly "unladylike," and claims that Greve was ashamed of her. He also feared her "sex radiance," and would have gladly "placed [her] in a harem" if he could have (*AB* 103). Wherever they went, he did his best to keep her contained by choosing relatively isolated places, like Wollerau near Zürich, Paris-Plage/Étaples near Paris, and Sparta, Kentucky, near Cincinnati. The exception to this rule was Berlin, where they lived an "artificial life" nearly devoid of social contacts, and where Greve made her wear a corset and false hair (*AB* 104). Greve's fits of jealousy and his suspicious mind were, according to Else, indicative of a deep-rooted lack of self-confidence. He suffered from hurt pride over her past affairs, and he was a "slave acting like a master" (*AB* 106, 108).

There were also power-struggles related to her fledgling creativity, when she started writing "the story of [her] childhood" which Greve would present as his second novel. Domestic violence erodes their union: when Else makes a swipe against Greve's "virtue-spiked" mother, he grows pale and almost hits her. Their relationship is one of "love-hate, to the killing point" (*AB* 107). Intimations of murderous brutality were already present in Fanny Essler's "Hand"-sonnet, and become, of course, concrete in Grove's *Settlers* when Niels shoots his wife. This gives the novel yet another therapeutic layer: Greve likely did come close to killing Else in Kentucky, and he has his *alter ego* live out a wishful fantasy.

Related to FPG's ideal of womanhood is the obvious polarization of "bad" and "good" women in Grove's oeuvre. The prototype for the blonde and blue-eyed Kirsten in *In Search of Myself*, Ellen in *Settlers*, "Margaret" in the *Faust*-like epic poem "Konrad the Builder," or Catherine Wiens Grove in real life can be found in Else's report about Greve's infatuation with what she calls the "travelling virgin" in 1902. Everything points to the sister of the influential philosopher Ludwig Klages, whom Greve had courted in Munich before Else's time.[41] According to Else (*AB* 58), Helene Klages had held out on Greve while travelling with him, and was the reason why he moved to Berlin. Not long afterwards, she had an illegitimate child, which catapulted her into the "Madonna" role at various George-Circle festivities.[42]

While the gossip of Munich's Bohemians is of little interest here, Else's violent reaction to this story provides the key to the second reason why the marriage was ultimately destined to fail. First, it unleashes a diatribe against virginity and its overrated value in society in general (*AB* 59).[43] Then it is linked to the personal issue of Greve's revival of the virgin ideal in America (*AB*, 98). This was part of a Rousseau-like "back to Nature" trend on his part. Engaged in "a primitive struggle for life" by toiling on the soil, Greve declared that he didn't need women, and practiced abstinence (*AB* 72). His attitude seriously complicated the couple's reunion in 1910/11; "it was murder, hate" (*AB* 98), resulted in tension, confrontation, occasional violence, and finally led to the "terrible, disgraceful" dissolution of their decade-long relationship (*AB* 63, 30). She calls his third and final abandonment, which left her destitute in the Kentucky "wilderness," the inexplicable act of "a desperado," and darkly predicts that it would come to haunt him (*AB* 98)

In reminiscence of their old "Fanny Essler" collaboration, Else managed to place an out-of-character 1840 lithograph[44] of the Romantic Viennese dancer Fanny Elssler[45] in the same 1922-23 volume of the avant-garde journal *Broom* that contained her illustrated poem "Circle."[46] About the *Fanny Essler* novel, she had this to say:

> Felix had written two novels. They were dedicated to me in so far as material was concerned; it was my *life and persons out of my life*. He did the executive part of the business, *giving the thing the conventional shape and dress*. He esteemed Flaubert highly as stylist . . . so he tried to be Flaubert . . . .He took it all outwardly as mere industry, except for the material in it. They must be fearful books as far as art is concerned.
> (*AB* 34-35, emphasis mine)

In the same context, she mentions Greve's outstanding marketing skills: "He even thought of himself as a genius, art genius . . . until the end when he broke off, or down, his career deciding to become a business genius, or potato king in America" (*AB* 34). In her judgement, Greve lacked the truly artistic temperament and inspiration of the creative "genius" he thought he was. He was, however, an accomplished master of form and craftsmanship. Her opinion finds confirmation in FPG's life-long emulation of Flaubert's symbolic realism in his prose, the practice of Stefan George's poetic techniques in his poetry, and the use of Nietzsche's rhetoric in his essays.

Notes

1. For a biographical sketch, see http://www.umanitoba.ca/libraries/archives/collections/fpg/bio/bionarr.html.

2. A bibliography of FPG's works, including available online editions, can be found at: http://en.wikipedia.org/wiki/Frederick_Philip_Grove.

3. See http://www.umanitoba.ca/libraries/units/archives/collections/complete_holdings/rad/mss/grove.shtml for a description of the Grove collection. For the complete Finding Aid see http://www.umanitoba.ca/libraries/units/archives/collections/complete_holdings/ead/html/grove.shtml.

4. FPG & FrL website: http://www.umanitoba.ca/libraries/archives/collections/fpg/fpglib/index.html.

5. See these ca. 155 letters online at: http://www.umanitoba.ca/libraries/archives/collections/fpg/corr/Phelps/INDEX.htm.

6. The typescript of Freytag-Loringhoven's *Autobiography*, University of Maryland, College Park (205 p.) and the abbreviation "AB" have been used here throughout.

7. Claude Martin's 1976 edition of Gide's original 1904 drafts has been made available in 2001 at http://www.umanitoba.ca/libraries/archives/collections/fpg/gide_conv/index.html.

8. Grove's poem "Questions Reasked" is a transparent imitation of Goethe's "Gott, Gemüt und Welt," which is annotated in Grove's personal copy of Goethe's *Poems*, Boston, [1899], 26-28.

9. The importance of Nietzsche's influence on FPG has been confirmed in the March 2008 discovery of a late 1901 bound manuscript poetry collection by Greve in which four poems are explicitly dedicated to the philosopher, and several more imitate the rhymeless *Zarathustra* "Dithyramben." See the full table of contents of this remarkable recent acquisition to the University of Manitoba archival collections at: http://www.umanitoba.ca/libraries/archives/collections/fpg/pEd/1gre1901JahrDWende_mar08/index.html.

10. Spettigue, *FPG* 144. Grove's untitled manuscript poem is "Die Dünen fliegen auf..."; his own translation, "The Dying Year," is mistakenly cited as "The Flying Years."

11. A 1983 article by Lynn DeVore about Djuna Barnes' *Nightwood* led Spettigue to the University of Maryland FrL collection.

12. *Poems/Gedichte* by/von Frederick Philip Grove, Felix Paul Greve und "Fanny Essler" was published in December 1993, and made available online in 2007 at http://www.umanitoba.ca/libraries/archives/collections/

fpg/pEd/index.html.

13. Greve's October 1904 letter (eng. tr.) is part of Gide's "Conversation" at http://www.umanitoba.ca/libraries/archives/collections/fpg/gide_conv/ conv04e.html#let2.

14. See the bilingual 100th Anniversary edition of Greve & Else's "Fanny Essler" Poetry Cycle at http://home.cc.umanitoba.ca/~divay/FEPoems05/ index.html#toc.

15. In a letter to Gundolf, Wolfskehl mentions Greve's "Münchhausiaden" (imposturous adventures), and wonders if he is ill ("Ob er krank ist?" 4.2.1902).

16. "Et de moi-même. Il me faut travailler d'une façon bien singulière. Je ne suis plus une personne, j'en *sommes* trois: je suis 1. M. Felix Paul Greve; 2. Mme Else Greve; 3. *Mme Fanny Essler*. La dernière dont je vous enverrai prochainement les poèmes, et dont les poèmes—encore un secret—sont adressés à moi, est *un poète* déjà assez considéré dans certaines parties de l'Allemagne" (17.10.1904, BAAG 40, emphasis mine). See also: http:// www.umanitoba.ca/libraries/archives/collections/fpg/gide_conv/fp-g17oct04_fre.html.

17. They were believed lost, since only the empty envelope of Greve's submission was acknowledged in the 1962 edition of Gundolf's correspondence with George, who judged it "insufficient" ("zu wenig," 3.9.1902, 120, n. 3).

18. Notably, sonnets from Dante's *Vita Nuova*, ca. 1898, a Browning translation, excerpts of Oscar Wilde's aphorisms as "Lehren und Sprüche," Wilde's *Fingerzeige* (*Intentions*) with dedications to George or Wolfskehl, etc. Copies were obtained from archivist Dr. Ute Oelmann.

19. A facsimile of the three "Fanny Essler" sonnets can be found at http://www.umanitoba.ca/libraries/archives/collections/fpg/ill-pgs/ill_ FEsonnets1904.html.

20. See a side-by-side comparison of the three German poems in question at: http://www.umanitoba.ca/libraries/archives/collections/fpg/ill-pgs/ txt_frlSchalkFEsonsFPG1stSturm.html.

21. See the vivid description of this episode in ASA, Book II, The Relapse, Chapter 5, "I join a new company": http://www.umanitoba.ca/librar-ies/archives/collections/fpg/etexts/Search-America2005/htm_txt/chap2-5.htm.

22. For the text and a commentary of the brief NYT note see http://www. umanitoba.ca/libraries/archives/collections/fpg/bio/cri_pittsbNYT-sep1910.html. For a facsimile, see http://www.umanitoba.ca/libraries/ar-

chives/collections/fpg/ill-pgs/ill_pittsbNYTsep1910.html.

23. See the December 1915 NYT coverage of artists' model FrL, at http://www.umanitoba.ca/libraries/archives/collections/fpg/frl/ill_frlNYT5d-ec1915doc.html.

24. FrL photo, ca. 1915, at: http://www.umanitoba.ca/libraries/archives/collections/fpg/frl/ill_nyLCwClaudeMcKay.html.

25. FrL as the capital letter "A" in Man Ray's pun "La mer de la mer.... de l'Amerique" to Tristan Tzara, 1921: http://www.umanitoba.ca/libraries/archives/collections/fpg/frl/ill_frlLettA_ManRay1921.html.

26. *Jane Atkinson* was chosen for its references to Greve's Munich days in Karl Wolfskehl's hospitable salon in 1902, and a self-quotation from his 1905 *Fanny Essler* novel.

27. Thomas Mann acknowledges, from his new home in Princeton, receipt of ASA and Grove's brand-new novel *Two Generations*.

28. This memorable event was spearheaded by Carol Shields in late September 1998. Included are some full-text presentations, and digitized video proceedings of all twelve sessions.

29. Oral communications by Richard Ottenbreit, 1994, and Mary Grove, 1998, respectively.

30. Grove to Isaac J. Warkentin, 10.2.1914, *Letters*, 13: "As for my marriage, that has gone to smash; something I have been working for for the last five years. I don't blame the girl—I merely don't understand her. Difference of age was considerable; she was my pupil before she went to college. At Christmas I went down to Arkansas—into the hospital!! And when I came out after a week of raging fever, I did not know my world any longer!"

31. Friedrich Michael, "Verschollene..." A81: "Jahre später wurde Kippenberg von einer New Yorker Klinik benachrichtigt, in der Greve Aufnahme gefunden hatte." ("Years later, Kippenberg was notified by a New York clinic where Greve had been admitted.")

32. O. A. H. Schmitz, Diaries, DLA, Marbach, 13.1.1908 and 30.1.1908.

33. Kippenberg's reply is dated 29.9.1909 (*Letters*, 548ff.).

34. FrL, *AB 72*, mentions that he had brought her to America. He was not interested in sex anymore due to his Rousseau-like "back to nature" conversion, and he left her "within a year."

35. Palermo is also mentioned in *ISM*, 80, and in *ASA*, 10.

36. Grove to Phelps, 13.12.1924: http://www.umanitoba.ca/libraries/archives/collections/fpg/corr/Phelps/let029.htm

37. Grove about *Settlers*: "Its publication became a public scandal. . . .[I]t was

the old story of Flaubert's *Madame Bovary* over again. A serious work of art was classed as pornography; but with this difference that the error, in Flaubert's case, increased the sales; he lived in France. In my case, and in Canada, it killed them." (http://www.umanitoba.ca/libraries/archives/collections/fpg/etexts/Search-Myself/pt4_AB10.html).

38. This is the one and only reference to the precise Kentucky location on the Ohio River, between Cincinnati and Louisville. When Spettigue and Hjartarson investigated Freytag-Loringhoven's autobiography, poetry, and correspondence, they seem not to have looked at her German poems and letters—many of them still labeled "unidentified" at the time, so, that they missed the many "FPG" dedications and notes.

39. For a detailed discussion of the "Fanny Essler" complex, see my introduction to the edition of Greve/Grove's *Poems/Gedichte*, and the 1994 *Arachne* article "Felix Paul Greve's Fanny *Essler* Novel and Poems: His or Hers?"

40. This note also mentions her situation after Greve was in prison thanks to his "English friend" (Kilian), his translation career while incarcerated, and her meeting him in Köln upon his release: http://www.umanitoba.ca/libraries/archives/collections/fpg/frl/ill_frlWolkzugPal+Note1903Kent.html.

41. Greve mentions her several times in his correspondence with Wolfskehl, and the dedicatee of his closing poem in *Wanderungen*, "Irrender Ritter": *** ** matches the sound of "Helene Klages." In November 2007, manuscript poems from a previously unknown collection entitled "Helga," which is likely an anagram of her name, surfaced in the DLA Wolfskehl collection, and will soon be incorporated in the e-Edition of FPG's poetry.

42. Helene Klages' "spring-like blondness" and her Madonna-status are documented in Jürgen Kolbe's excellent book about the Munich Bohemians, *Heller Zauber*, 1987, 180. On page 178, Thomas Mann's younger brother Viktor's hilarious description of "the holy act" of a public breastfeeding ceremony at Wolfskehl's is cited at length. FrL says in connection to Klages and her child that "virgin—baby—nunnery" was a "career much admired in Munich" (*AB* 60), which also held true to Franziska "Fanny" von Reventlow's experience a decade earlier (her son was born in 1897). The "Madonna" in her satire *Herrn Dames Aufzeichnungen*, however, does not represent her own case, as is usually asserted. The 1904 timeframe makes Helene Klages' motherhood and her daughter Heidi a much more likely target.

43. *AB* 59: Greve was "impressed again with virginity" in America. She here defines it as "a freak growth of no sense."

44. Fanny Elssler 1840 Lithograph by Leybold in *Broom*: http://www.umanitoba.ca/libraries/archives/collections/fpg/frl/ill_frlBroom1840Fanny-ElsslerLithogr1922.html.

45. See http://en.wikipedia.org/wiki/Fanny_Elssler/.

46. "Circle," in *Broom*: http://www.umanitoba.ca/libraries/archives/collections/fpg/frl/ill_frlBroomCircle+ill1923.html.

Brian Johnson

•

Beyond Regionalism: Martha Ostenso's *Wild Geese* and the Northern Nation

A major popular success when it first appeared in 1925, Martha Ostenso's *Wild Geese* is now widely considered a landmark of prairie fiction whose use of realist and naturalist techniques to depict farming in northwestern Manitoba made a striking break with the conventions of regional romance that had dominated prairie writing until that point. Realism and regionalism invariably overlap and reinforce each other in critical accounts of the novel, for the "realism" of *Wild Geese* stems in large part from an "intensely local and specific" treatment of prairie space (Hammill 82) that is typical of regional literature. By Janice Fiamengo's definition, this genre "portrays regional experience, using 'the details of real-world geography' to assert the value of the particular" and "examines the impact of distinctive terrain, topography, and climate upon the people who experience them, sometimes suggesting quasi-mystical explanations for the force of geography" (242). How better to describe a novel whose characters are prone to ruminating upon "the strange unity between the nature of man and earth here in the north" (92) and whose narrator asserts that demonic patriarch Caleb Gare is "a spiritual counterpart of the land, as harsh, as demanding, as tyrannical as the very soil from which he drew his existence" (35)? The fact that the novel's depiction of homesteading in the fictional farming community of "Oeland" originated in Ostenso's experience as a rural schoolteacher in the Hayland district 160 km northwest of Winnipeg in 1918 has further reinforced the novel's regional significance and credentials, as has the fact that Ostenso seems to have based many of the characters in the novel on real families she met while living and teaching there (Atherton 2). Robert G. Lawrence's critical foray into imaginative cartography—a comparison of a map of the Hayland district to maps of "Oeland" and the Gare farm that he drafted, based on the novel's descriptions—is emblematic of the importance that region has assumed for situating Ostenso's fictive topography within studies of prairie fiction more generally.

Yet, despite the novel's meticulous examination of the deleterious psychological effects the prairie landscape has on its inhabitants, Ostenso's regionalism is less firmly rooted in place than it might seem. Anticipating the techniques of Sheila Watson, who transformed regional material into an archetypal pattern in *The Double Hook* (1959), Ostenso recounts the genesis of *Wild Geese* as a discovery of the universal within the particular:

> It was during a summer vacation from my university work that I went into the lake district of Manitoba, well toward the frontier of that northern civilization. My novel, *Wild Geese*, lay there, waiting to be put into words. . . .Here was human nature, stark, unattired in the convention of a smoother, softer life. (Qtd. in Thomas 40)

In keeping with this pronouncement, numerous critics have interpreted the novel's depiction of repression and violence on the northern prairie as a pre-text for what is in fact an archetypal or metaphysical examination of human isolation and existential homelessness—what the novel's narrator calls the "unmeasurable Alone surrounding each soul" (53). M. G. Hesse, for instance, argues that the novel is only superficially concerned with the melodrama of prairie patriarchy, and is more interested in elaborating "the eternal themes of good and evil, the search for identity and the freedom to be oneself" (48). Rosalie Murphy Baum's reading of the novel's naturalism similarly notes that the role of prairie landscape in *Wild Geese* is "symbolic and yet almost incidental," serving primarily as "a metaphor for life" that allows Ostenso to contemplate "the nature of existence" and its "mythic patterns" (132-33). To some degree, similar assumptions feature in virtually all interpretations of the role of place in the novel.

Further complicating the novel's "regionalism" is the way that its treatment of prairie settlement extends beyond the local but also falls short of the universal, evoking instead the national metanarratives of thematic "myth" critics like Northrop Frye and D. G. Jones. Interpretations that identify the novel's northern prairie landscapes with an incipient form of national allegory tend to be partial or implicit, but hints of such a reading are evident in many classic studies of the work. Laurie Ricou's seminal analysis of *Wild Geese* as a novel about "man's overwhelming loneliness in a barren, empty land," and whose "central concern is with the loneliness of the human heart" (74) anticipates the regional-universalist interpretations of later critics like Hesse and Baum. But Ricou's more general paradigm of prairie fiction—the solitary figure of "vertical man in a horizontal world" whose exposure to the "emptiness" of prairie geography "inevitably prompts the theme of man's aloneness in a hostile, or at least indifferent, universe" (6)—also resonates suggestively with Frye's notion that Canadian literature is dominated by the trope of a "garrison mentality" pitted against a hostile wilderness. To support his case, Ricou even makes reference to the "evocation of stark terror" prompted by the "frightening loneliness of a huge and thinly settled country" that Frye sees as characteristic of Canadian poetry in *The Bush Garden* (Ricou 6; Frye 138). Such a theorization of prairie fiction that overlaps with Frye's national poetics begins to complicate the regional-universalist reading of *Wild Geese* that Ricou actually advances.

In his influential study *Unnamed Country* Dick Harrison likewise locates a national metanarrative at the heart of prairie fiction, a regional literature which he repeatedly characterizes as an "extreme form" of the wilderness myth that pervades the depiction of landscape in Canadian writing more generally, from Sir William F. Butler's *The Great Lone Land* to Howard O'Hagan's *Tay John* (ix, 7). For Harrison, as for Ricou, prairie fiction's representation of landscape as "at once enticing and threatening to the civilized imagination" (7) necessarily puts this form of regional writing in conversation with broader discourses of national myth. In this context, it is perhaps not surprising that Ostenso's stark depictions of the northern prairie have been compared to the wilderness landscapes of the Group of Seven or to the austere nature poems of their modernist counterparts, F. R. Scott and A. J. M. Smith—visual artists and writers who were instrumental in creating the wilderness mythology that subtends the nationalist criticism of Jones and Frye (Harrison 35; Lenoski 281; Thomas 40; see Mackey 40-49).

My aim in this paper is to map the confluence of such regionalist, universalist, and nationalist discourses in *Wild Geese* from the perspective of a postcolonial pedagogy that seeks to unsettle the myths of settler-invader nationalism. Implicit in the novel's complication of realist regionalism with a universalist thematics of existential homelessness and with a nationally inflected wilderness myth are a broader set of preoccupations with indigeneity and the settler-invader dilemma of belonging. These become particularly visible in the novel's residual Gothicism and in its pervasive evocation of what Sherrill Grace, following Glenn Gould, calls "ideas of North" (xii). The novel's Gothic tropes may be read as symptoms of the bad conscience that accompanies the novel's substantial investment in settler-invader narratives of indigenization. Subsequently, the reader will note how the novel's complementary investment in discourses of nordicity constitutes a national ideology of belonging the function of which is to assuage colonial anxieties about settlement. This is done by projecting a counternarrative of Nordic "indigeneity" that tacitly legitimates the dispossession of the prairie's Native inhabitants. By examining the ways in which Ostenso's novel manifests a discourse of northern nationalism that symbolically replaces the "unhomely" (*unheimlich*) homestead of archetypal settler-invader Caleb Gare with a new mode of national dwelling suggested by the text's idealized Nordic homes and northern European characters, we can see how the regionalist and universalist aesthetics of *Wild Geese* conceal a powerful nation-building ideology and a legitimizing allegory of settler-invader national formation.

As Margot Northey's *The Haunted Wilderness* and my own "Unsettled Landscapes" both suggest, there are strong currents of Gothicism and the uncanny in *Wild Geese* that inhere particularly in the enclosed and repressive space of Caleb's household and in the novel's presentation of the prairie as an animistic, often malevolent site for the projection of unconscious fears and repressed desires. This Gothic dimension implicitly attests to the novel's embedded national themes, for, as Cynthia Sugars has argued concerning "the unhomeliness of the Canadian locale," settler-invader culture occupies an essentially uncanny space due to a colonial history whose legacy is an "intangible sensation of unbelonging" (xix-xx). In Alan Lawson's influential formulation of this condition, the colonial settler's sensation of being permanently and paradoxically "unsettled" stems from his or her ambiguous position within a "postimperial" culture "suspended between 'mother' and 'other', simultaneously colonized and colonizing" (155). A major consequence of this ambivalent position is the proliferation of settler-invader narratives that inscribe "the suppression or effacement of the Indigene, and the concomitant indigenization of the settler who, in becoming more like the Indigene whom he mimics, becomes less like the atavistic inhabitant of the cultural homeland whom he is also reduced to mimicking" (158). In other words, as Terry Goldie has shown, settler-invader cultures characteristically seek symbolic legitimization for their presence on foreign ground by appropriating the authenticating signs of indigenous identity—a fantasy of cross-cultural inheritance that has historically involved a double-pronged strategy of "going Indian" while asserting the "death" or extinction of Native cultures. The fact of ongoing Native presence and anti-colonial resistance in Canada ensures that such ideological gestures can never have the final word, and, as such, require frequent, indefinite repetition; in this way, narratives that appear to "settle" the question of the settler's indigenization nonetheless remain haunted by the very cultural groups whose absence they falsify and whose aura of belonging they appropriate. Representations of a menacing Gothic wilderness in Canadian settlement literature are often symptomatic of such national haunting. That is because, in keeping with Freud's conception of the uncanny as a return of the repressed—"that class of the frightening which leads back to what is known of old and long familiar" (Freud 340)—representations of Gothic wilderness recall the conventional association of Native peoples with wild nature. This association can suggest the return of a resistant Native presence that the disavowals and appropriations of indigenizing narratives attempt to occlude.

Such a haunting of settlements by their repressed colonial history is evident in *Wild Geese*, a novel in which Native characters appear primarily in the margins as "half-breeds" who work as hired men and "h[a]ng about" Yellow Post with "leering eyes" (100), gazing at the women of the settlement and gossiping about "bad omens" (174). Despite their marginal involvement in the plot, the significance of their presence is suggested on the first page of the novel when Oeland's new schoolteacher Lind Archer recalls, "with increasing discomfort, the short, scornful grunt of John Tobacco, the mail carrier, when she had sought from him what manner of being she might expect in Caleb Gare" (7-8). As the narrative soon demonstrates, Caleb is an archetypal settler-invader who treacherously and single-mindedly seeks to appropriate all of the land in the area in a compulsive repetition of the colonizing impulse; that the novel's first judgment about him is provided by the "short, scornful grunt" of a peripheral Native character suggests both the broader colonial context of Caleb's prairie dominion and the virtual silencing of the indigene that such a dominion entails and perpetuates. John Tobacco's role as mail carrier, a job that makes him paradoxically central and yet largely invisible to the settler-invader community whose messages he delivers in a symbolic substitution of his own voice, hints that, despite its de facto marginality, Native presence in the novel is considerably more significant than it seems.

In fact, *Wild Geese* is a novel preoccupied with indigeneity and, in its Gothic mode, anxious about the settler's prospects for indigenization. Not only are most of the Gares plagued by the problem of feeling existentially homeless in a hostile landscape whose tyranny is embodied in Caleb's domination of the family; this concern is also at the heart of Caleb's complex relation to his land, which he attempts to dominate, but, in a curious way, also desires:

> Caleb would stand for long moments outside the fence beside the flax. Then he would turn quickly to see that no one was looking. He would creep between the wires and run his hand across the flowering, gentle tops of the growth. A stealthy caress—more intimate than any he had ever given to a woman. (147)

Such libidinally charged language in relation to a feminized prairie recalls Daniel S. Lenoski's perceptive reading of how the novel exploits conventional stereotypes of the Indian's "closeness to nature" and repeatedly identifies Native characters with the landscape in order to symbolize a sought-after "connection between man and prairie space" (286). More particularly, this image of the prairie as sexualized and animistic recalls Goldie's point that "[t]he female indigene as emanation of the land is a source of indigenization," one of whose characteristic manifestations is a figure that suggests "the possibility that the white [male] might find within the apparently inimical land an element that will save him" (73). Native women who might serve as symbolic intermediaries for masculine indigenization are absent from the text, and this function is subsumed within the strange figure of an eroticized landscape in Caleb's story. Ostenso thus effectively dramatizes the desire for an indigenization whose Native object has been subtly disavowed through processes of displacement and idealization.

This substitution also suggests a discomfort with the sexual rhetoric of indigenization with which Caleb's "stealthy caresses" flirt—a discomfort evident too in the refusal of a "half-breed" suitor by Caleb's dutiful daughter Ellen. As Goldie points out, such ambivalence with regard to the sexual economy of Native stereotypes is not unusual:

> [t]he essence of the indigene maiden is a sexual interest
> but also a sexual restraint. In many instances there is no
> overt reference to any sexual interaction. It is an example
> of the repression of miscegenation . . . [that] cloaks the is-
> sue in an ethereal aura which suggests the impossibility of
> sexual congress with a spiritual entity. . . .The text's associ-
> ated comments on the land are usually positive, with many
> references to the attractions of the topography. (68)

From this perspective, Caleb's idealization of the flax field and its topographic attractions acquires a more profound significance than the notion that it is merely a sublimation of his "inability to possess" his wife Amelia or a perverse offshoot of his obsession with working the land (Arnason 306). The secretiveness and apparent shame of Caleb's transgressive "caress[ing]" of the idealized feminine landscape can also be explained as signs of "the repression of miscegenation" within a sexualized indigenization narrative, as well as of its "cloak[ing] . . . in an ethereal aura."

At the same time that Caleb's narrative dramatizes both the settler-invader's acquisitive attitude towards land and his use of the landscape as a Native proxy to disavow his desire for indigenization, the narrator also reminds us that "the Indians were always ready to predict evil for the white settlers" (174). Such a readiness to spread a counterdiscourse of "rumours" (174) subversively doubles John Tobacco's official capacity as mail carrier and gives fuller voice to the unspoken sentiments behind his "short, scornful grunt" about Caleb

Gare. Further underlining the Natives' potential resistance to settler narratives of appropriation and indigenization is the text's tacit identification of the vengeful landscape with the resentful Indians of Yellow Post. Some time before the climactic scene in which Caleb drowns in the muskeg—the one region of the prairie that remains constitutively beyond his considerable powers to exploit—the Indians at Yellow Post trade "rumors of bushfires to the north" that could threaten Caleb's crops; the narrator, focalized at the time through Caleb, dismisses this possibility as malicious Native gossip: "It meant nothing" (174). Yet, the Indians' "bad omens" are at least partially borne out when Caleb meets his end in another bushfire that drives him into the muskeg where he drowns trying to save his beloved field of flax. As the proximate cause of Caleb's death, the anthropomorphized muskeg—described throughout the novel as "bottomless and foul," "the sore to Caleb's eye" (17), "black and evil and potted with water holes," "rotten land" (156)—seems to enact the murderous implications of the Indians' eagerness to "predict evil for the white settlers," figuring a revenge of the silenced indigene against the violence of the archetypal settler-invader.

Significantly, this revenge is figured as a Gothic inversion of the sexual economy of indigenization represented by the ethereal femininity of the flax field. The notorious eroticism of Caleb's death scene, as he is sucked into the "silky reeds" (298) of the feminized muskeg and is crushed in "the over-strong embrace of the earth" (299), could be said to enact not just the failure of the indigenizing narrative, but a parody of its ultimate consummation. Caleb's death, in other words, might plausibly be read as a grotesquely displaced fulfillment of the repressed miscegenation impulse that underpins his indigenizing "desire" for the flax. In this way, Caleb's narrative reaches an ambivalent climax that hints parodically at the indigenization he fails to achieve while transforming him into a scapegoat whose symbolic death frees the remaining settlers of their burden of colonial guilt.

The fact that *Wild Geese* figures indigenous resistance to invasion and appropriation only in veiled terms as a Gothic allegory of the settler's losing battle with the soil is revealing of the novel's own ideological investments. Although Ostenso's work provides a romantic critique of Caleb's "Cartesian" and "Judeo-Christian" attempt "to rationalize and temporalize the space of Northern Manitoba" (Lenoski 290-91), it does not do so in the name of anticolonial critique, despite the passing references to Native resistance already noted. Quite the contrary: such textual irruptions are symptomatic of the novel's own bad conscience. That is, they represent problems to be managed and ultimately dismissed by the logic of the novel's own investment in settler-invader narratives of indigenization. This investment is evident in the way that Caleb's death makes possible the happy resolution of a romance plot between Lind Archer and Amelia Gare's illegitimate son Mark Jordan that culminates in an uncritical celebration of conventional forms of indigenization. Thus, on the same night that the novel's representative settler-invader meets a symbolic Native comeuppance in the muskeg, enacting a grotesque parody of the indigenizing narrative, Lind and Mark plan to attend the harvest jubilee masquerade with the help of "old John Tobacco" who provides "an outfit of doeskin and feathers for Mark, and a costume for Lind ornate with beads and feathers" (268). The lovers' symbolic indigenization under the approving eye of John Tobacco at the same moment that the novel's villain is dispatched by the plot to ensure their union leaves little doubt about the novel's ideological commitments.

Equally significant is the fact that the indigenized space of the harvest masquerade is the narrative means by which Ostenso secures the freedom of Caleb's daughter Judith Gare, the novel's already indigenized heroine who seems intuitively to embody Goldie's trope of the "female indigene as emanation of the land." For instance, in an earlier scene of erotic communion with the landscape, "not knowing fully what she was doing, Judith took off all her clothing and lay flat on the damp ground" to discover

> how knowing the earth was, as if it might have a heart and
> a mind hidden here in the woods. The fields that Caleb had
> tilled had no tenderness, she knew. But here was something
> forbiddenly beautiful, secret as one's own body. (61)

Coupled with the subsequent departure of Lind and Mark from Oeland, Judith's use of the harvest masquerade to escape from Caleb and to flee with her lover to the city is clearly meant to convey the consecration of a new order represented by the "New House" that Caleb's son Martin builds on the prairie to replace the rickety Gare homestead following Caleb's death. The emergence of this new order during "the languid peace of an Indian Summer" (300) reinforces the sense that Martin's dwelling carries the sanction of "old John Tobacco" in the same manner as Lind and Mark's Indian masquerade.

Complementing and reinforcing the indigenizing narrative of *Wild Geese* is the novel's striking identification of prairie space with nordicity—an identification that stems from the perspective of the novel's primary focalizer, Lind Archer. An outsider to the region whose point of view recalls Ostenso's own southern Manitoba perspective on the more northerly district of Hayland, Lind sees Oeland as an "isolated spot in the north country" (10), characteristically referring to the prairie setting simply as "the north" (26). In many ways, the "northerliness" of Oeland is conventionally metaphorical; it plays on the cliché of Nordic barrenness to present the prairie as a mythic waste-land awaiting succor. Moreover, a lengthy philosophical exchange between Lind and Mark Jordan, in which "[t]hey talked of the strange unity between the nature of man and earth here in the north" (92), links Oeland's northerli-ness to an environmentally-determinist analysis of the way the land "sap[s] all [the] passion and sentiment" from the inhabitants (92). However, just as the "northerliness" in *Wild Geese* connotes more than regional specificity, it also functions as more than a metaphorical buttress to Ostenso's "naturalist" exploration of the impact of environment on personality (Baum 125-28).

Ever since the Canada First group articulated a "new nationality" for the Dominion of Canada based on Robert Grant Haliburton's vision of a distinct-ly "Northern country inhabited by the descendants of Northern races" in the late 1860s, ideas of north in Canada have been profoundly tied to the cultural project of imagining the nation (Berger 52; Haliburton qtd. in Berger 53). Rooted in eighteenth- and nineteenth-century assumptions about the invigo-rating effects of cold climates on "racial stock" and fed by Nordic antiquarian-ism's "revival of interest in the sagas of the Northmen and the myths of primi-tive people," Haliburton's Confederation-era northern racialism "equat[ed] the adjective northern with toughness, strength, and hardihood to construct Canadians as "the Northmen of the New World" (Berger 51, 53). As this phrase suggests, although Canada First's northern nationalism emphasized the common "northern ancestry" of "the diverse nationalities within Canada," British and northern European immigrants nonetheless acquired additional symbolic capital within this nation-building metanarrative, leading to their status as "preferred nations" in official immigration policy during the first half of the twentieth century (Berger 53; Elliott and Fleras 55). So pervasive has the northern myth become that Sherrill Grace has recently asserted that "no matter who, or when, or where we are, we are shaped by, haunted by ideas of North, and we are constantly imagining and constructing Canada-as-North, as much so when we resist our nordicity as when we embrace it" (xii).

Although Canada First's northern nationalism was conceived as an impe-rialist strategy to distinguish Canada from the United States and to unify its immigrant population under the ideology of a common northern ancestry, its defense of Canadian imperial sovereignty on the basis of a natural "Nordic" inheritance in the "New World" made it a powerful legitimizing discourse that could help to allay the anxieties about indigenization and colonial guilt that plagued settler-invader culture's relation to the indigene. In fact, the ra-cialist basis of its appeal reveals northern nationalism to be an inverted and complementary form of indigenization discourse; rather than announcing the inevitable "death" of the races whose indigeneity it covets, northern nationalism tacitly implies that the immigrant settler-invader is always already indigenous to this place because he or she is always already "northern."

Such a nationally-inflected discourse of Canadian nordicity emerges in *Wild Geese* in Mark's recollections of his upbringing by Catholic missionaries in a region farther north" than Oeland (93). These recollections of a boyhood in the north reinforce, but also begin to complicate the trope of the austere northern wasteland and its psychological effects, ultimately bringing the indigenizing promise of northern identity to the fore:

> That's a country for you. If there's a God, I imagine that's where he sits and does his thinking. The silence is awful. You feel immense things going on, invisibly. There is that eternal sky—light and darkness—the endless plains of snow—a few fir trees, maybe a hill or a frozen stream. And the human beings are like totems—figures of wood with mysterious legends upon them that you can never make out. The austerity of nature reduces the outward expression of life, simply, I think, because there is not such an abundance of natural objects for the spirit to react to. We are, after all, only the mirror of our environment. (93)

These reflections, which immediately follow and directly gloss Mark and Lind's observation about "the strange unity between the nature of man and earth here in the north [i.e. in Oeland]" (92), identify the northern prairie of Oeland with the "far" north of Mark's youth, a comparison whose import is signaled by Lind's speculation that "perhaps human life, or at least human contact, is just as barren here as farther north" (93). Mark's observation that in the frozen immensity of the far north "the human beings are like totems," virtually free of "the outward expression of life," similarly recalls Ostenso's authorial disclosure that what she found during her time as a teacher in Hayland was "human nature, stark, unattired in the convention of a smoother, softer life" (qtd. in Thomas 40).

At the same time, however, Mark's sublime vision of the north as a place of metaphysical mystery, where intimations of a rather remote-sounding Judeo-Christian God are curiously linked to a simile drawn from Native cultures ("human beings...like totems—figures of wood with mysterious legends upon them that you can never make out"), hints at the transformation of settler-invaders into indigenized inhabitants of northern space. Mark's culturally hybrid vision of the north, in other words, is a double-faced parable that looks

towards the future at the same moment that it characterizes the present situation in Oeland. In its dramatic context, the parable alludes to Caleb's role as
repressive "God" of the Gare farm whose tyranny reflects the landscape's and
who reduces his family to "frozen" and inscrutable "figures of wood." However—and although Mark and Lind do not realize it—the image of northern inhabitants becoming Native "totems" also foreshadows the indigenization that
will become possible once Caleb's reign has ended. A similar pattern is evident
in the novel's multivalent use of the image of the wild geese whose initial flight
"farther north, to a region beyond human warmth . . . beyond even human
isolation" (34) is succeeded by the more complex and more positive image of
"a magnificent seeking through solitude—an endless quest" (53, 302)—a description that appears twice, first in Caleb's absence after Lind spends an eve-
ning with a family of Icelandic settlers, the Bjarnassons, and again after Caleb
has died and a new order has taken root. What the plot's transformation of the
prairie setting from uncanny frozen wasteland into habitable and indigenized
northern landscape dramatizes, in other words, is not simply a regionally-
based mythic journey to overcome the "unmeasurable Alone surrounding
each soul," but an allegory of the settler-invader's national formation.

The integration of northern nationalism and indigenization that such an
allegory entails is particularly evident in the aborted romance between Caleb's
obedient daughter Ellen and a former hired man named Malcolm, who is
Scottish with "Indian blood in his veins" (48), "Cree blood two generations
back" (163). Ellen's "half-breed" suitor, who returns after several years to the
Gare farm riding an "Indian pony" (162) and offers her the chance for a new
life in the north, is in every sense her father's opposite: the archetype of the
existentially secure, indigenized northern settler. Evoking the novel's peren-
nial association of horses with passional freedom, Malcolm promises:

> I'd buy a horse for you—we'd go slow, and sleep out nights
> all summer under the stars, Ellen, and in my silk tent when
> it rains. I've got an old cabin up north—make lots of money
> on furs—you wouldn't be needin' for nothin'. (168)

The prospect of dwelling in existential security in the cabin "up north" in
this promise tellingly infuses northern discourse with allusions to Malcolm's
indigenous heritage: the silk tent suggests a teepee just as trapping recalls
a Native mode of subsistence. Similarly, an earlier reference to Malcolm as
"a wanderer, hearing ever a call in the wind, a summons to far lakes and
lonely forests" (166) alludes to Romantic conceptions of the "nomadism" of
Native societies, and reinforces Malcolm's function as a potential means of
indigenization for the settler-invader culture whose alienation and stunted

growth Ellen embodies.

Like Lind and Mark's failure to see the indigenizing potential of an identification with areas "farther north" at the midpoint of the novel, Ellen's rejection of Malcolm's courtship marks the distance that the novel's national
allegory will have to travel before nordicity becomes a sign of habitation rather than exile. In its favourable evocation of a northern home for the settler,
the failed national romance between Ellen and Malcolm begins the process
of rewriting Mark's vision of an austere and deadening northern immensity
into the more vigorous and optimistic script of indigenized Nordic nationalism that his vision simultaneously anticipates. In fact, Ellen's response to
Malcolm's proposal—under the pressure of imagining such a betrayal of her
father "she could neither move nor speak" (169)—figuratively transforms her
into one of the "totems" of Mark's narrative, as if her immobility was the index of a still "frozen" process of indigenization. Her subsequent reflections,
after she has refused Malcolm's offer and her suitor has departed on "the trail
north" (168) without her, confirm the rewriting of Mark's barren discourse
of nordicity by Ellen's narrative, even if she does not actually experience the
idealized north she imagines. "Perhaps it would have been delightful to have
gone away with Malcolm. The northern lakes would have been deep and blue,
and there would have been infinite rest beside them at night, under the stars"
(271), she speculates, echoing but also making habitable Mark's far chillier
and more barren vision of northern infinity with its "eternal sky—light and
darkness—the endless plains of snow—a few fir trees, maybe a hill or a frozen
stream."

Ellen's fantasy of "infinite rest" in the north receives more concrete expression in the novel's depiction of Oeland's northern European immigrants.
As with Malcolm, the principal function of these characters is to critically
undermine and present an alternative to the crudely colonizing attitude and
alienated mode of dwelling symbolized by Caleb and his homestead. Like
Malcolm, moreover, they are hybrid figures whose textual authority and existential security reflect their synthesis of nordicity and indigeneity. The "great
clan" of the Icelandic Bjarnassons and their "great stone house on the lake," in
which four generations dwell in comparative harmony under the guidance of
a patriarch who is "eternal in endurance . . . in warmth and [in the] hospitality
of nature" (49), provide a pointed contrast to the claustrophobic, treacherous,
and inhospitable household of the Gares where Caleb "hold[s] taut the reins
of power, alert, jealous of every gesture in the life within which he moved
and governed" (36). Thus, whereas Lind experiences the Gare household as a
Gothic space demonically illuminated by the red glow of the stove, where "the

rough, cobweb-hung rafters leaned down upon you" and where "on a wild
night a jet of wind would ripple over your cheek if you lay with your face to
the wall" (16), she arrives at the dwelling of the Bjarnassons to discover that
"[i]n all that region, there was not another house like it. Like a welcome,"—
and in contrast to the Gare's glowing red stove—"its western windows were
aflame with light from the red sun" (49). Moreover, the great stone house is
a metonymy for its maker, the eternally warm and hospitable patriarch, Mat-
thias Bjarnasson:

> The house he had built with his own hands was like him,
> was a square stone image of him. He had excavated the
> earth and built its rugged, lasting foundation; had hauled
> stones in slow wagonloads, and with the care and fineness
> of a woman patterning lace, had fitted them together in the
> mortar and had built four broad walls to the blue. (49)

Such an identification of the inviting and secure stone house on the northern
prairie with its Icelandic architect is one of the ways that the novel's representation of northern European immigrants constructs an alternative legitimating discourse of prairie settlement whose assumptions reflect the racialist
economy of Canada First's northern nationalism.

The "lasting foundation" of the Bjarnassons' existential comfort as inhabitants of prairie space is reinforced by the indigeneity that is implicitly attributed to them as symbolic stand-ins for, or natural inheritors of, Native cultures. As Lind observes of the family in which an "ancient lady" tells fortunes
(50) and in which nights are passed telling "tales of supernatural events, of
visions and omens" (52), "Superstition here lay along life in a broad vein" (51).
In contrast to the Christianity that Caleb hypocritically distorts and exploits
to ensure his family's unswerving devotion to the farm, the "clan's" various
"superstition[s]" associate them with the cosmologies of people that Caleb
dismisses as "heathen" (255). Similarly, in contrast to Caleb and in keeping
with the animism of Native spirituality, the Bjarnassons invest the landscape
with spiritual and historical meanings that they prioritize over its use value.
As young Erik Bjarnasson explains to Lind:

> The lake has two of our family. One, my brother Gisli, one
> my sister Althea's promised husband. They were friends,
> and they quarreled. They carried their quarrel into the lake
> in two boats. It was a storm—the lake took them. We have
> not yet found any of them—not a small sign. Until so, we
> do not let others fish in the lake. Caleb Gare, he says, yes, he
> shall fish. We say no. We are a family, Mees Archer—a great

> family. We shall not let others in to fish where our dead is
> buried. (52)

The "sacred lake of the Bjarnassons" (180) thus suggests the family's indigenization both because its sacral quality recalls the animate landscapes of
Native cosmologies, and because it simultaneously evokes the trope of the
Native burial ground whose sacred space the settler-invader is indifferent to
disturbing.

The novel's treatment of Fusi Aronson, another Icelandic neighbour of
Caleb's, develops the symbolic role of the Icelanders as indigenized north-
erners in a more complex way that bears heavily on the novel's outcome and
ideology. As I have already argued, Caleb's death in the muskeg provides the
novel with an ambiguous, multivalent climax. It may be read as an anti-colonial allegory of the Native's revenge upon the settler-invader, and as such
constitutes the "bad conscience" of the novel. However, its function within
the plot, which is to make a scapegoat of the only settler whose violence directly exposes the "invasiveness" of colonization, ultimately silences this bad
conscience and recuperates indigenizing ideologies by making possible the
novel's concluding exchange of uncanny affect for national romance: Caleb
dies, freeing two pairs of indigenized lovers to unite. In this way, resistance
to the novel's nationalist ideology (Native revenge) is neutralized by the plot,
whose machinations convert resistance into the very means of securing ideological closure. Fusi's desire to take revenge on Caleb for the latter's role in the
death of his two brothers is inseparable from the double movement of this
narrative.

Like the Bjarnassons, Fusi is a northerner identified strongly with the
landscape and with indigenous peoples; he is like "a solitary oak on the prairie" (33), yet he "strides across the country, like some giant defender of a forgotten race" (82). Which "forgotten race" is he defending? It is not simply
his own "race"—that is, his dead brothers—for Fusi's account of the circumstances surrounding Caleb's role in their deaths by exposure hints at another
substitution:

> [Caleb] took the lives of two of my brothers. There was an
> epidemic here with the Indians some years back. It was a
> snowstorm and my brothers asked in at his door. They were
> blind from the storm. They were not sick—my brothers.
> But Caleb Gare feared the sickness—he feared for himself.
> And he closed the door in their faces. (33)

The "epidemic here with the Indians" is a detail that suggestively identifies
Caleb's self-protection and responsibility for the deaths of these Northmen

with a major signifier of colonial violence. As such, Caleb's fatal action and Fusi's determination to kill him in retribution symbolically dramatizes the unresolved historical conflict between colonizer and colonized, settler and Indigene. Fusi's role in precipitating the crisis that destroys Caleb—he has inadvertently started the fire that threatens Caleb's flax—further confirms the status of his revenge as a proxy for Native resistance; in fact, by this point in the narrative, he has actually acquired the worthless muskeg after being blackmailed into a property exchange by Caleb. Thus, moments before disappearing into the muskeg, Caleb is haunted by the image of "Fusi Aronson, on whose land he was about to die" (299).

Fusi's role as a displaced agent of Native vengeance constitutes a now familiar synthesis of nordicity and indigeneity. In conjunction with the symbolic indigeneity of the muskeg itself (the proximate cause of Caleb's death), Fusi's role in precipitating the crisis makes the novel's concluding transformation of Oeland into an idealization of indigenized northern dwelling dependent on both northern and indigenous agents. If the accidental nature of Fusi's fire-setting seems curiously anti-climactic and makes Fusi an unusually passive, ambiguous source of Nemesis, that is perhaps because the metaphorical indigeneity of his doubled identity requires that his role in bringing about Caleb's death be subtly disavowed at the same moment that it is asserted. On the one hand, Fusi's intention to avenge his dead brothers must be asserted at the level of plot in order to make legible the colonial allegory he enacts and the indigenous identity he appropriates. On the other hand, his identification with a figure of Native revenge risks undermining the legitimating ideology of indigenized northern nationalism that the doubling of his identity is meant to support. Fusi's "accidental" role in bringing about the demise of the scapegoat is the token of the disavowal that is necessary to mediate this complex rhetorical situation that emerges at the novel's conclusion.

The novel's reach beyond regionalism to articulate a collective fantasy of national northern space that would disguise the founding violence of colonial "settlement" is finally confirmed by the southerly movement of the two pairs of lovers who depart from Oeland at the novel's conclusion. The escape of Caleb's rebellious and now pregnant daughter Judith with her Norwegian lover Sven to the city in the south at the end of the novel significantly widens the geographical scope of the novel's poetics of dwelling. As Lenoski observes, "since the pregnancy is quite definitely the result of [Judith's] indenture to the region, she may even be said to carry symbolically the bounty south to the city, just as the geese carry the cry of the Northland there" (285). In thus embodying "the cry of the Northland" in her unborn child and in communicating it to the city, Judith's flight suggests that the real significance of the becoming-indigenous of the northern prairie lays not in the rural north, but in the urban south—or, at least, in what southerliness represents in the novel's expanding symbolic geography. Such a reading helps to answer the common complaint that Ostenso has "misunderstood" her earthy heroine Judith by forcing her into a conventional marriage in the city at the end of the novel, when her passionate connection to the landscape's hidden fecundity so obviously dictates a rural fate for Judith (Harrison 113-14). Judith's "happy ending" is only surprising, however, if one insists on reading the novel in regional or conventionally romantic terms; in light of the novel's nationalist subtext, the circulation of the indigenized and now pregnant northern heroine through the urban world to the south to symbolically complete the dissemination of a Nordic national ideology is a logical, even inevitable conclusion.

The nationalist implications of Judith and Sven's departure from the north are even more powerfully present in the parallel departure of Mark and Lind at the novel's end. Both are outsiders to Oeland, so their return to the southern city, following the circular path of the wild geese in their "endless quest" (302), gives the northern prairie of Oeland the quality of an adventure space whose value is primarily to serve the emotional and epistemological needs of its southern visitors. As Mark reassures Lind shortly before their departure, while they are walking in the "weird" space of the dried lake-bottom near the muskeg, "We'll be away in a few weeks, now, and this life will seem like a dream" (275)—a surreal scene whose evocation of the landscape as a hallucinatory "dream" foregrounds the value of the region as a symbol and mental abstraction, the projection of a southern consciousness that answers southern needs. In fact, this is precisely Oeland's function for Mark, an architect with "raw nerves" who tires of his urban colleague's "everlasting talk of art and the City Beautiful of Tomorrow" and who has come north for a rustic "jump cure" on doctor's orders (54-55). The way that Mark's "raw nerves" interfere with his architectural work suggestively recalls the paradigmatic anxiety of the settler-invader whose existential insecurity produces the need for compensatory narratives of indigenization if he is to imagine a "homely" mode of national dwelling.

Significantly, what Mark finds in the north is not the truth about the shameful secret of his birth—that he is the illegitimate and unacknowledged son of Caleb's wife Amelia. Rather, he finds a solution to the problem of solitude in his romance with Lind Archer, a woman who is privy to a supernatural guarantee that the shameful secret of Mark's origin, like the shameful "secret" of the nation's birth, will remain hidden. As she is told when she has her fortune read in the great stone house of the Bjarnassons, "you will have a lover very soon. . . .There is a shadow of him. You will never know the secret of him. But you will be happy. That is all—" (50-51). And the novel's conclusion bears out this prediction, for the "mystery . . . at the Gares'. . . seemed to vanish with Caleb" (302), who had been using his knowledge of Mark's birth to blackmail Amelia into submission. What Mark finds, in short, without knowing it, is a saving lie whose very existence as a "lie" is unrecognized—a personal version of the indigenizing northern metanarrative that consoles or "cures" through mystification and disavowal. With Caleb dead, only Amelia knows the secret of Mark's parentage, and for that reason, perhaps, the narrative leaves her behind to mind the farm in Oeland as the novel's perspective shifts, with that of the younger characters, to the new locale of the southern city. In this way, like the flight of Judith and Sven, Mark's eventual departure with Lind from the northern rural community of Oeland for the city is a contrived "happy ending" that symbolizes the dissemination of the national ideology of indigenized northern dwelling that Malcolm's "cabin up north," the Bjarnasson's "stone house," and Martin's "New House" variously represent.

Ultimately, the national ideology that I have been tracing is signaled by the central symbol and most haunting image of the novel:

> From the northern swamps came a solitary hollow call, as if
> it was blown by a wind. It was the honking of a belated wild
> goose, the last to fly over the land to the half-frozen marsh-
> es of the remoter north. Lind and Mark listened, standing
> still, then looked at each other. Suddenly, it seemed, the air
> had cleared, and the night stood over them, wide, infinite,
> transparent as a strange dream. . . .(77)

What is the "strange dream" of *Wild Geese* but settler-invader nationalism itself? For the lovers, Lind and Mark, the "hollow call" of wild geese that echoes through the text signifies both the existential chill of human isolation and, in the final words of the novel, "a magnificent seeking through solitude . . . an endless quest. . . ." to overcome this condition (302). Laurie Ricou, in his key study of the work, agrees: "these wild geese come to represent both the mystery, the great imponderable at the heart of human existence, and the human impulse to seek an understanding of this mystery" (79). But as I have argued, this cosmic "mystery" around which all archetypal and metaphysical readings of the novel's regionalism circle, might be less mystery than mystification: a "strange dream" that perpetuates the novel's finessing of the settler's complicity with colonial violence and its instantiation of a consoling counternarrative of northern legitimacy and national romance. The "endless quest" of Ostenso's

wild geese, whose movement in and out of northern space so memorably figures both solitude and existential longing, may thus, from the perspective of
a postcolonial pedagogy, serve as an equally striking figuration of the settler-invader's "endless quest" to escape the anxiety of dwelling in an uncanny
national space haunted by indigenous ghosts.

Diane Beattie

•

"An Eventful Year":
Sinclair Ross's *As for Me and My House* as a
Reflection of its Era

"Canadian poetry . . . is altogether too self-conscious of its environment, of its position in space, and scarcely conscious at all of its position in time," wrote A. J. M. Smith in 1928. "This is an evident defect,
but it has been the occasion of almost no critical comment. Yet to be aware of
our temporal setting as well as our environment, and in no obvious or shal-
low way, is the nearest we can come to being traditional" (33). Smith's remarks
have been as true of Canadian fiction as of Canadian poetry and criticism
and rarely more so than in the case of prairie fiction and, in particular, the
work of Sinclair Ross. With some notable exceptions, most recently by critics
informed by Queer Theory, Ross's masterpiece *As for Me and My House* has
been studied as a regional novel that reflects its environment more realistically than most, if not all, works written before or since. This is not to say
that critics have ignored the fact that the novel is precisely situated in time as
well as place: the year and a few days covered by the diary of its protagonist,
Mrs. Bentley, runs from 18 April to 12 May five to six years after the onset
of the Great Depression (Ross 26). However, it is the spatial dimension of
the Depression setting—the drought-ridden and wind-swept landscape of
the prairies in the mid-thirties—that has been of primary interest to critics,
one result of this being that little attention has been paid to other elements
of the novel that are more widely characteristic of the period in which it is
set—the period of radio sermons, "bright young modernists," Jazz-Age bands
with "saxophone" and "drum," and, my principal concern here, "book[s] on
popular psychology" and papers on "marital success" (174, 12, 64, 114, 15 and
see 127-29). There are no political references or overt social commentaries in
As for Me and My House, but the "sombre environment" of the novel, like that
of such paintings as Caven Atkins' *Political Discussion, Depths of Depression,
Winnipeg* (1932) (Ring 73), is as much a reflection of the collapse of the economy of the prairies during the depression as it is of the state of the landscape
during the same period.

    In his article titled "Psychoanalytical Notes upon an Autobiographical
Account of a Case of Paranoia (*Dementia Paranoides*): Mrs. Bentley in Sin-

clair Ross's *As for Me and My House*," D. M. R. Bentley convincingly argues that Ross constructed his unreliable narrator as a paranoiac whose symptoms grow increasingly acute and pronounced as the novel proceeds and effectively come to a climax in her megalomaniacal subjugation of her husband Philip through the adoption of the child that he has fathered with Judith West.[1] Sigmund Freud's *A General History of Psychoanalysis* (1927) "contains all the material that Ross needed to construct Mrs. Bentley as . . . [an] extremely complex and complexly unreliable I/eye," writes Bentley as he proceeds to demonstrate that she exhibits all the symptoms of paranoia as well as its underlying causes—namely, sexual frustration and, more tentatively, same-sex attraction to Judith (864 ff.). Bentley's reading of *As for Me and My House* is as illuminating as it is convincing, and one of its additional merits is that, like David Stouck's more recent use of Freud in his biography of Ross, it invites further consideration of the novel in terms of the Freudian concepts that were in circulation in Canada, as in Britain and the United States, when it was written in the late nineteen thirties and early nineteen forties and published, in the United States, in 1941.[2] Did Ross draw on Freudian sources other than Freud himself for the construction of Mrs. Bentley, and is she perhaps even more complex from a Freudian perspective than D. M. R. Bentley so successfully demonstrates? By exploring these and other questions, I want to shed light on Mrs. Bentley as a representation of an embodied and emplaced—settled as well as unsettling—psyche and to ask how and on what post-Freudian basis Ross made her one of the most compelling characters in prairie fiction.

Much of Mrs. Bentley's complexity lies in the fact that Ross weaves several strands into her character, each with its implicit assumptions about female behaviour and male expectations with respect to such matters as female dependence and autonomy, reticence and revelation, and propriety and impropriety.[3] As a minister's wife, Mrs. Bentley is expected to "exhibit a genteel kind of piety, a well-bred Christianity that will serve as an example to the little sons and daughters of the town" (Ross 5). As a wife *per se* in small-town Canada in the nineteen thirties, she is expected to confine herself to traditionally feminine tasks such as cooking and cleaning and permit her husband to be "the man about the house" by doing heavier tasks such as "putting up stovepipes and opening crates," and digging the garden (5).[4] As an accomplished pianist of the same time and place, she is expected to confine herself to modest performances, preferably (because she is the minister's wife and the church organist) of uplifting religious music. As a female diarist, again of her time and place, she is expected to record only those events and thoughts that would not be a source of embarrassment to her husband and to herself in the event that he or someone else were to find and read her diary.[5] The sum of these parts is a richly composite figure who displays a myriad of contradictions and conflicts stemming from frequent disjunctions between what she knows she should be doing in accordance with the small-town laws of "Propriety and Parity" (9) and what she needs and wants to do. Never more than an unwilling inhabitant of the role of minister's wife in a small town, Mrs. Bentley's habitual condition is one of neurotic tension between her public and private selves, a tension that occasionally results in the alienation from self that leads her to describe herself in the third person as a "parson's wife" (29, 30, 31).

The fact that she never reveals either her "Christian" name or her "maiden name" is indicative of her subordination to her husband (and the patriarchy),[6] but the novel's recurring trope of "false fronts" suggests that her acceptance of the respectability and responsibilities of bourgeois marriage is a mask for psychic tumult and anarchic desire. It also suggests a continuous alienation from her non-Bentley self—the self that existed before her marriage to Philip and that, as the novel proceeds, manifests itself in forms of behaviour that sometimes appear conscious and at other times reflect her paranoia. The fact that Philip has sex with Judith in the "lean-to shed" that he has added to the parsonage as a bedroom for Steve (162) is but one indication of the homology in the novel between the false fronts of the small town and the superficial respectability of middle-class marriage: behind the façades of both houses and marriages are absences as well as habitations, and spaces that contain dark and dangerous secrets—indeed, storeys and stories.

Of course, the entries in Mrs. Bentley's diary are the only source of the reader's knowledge of her thoughts and activities and of the events that surround her. Written largely in the first-person singular and from a first-person ("I/eye") perspective, all of the entries in the diary are personal in content as well as style. Nearly all are written *post facto*[7] and all rely on eyewitness and/or hearsay evidence, the consequence being that they are the product of a combination of direct or indirect observation and meditation or interpretation. Designed by Ross to permit the reader to follow her activities and responses, they show her moving from one notable incident and emotion to the next and conjure up a character constituted and constrained by the routines of a minister's wife in a small town. Mrs. Bentley's text exhibits the frustrations of a loveless marriage to a man who appears to be a philandering bisexual with pedophile tendencies. The diary entries are also punctuated by incidents of spontaneity such as the ride with Judith on the railroad hand car (102-03) that confirm Mrs. Bentley's emotional nature, her need for self-expression, and the sense that, in Freudian terms, she is libidinally repressed and, hence, given to anarchic outbursts of energy in acts that do not conform to social norms and expectations, and, in fact, violate these norms and expectations in ways that court and sometimes prompt rebuke. Instances of this include her lack of restraint at the piano (see, for example, 77 and 128-29). The incident with the two men on the handcar causes Philip to frown and, despite telling her that she "shouldn't concern [her]self so much about the opinion of the town," Mrs. Bentley reports that he "clenched his jaws again, and squared his shoulders belligerently" (103).

In recording and, at times, analyzing her thoughts, feelings, motives, and fantasies in her diary, Mrs. Bentley uses her writing as a tool for cathartic self-assessment. Thus understood, Mrs. Bentley's diary-keeping is a consciously psychoanalytical activity, as she herself intimates when she quotes a remark about "popular psychology" and uses the term "repression" (15-18). In this light, the diary's inclusions and exclusions reflect Mrs. Bentley's awareness of her own neuroses and, at times, psychosis, and explain her recourse to such terms as "nerves" and "dread" (34) to describe and explain moments of heightened psychic distress.[8] Ross constructs his protagonist as a paranoid, but he also credits her with the capacity to discern and register psychological symptoms that the diary helps her to investigate and manage. Denied lengthy and profound conversations with her husband (let alone access to a psychiatrist), Mrs. Bentley undertakes her own self-analysis, describing her psychic strengths and weaknesses, taking stock of her relationships, and articulating her hopes and plans. In short, she is her own analyst and analysand, who enacts her self-analysis in the realm of her writing. *As for Me and My House* stands firmly in the modern tradition of the psychological and psychoanalytical novel to which Margaret Atwood's *Surfacing* and Margaret Laurence's *The Diviners* also belong: precisely to the extent that she does not fully name herself, Mrs. Bentley is an ancestor of the nameless protagonist of Atwood's novel, and precisely to the extent that she is versed in psychoanalysis she is the ancestor of Laurence's thoroughly Jungian Morag Gunn.

Ross also embeds a telos in Mrs. Bentley's diary entries that takes her from a condition of (feigned) powerlessness and delegated power to one of empowerment and control. Her first comment about herself is that she can "use the pliers and hammer twice as well" as Philip but allows him to be "the man about the house" for the sake of propriety (5). Her last words in the novel are an explanation of her decision to name Philip's and Judith's illegitimate child after him: "'That's right Philip. I want it so'" (216). Throughout the diary, Philip is at once a source of pain and insecurity and the object of desire and manipulation who must be indulged, protected, and controlled if he is to be retained as a husband and provider.[9] As a teleological whole Mrs. Bentley's diary is the record of a victorious campaign to bring her wayward husband to heel and save her marriage. As it proceeds she emerges from behind her mask of deference to become very obviously the controlling power and rule-maker in the Bentley household. Capitalizing on her knowledge of Philip's sexual desire for Steve, the boy whom the Bentleys temporarily adopt, as well as for Judith, Mrs. Bentley dethrones him not only by engineering this adoption of Judith's baby, but also by presenting him, in the form of a "pipe and . . . tobacco," with a symbol of what he had denied himself in accordance with his religious vocation (215). As she contemplates the future that lies beyond the end of the novel, Mrs. Bentley reasons that she will not work beside her husband in the second-hand book shop that they plan to run because "I'm so much more practical and capable than he is that in a month or two I'd be one of those domineering females that men abominate" (210). In fact, this is precisely what she has always been and, from the outset, abundantly and increasingly demonstrated.

One area in which she has ceaselessly done so is the arts. In addition to using piano-playing to manipulate the males in her life (more of which in a moment), Mrs. Bentley uses her diary entries to dominate Philip's art—drawing and painting—through interpretation and misprision. He is adamant that art and religion are entirely compatible and repeatedly draws upon the theories of Clive Bell and Roger Fry to argue for their homologous nature.[10] Not only does Mrs. Bentley perversely disregard his arguments and the evidence that supports them, but she also consistently disregards whatever significance his drawings hold for him as a Modernist and, instead, imposes her own Romantic readings on them. Thus a sketch of a Main Street on the back of a sermon becomes, not a work of "significant form" (the catchphrase between the wars for the aspects of a work of art that generate an aesthetic response)[11] but "a single row of smug, false-fronted stores [with] a loiterer or two" and "the prairie in the distance" and, later, a drawing on the table beside his Sunday sermon becomes "[a] cold, hopeless little thing" with a "solitary street lamp, pitted feebly against the overhanging darkness" (7, 23). Philip's aspiration to transcend (feminine) emotiveness and subjectivity through a combination of art and religion runs counter to Mrs. Bentley's interest in subject matter and remembered experience, and his concentration on form, which has a parallel in the concern "with a metaphysical concept of form" (Ring 78) in such paintings as *Doc Snyder's House* (1931) by the prairie artist Lionel MeMoine Fitzgerald, strikes no answering chord in his wife, who reacts to his work with a romantic (and Romantic) intensity of feeling that verges at times on sentimentality.[12] While he wants his art to be released from its environment into the realm of form and design, she wants to keep his drawings rooted in the circumstances of their production and, despite his protestations, succeeds to her own satisfaction in doing so: his generalities about the compatibility of art and religion are allowed into the diary, but not his interpretation of individual pieces of his [surely his?] art; these come entirely from Mrs. Bentley, who thus exercises ultimate control over their meaning. More than this, she ultimately gains control of the medium of his art. Almost a year before her diary ends she surreptitiously orders enough "[p]aints and brushes and canvases" to "start him up again" in oil painting, a medium that, like his pipe, he had abandoned when he became a minister (106). As the diary draws to a conclusion, she records that she has "persuade[d] him" to redo a sketch "in oils" and that he "started another picture yesterday in oils, worked hard at it all morning" (106, 202). Despite the fact that Mrs. Bentley "coaxed and admired and upbraided," the latter painting remains unfinished, but Mrs. Bentley's control over Philip's art is nevertheless almost total: never his muse, she is now his master.

Given Ross's association of Mrs. Bentley with Chopin and, especially, Liszt, one could be forgiven for leaving the contrast between her art and Philip's at the level of Romantic versus Modern, an opposition that is certainly consistent with other conflicts and tensions in their relationship. But rather than pursue this contrast, I wish to suggest that Ross's construction of Mrs. Bentley is more complex than can be captured by the term Romantic, at least in its popular sense of emotional and subjective rather than intellectual and objective. Is there perhaps an other-than Romantic conception of art and the artist at work in *As for Me and My House*? What is to be made of the fact that few of Mrs. Bentley's diary entries read as the product of a Romantic sensibility while many read like the utterances of a self-reflective obsessive neurotic? D. M. R. Bentley has noted the relevance to the novel of Freud's conception of art as sublimation, but it is worth pursuing further here, I think, in light of its underlying assumption that psychic illness or failure is a precondition of creativity. Art, specifically in Mrs. Bentley's case, piano-playing and diary-writing, appear to serve as an outlet for neurosis, a repository into which sexual energy is channeled and released in another form. With Mrs. Bentley's piano-playing, however, the matter is more complicated than this because her piano-playing is more than merely a product of sublimated sexual energy. It is a means by which she uses a combination of her musical choices and her performance of them—her physical form and movements—to manipulate her listeners, especially, as intimated earlier, the males in her life. Early in the novel Paul Kirby, the young school teacher who is infatuated with Mrs. Bentley, explains the source of her musical power succinctly when he explains that he goes to church, not for religious reasons, but for "'the music—and the way Mrs. Bentley plays'" (12).

Instances of the powerful effect of Mrs. Bentley's piano-playing on males young and old abound. In her diary entry for 13 May, she states that earlier in the day she had played "brilliantly" so that Philip would "see how easily if [she] wanted to [she] could take the boy [Steve] away from him" (63). On 30 May she does precisely that: "forget[ting] all about Philip and [her] good resolves" to play only "the driest Bach" that she knows and initially plays for Steve, she plays instead "Chopin waltzes and mazurkas, finally some of the gypsy-Hungarian themes from the Liszt rhapsodies" in a manner that first "excite[s]" the boy and eventually leaves him mentally exhausted and, perhaps, sexually aroused: "when I finished," she records, "he sat still for a minute his lips white and then without speaking shipped away to bed" (90-91).[13] On 2 December, after a concert in which she plays Liszt with a showy emphasis on the "octave and arpeggio work" in the "brilliant parts," Philip accuses her of practicing for the purpose of impressing Paul Kirby. If this was indeed her conscious or unconscious goal, she succeeds brilliantly, noticing Paul's "face like a cool white rent in the slowly wheeling crackle of applause" and capping her performance by making physical contact with him or, as she puts it, "pretend[ing] to stumble squeezing past him to[her] seat" (189-90). It comes as no surprise to discover that it was at a concert that Mrs. Bentley got the attention of Philip and, after meeting him, abandoned her ambition to be a concert pianist in favour of "another goal"—that of making him her husband, or, to put it more strongly, gaining control over him (142).

Nor is the incident at the concert the only instance of Mrs. Bentley's seductive behaviour towards Paul. A particularly striking example of such behaviour occurs half-way through the novel when Paul brings "a basket of strawberries" to share with the Bentleys and, in a scenario reminiscent of the lobster-eating episode in *Tom Jones*, she sets out "saucers of sugar" so that the three can eat them in an "informal way," which is to say, by picking them up with their fingers, dipping them in the sugar, and putting them in their mouths (111). This technique makes Philip "self-conscious" and Paul "ill at ease." It also leads to an awkward conversation about religion in which Mrs. Bentley's obtuse responses leave Paul frustrated and distracted: "[h]e started pressing his fingers into the sugar that was left in his saucer, and taking absent-minded little licks at his fingers" (111). In the closing pages of the novel, the sexual tension between Mrs. Bentley and Paul becomes almost unbearable for him when, standing next to each other at a ravine outside the town with their hands "side by side on the railing, two or three inches apart," no physical contact is made and he fully and finally realizes that either she does not or will not respond to his desire (208). As she recalls and records, "He turned and looked at me a moment, fixedly, humbly, without heed of my response, as if I were asleep, or a curious stranger. Then he said [in response to her earlier statement, 'It's getting late. . . .There's Philip's supper'], 'He'll be wondering where you are. We'd better go'" (208).[14]

Given the other Freudian elements in the novel, the tense pairing of Mrs. Bentley and Paul, and her ultimately and crushingly negative responses to his romantic overtures, it is tempting to associate them with the two types of ego-instincts identified by Freud in "The Ego and the Id" (1923; trans. 1927)—he with the sexual instinct (Eros), whose task it is to "prolong," "complicat[e] and . . . preserve" life, and she with the death instinct (Thanatos), whose "task . . . is to lead organic life back into the inanimate state" by "exercis[ing] pressure towards death" (316, 380-81). Indeed, there is some evidence in the novel to support these alignments. Paul's attempts to make Mrs. Bentley sexually aware of him include an explanation of the etymological origins of "cupidity" in "Cupid," "venereal" in "Venus," "aphrodisiac" in "Aphrodite," and, of course, "erotic" in "Eros" (100-01). Evidence for aligning Mrs. Bentley with Thanatos comes in two main forms: not long after her marriage to Philip, she gave birth to a still-born baby (45), and she plants and tends flowers and vegetables but, after some initial success, they all die, some as a result of forces beyond her control (parching sun, smothering dust, chickens, the Bentley dog) and others as a result of her neglect ("I forgot last night to take the fuchsias and geraniums out of the windows, and this morning they were frozen stiff as boards" [186]). In both cases, she is closely associated with the return of "organic life . . . to the inanimate state."

But it would be simplistic, I think, to view Mrs. Bentley as an anti-life force. Her pregnancy as such, her very desire to grow plants, her flirtatious interactions with Paul and with other men,[15] and the fact that on at least one occasion in the past she persuaded Philip to have sex with her in the afternoon (see 102) all suggest that she is a strongly sexual being who is aligned at least as much with Eros as with Thanatos. Relevant to this aspect of Ross's construction of her is a further Freudian concept that works in tandem with her perfectly understandable anger on the discovery of Judith's pregnancy, and helps to explain her deliberate and repeated cruelty to Judith in the closing pages of the novel. According to "Beyond the Pleasure Principle" (1920; trans. 1922, 1924), the "sexual instinct" contains a "sadistic component" (327). This could be related to the narcissism instanced by Mrs. Bentley's paranoia. Precisely to the extent that Mrs. Bentley is attracted to and affectionate towards Judith as a fellow outsider and possibly, as an object of desire, her feelings and impulses would (on the Freudian model) mutate into sadism, "whose aim is to injure the object" (327). "I sat thinking of her during the sermon, hating myself for the little gift I sent her yesterday," writes Mrs. Bentley on 24 December. "I did it deliberately to hurt her, and I'm sorry now" (193). Despite this expression of regret, she sends Judith another gift and appears to relish its devastating effect: her diary entry for 8 February records her calculated, insouciant questioning of Philip about Judith:

> "And Judith?" I asked at last, pouring myself out another cup of tea to drink with him. "How was she? Didn't she send a message?"
>
> It seemed as he looked up at me that something in his eyes broke. "Next time," he said, "you'd better not send or-anges. . . .She cried when I told her they were from you—all afternoon . . ."(201)

The terms in which Mrs. Bentley later expresses her decision to adopt Judith's baby are also consistent with Freud's conception of a sadistic element in Eros:

> "I've always liked Judith. Better than anyone else's I think I could take her baby and forget it isn't mine". . . .I looked ahead and the prospect brought a bitterness. I felt my blood go thin, and my lips set hard and cruel.
>
> I told him he must make her understand that once we take the baby she is never to see it again—that she is never to see even me. I want it to be my baby—my son. (203-04)

When Mrs. Bentley's friend, Mrs. Bird, mentions that she and her husband, the town doctor, have written papers on "marital success" that point to the need for a woman not to "'distress' [her husband by] 'letting him see [her] cry'" (114), she indicates the existence during the era in which *As for Me and My House* is set of a large and growing post-Freudian periodical literature that would have been readily accessible to Ross through friends at the University of Manitoba. One "paper" that casts a bright light on Ross's construction of Mrs. Bentley is "Womanliness as a Masquerade" by Freud's English translator, Joan Riviere. First published in the 1929 volume of the *International Journal of Psycho-Analysis*, Riviere's paper addresses "types of men and women . . . who, while mainly heterosexual in their development, plainly display strong features of the opposite sex," specifically "women who wish for masculinity [and] may put on a mask of womanliness to avert anxiety and the retribution feared from men" (303). Among the behaviours exhibited by such women are "flirting and coquetting" after "public performance[s]" that demonstrate their masculine-like expertise, a defensive and compulsive assumption of "a menial rôle (washing clothes) and . . . *washing off* dust and sweat," and the adoption of what Riviere variously calls a "mask," "disguise," or "feminine guise" of "womanliness" as a "masquerade" to conceal the possession of "masculinity" (304-05, 306-11, emphasis in original).

Precisely because it is focused on a female "type" in the period between the two world wars, Riviere's analysis resonates loudly with the characteristics and behaviours that Ross gives to Mrs. Bentley. As already observed, Mrs. Bentley represents herself at the outset of the novel as capable of performing male tasks "twice as well" as her husband and later records in one of her last diary entries that she will not work beside him in the book store because she is "so much more practical and capable than he is"(5, 210). At various points in between she observes that when she was striving to become a concert pianist her ambition made her "self-sufficient, a little hard" and that one of her piano teachers used to wonder at what he called her "masculine attitude to music" (22, 198). Moreover, even as she repeatedly criticizes conventional feminine behavior, she assumes a "menial rôle," throwing herself into compulsive scrubbing to rid the parsonage of odours that give her "a vague suggestion of musty shelves, repression and decay" (18, and see 35). And, of course she repeatedly uses "public performances" to play to and on the sexual desires of Philip, Paul, and others. Only once in the novel, and then only in relation to Judith West, does she use the word "mask" (164), but her "false front" functions in ways that are similar to the "mask of womanliness" that Riviere observed being worn by "women who wish for masculinity" (303). The sense of "acting a part" that Riviere finds in one such woman also resonates with Mrs. Bentley's numerous references to drama and the dramatic (see, for example, 74, 78, 124, 157, 184, and 210) as well as with comments throughout her diary that reflect her awareness of merely playing the part of a minister's wife. (It is arguable that Mrs. Bentley stages the relationship of Philip and Judith as a drama with herself as director and heroine, Philip the tormented male protagonist, and Judith the pathetic victim.) Finally, her admission that she has difficulty establishing relationships with women ("I've never got along with women very well . . . I was always impatient of what seemed their little rivalries"[102]) is consistent with Riviere's account of the "relations" of one of her female patients with members of her own sex:

> She was conscious of rivalry of almost any woman who had
> either good looks or intellectual pretensions. She was con-

scious of flashes of hatred against almost any woman with
whom she had much to do, but where permanent or close
relations with women were concerned she was none the less
able to establish a very satisfactory footing. Unconsciously
she did this almost entirely by means of feeling herself superior in some way to them. . . .(309)

The elements of "bisexuality," "sadism," and "megalomanic . . . necessity for
supremacy" that Riviere sees behind the "mask of womanliness" (304, 312,
311) can all be discerned in Mrs. Bentley's attitudes and behaviour, especially
in the portions of her diary that deal with the relationship between Philip and
Judith. Riviere argues that the women she is analyzing tend to "play the part
of devoted and disinterested mother-substitutes" (304), which Mrs. Bentley
arguably does with Judith in the early stages of the relationship.

As for Me and My House conveys a vivid sense of small-town life on the
prairies during the deprivation and sterility of the Depression, but it also contains in the form of Mrs. Bentley the literary incarnation of a recognizable
period "type" whose psychic states are discernable in and behind the "mask"/
"false front" that she places on view in her diary. In Mrs. Bentley, Ross appears
to draw both directly and indirectly upon the theories of Freud to construct
a character whose psychic illness and distress is the source not just of anxiety,
cruelty, hypocrisy, and a will-to-power, but also of art—a figure who anticipates by several years Lionel Trilling's famous "Art and Neurosis" (1945), the
essay that more than any other formulated for his times the idea of the artist as
a neurotic social misfit. It is because Ross was a writer of his time as well as his
place that Mrs. Bentley anticipates Trilling's formulation and finds parallels
in other treatments of the figure of the artist in modern Canadian literature,
most notably A. M. Klein's "Portrait of the Poet as Landscape," which was first
published in 1948. A. J. M. Smith's contention twenty years earlier that Canadian poetry is "altogether too self-conscious of . . . environment" can only be
applied to Ross's novel in ways that scant its temporal dimension, for *As for
Me and My House* is a product and a reflection not just of its place, but of its
time and the ideas that were then in circulation. It is a novel of the prairies
certainly, but it is also a novel of the post-Freudian era of Trilling and A. M.
Klein, books on popular psychology, papers on "marital success," and, as I
have tried to show, studies of "womanliness" and its disguises.

In this essay I have looked at Mrs. Bentley as a carefully constructed and
highly complex character who is situated in space and a product of the inter-
war era. With the start of World War II, the Depression came to an end and
allowed writers such as Ross to begin to view the period with a degree of de-

tachment as a distinctive period in prairie life that could be used as a setting against which to explore such themes as marital tension and psychological disturbance. It has been my intention to build upon D. M. R. Bentley's diagnosis and analysis of Mrs. Bentley's psychic illness in ways that emphasize the importance of Freudian and post-Freudian ideas for an understanding of her character and the novel as a whole. In no way has it been my intention to diminish the degree to which she remains enigmatic and, for this reason as well as many others, remains a source of puzzlement and fascination nearly seventy years after *As for Me and My House* was first published. It is because, like Mrs. Bentley herself, Sinclair Ross's masterpiece both unfolds and withholds meaning that it remains tantalizingly resistant to resolution and an enduring classic of prairie and Canadian fiction.

Notes

1. Wilfred Cude makes the essentially Freudian argument that by the end of the novel Mrs. Bentley has all but castrated her husband. Robert D. Chambers provides a typical instance of the tendency to locate the novel and its narrator in space rather than time—and, indeed, to allegorize its spatial relationships—when he observes that "Ross often places [Mrs. Bentley] at th[e] midpoint between town and wilderness, between the order of reason and the chaos of insanity" (38). Chambers also suggests that the "strongly deterministic quality" of the characters of Ross's short stories means that "we tend to take greater interest in their situations than in their individual psychologies" (25).

2. As Keath Fraser observes in his memoir of Ross, the novel was largely written in 1939 when he was "living with his mother" (51). Fraser speculates that Mrs. Bentley is "a kind of anti-Mrs. Ross."

3. I would like to acknowledge a general debt to Mary Poovey's *The Proper Lady and the Woman Writer* for my conception of Mrs. Bentley's dualistic nature.

4. "For a man I think is like that," Mrs. Bentley writes in her diary entry for 27 May concerning a tense moment with Philip. "Where a woman is concerned he likes to be able to respect himself, feel chivalrous, superior" (86). In her diary entry for 21 June, she reports that, following another tense moment, she "dropped beside him, and put [her] arms around his knees and buried [her] face"(113), a melodramatic act fully consistent with her cultivated femininity, and in her diary entry for 9 August she reports having seen in him "a deep, uncontrollable aversion to any household task ordinarily performed by a woman"(159), a further instance of

her recognition and internalization of the gender roles institutionalized by (bourgeois) marriage. Given her double nature, it is scarcely surprising that on 11 September, Mrs. Bentley admits to being "a little proud" of Philip when he helps to fight a fire but on 29 September hurls abuse at him for failing to "get the heater up in the living room" (170, 175).

5. See 38, 158, 199, where the absence of explicit reference to the sex act can suggest either that it did not occur or that Mrs. Bentley prefers to draw a veil of silence over it. The absences and evasions in Mrs. Bentley's diary are not just gaps in which the reader's speculations and suspicions are activated. They also correspond to the voids that Melanie Klein identifies in "Infantile Anxiety Situations in a Work of Art and in the Creative Impulse" (1929) as sites in which an experience of loss rooted in infancy is activated by omission or metaphorically. Of course, the diary as such is a traditionally female medium of self-expression.

6. The association of Philip with the crucified Christ in the opening paragraph of the novel that is remarked by Robert Kroetsch ("His first appearance evokes recollections of the Pietà " [218]) has a counterpart in Mrs. Bentley's much later association of herself with Christ on the cross ("I stood against the south wall of the elevator, letting the wind nail me there" [209]), and together the two allusions suggest that she usurps his patriarchal position as Father of the Law. See Helen Buss for an astute application of feminist theory to the novel.

7. A notable exception is the diary entry for 24 April, which is partly written in the present tense, perhaps because Mrs. Bentley is under extreme psychological pressure and exhibiting the full-blown symptoms of the paranoia diagnosed by D. M. R. Bentley (see 34-37).

8. In several diary entries, Mrs. Bentley records her dreams and fantasies; see, for example, 21-22 (a dream in which Philip vainly searches for a biblical text and then throws his Bible "among the pews" in church), 31-32 (where she has a "curious sense of leaving imprints of herself"as she crosses the town), and 47 (where she has a "queer, helpless sense of being lost miles out in the middle of [winter]") (and see also 34, 64, 126, 131, 162, and 189). The majority of Mrs. Bentley's dreams and fantasies occur at times of psychic trouble and reflect her narcissistic tendencies.

9. One of Mrs. Bentley's finest moments comes when Philip, faced with the Church Board's attack on Steve, is on the verge of losing his temper (and, perhaps, admitting his homosexuality?) and she steps in to save him from disgrace and her marriage from disaster: "I took my place beside him, and as he groped for words began explaining the situation as it re-

ally was" (96). Much later in the novel she identifies herself as "a fungus or parasite whose life depends on his" (199).

10. See 105-06, 148, and 202 for Philip's emphasis on pattern in art and his insistence on the similarities between art and religion, and D.M.R. Bentley, "As for Me and Significant Form" for the indebtedness of Philip's theories about art to the work of Clive Bell and Roger Fry.

11. See Bentley, "As for Me and Significant Form."

12. The paintings by Atkins and Fitzgerald mentioned in this paper can be viewed in Dan Ring's *The Urban Prairie*.

13. See also Mrs. Bentley's diary entry for 16 April where she forgets her "good resolve" not to outshine the piano playing of a young boy but does so and, in the process, "releas[es] [herself] after so many pent-up days in th[e] tight, depressing little parsonage" (27-28).

14. Only in her closing diary entries does Mrs. Bentley acknowledge Paul's infatuation with her (207, and see 213) despite the fact that it has been obvious from the start, especially in the body language that she continually observes and reports.

15. See especially her flirtation with the young cowboy while on holiday at Laura's ranch (128-29), where she sleeps in a bed above which hangs a picture of a Hereford bull whose calf is named "Priapus the First" (130).

Brenda Beckman-Long

•

Nationalism and Gender:
The Reception of Margaret Laurence's *The Diviners*

In her last novel, *The Diviners,* Margaret Laurence uses divining as a symbol for the creative gift. The trope of the title refers to the practice of water divining with a willow wand, but it also refers to novelist Morag Gunn's ability "to see, in writing" (*Diviners* 438). Critics have referred to Laurence's divining metaphor as "the logocentric quest for hidden truth" (McLean 102) and the romantic conception of the writer as a "prophet" (Fabre 248).[1] Whether interpreted internally or in terms of forces outside the text, this metaphor is not always helpful if one wants to investigate relations between the text and the social context from which it emerges and which sustains its meaning. While Laurence knows that the woman writer does not work in a vacuum, the divining trope cannot explain the material processes of literary production.

French sociologist Pierre Bourdieu is, however, helpful in this regard. Bourdieu's essays "The Field of Cultural Production" and "The Production of Belief" offer a model that allows us to examine the complex network of social relations from which a literary text emerges, including not only the writer who is the producer of the work, but also the artistic mediators, such as publishers, reviewers, and critics, who become joint producers of the meaning and value of the work (76-77). Bourdieu posits homologies, or correspondences, between the field of literary production and the broader fields of class and power relations, such that "each work becomes a manifestation of the field as a whole" (Johnson 11). Feminist theorist Toril Moi adds to Bourdieu's category of power relations the category of gender (1019). In a Bourdieuian analysis, Laurence's *habitus*, particularly her Scottish origins and her portrayal of Canada as the "real country [w]here I was born" (*Diviners* 415), coincides with literary and political structures that may account for the novel's acclaim, especially among Canadian critics. Bourdieu thinks that to play the literary game "one must possess the *habitus* which predisposes one to enter that field" (Johnson 8). At the same time, the novel's publication in 1974 corresponds to the rise of the Women's Movement. Although these aspects of the novel's history may be well known, they are seldom examined together in an effort to understand its reception. By applying Bourdieu's model in conjunction with Moi's, we may see how adeptly *The Diviners* was positioned such that it coincided with political and critical debates about both a developing national literature and gender equality. Like Marian Engel's *The Honeyman Festival* (1970) before it or Margaret Atwood's *Lady Oracle* (1976) after it, *The Diviners* portrays a woman writer's experience, but with greater combined emphasis on nationalism and feminism. I would argue that by creating a novel about the development of a woman writer, Morag Gunn, Laurence was challenging gender politics from within the literary institution. As Moi argues, "feminists struggle to *transform* the cultural tradition," of which they are "the contradictory products" (1018, emphasis in original). Furthermore, feminist critics who were in the ascendancy during the university expansion in Canada of the 1970s supported the challenge. By surveying reviews of *The Diviners* and by drawing upon Bourdieu and Moi, I will examine Laurence's bid for power to legitimize women's authorship in Canada.[2]

Before proceeding, however, we must consider the historical and sociopolitical contexts of Laurence's work. Bourdieu contends persuasively that both the production and reception of literary works are historically constituted. An exclusively literary critical focus on the individual writer or work ignores the structural relations between "social positions that are both occupied and manipulated by social agents . . . [and] institutions" (29). In other words, "no cultural product exists by itself" (32). The literary field may, therefore, be seen as a competitive field of "position-takings" (34). It becomes a site of struggle for legitimacy and domination, a struggle in which Laurence participates. Moreover, this field generates its own *habitus*, a system of "dispositions" (71) and "awareness of the logic of the game" (72). This awareness, varying in degree of consciousness, depends upon a social agent's position and trajectory within the field. Bourdieu defines a writer's "social trajectory" as "the set of successive movements of an agent in a structured (hierarchized) space, itself subject to displacements and distortions" in economic and cultural fields (276). Before examining the reception of *The Diviners*, particularly its reviews, it is therefore crucial to consider her *habitus* within the literary field in Canada.

According to Bourdieu's model, the contextualization of a work involves the author's individual and class *habitus* as well as position and social trajectory within the literary field. Even a brief summary of Laurence's upbringing, education, and career will indicate a predisposition "to enter that field" (Bourdieu, qtd. in Johnson 8).[3] She was born in Neepawa, Manitoba in 1926 and much has been made of Laurence's small-town roots as the source of the rural setting for much of her fiction, reflecting a Canadian tradition that encompasses Frederick Philip Grove, Stephen Leacock, and Alice Munro, among others. Even more significant to a Bourdieuian analysis, however, is Laurence's class. She was born into a middle-class family, and although she lost both parents by the age of eleven, she was raised by her father, lawyer Robert Wemyss, and her stepmother, schoolteacher Margaret Simpson Wemyss. Her class inclined Laurence toward a university education and she graduated in 1947 with a degree in English from United College at the University of Manitoba. Her contacts there would become important connections or social capital. One of her professors was Malcolm Ross, who promoted an academic interest in Canadian literature, and her closest friend was future novelist Adele Wiseman, who also attended Ross's seminars. The student newspaper, moreover, printed Laurence's first published stories.

Her education at United College prepared her professionally to write for two Winnipeg newspapers, *The Westerner* and *The Winnipeg Citizen*. Her experience at United College also influenced her politically because of its roots in the Social Gospel movement which produced politicians J. S. Woodsworth, Stanley Knowles, and Tommy Douglas (Laurence, *Dance* 91). She was "a Christian Social Democrat" who embraced not violent revolution, but rather "a need for social justice" (Laurence, *Dance* 107). Laurence also worked in Winnipeg as a registrar for the Young Women's Christian Association, where she met local activists for women's rights. Shortly after her marriage to civil engineer Jack Laurence, she moved to Somalia and Ghana, where the couple lived from 1950 to 1957. Her encounter with African colonial rule in Ghana reinforced her concern for social justice and stimulated her reinterpretation of Canada as a colonial society. She was also politically motivated to translate Somali stories to refute claims that Somalis had no literature of their own. She was subsequently able to take the initiative to publish her own fiction in *Queen's Quarterly*, edited by her former teacher Malcolm Ross, as well as in other literary journals.

After she returned to Canada in 1957, her work was recommended to publisher Jack McClelland in 1959, at a moment when his interest in promoting Canadian authors converged with the federal government's support of Canadian culture following the 1951 Massey Commission, which called for urgent attention to the arts in Canada. McClelland published a novel and a travel memoir by Laurence and he continued to be her publisher. After Laurence separated from her husband in 1962, she moved to England, where she wrote three more novels, including *A Jest of God*, winner of the 1966 Governor General's Award for Fiction. On the strength of her publications, she served as a writer-in-residence at the University of Toronto, the University of Western Ontario, and Trent University between 1969 and 1974. She also received her first honorary degree from McMaster University in 1970. These awards and honours increased her symbolic capital and strengthened her ties within the Canadian literary institution. She was made a Companion of the Order of Canada in 1972. Laurence was at the height of her career in 1974, and in a position to become a "consecrated" writer (Bourdieu 51), when *The Diviners* won another Governor General's Award. Although she subsequently published several children's stories, *The Diviners* was her last novel and many consider it her most distinguished work. The acclaimed novelist died in Lakefield, Ontario in 1987.

In addition to her class, education, and social trajectory, Laurence's Scottish origins gave her a privileged position in Canada's literary and cultural fields. In her essay "A Place to Stand On" (1970), she traces her roots to the "pioneers of Scots-Presbyterian origin" immigrants who were among the first European settlers in southern Manitoba (16). An early critic of Canadian women writers, Clara Thomas, comments that the "passing on of the authentic heritage of their people is a central preoccupation of writers today, particularly of the post colonial nations" ("Myth" 115). She links this myth-making to Laurence's interest in assimilating into her fiction a sympathetic view of the Selkirk Settlers and the Métis, as derived from Laurence's reading of W. L. Morton's *Manitoba: A History* ("Myth" 116-17). Laurence's Scottish heritage aligns her with Scots who were "inventors of English Canada" and leaders in business, politics, religion, and education (Coleman 5-6).[4] In *The Vertical Mosaic*, John Porter identifies "a reciprocal relationship between ethnicity and social class in Canada" (63), and he finds that those with British origins were the leading ethnic group in the prairie provinces by 1961 (77). Although Canada has two charter groups, English and French, in addition to many aboriginal peoples and immigrants from other cultures, Porter observes that "Canada's political and economic leaders were British and were prepared to create a British North America" (62).

Laurence's claim of a Scottish identity generates, however, productive contradictions—that is, multiple identities—which were crucial to her literary development. She was "proud of her Scottish ancestry" (King 1997, 10), but as a Canadian she was ambivalent about a British identity. In "A Place to Stand On" she discusses her roots in the contexts of English "colonialism" and her experience in Africa (15). Because of the dispossession of the Scots by the lairds in Sutherland, she identifies with the dispossession of Africans by the English in Ghana. She subsequently relates her theme of dispossession to Canada's colonial past and, with a concern for social justice, she extends the theme to the Métis. Speaking of her Canadian fiction in the essay "Ten Years' Sentences" in 1969, she states, "I imagined the theme was probably the same as in much of my African writing—the nature of freedom" (32). This theme was well received in a nationalistic, Canadian environment. Clara Thomas emphasizes Laurence's "deep involvement in Canadian cultural nationalism" ("Myth" 104), a nationalism also discussed by later critics such as Colin Nicholson and Angelika Maeser Lemieux.[5]

In addition to the author's individual and class *habitus*, our contextualization must also take into account the larger field of power relations, which includes political, economic, and gender relations (Moi 1019). The 1951 Massey Commission set a government agenda of supporting high culture. With the subsequent founding of the Canada Council for the Arts, for example, federal support of professional artists became part of national efforts to distinguish Canada internationally, thereby shedding a colonial past and defending Canada from the encroachments of American culture (Berland 15). On the one hand, Laurence benefited to some degree from federal support. In 1964 she received a Canada Council travel grant, for example, to return to Manitoba while working on *A Jest of God*, and in 1966 after winning a Governor General's Award, she received another grant. On the other hand, she struggled financially as she attempted to become a professional writer and she was acutely aware of her gender. She knew, for instance, that grants were not easily given to married women, as she complained in a letter to novelist Ernest Buckler when her grant application was turned down in 1963 (qtd. in King 1997, 179). She was nevertheless influenced by some of the Massey Commission's key messages, such as the promotion of Canadian literature in educational institutions. In an interview in 1974, she asserted that "kids in Grade 12 and 13 are very interested in finding out about the writing of their own country" (Lever 32).

Burgeoning studies in Canadian Literature at the time also demonstrate the Commission's influence on academic reception of Laurence as a writer who was exemplary of a developing national literature. In *Articulating West: Essays on Purpose and Form in Modern Canadian Literature* (1972), W. H. New sees Laurence's *The Stone Angel* as typical of the "Canadian mode" and he identifies "freedom" as "a key word in the fiction of the decade" (143). In *The Canadian Novel in the Twentieth Century* (1975), George Woodcock similarly recognizes an "emergent tradition of Canadian criticism" (xi), and he includes an essay by Laurence in his anthology to mark "a period of coming of age," with fiction writers "at the forefront" (x). In *The Canadian Novel: Here and Now* (1978), John Moss also names Laurence, along with Margaret Atwood, Robertson Davies, Alice Munro, Mordecai Richler, and Rudy Wiebe, as possessing "a voice and a vision that is recognizably Canadian, informed by common traditions and common culture that make us a people, however variegated we may be" (7); in fact, Canada "through their work achieves definition" (8). By 1980, Woodcock describes Laurence as "the best living Canadian novelist" to embody "our roots in Canada" (157). These literary critics see Laurence's works in terms that are highly aligned with the Massey Commission's objectives, indicating the homologies or correspondences that existed between Laurence's literary production and the literary establishment. Critics engaged in nationalist discourses during Canada's university expansion in the seventies.

Laurence internalized the nationalist *habitus* of the literary field, while appearing to be almost unconscious of its effect: "A strange aspect of my so-called Canadian writing is that I haven't been much aware of its being Canadian, and this seems a good thing to me, for it suggests that one has been writing out of a background so closely known that no explanatory tags are necessary" ("Ten" 33). Interestingly, her example corresponds in this respect to Robert Lecker's recent depiction of the literary institution in *Making It Real: The Canonization of English Canadian Literature* (1990). He finds a conjunction of government, academia, and the publishing industry in efforts to promote a national literature (26). He also identifies in Canadian literature the recurring themes of Canadian identity, history, and survival, as well as a "realist-nationalist impulse" (38). These are literary values which Laurence also professes.

In light of the historical and socio-political contexts of Laurence's work, we may now examine critics' reviews of *The Diviners* for traces of the conflicting nationalist and gender discourses which would affect her reception unevenly. In the *Antigonish Review*, critic and poet R. J. MacSween lauds Laurence's "sense of place" (107). In *The Tamarack Review*, poet Phyllis Gotlieb emphasizes the Canadian settings, ranging from small-town Manitoba and rural Ontario to Vancouver and Toronto (80). Morag's travels to England, Scotland, and back to Canada become a search for Canadian identity, as Morag "works to absorb and resolve her identity" (80). Gotlieb calls Morag a "survivor," alluding to Margaret Atwood's *Survival: A Thematic Guide to Canadian Literature* (1972). Pique represents Canada's future; she is a "product of the land . . . who has found by chance and desperation the way to join the currents of its history" (81). While Gotlieb notes that Pique is a "halfbreed," she avoids discussing Pique's Métis origins, reflecting a shift in nationalist discourses away from "racial assimilation" and toward cultural integration (Day 171, 175). In *The Journal of Canadian Fiction*, critic and poet Bernice Lever similarly states, "Morag's troubled child of two cultures [British and Métis] emerges as a budding artist who can . . . be seen as a symbolic answer to reconciliation for Canada" (96). She finds in Laurence's fiction a settler narrative: a "solid background of Manawaka pioneer lives – the first Scot and Ukrainian settlers and the Métis people – who co-exist and multiply" (94). Her description recalls nationalist discourses, in which class and racial hierarchies are erased, and aboriginal and Métis identities are subsumed by an emerging Canadian identity (Day 174). In *Books in Canada*, author and critic David Helwig argues, conversely, that history cannot be erased because the past is a "perpetual present": "The symbolic structure of the book is intricate, Morag living out in her own life the dispossession of her Scottish ancestors just as Skinner Tonnerre, her half-breed friend lives out the dispossession of his people" (7). He refers of course to the dispossession of Scottish highlanders in Europe and Indians and Métis in Canada. It must be noted, however, that the dispossession of the Scots who gained land as settlers in Western Canada is quite a different matter from the dispossession of the Indian and Métis who were displaced from the land: Helwig's comment obfuscates the colonization of aboriginal peoples by European Canadians.

Other reviewers also acknowledge the historical marginalization and poverty of Indian and Métis peoples. In *The Canadian Forum*, Phyllis Bruce, editor of *15 Canadian Poets* (1970), notes that Jules lives on the "fringes of society," while his sister Piquette lives in a shack where she is "burned alive with her children" (16). Similarly, Brita Mickleburgh, who is also the editor of *Canadian Literature: Two Centuries in Prose* (1973), notes in *The Fiddlehead* that "class and racial lines" are "sharply drawn" in Manawaka (113), and "Jules' Métis ancestors were ruined by westward colonization" (114). Allan Bevan, editor of *The Dalhousie Review*, also notes that the Tonnerres live "on the edge of white society" (262), and Pique goes to Galloping Mountain, where her uncle lives as "the sole survivor of the five children of Lazarus" (362). Moreover, Jules writes ballads for his grandfather, who fought with Louis Riel in the North West Resistance, Canada's forgotten civil war; Bevan asserts that history is "inescapable" (361). Significant to then-current debates about Canadian identity is Laurence's dispossession theme that encourages readers' identification with a racialized other as well as a gendered other.

From these reviews it is evident that nationalist elements of Laurence's *habitus* were emphasized by academics and writers with an interest in establishing a national literature at a time when many small literary journals and magazines were fostered by federal government support. In retrospect, we can see that Laurence's place in the first ranks of Canadian literature is connected to her novel's critical reception as an embodiment of Canadian values. The entry on Laurence in *Contemporary Literary Criticism* states, "Laurence's status as a leading chronicler of Canadian life has endured in the years since her death. . . .Her Manawaka cycle is widely considered among the most poignant and important depictions of life in Canada in the twentieth century." Her main character "symbolizes Canada itself, investigates and mythologizes her Scottish heritage and matures under the domination of her English husband, but she eventually rejects him for the authentic love of a Canadian Indian, who begets a feisty personification of the racially and culturally unified Canadian future" (CLC 266). The formation of Morag's identity parallels Canada's assertion of its independence from English imperialism: "Laurence brought to her Canadian fiction a wise sympathy for the plight of the individual in a young nation" (Staines 267). The idea of Canada as a "young nation" has, of course, been challenged by many critics and writers. In any case, Laurence became a classic Canadian writer, one who envisions Canada as a progressive, ethnically diverse, yet "unified" nation. This vision recalls the mosaic metaphor which has played a part in Canada's "nation-building" (Day 149). In reviews of The Diviners we find a rhetoric of equality and integration, reflecting nationalist discourses in postwar Canada (Day 162, 171). In this political climate, The Diviners is received with nationalist fervour. Reviews are primarily favourable, establishing Laurence's reputation as a preeminent Canadian writer.

Even in the popular press reviewers credited Laurence with a Canadian classic. In The Globe and Mail, literary critic Phyllis Grosskurth celebrates a "Canadian theme" of "coming to terms with your own past" (Grosskurth 35). She refers to Atwood's Survival and the familiar setting of the small, rural town. In The Toronto Star, arts critic Robert Fulford similarly writes, "The Diviners also plants itself firmly within a strong recent tradition in Canadian novels . . . the turning back to root experiences of time and place." These reviewers perhaps allude to novels such as Robert Kroetsch's Studhorse Man (1969), Robertson Davies's Fifth Business (1970), and Rudy Wiebe's The Temptations of Big Bear (1973). Fulford adds that Pique "plays a symbolic role as a kind of reconciliation between the native peoples of Canada and the whites who conquered them." Both Grosskurth and Fulford, however, criticize the novel on aesthetic grounds. Grosskurth finds that "the structure takes a little getting used to," while Fulford sees "enormous flaws" in terms of "style and structure." He adds, "It's hard to believe a good editor ever looked at the manuscript." Laurence was "particularly stung" by both reviews (King 1997, 324). Her objections indicate not only her struggle to position herself within the literary field, but also to assert women's right to interpret their sexual experiences. She was especially offended by the Globe's headline, "A looser, more complex, more sexually uninhibited Laurence." She was even more outraged by Fulford's review: "He does not seem to understand the form of the damn thing at all. Well, the hell with it. Screw him" (qtd. in King 1997, 324). Ostensibly he faults her work on an aesthetic level, but Fulford, who was also the editor of *Saturday Night* and a member of the male-dominated literary establishment, betrays a lack of sympathy for Laurence's feminist stance. Laurence perceives his review as a veiled attack: she claims that "he had interviewed her on the CBC on May 17, the day before his review was published, and not voiced any of the objections which made their way into print" (324).

Conversely, Marci McDonald in *The Toronto Star* credits Laurence with "an awareness of feminist issues," for "every one of her heroines [is] locked into a struggle for survival in an alien world, chafing at the bodies and roles that bind" (H5). Other women writers with feminist views are equally sympathetic. Novelist Marian Engel finds in *Chatelaine* that some "Toronto critics" are "terrified of the monumental, particularly in the works of women." She believes that the novel's "polite surface was certainly invented to minimize tension" (237). Poet Marge Piercy in *The New York Times* praises Laurence for "a strong breed of women characters." She calls attention, however, to often fraught relationships between women writers and publishers, critics, or funding agencies by finding Morag's situation "romanticized":

> Unlike writers in my experience who write for a living, Morag never changes publishers, feels her agent is neglecting her, worries about the size of other writers' advances, or has any truck with universities. Author Laurence thanks the Canadian Council on [sic] the Arts for the award that enabled her to write this book, but writer Morag never fusses about grants. (213)

Piercy makes a valid point about potential conflicts between women writers and publishers and we will return to this point shortly.

In contrast to Fulford, most literary critics appreciated the novel's aesthetic value. Allan Bevan thinks that *The Diviners* is "a complex and skillfully-constructed novel" (363), involving two levels of narration – past and present – which by the end converge (362). Barry Cameron agrees in *Queen's Quarterly*: "The method of presentation also stresses the ways in which past and present, fact and fiction, history and myth, ever penetrate each other, reshaping and reinterpreting each other and, in so doing, reconstituting reality" (639). He sees the novel as self-reflexive: "a novel that is essentially about itself as a novel." Other critics concur in *Canadian Literature*, *The Canadian Forum*, and *The Fiddlehead*. *The West Coast Review*, an avant-garde journal which favours experimental writing, finds that "the implicit questioning of art itself, its efficacy, its value, makes this a much stronger book than any [Laurence] has given us before, one certainly that other writers will value highly" (Stouck 46). David Stouck's evaluation of *The Diviners* as "art for artists" confers prestige and "symbolic capital" (Bourdieu 51, 76) on the "classic Canadian writer" (Stouck 43). This review and nine other positive evaluations of Laurence's experiments with narrative technique, such as perspective, genre, embedded tales, the Snapshots and Memorybank Movies, secure her position as a "consecrated producer" (Bourdieu 107). (See reviews by Bevan, Bruce, Cameron, Grosskurth, Helwig, Lever, Piercy, Thomas, and Mickleburgh.)

At the same time, Stouck is representative of a gender bias in the Canadian literary institution. He praises *The Diviners* for calling into question "the writer's facile assumption about *his* craft" (44-45, emphasis mine). He denounces "Mrs. Laurence's" earlier novels, however, for their "popular appeal" and heroines who "cannot sustain *our* lasting interest," by which he assumes a universal male reader. On the contrary, many women writers and academics recognize the gender politics of Laurence's work as significant in relation to the Women's Movement. In *Canadian Literature*, Audrey Thomas praises the novel's emphasis on the woman artist (90). In *The Tamarack Review*, Phyllis Gotlieb states, "Margaret Laurence certainly knows and can put down what women feel in our times and our places. . . .She knows what women like about men and what they find sexually attractive" (80). For *The Canadian Forum*, Phyllis Bruce writes that Laurence has a "gift of delineating the conscious and unconscious processes of the feminine psyche" (15). Brita Mickleburgh expands this idea in *The Fiddlehead*: "It is difficult not to be aware of the number of seventies' causes that have found their way into *The Diviners*: the Métis, women's liberation . . . the horrors of war" (113). It is important to note that some male reviewers, such as Bevan and Helwig, similarly identify portrayals of women's sexuality and single motherhood as strengths of the novel. Even in the *Globe*, Grosskurth finds Laurence's representations of Morag's experience typical of "women in Western cultures" and comparable to the work of Doris Lessing, for whom the personal is political (13).

Laurence's gender politics nevertheless provoked public controversy. Despite her critical acclaim, her portrayal of Morag's sexuality was attacked in the *Peterborough Examiner* and the book was banned in the city's schools in 1976. The censorship almost paralyzed Laurence and she became increasingly reclusive in her Lakefield home. In her autobiography, *Dance on the Earth*, she later defends her work:

> In 1976, to my total horror and surprise, *The Diviners* was
> attacked as being pornographic. . . .I knew, as many other

people did, that this novel was and is, to the best of my ability, an honouring of my people. . . .The problem of the people who attacked me, as I see it, is that they are extremely
unskilled readers. (214)

In contrast, Jack McClelland, a publisher who welcomed the publicity to
boost sales, told her that he wished the newspaper would report bans on all
her books (King 1999, 343).

To return to Piercy's comment about relationships between women writers and publishers, Laurence's publisher reflects not only a commercial interest, but also a gender bias. For Laurence, publication was largely mediated
by men. Laurence got her "big break" in 1947 with Bill Ross, editor of *The
Westerner* in Winnipeg. The paper folded only a year later but she landed
another job with *The Winnipeg Citizen*. Its editor later fired her for "being a
communist" (King 1997, 68), although she was in fact a social democrat. In
1952 Laurence had a short story published by Whit Burnett at *Story* and he
encouraged her to begin a novel. She offered him a collection of short stories but he said they were "hard selling" (King 1997, 106). Malcolm Ross, her
former professor and future editor of the New Canadian Library paperback
series, accepted a short story for *Queen's Quarterly* in 1953. In 1960 Jack Mc-
Clelland published *This Side Jordan* after receiving a tip from a University of
British Columbia professor, George Elliott, for whom Laurence had worked
as a marker (1997, 136). Despite her success as a writer, McClelland described
her to a New York agent as "a housewife," claiming that "when I read it I found
it hard to believe that the novel had been written by a woman" (1999, 83). He
would publish it only if he could find American or English publishers to print
it simultaneously, making the project financially viable (1997, 138). In Alan
Maclean at Macmillan, Laurence found "a publisher who was . . . more keen
on her work than Jack" (1997, 181). He agreed in 1963 to publish *The Stone
Angel*—with a title change from *Hagar*—and a package of three books in 1964,
including a novel, travel memoir, and short story collection. He got McClelland and American publisher Alfred Knopf on side. Knopf had previously
rejected the collection because of one reader's sexist report about "an average
Canadian housewife's view of an exotic land" (1997, 187). McClelland initially
objected in writing to Laurence, "What in hell goes on at Macmillan's?. . . .
Even if you were the second coming of Christ, it would be foolish to publish
three of your books in one season" (1999, 151). He urged Laurence to demand
that Macmillan cease production but she refused.

Laurence's relations with McClelland were complex and complicated by
gender ideologies. After meeting her at the launch of her first novel in 1960,

he helped her to become a professional writer by suggesting an agent, and he directed her toward Canadian subject matter by sending her a novel by Manitoba writer Patricia Blondal (1999, 152). He made Laurence one of the top writers on his list and he told his editorial staff, "Laurence . . . can do no wrong" (174). However, she balked at his marketing and domineering. She quarreled with the "Boss" and complained about a publicity tour for *A Jest of God*: "when McClelland said 'a working trip,' he sure wasn't kidding. In the two months, I did a total of 17 radio interviews, and gave 4 talks" (1977, 153). He eagerly launched *The Diviners* with a divining contest on the grounds of the Ontario Science Centre, while Laurence needed a tranquillizer to get through the day (1977, 332). He made her a household name; however, in her autobiography Laurence credits not McClelland, but rather women writers, such as Adele Wiseman and Ethel Wilson, as her best supporters. She was, in turn, able to persuade McClelland to publish Wiseman's *Crackpot* and Marian Engel's *Bear*. He respected Laurence enough, despite their differences, to appoint her to the board of McClelland and Stewart, but in order to promote solidarity among writers, she had to "go behind his back" to agitate for the Writers' Union of Canada, an institution to which he was "extremely hostile" (1999, 319). The organization undoubtedly gave writers more negotiating power with publishers, and many were women, including the founding Chairperson, Marian Engel.

At the same time, McClelland may be credited with creating a climate for "experimental fiction by young Canadian novelists" (King 1999, 219). After he had returned from naval service in World War II, he declared himself a nationalist and determined to make his father's publishing house "*the* Canadian publisher" (1999, 29). He had the economic and social capital to do so. On the strength of his reputation he later secured federal funding. The alignment of Laurence's and her publisher's positions produced an award-winning bestseller; to some extent, they shared the nationalist and aesthetic values of their time. However, McClelland's economic interests, in addition to his gender bias, complicated the relationship. For example, when he released Bantam paperback editions of Laurence's books, of which *The Diviners* sold 210,000 copies in Canada alone, Laurence complained that her royalties decreased by 50 percent (King 1997, 360). To ease financial stress at McClelland and Stewart, the publisher had allied himself with Bantam, an American mass-market, paperback house. Laurence's sometimes strained relationship with her publisher indeed belies the ease with which Morag authors her book in *The Diviners*. Still, the commercial success of *The Diviners* is yet another indicator of legitimation and of Laurence's alignment with the fields of power and gender relations that shaped the literary field in 1974. It was on the national bestseller list for twenty-nine weeks by late 1975 (Mickleburgh 114). Linda Svendsen later produced a television screenplay for the CBC in 1993.

In discussing nationalism as a contributing factor to Laurence's publishing success, we must also recognize that nationalist discourses are not by any means homogenous. A review in Quebec's *Le Devoir* focuses not on her representation of Canadian identity, but rather her representation of the Métis. Columnist Naim Kattan notes that Jules "remembers" Riel, choosing a word with political connotations in a province where the Métis leader is often regarded as a champion of French minority rights. In fact, "Jules Tonnerre se souvient" echoes the Quebec motto "Je me souviens." Kattan concentrates on "l'empreinte de l'histoire" or the stamp of history and the historical implications of Morag's alliance with Jules in a search for her origins and birthright: "Dans cette petite ville de Manitoba, nous sommes au coeur d'un Canada qui fait sa propre histoire, qui recueille ses héritages britanniques, français, indiens, inconsciemment, avec réticences et parfois en les rejetant." Kattan calls Laurence one of the most prestigious novelists of Canada in a review which appears, ironically, under the heading "les Lettres étrangères."[6]

In contrast to the nationalist perspective in the Canadian press, some alternative and sometimes surprising views of the Canadian context come from American reviewers. Piercy recognizes correctly a "buried history" in the conflicts of "different ethnic peoples" in Canada. She accurately describes the Métis as "half French, half Indian people whose land was taken," although she locates Manawaka in "Southern Ontario's plains" instead of Manitoba. In the *New Republic* Sheldon Frank discusses Laurence as a Canadian author but to him Manawaka resembles an American "frontier town":

> Alberta, Saskatchewan, Manitoba. What happens in these huge areas that dwarf our largest states? Who lives there? What kinds of lives do they lead? It has become commonplace to remark that for most Americans, Canada is still an unknown country filled with Mounties and a few huskies. (28)

Discussing Morag and Jules, he avoids racial differences by focusing on "an affair that left her pregnant." In Boston's *The Atlantic Monthly*, Edward Weeks comments perceptively on issues of history and class: "Manawaka was settled by Scots, descendants of those driven from Sutherland when the lairds enclosed the land, but the community long since has been stratified, and those who live on Hill Street, where Christie dwells, are the failures, on a level with the Indian half-breeds" (108).

Ultimately, because of her *habitus* and position as a "consecrated" writer in Canada, Laurence was able to challenge the literary institution in terms of gender politics. In *The Diviners* Laurence exposes gender relations as playing a part in power relations. In her essays and in an address at the University of Toronto in 1969, she also states that the treatment of time and the narrative voice, particularly the "female" voice, are "of paramount importance" to her fiction ("Time" 155). In fact, her narrative form evolves from these concerns ("Gadgetry" 80). If the literary field is not only a field of forces, such as political and economic forces, but also a field of struggles, such as those between writers and publishers or critics or other mediators of culture, as Bourdieu suggests, then the very "definition of the writer" is at stake (30, 40). I would argue, therefore, that Laurence's position-taking in the field challenges male dominance and "monopoly of literary legitimacy" (42). Toril Moi insists that the concept of *habitus* is "crucial for feminism" (1034), as she draws upon Bourdieu to "reconceptualize gender as a social category" and part of the field of power relations, which includes socio-political and economic relations (1019). When viewed in this way, Laurence's challenge clearly takes place not only on an aesthetic level, but also on political and social levels.

On a political level, Laurence writes in a period when homologies exist between the literary field and the broader field of power relations in terms of nationalism, as we have seen. She also writes in the context of the Women's Movement. In 1967, Prime Minister Lester B. Pearson appointed a Royal Commission on the Status of Women to "inquire into and report upon the status of women in Canada and to recommend what steps might be taken by the federal government to ensure equal opportunities with men in all aspects of Canadian society."[7] The final report, which was released in 1970, documents the Women's Movement and its struggles in Canada for women's rights to work outside the home, as well as pay equity and child care. One issue raised is that any occupation should be open to women. Laurence's depiction of Morag as a woman writer and single mother resonates with the times. Its positive reception by academics, such as Thomas, Grosskurth, Helwig, and Bevan, furthermore reflects a corresponding shift in the field of power relations. Because the literary institution is situated within the field of power relations, position-takings like Laurence's, which "clash with the prevailing norms of production and the expectations of the field . . . cannot succeed without the help of external changes" (Bourdieu 57). Laurence's representations of Morag's creativity and sexuality are legitimized by critics who acknowledge the wider social shifts that are effected by the Women's Movement. Clara Thomas, like subsequent critics Helen Buss, Barbara Godard, and Gayle Greene, recognizes Laurence's revision of masculine literary models (Thomas, "Planted" 14).[8]

These feminist critics accept Laurence's appropriation of the genre of the *Kün-stlerroman* to the development of the *woman* artist, emphasized by the "Portrait of the Artist as a Pregnant Skivvy" (*Diviners* 316). On an aesthetic level, Thomas also lauds Laurence's allusions to canonical texts, including Milton's *Paradise Lost*, Shakespeare's *The Tempest*, and Joyce's *A Portrait of the Artist as a Young Man* ("Myth" 115). Other Canadianists, such as Barry Cameron, praise *The Diviners* for being "about the act of writing fiction" (639). Neither aesthetic nor gender issues remain uncontested, however, as demonstrated by Robert Fulford or those who would later call for censorship. The novel is nonetheless legitimized by critics who, like David Stouck, value the novel's art and self-reflexive experimentation. In a convergence of art with political and social shifts, *The Diviners* is accepted as part of a growing national literature.

Laurence's position-taking is perhaps best illustrated in relation to Canadian writer and feminist Margaret Atwood. In an interview in 1974 Atwood characterizes Laurence as formidable: "My first reaction is 'This is not someone I would ever want to get into a fight with'. . . .The combination of the photograph and the strength of the book itself is enough to strike terror into any young novelist. . . .By this time she was almost a legendary figure" (20). Laurence states that she was always "writing about the situations of women" (22), and tells Atwood, "I was dealing with a lot of the stuff Women's Lib is talking about right now" (23-24). These comments suggest Laurence's competitiveness with Atwood, a writer who occupies a similar position in the literary field. They occupy the same *habitus* and feminist critique and both received the Governor General's Award in 1966, Laurence for fiction and Atwood for poetry. In fact, Laurence wrote to Ernest Buckler in 1974, "I was talking, in my fiction, about survivors, long before Peggy Atwood said this was one main theme of Canadian fiction" (291-92). Their rivalry signals similar position-takings by Laurence and Atwood in a maturing literary field. This rivalry is probably part of the reason for Laurence's objection to the title of the *Globe*'s review: "A looser, more complex, more sexually uninhibited Laurence. And never an Atwood victim." That review goes on to compare Laurence's work to Atwood's *Survival*. The rivalry peaked when Atwood, who chaired the Writer's Union of Canada in 1981, questioned Laurence's drinking habits and Laurence angrily resigned from the Union. As her biographer, James King, points out, "Laurence . . . was threatened by [Atwood] and was, in turn, resentful" (1997, 366).

Laurence's final novel constitutes a successful bid to establish women's authorship in national and even international fields of cultural production. Her *habitus*, to borrow a term from Pierre Bourdieu, corresponded to the nationalist values of academics, reviewers, and publishers such as Jack McClelland, although it did not always parallel them exactly. In particular, Laurence's work is remarkable for the way in which it coincides with the Women's Movement and with increased attention for state support of the arts. For perhaps the first time in Canada's cultural history, the nationalist and feminist positions of influential artists, critics, politicians, and academics powerfully converged to redefine and encourage the field of literary production in Canada. *The Diviners* was published at a time when Laurence possessed the necessary social and symbolic capital to mount a challenge to a male-dominated literary establishment, and for these and many and complex reasons, the novel has become Laurence's most acclaimed work.

Notes

1. Having made this point, as many critics do, Fabre goes on to discuss the diviner as an "interpreter" of cultural codes (267), perhaps coming closest to a Bourdieuian analysis.

2. I would like to thank Paul Hjartarson at the University of Alberta for his insightful reading of an earlier draft of this paper.

3. For detailed biographies, see James King's *The Life of Margaret Laurence* (Toronto: Vintage Canada, 1997); Lyall Powers' *Alien Heart: The Life and Works of Margaret Laurence* (Winnipeg: U of Manitoba P, 2003); Donez Xiques' *Margaret Laurence: The Making of a Writer* (Toronto: Dundurn Press, 2005); and Noelle Boughton's *Margaret Laurence: A Gift of Grace: A Spiritual Biography* (Toronto: Women's Press, 2006).

4. For further discussion, see Daniel Coleman's "The Enterprising Scottish Orphan: Inventing the Properties of English Canadian Character" (in *White Civility* [Toronto: U of Toronto P, 2006], 81-127).

5. See Nicholson's article "'There and not there': Aspects of Scotland in Laurence's Writing" and Maeser Lemieux's "The Scots Presbyterian Legacy."

6. Kattan's statement may be translated roughly as follows: In this little Manitoba town, we are in the heart of a Canada that makes its own history, which collects its British, French, and Indian heritages, unconsciously, with reservations and at times dismissing them (translation mine).

7. See the full report at http://www.library.utoronto.ca/robarts/microtext/collection/pages/ carylcos.3html.

8. See Helen Buss's "Margaret Laurence and the Autobiographical Impulse" (in *Crossing the River: Essays in Honour of Margaret Laurence*, Kristjana Gunnars, ed., [Winnipeg: Turnstone Press, 1988], 147-68); Barbara Godard's "Caliban's Revolt: The Discourse of the (M)other" (in Critical

Approaches to the Fiction of Margaret Laurence, Colin Nicholson, ed., [London: Macmillan, 1990], 208-27); Gayle Greene's "Margaret Laurence's *The Diviners:* The Uses of the Past" (in *Critical Approaches to the Fiction of Margaret Laurence*, Colin Nicholson, ed., [London: Macmillan, 1990], 177-207).

Nora Foster Stovel

•

"Canada Via Africa": *The Stone Angel* as the Missing Link Between Margaret Laurence's African and Canadian Writing

Margaret Laurence (1926-1987), called "Canada's most successful novelist" by Joan Coldwell in *The Oxford Companion to Canadian Literature* (1983), is most famous for her Canadian fiction set in her mythical microcosm of Manawaka. Canadians do not think of Laurence as an author of African texts, although she does deserve that title, because she actually wrote as many books about Africa as she did about Canada. The fame of her Canadian fiction has overshadowed her earlier African work, however, and the two sets of texts are not always considered together[1]—unfortunately, because her African experience, I argue, helped make her a great Canadian novelist.

While she wrote five fictions set in Canada—*The Stone Angel* (1964), *A Jest of God* (1966), *The Fire-Dwellers* (1969), *A Bird in the House* (1970), and *The Diviners* (1974)—she wrote an equal number of books about Africa, four of them before she ever wrote a novel set in Canada. Her first published book, *A Tree for Poverty: Somali Poetry and Prose* (1954), the first ever translation or publication of Somali folk literature; her first novel, *This Side Jordan* (1960); her first collection of short stories, *The Tomorrow-Tamer and Other Stories* (1963); her first memoir, *The Prophet's Camel Bell* (1963); her first and only critical study, *Long Drums and Cannons: Nigerian Dramatists and Novelists, 1952-1968* (1968), were all written out of Africa, where she lived from 1951 to1957. Margaret and Jack Laurence lived for a year and a half in the British Protectorate of Somaliland, later the Republic of Somalia, and five years in the Gold Coast, soon to become Ghana. This African experience that she labelled "my seven years' love affair with a continent" ("Ten"18) influenced her Canadian writing indelibly. As Patricia Morley states in *Margaret Laurence: The Long Journey Home*, "The way to Manawaka lay through Ghana, Nigeria, and the searching desert sun" (39).

The Stone Angel was hailed as Laurence's first Canadian novel—the work that was judged by William H. New to be "one of the most illuminating literary experiences in recent Canadian fiction" (141). When Malcolm Ross, as editor-in-chief of the New Canadian Library series, asked Canadian academics to rank the best hundred Canadian novels in 1982, *The Stone Angel* topped the list.[2] But *The Stone Angel* could also be considered her last African novel. George Woodcock observes in *Introducing Margaret Laurence's The Stone Angel: A Reader's Guide*, "just as *The Stone Angel* looked forward to the Manawaka novels, and in some ways set a pattern for them, it also looked back to Margaret Laurence's African experiences and bore their traces" (54). Fiona Sparrow states in her excellent 1993 study, *Into Africa with Margaret Laurence*: "the effects of her journey in Africa are evident not only in her African writing but also in the Manawaka works that brought her writing career to its climax" (206). In this essay I will investigate the truth of Woodcock's observation by exploring unexpected ways in which Laurence's first Canadian novel could also be seen as her last African fiction.

It is not surprising that *The Stone Angel* parallels Laurence's African writing because it was composed simultaneously with it. Her journal for 30 August 1986 records, "I wrote *The Stone Angel* in the first draft in 1961" (qtd. in King 160). Laurence wrote that first draft in Vancouver while she was revising her Ghanaian stories and editing her Somali journal (King 160). In *Dance on the Earth: A Memoir* (1989), she explains that she set aside *The Stone Angel* to prepare her Somali travel memoir, *The Prophet's Camel Bell* (157). Knopf, in an unusual publishing manoeuvre, published *The Stone Angel* simultaneously with two of Laurence's African books—*The Prophet's Camel Bell*, titled *New Wind in a Dry Land* in its American edition, and *The Tomorrow-Tamer and Other Stories*—on the same day in June 1964.

The Stone Angel is thus Laurence's transitional novel. She writes in her 1978 essay, "Ivory Tower or Grassroots? The Novelist as Socio-Political Being": "I had come back home to *Canada via Africa*, both physically and spiritually" (157, italics mine). In a 14 February 1963 letter to Adele Wiseman, she affirms that *The Stone Angel* "meant the transition from writing about Africa to writing about my own people, the only ones I know from the inside, so on that level also it had almost too much significance for me" (Lennox and Panofsky 156). In her original, unpublished introduction to *Long Drums and Cannons*, finally published in my 2001 edition, she explains how she found her voice in moving from Africa to Canada in fact and in fiction:

> My own first novel and a subsequent book of short stories were set in Ghana, where I lived for a number of years. I began to realize, however, that if I wanted to go on as a novelist, I could really only write about people whom I knew from the inside, my own people who came out of the same background as myself—Scots Presbyterian, in a Canadian prairie town—people who were (as Muslims say about Allah) closer

to me than my own neck-vein. It was probably fortunate that
I came to this conclusion at the moment I did, for the time
for outsiders to write about Africa was then nearly over.[3]

In a 29 June 1963 letter to Jack McClelland, she writes of *The Stone Angel*: "It seems to me to be the only really true thing I have ever written—this because it is the only thing written entirely from the inside, with the kind of knowledge that one can only have of one's own people, who are, as the Muslims say about Allah, as close to you as your own neck vein. I do not know why I had so many doubts about *Hagar*, initially—possibly because I wasn't sure I could write about anything in which the theme was all inner, not outer" (King 184). In her 1970 essay "Sources," retitled "A Place To Stand On" in her collection of travel essays, *Heart of a Stranger* (1976), she says, "I always knew that one day I would have to stop writing about Africa and go back to my own people, my own place of belonging" (6).

When Laurence moved from Africa to Canada in her fiction, however, she brought with her all that she had learned from translating Somali folk-literature for *A Tree for Poverty* and critiquing Nigerian writing in *Long Drums and Cannons* that enhanced her Manawaka fiction—particularly issues that she emphasizes in essays and interviews as being most central to her writing—character, dilemma, theme, individual voice, and narrative structure.

It is worth noting here that her transition from Africa to Canada is simultaneous with her transition from a male to a female protagonist. Referring back to Nathaniel Amegbe, protagonist of *This Side Jordan*, Laurence acknowledges, in her 1969 essay, "Gadgetry or Growing: Form and Voice in the Novel," "I actually wonder how I ever had the nerve to attempt to go into the mind of an African man" (82). In fact, Hagar *is* masculine: in trying to be the strong son her father, Jason Currie, never had, the motherless Hagar becomes a patriarch in petticoats, as I have argued in " 'A Holy Terror': Hagar, Hero(ine) of *The Stone Angel*" in *Divining Margaret Laurence: A Critical Study of Her Complete Writings* (2008). Hagar is, of course, the first in what may be the most famous gallery of portraits of powerful women in Canadian literature, including Rachel Cameron, Stacey MacAindra, Vanessa MacLeod, and Morag Gunn.

The fact that Laurence wrote *Long Drums and Cannons* during the decade when she composed her Manawaka cycle is relevant, and a few discerning Canadian critics have observed parallels between Laurence's fiction and the African writers she discusses in *Long Drums and Cannons*: Wole Soyinka, Chinua Achebe, Amos Tutuola, Cyprian Ekwensi, John Pepper Clark, and six promising new writers—T. M. Aluko, Elechi Amadi, Nkem Nwankwo,

Flora Nwapa, Onuora Nzekwu, and Gabriel Okara. Clara Thomas judges, in "'Morning Yet on Creation Day': A Study of *This Side Jordan*," "She was particularly influenced then, I believe, by her recent work in *Long Drums and Cannons* on the Nigerian writers, especially Achebe, Soyinka and Okigbo" (104). James King judges, in *The Life of Margaret Laurence*, "It is obvious that in the work of Wole Soyinka, Chinua Achebe, Amos Tutuola, Flora Nwapa and their contemporaries Margaret Laurence also saw reflected many of her own themes" (221). Patricia Morley asserts, in *Margaret Laurence: The Long Journey Home*, "Because she feels a sympathetic identification with many Africans, her comments on their work reveal many of her own attitudes towards writing" (35). In "'Canada, Africa, Canada': Laurence's Unbroken Journey," Morley concludes: "*Long Drums and Cannons* (1968), published in the middle of the decade in which her Manawaka works were produced, is as much a spiritual autobiography as is her earlier travel memoir, *The Prophet's Camel Bell*. Through an analysis of Nigerian dramatists and novelists, Laurence reveals her own way of seeing, a vision which proves to have surprisingly close parallels with those of modern Nigerian writers" (81-82). In "Margaret Laurence and Africa," Craig Tapping claims that *Long Drums* "sheds further light on Laurence's literary mission in Manawaka and environs," for "the critical terms with which Laurence describes Achebe's early achievement prefigure her own Manawaka cycle. Canadian literature is the sleeping giant behind the description of Nigerian literature in *Long Drums and Cannons*," because "Laurence's critical endeavours on behalf of African literature determine what she will attempt on returning to Canada" (70-73). In this essay I will investigate the truth of Tapping's sleeping giant metaphor.

When Laurence finally returned to her own people in her fiction, however, it was to her grandparents' generation: "I had to begin by approaching my background and my past through my grandparents' generation, the generation of pioneers of Scots-Presbyterian origin who had been among the first to people the town I called Manawaka." She adds, "Hagar, in *The Stone Angel*, was not drawn from life, but she incorporates many qualities of my grandparents' generation. Her speech is their speech, and her gods their gods" (*Heart* 6-7). Laurence wrote to Jack McClelland on 29 June 1963, "Personally, I think she is a hell of an old lady! Of course, I may be prejudiced. Anyway, for better or worse, the voice in which she speaks is all her own, and I think now that I can't ever again be content to write in anything except this idiom, which is of course mine" (King 184). She affirms, "*The Stone Angel* is the first book that I had written about my own country of the heart" (Arnason 33). But Canada, her country of the heart, reflects Africa in *The Stone Angel*.

The first clue to *The Stone Angel* as Laurence's transitional novel is the name "Hagar." Hagar Currie Shipley, heroine of *The Stone Angel*, owes much, of course, to her biblical namesake—the Egyptian handmaid who is driven into the wilderness by Sarah, Abram's barren wife, after she conceives Ishmael, in Genesis 16, as numerous critics, including William H. New, Sandra Djwa, and Patricia Koster, have observed. New parallels *The Stone Angel* with Paul's discussion of Hagar in Galatians 4: 22-27 in his introduction to the 1968 NCL edition (viii), and Djwa says the novel "moves through the Genesis account of Abram (Bram) and Hagar into the New Testament allegory of the covenant of grace as opposed to the covenant of the law" (47). Patricia Koster debates "Hagar's identification of herself as Egyptian" (41) in "Hagar 'The Egyptian': Allusions and Illusions in *The Stone Angel.*" This biblical desert association is emphasized when Hagar refers to herself as an "Egyptian" (40) and as "Pharaoh's daughter" (43). Laurence says *The Stone Angel* "parallels the story of the biblical Hagar who is cast out into the wilderness" (Sullivan 68), but adds, "in the case of my Hagar the wilderness is within" (Fabre 198).[4]

But "*hhagar*" is also the Somali word for "thorn-bush," the only form of vegetation that flourishes in the desert landscape of Somalia. Laurence declines to translate the word "*hhagar*," preferring to let it stand, but framing it in quotation marks to signal its Somali origin. In her translation of the Somali *gabei*, "To a Friend going on a Journey" by Mohamed Abdullah Hassan, she writes of "airless forests thick with 'hhagar' trees" (*Tree* 53). And in translating Salaan Arrabey's "*gabei in ħ*" "To a Faithless Friend," she writes, "'hagar' bushes tore my flesh" (*Heart* 189). What moniker could be more appropriate for the cantankerous Hagar Currie Shipley? Like the word "*sabra*"—the Hebrew word for *cactus*, prickly on the outside, but juicy on the inside, that has come to represent the tough-but-tender Israeli people—"Hagar" suggests this aging termagant's prickly personality.

So much did she dominate the narrative that Laurence titled her embryo novel simply *Hagar*, until, on the eve of publication, her editors objected. They thought it sounded too much like "an Old Testament tale" (Lennox 156) and suggested the title *Old Lady Shipley* instead (*Heart* 145). Laurence says in her essay, "Living Dangerously . . . by Mail," in *Heart of a Stranger*, "I've had more trouble with titles than a prospective peer. And I've defended my titles more often than a middleweight boxer." She claims, "A title should, if possible, be like a line of poetry—capable of saying a great deal with hardly any words. The title of a novel should in some way express the whole novel, its themes and even something of its outcome. It should all be there, in a phrase" (144). Desperate at the prospect of having her novel titled *Old Lady Shipley*, she re-

read the Psalms, seeking a title and coming up with *Sword in my Bones*, which sounded, she realized, like "a tale of pirates and buried treasure" (145). In a 26 August 1963 letter to McClelland, Laurence says, of "Sword in My Bones," "This title seemed to me to suggest either a who-dun-it by Mickey Spillane or some kind of blood-and-thunder story" (King 190). She also considered "Rage Against the Dying" from Dylan Thomas' villanelle, "Do Not Go Gentle into That Good Night," for her title. Finally, she read the manuscript of the novel, and there it was in the first sentence: "Upon the hill brow, the stone angel used to stand" (3). "The title, the real and true and only possible title had been there all the time, in the first line of the book" (*Heart* 145).[5] *The Stone Angel* was indeed the perfect title, for, as Laurence says, "it does dominate the book like an imposing symbol" (Fabre 199). It is also the perfect title for Hagar's story, for Hagar *is* the stone angel, as I argue in my chapter on *The Stone Angel* in *Divining Margaret Laurence*.

So powerful was Hagar, in fact, that she almost broke up the Laurences' marriage. Jack did not like *The Stone Angel*, but Margaret recalls in *Dance on the Earth: A Memoir,* "for me it was the most important book I had written, a book on which I had to stake the rest of my life" (158).[6] In 1962 Margaret embarked for London with her two children and "the old lady"—her two kinds of offspring—while Jack went to Pakistan: "Strange reason for breaking up a marriage: a novel. I had to go with the old lady, I really did, but at the same time I felt terrible about hurting him" (158). While we know from recent biographies by James King, Lyall Powers, and Donez Xiques that there were various reasons for the Laurences' separation in 1962, we can well believe that Hagar had a hand in it.

Hagar is possibly the most powerful character in Canadian literature. As Constance Rooke says in "Hagar's Old Age: *The Stone Angel* as *Vollendungsroman*," "In Canadian literature, Hagar is reigning still as Queen of all the characters" (25). Clearly, character is the most important element for Laurence's fiction. She affirms, in numerous essays and interviews, the paramount importance of *characterization* to her novels. She calls herself a "Method writer" in her 1972 essay "Time and the Narrative Voice" (157), because she is possessed by her protagonists—like the dancers possessed by spirits of the ancestors in Nigerian masquerade drama or the storytellers whose tales she translates in *A Tree for Poverty*. She says in her 1973 interview with Donald Cameron, "The Black Celt Speaks of Freedom," "I write what I would call a Method novel. Like a Method actor, you get right inside the role. I take on, for the time I'm writing, the *persona* of the character" (102).[7]

Writing *The Stone Angel* was like taking dictation from a determined ghost;

she recalls, "The novel poured forth. It was as if the old woman was actually there, telling me her life story, and it was my responsibility to put it down as faithfully as I could" (*Dance* 156). She wrote to Adele Wiseman on 5 September 1961, Hagar is "one hell of an old lady, a real tartar. She's crabby, snobbish, difficult, proud as Lucifer." She adds, "She's also . . .dying" (Lennox 135). She recalls in her memoir that a British reviewer called *The Stone Angel* "'The most telling argument for euthanasia' which he had ever read" (*Dance* 166).

Hagar also calls herself "proud as Lucifer" (191), the rebel angel, for she is proud to a fault. In fact, pride is her tragic flaw, as numerous critics have observed. On her deathbed she realizes, "Pride was my wilderness, and the demon that led me there was fear" (292). Pride, in a positive sense, is also the distinguishing feature of the Somali people, according to Laurence. She believes that pride is their survival mechanism: in *The Prophet's Camel Bell* she says, "The Somalis are proud, not groveling, and in their own eyes, they are aristocrats and warriors" (186). Even the women, who initially appear to Laurence to be meek and modest, are, she soon discovers, "meek as Medea" (13).

In essays and interviews, Laurence explains that what interests her primarily about character is what she calls the human *dilemma*. In "Ivory Tower or Grass Roots?" she writes, "Fiction has many facets. . . .It speaks first and foremost of individual characters, and through them it speaks of our dilemmas. . . ." (259). In *Long Drums and Cannons* she defines dilemma as "the individual's effort to define himself, his need to come to terms with his ancestors and his gods" (181). For Nigerian writers, such conflicts involve "the clash between generations" (12). She affirms, in a 1973 interview, "I like to think that my books basically deal with human dilemmas which could be understood by somebody in Africa or New Zealand. But at the same time, there is a kind of cultural thing, which is deeply related to one's own people, one's ancestors" (Gibson 193).

This "clash between generations," between the past and the present, is of paramount importance for Hagar. Just as Laurence's character, Nathaniel Amegbe, protagonist of *This Side Jordan*, is torn between yesterday and tomorrow—between his past as son of the *kyerema*, the drummer, in an Ashanti village and his present as the history teacher at the Futura Academy—so Hagar, too, "is rampant with memory" (5) in *The Stone Angel*. She is "remembering furiously" (6), living as much in the past as in the present, now that "time has folded in like a paper fan" (250), in her own words.

Hagar's memories dictate the structure of *The Stone Angel*, as the narrative method alternates between past and present. In "Time and the Narrative Voice," Laurence explains "the relationship between the narrative voice and the treatment of time," claiming "it is the character who chooses which parts of the personal past, the family past, and the ancestral past have to be revealed for the present to be realized and the future to happen" (160). She explains in *Dance on the Earth* that she planned "to record Hagar's life in time present, and encompass her long past in a series of dramatic memories by having each one of her memory sequences triggered by an event in her present" (157).

This flashback technique not only determines the structure of the narrative, but it also dictates Hagar's voice, for Hagar is double-tongued. She has two voices: a prosaic spoken voice and a poetic inner voice. In *Dance on the Earth*, Laurence recalls that "Hagar's description of places and events and her inner feelings were emerging in a kind of poetic, even rhythmic, prose, whereas her speech to others was brusque, down-to-earth, testy and cranky" (156). Like Nathaniel Amegbe's eloquent inner monologues in *This Side Jordan*, Hagar's memories are so poetic—perhaps reflecting the influences of the Somali poetry Laurence translated for *A Tree for Poverty*—that Laurence feared it was unrealistic. Laurence translates Somali poetry using alliteration and assonance on stressed syllables, rather like Anglo-Saxon poetry: for example, in her translation of a *belwo*, she writes, "Woman, lovely as lightning at dawn, / Speak to me even once" (48). Similarly, Hagar compares herself to "prissy Pippa as she passed" (5). Hagar's reminiscences are lyrical: at the outset of her narrative she imagines the prairie past, "before the portly peonies and the angels with rigid wings, when the prairie bluffs were walked through only by Cree with enigmatic faces and greasy hair" (5). In fact, Walter Swayze observes, in his essay "Margaret Laurence: Novelist-as-Poet," that the opening of *The Stone Angel* is only considered prosaic because it is printed as prose: if read aloud, it sounds like poetry (5).

The parallels between Laurence's African and Canadian work are evident not only in her characterization and narrative method, but also in her themes. Indeed, one could argue that Nigerian literature influenced Laurence's Canadian writing in general, as I have done elsewhere.[8] None of her Manawaka novels, however, exhibits such direct parallels with her African work as does *The Stone Angel*. Pride is not the only thematic parallel between Laurence's Canadian protagonist and African literature, of course. Many themes in *The Stone Angel*, and indeed in all the Manawaka novels, have parallels in African writing, especially in the Nigerian literature that Laurence critiques in *Long Drums and Cannons*, and particularly that of novelist Chinua Achebe and dramatist Wole Soyinka. One need only think of the importance of freedom and bondage, communication and solipsism, strength and weakness, pride and submission, survival and despair to both bodies of work in order to recognize the importance of these parallels. As Paul Comeau writes in *Margaret Laurence's Epic Imagination*, Laurence "recognized the tremendous influence of Africa as the crucible for such central themes in her later work as survival, exile, independence, tribalism and communication, to name but a few" (15).

Freedom is a major theme for Laurence, and freedom is closely related to the value of the past, for one must appreciate the past while freeing oneself from its fetters. In both her African and Canadian fiction, Laurence writes about her characters' struggle with the past, because "the past and the future are both always present," as she asserts in "Time and the Narrative Voice" (157). In *Heart of a Stranger*, she affirms, "My writing, then, has been my own attempt to come to terms with the past. I see this process as the gradual one of freeing oneself from the stultifying aspect of the past, while at the same time beginning to see its true value" (8). In *Long Drums and Cannons*, Laurence explores Nigerian writers' progress toward independence in terms of each protagonist's "perpetual battle to free himself from the fetters of the past" (181). She cites the "quest for freedom" ("Ivory" 258) as central to her own fiction. As Donez Xiques writes in *Margaret Laurence: The Making of a Writer*, "Laurence's own writing may be construed as an examination of the question of freedom through the prism of fiction" (207). "Free-Dom" [sic] is the watchword of Laurence's Ghanaian fiction, as she traces the process of Africanization—training African workers to replace British colonials—and the emergence of Ghanaian independence in both *This Side Jordan* and *The Tomorrow-Tamer*. We remember that Laurence lived in Somalia and Ghana when both those countries were on the verge of declaring independence. In fact, Laurence was invited back to Hargeisa to participate in the Somali independence celebrations in 1966. She also concludes *The Tomorrow-Tamer* with Mammii Ama chanting "Free-Dom" in her final story, "A Gourdful of Glory" (242).

Freedom is closely linked to the concept of personal and political independence. As Barbara Pell writes in "The African and Canadian Heroines: From Bondage to Grace," "In the cultural upheaval of the new Africa on the verge of independence . . . Laurence also saw images that she associates with the end of the heroine's pilgrimage out of bondage, freedom, dignity, and spiritual grace" (36-37). She argues that the three stories with female protagonists in *The Tomorrow-Tamer* "encapsulate Laurence's themes of bondage and freedom—both colonial and feminist" (43) and that "A Gourdful of Glory" concludes *The Tomorrow-Tamer* "with optimism and exaltation for the future of Africa, expressed by a 'liberated' woman who foreshadows Laurence's Canadian heroines" (45).[9]

Freedom is crucial to Laurence's Manawaka heroines. Hagar's tragedy is her failure to be free: on her deathbed, she says, "I lie here and try to recall something truly free that I've done in ninety years" (307). Before her death, she achieves two free acts: when she reaches the bedpan, a comic grail, for her suffering young roommate, Sandra Wong, and when she tells a loving lie to her long-suffering son, Marvin. Although she dies, Hagar achieves what Laurence terms "the promised land of one's own inner freedom" ("Ten" 14).

Hagar also cries out on her deathbed, "When did I ever speak the heart's truth?" (292). The theme of communication is closely related to that of freedom, and communication is clearly crucial to an author whose first published book was a translation of folk literature in a language with no orthography. Speaking of Chinua Achebe's fiction in *Long Drums and Cannons*, Laurence asserts, "we must attempt to communicate, however imperfectly, if we are not to succumb to despair or madness" (112). In *Dance on the Earth,* she writes, "Knowing that, in our different ways, Achebe and I have been trying to do much the same sort of thing all our writing lives, I recognized that communication [between African and western writers] could be possible" (153). G. D. Killam, in his 1974 introduction to *A Jest of God,* claims "the problem of communication is central in Margaret Laurence's novels" (np). The problem of communication between her African characters and her British colonialist characters, such as Nathaniel Amegbe and Miranda Kestoe in *This Side Jordan,* or Constance and Love in "A Fetish for Love" in *The Tomorrow-Tamer,* is central to her Ghanaian fiction. Hagar, too, has never been able to communicate her "heart's truth" to the people she loves. In the shadow of death, she finally speaks truly when she confesses, "Marvin, I'm so frightened" (303). Indeed, she speaks truer than she knows when she voices her loving lie, "You've been good to me, always. A better son than John" (304).

Survival is a theme that is central to both Laurence's African and Canadian fiction. In "Ivory Tower or Grass Roots?" she asserts, "The quest for physical and spiritual freedom, the quest for relationships of equality and communication—these themes run through my fiction and are connected with the theme of survival, not mere physical survival, but a survival of the spirit, with human dignity and the ability to give and receive love" ("Ivory" 258). In "A Place to Stand On," the opening essay in *Heart of a Stranger,* she says of her ancestors, "They were, in the end, great survivors, and for that I love and value them" (8). She discovers, after the suicide of Sylvia Plath in 1963, Laurence's first winter in England, that, despite her anxieties, she is a survivor (*Dance* 163). She writes to Gordon Elliott on 25 November 1962, "I am a survivor at heart" (qtd. in Xiques 301).

Survival is a challenge in the Somali desert. In her introduction to *A Tree for Poverty*, Laurence writes of the nomadic Somalis, known as "the people without a pillow," "Life is utterly hard and utterly insecure" (45), and "the actual process of survival demands so much effort and tenacity from each tribesman" (47) that "Individualism and independence are a necessary step to survival" (40). In her 1969 essay, "Ten Years' Sentences," Laurence claims that the "theme of survival" (*Heart* 8), which became the subject of Margaret Atwood's 1972 *Survival: A Thematic Guide to Canadian Literature*, is also the central theme of *The Stone Angel*. Indeed, George Woodcock concludes in *Introducing Margaret Laurence's The Stone Angel* that Hagar "is a universal personification of the urge to survive" (25).

Later, in her 1970 essay "A Place to Stand On," she refines that definition, explaining that, by the "theme of survival," she means "survival not just in the physical sense, but the survival of some human dignity and in the end the survival of some human warmth and the ability to reach out and touch others" (*Heart* 15). For Hagar, Laurence claims, it is spiritual rather than physical survival: the point is "to survive with some dignity, toting the load of excess mental baggage that everyone carries, until the moment of death" ("Ten" 21).

Survival is clearly a crucial issue in the Somali desert, but Hagar's situation in the Canadian prairie seems a different case. Laurence, however, parallels these two unlikely locales explicitly in *The Prophet's Camel Bell*, affirming, "when we lived in Somaliland in the desert, this was a kind of country I took to right away because, as in the prairies, you can see from one side of the horizon to another" (33). Laurence's description of the Canadian prairies, during the "Dirty Thirties" when "The Drought and Depression were like evil deities," as she writes in her essay "Where the World Began" in *Heart of a Stranger*, parallels her descriptions of the Somali desert, especially during the *jilal* or dry season, when the land lies parched by the sun (*Heart* 170). Hagar's description of "the sun that grinds bone and flesh and earth to dust as though in a mortar of fire with a pestle of crushing light"(54) is just as applicable to the blazing sun of the Haud desert "steeped in heat, stifling and dry" (*TP* 53) during the *jilal*, or drought, as it is to the prairie summer. In discussing Hagar's biblical associations in his introduction to the 1968 NCL edition of *The Stone Angel*, William H. New notes the "numerous desert images" in the novel, adding, "the prairie in drought is a desert" (viii) .The social structure has parallels too, as Laurence, in various essays and interviews, compares Somali tribal culture with Canadian small-town society, which she affirms can be both protecting and stifling, both a fortress and a prison.

The crucial importance of water in such arid landscapes is emphasized by

Laurence's description, in *The Prophet's Camel Bell*, of the time she and Jack stopped their jeep to offer water to a young mother and child dying of thirst while crossing the desert. Laurence writes, "In her hands she held an empty tin cup. She did not move at all or ask for water. Despair keeps its own silence" (65). After Margaret and Jack stopped to give her some water from their spare tank, "She did not say a word, but she did something then which I have never been able to forget. She held the cup for the child to drink first. She was careful not to spill a drop. Afterwards, she brushed a hand lightly across the child's mouth, then licked her palm so that no moisture would be wasted" (66). Laurence was haunted by this scene: "what I felt, as I looked into her face, was undeniable and it was not pity. It was something entirely different, some sense of knowing in myself what her anguish had been and would be, as she watched her child's life seep away for lack of water to keep it alive. For her, this was the worst the *Jilal* could bring. In all of life there was nothing worse than this." She adds, "What we could do here was only slightly more than nothing" (66).

But she did not do nothing. She wrote about it in *The Prophet's Camel Bell*, and the cup of water surfaces as a kind of grail when Hagar, proud as ever, even on her deathbed, wrests the water from the nurse in the final scene of *The Stone Angel* (308). As Fiona Sparrow notes, "Water was as precious in the dusty Prairies as in the desert wilderness. . . . Water is a sign of God's mercy for Bram Shipley's Hagar as it was for Abraham's Hagar in the desert" (207). Holding the redemptive cup of water in her own hands, Hagar gives birth to herself as a woman and to Laurence's gallery of Manawaka heroines. Finally, the angel is freed from the stone.

Thus, *The Stone Angel* links Laurence's African and Canadian texts as it reflects her experience observing independence movements in African countries, and it also presages her portrayal of the empowerment of female protagonists in the Manawaka cycle. As Barbara Pell concludes, "Laurence's Canadian heroines were born in Africa" (46).

Notes

1. For example, Christian Riegel's *Writing Grief: Margaret Laurence and the Work of Mourning* (2003) and Paul Comeau's *Margaret Laurence's Epic Imagination* (2005) focus exclusively on the Manawaka Saga, and the vast majority of scholarly articles on Laurence focus on one or more of the Manawaka texts.

2. See Charles Steele, *Taking Stock: The Calgary Conference on the Canadian Novel.*

3. Laurence's original, unpublished introduction to *Long Drums and Can-*

nons is in the Laurence Archives at McMaster University. In her interview with Rosemary Sullivan, Laurence explains, "I really knew that I didn't want to go on writing about Africa, because otherwise my writing would become that of a tourist. I had written everything I could out of that particular experience, and I very much wanted to return home in a kind of spiritual way" (68).

4. As Joan Coldwell observes, "Incorporating many biblical allusions, the novel offers a modern version of the archetypal quest for spiritual vision" (OCCL 1098).

5. The typescript of the novel at McMaster University shows that, in fact, Laurence emended that first sentence more than once.

6. In a 14 February 1963 letter to Wiseman, in which Laurence reports that Alan Maclean, editor for Macmillan, likes *Hagar*, she writes, "I feel as though my faith in life, in myself, in everything, has been miraculously restored to me. Of course, this novel meant a lot more than it should have done, to me, as in a way it was (or became) a whole test of my own judgment" (Lennox 156).

7. She affirms, in a 24 January 1965 letter to Wiseman, "*The Stone Angel* was written in a way similar to the Stanislawski (sp?) Method [sic]" (Lennox 192-93).

8. "'The Sleeping Giant': The Influence of Nigerian Literature on Margaret Laurence's Manawaka Fiction."

9. While I agree with Pell on most points in her very perceptive essay, I would question her reading of "A Gourdful of Glory" as entirely optimistic. Laurence definitely qualifies or ironizes the optimism in this story.

Wolfram R. Keller

•

Discovering Strangeness:
Metaphor, Allegory, and Cultural Otherness
in Rudy Wiebe's *A Discovery of Strangers*

E ver since George Lakoff and Mark Johnson's *Metaphors We Live By* (1980), conceptual metaphor theory has been fruitfully applied in many arenas beyond linguistics, for instance, in psychology, the social sciences, and anthropology. Perhaps surprisingly, given the prominence of metaphor in poetics, literary scholarship has relatively rarely engaged with recent work in cognitive linguistics. Moreover, its role in the teaching of literature remains largely unexplored. After a short review of the application of conceptual metaphor theory in language teaching, I argue for the benefits of engaging with conceptual metaphor theory in the literature classroom. More specifically, I contend that Rudy Wiebe's novel *A Discovery of Strangers* not only raises students' awareness of the metaphoric structure of conceptual systems but also questions the epistemological validity of mapping one domain onto another, of conceptualizing the foreign in terms of the familiar. *A Discovery of Strangers* generates an important conversation about alternative ways of negotiating and discovering cultural difference, advancing an epistemology that ultimately promotes allegory as a trope of difference over metaphor as a trope of identity—a kind of allegorical mapping that I refer to as conceptual allegory. Instead of collapsing the domains involved in the mapping process, as does metaphor, the novel develops an allegorical model that enables multiple mappings across several domains while maintaining those domains as separate entities. As such, *Discovery* engages with questions of otherness and cultural difference on multiple levels, involving students in a meta-reflection regarding conceptual metaphor theory and its capability to map other signification systems.

•

The translation of Paul Ricoeur's monograph on metaphorical language, *The Rule of Metaphor* (1977), could not have been more appositely titled. With Lakoff and Johnson's *Metaphors We Live By*, the conceptual function of metaphor has firmly filled the containers of our analogical imaginations, superseding earlier, and supposedly reductive rhetorical theories of figural language, which nevertheless saw in "rhetorical" metaphor "The most elaborate of tropes" (Dupriez 276; Lanham 101; Lausberg 1: 285-91).[1] According to Lakoff and Johnson, our entire conceptual system is largely metaphorical in that "the way we think, what we experience, and what we do every day is very much a matter of metaphor" (*Metaphors* 3). Metaphor, understood as conceptual mapping process, is consequently defined as an "understanding [of] one conceptual domain in terms of another conceptual domain," represented in studies of conceptual metaphor as "CONCEPTUAL DOMAIN (A) IS CONCEPTUAL DOMAIN (B)" (Kövecses 4). Provided that the human mind classifies items analogically, Lakoff and Johnson elaborate a number of conceptual metaphors, such as LIFE IS A JOURNEY, IDEAS ARE CONTAINERS, or ARGUMENT IS WAR, which in turn are the basis for all metaphor use. The authors grant that metaphorical understandings are culturally embedded, since "there can be no coherent view of the self without personal ritual. . . .Just as our personal metaphors are not random but form systems coherent with our personalities, so our personal rituals are not random but are coherent with our view of the world and ourselves and with our systems of personal metaphors and metonymies" (*Metaphors* 235). In epistemological terms, simply put, individuals navigate unknown worlds *qua* the known by means of conceptual metaphor.

Because of its cultural embeddedness, conceptual metaphor is very useful to language acquisition (Cameron and Low; MacLennan), specifically regarding awareness raising. Many cross-cultural learning experiments involving metaphor point to the value of conceptual metaphor theory (CMT) for the acquisition of vocabulary and idioms. Not surprisingly, this primarily exploits the aspect of identity rather than difference. Although Frank Boers, for example, concludes that "language learners' lexical resources benefit from an enhanced metaphor awareness" (562), his research also illustrates that CMT facilitates vocabulary retention only when employing semantically transparent experiments. This underlines metaphor's drive to likeness, not difference—and it is certainly the emphasis of difference that is conducive to raising awareness of cultural variance. Boers acknowledges this in concluding that "metaphor awareness is not meant to be used by the learner as a 'generator' of the conventional figurative expressions of the target language. Instead, its primary use proposed here is as a channelling device for learners to organize the stream of figurative language they are exposed to" (564). Tellingly, the usage of metaphor awareness in order to recognize "possible cross-cultural differences in metaphoric themes" ranks fourth among five possibilities (566; see Barcelona, "On the Systematic Contrastive Analysis").

There are scholars, however, who take exception to the rule of identity. Thus, with reference to different metaphorical expressions realized from the same conceptual metaphor as an aid to learning idioms—and with reference to MacLennan—it has been argued that "The aim is that students should think about frequent metaphors in their L1 [source language] at a conscious level, and become aware that, although some expressions operate in a similar way in L2 [target language], the existence of similar metaphors in L2 cannot be taken for granted" (Deignan, Gabryś, and Solska 356). Lakoff and Johnson already draw attention to cultural differences concerning conceptual metaphors. While in most Western cultures ACTIVE IS UP and PASSIVE IS DOWN, "there are cultures where passivity is valued more than activity" (*Metaphors* 24).[2] Zoltán Kövecses and Péter Szabó likewise suggest that there are problems with difference: "A major, and expected, complication is that the figurative idiomatic structure of one language will not coincide with that of another. Which metaphors and metonymies and which aspects of conventional knowledge are universal and which are not?" The authors believe that a "systematic answer" to this question can be and should be provided by future research (351-52). And yet, the vexing question concerning the construction of identity where none may exist is generally neglected in CMT. As concerns the acquisition of vocabulary and idioms, though, this poses few problems; after all, as Antonio Barcelona emphasizes, "an important advantage for L2 learning is the existence of the same basic metaphor[s] in both the target and the learner's language" ("On the Systematic Contrastive Analysis" 140). As concerns idioms, for example, Kövecses and Szabó demonstrate that orientational metaphors like INVENTION IS UP, DYSFUNCTIONAL IS DOWN, and HEALTH IS UP, which are current in English, likewise apply to Hungarian (esp. 345-51; but cf. Deignan, Gabryś, and Solska 354, for different conceptual metaphor use in English and Polish). Whereas conceptual metaphors undoubtedly aid the teaching of languages, using literary texts in the classroom can facilitate an awareness of cross-cultural communication while emphasizing cultural difference and complicating CMT's drive towards identity. A literary approach to CMT would lend itself to raising our awareness for what Cameron and Low describe as an inherent risk in cognitive linguistics, namely, "the tendency to discuss metaphors in the reduced schematic form A Is B," and that "insufficient attention is paid to variations in the grammatical form of metaphor that carry significance in discourse" (79). Rudy Wiebe's *A Discovery of Strangers* not only yields insights into the ubiquity of metaphorical conceptions, but also theorizes the limitations of metaphor in offering an allegorical scenario for non-essentialist cultural mappings. The novel thus points beyond strictly linguistic applications of CMT and contributes to a contentious discussion about cultural metaphor theory within cultural studies.

While metaphor is acknowledged as the *sine qua non* for conceptualizing other cultures in the realm of cultural studies and anthropology, recent work underscores philosophical problems regarding CMT. Despite the fact that all binary systems imply difference to some extent, scholars have reservations about the homogenization of cultures through metaphor. Fittingly, Angus Fletcher describes metaphor as a trope of "momentary masking" ("Positive Negation" 161; see further Burke 503-04; Frye, *Great Code* 7-8)—metaphorical mappings mask difference. Lakoff and Johnson themselves grant that metaphors occlude as much as they reveal, and they concede also that conceptual metaphor use "in a political or economic system" can lead to "human degradation" (qtd. in Mühlhäusler 281). Discussing political responses to the 1979 energy crisis, they observe that "New metaphors, like conventional metaphors, can have the power to define reality," irrespective of the truth of the mappings. This can have problematic consequences: "Though questions of truth do arise for new metaphors, the more important questions are those of appropriate action. In most cases, what is at issue is not the truth or falsity of a metaphor but the perceptions and inferences that follow from it and the actions that are sanctioned by it" (*Metaphors* 158). A prominent example of the problematic consequences of doubtful mappings is Susan Sontag's observation that the conceptual metaphor "CANCER IS DEATH" has prevented many patients from seeking treatment (23; see further Glassner 153). Less severely, but nevertheless pivotal for my argument, anthropologist Naomi Quinn quibbles that "thinkers ordinarily know the structure of the domain that is the target of their metaphor," and subsequently assume the identity of domains without validation, since the target domain is (seemingly) consistent with already existing cultural models (65, 77). She concludes, "there is more to culture than just metaphor" (56-57). If the suspicion is correct that metaphors not only uncover existing domain mappings but construct them, literary discourse concerned with depicting otherness engages in an epistemologically doubtful enterprise. This doubly complicates the use of literary texts concerned with other cultures in the classroom, where it would be quite fitting to likewise introduce students to the "Metaphors Others Live By," as Peter Mühlhäusler has it.

In this context, it is interesting that neither literary criticism and literary theory nor postcolonial studies have taken on the challenge of CMT in any sustained or systematic manner, in spite of these disciplines' cavils with essentialist epistemologies. From the perspective of cognitive linguistics, however, several studies analyze literary texts, mainly in terms of mapping conceptual metaphors as they emerge in novels and poems—most prominently Lakoff and Turner in their *More Than Cool Reason* (1989). While such studies allow that "Original, creative *literary metaphors* . . . are typically less clear but richer in meaning than either everyday metaphors or metaphors in science," scholars such as Kövecses quickly return to the linguistically orthodox, default position, according to which "most poetic language is based on conventional, ordinary conceptual metaphors" (43-44, 47-51, emphasis in original). On the other hand, Uta Lenk, working within the framework suggested by Lakoff and Turner, argues that literary texts, specifically works by Smaro Kamboureli, Margaret Atwood, and Michael Ondaatje, include many metaphors that remain to be mapped, the analysis of which would point up the importance of linguistic approaches to literary texts. Also concerned with poetry, particularly with works by Emily Dickinson and Sylvia Plath, Margaret Freeman surmises that CMT contributes to literary studies in four ways: it can explain and "evaluate" multiple readings; it can illustrate the cultural factors of interpretation; it explicates a writer's conceptual world view; and it can thus form a basis "for an empirical study of literary interpretations" (480). Norman Holland's *The Brain of Robert Frost* anticipates this inherent quality of metaphors of reading and talking about literature insofar as his study elaborates several conduit metaphors, such as LITERATURE IS FORCE, LITERATURE IS A PERSON, and LITERATURE IS CONDUIT. "Active texts," Holland maintains, "insist on meanings, which inactive, unthinking readers take automatically into their thoughts. LITERATURE IS OTHER" (112-34, quotations at 126, 134). Along these lines, I would suggest that literary texts which explicitly (and implicitly) evoke questions of otherness in metaphor use are particularly useful for putting CMT to the test (and taking it to task) as concerns awareness raising for cultural difference in the classroom.[3]

As this brief survey of relevant approaches shows—I say *relevant* since approaches that shed light both on linguistic, cognitive processes, *and* add original insights in terms of literary criticism are rare—more work in this area promises to be valuable. So far, however, the discussion of conceptual metaphor within the realm of the budding field of cognitive poetics (e.g., Stockwell 105-19) is concerned mainly with the way in which one can approach literary texts from the perspective of CMT rather than how such readings may challenge (or advance alternatives to) existing work in CMT. Given that English Studies at most European universities often require students to study both linguistics *and* literature, it is remarkable that a fertile dialogue has been hitherto lacking, specifically since an exploding field such as CMT is implicitly concerned with issues of great interest to linguists and literary scholars alike. Moreover, it presents an opportunity to mutually enrich existing findings.[4] In my opinion, Wiebe's *A Discovery of Strangers* is a highly suitable text for pursuing such interdisciplinary work in that it at once raises students' awareness for conceptual metaphors as a way of understanding the world while simultaneously inviting a more critical perspective on how such processes affect our perception of other cultures and otherness more generally. The novel thus enables a discussion about possible limitations of metaphorical mappings, reflecting the cultural dimension of the language learning enterprise, but also pointing up the very limits of cross-cultural communication and understanding. Wiebe's *Discovery* is, in fact, an intricate and extensive critique of metaphor as an epistemological tool for perceiving and describing otherness.

——————————— • ———————————

Discovery is a historiographic novel re-imagining the cross-cultural encounter in the Canadian Arctic between members of the 1820 Franklin expedition and the Dene (the Yellowknife "Indians"). Whereas the novel imagines a mostly non-verbal encounter between both cultures in their mutual attempts to understand each another, *Discovery* also reflects the characters' attempts to map foreign cultures. Central to the novel is the tragic love story that unfolds between the Lancashire clergyman Robert Hood and Greenstockings, the daughter of the tribe's elder. It is the love story which first and foremost demonstrates the importance of metaphor for cultural understanding; it is crucially this love story which ultimately illustrates the failure thereof. In mapping the processes of cultural (mis)understanding, *Discovery* becomes what has been called a *megametaphor* (see Cameron and Low 83), a mapping that extends beyond the word and sentence level insofar as the entire text represents the representation of one culture in terms of another. Within the novel, mirroring functions on multiple levels. On the plot level, Hood and Greenstockings attempt to mirror each other's culture. On the narrative level, the author mirrors Dene and English cultures, both historically removed. Structurally, there is a further mirroring process in that the chapters appear to be roughly organized as inverse mirrors, the first chapter mirroring the thirteenth (animal/human understanding vs. indigenous/white misunderstanding), the second chapter mirroring chapter twelve (native version of the arrival of These English vs. White version of the exploration), and so on. The central chapter relates that moment of Greenstockings's and Hood's relationship in which both protagonists come closest to understanding the otherness of the other culture. It is through this multi-layered mirror that the reader encounters an extended meditation on the usefulness of metaphor since mirrors and metaphors are akin to the point of sharing the same plight—without mirrors (metaphors), Northrop Frye observes, self-reflection does not occur; with mirrors (metaphors), we only glimpse a highly subjective selection (*Words with Power* 75).[5] The novel's multiplicity of mirrors as well as its concern with metaphorizing otherness is announced right from the beginning when it adds yet another way of metaphorically mirroring the world, namely, the map. The map, however, also signals the anthropological paradox that depicting otherness primarily represents one's own culture rather than the *other* culture (Engler; James 84).

The Canadian edition of *A Discovery of Strangers* fittingly opens with a map of the Dene territories—that is, the Canadian Arctic—in the 1820s, which alerts readers to the important role of maps as mirrors in this cross-cultural narrative. In fact, it is Robert Hood's job to provide the necessary double narrative for the Franklin expedition. He maps topography, but he likewise has to provide sketches of land and people, drawings which, according to Franklin, are of pivotal importance to the expedition insofar as they

> will form part of the extremely detailed report he must
> present on his return to England . . .; drawings as essen-
> tial as the magnetic-needle readings and declensions, the
> endless longitudes and latitudes, the flora and fauna, the
> temperatures and lists of aurora borealis sightings they
> have each, separately, recorded so meticulously day by day
> despite notebooks lost and other indescribable difficulties
> and hardships endured. (Wiebe 142)

Hood is especially talented in both needle-reading *and* "culture-drawing"; Doctor Richardson, the expedition's physician, stresses Hood's accomplishments when reporting that Hood was the "finest navigator among" them, and that his "talent in scientific observations, together with his maps and drawings . . . must have rendered him a distinguished ornament to his profession" (183). Needless to say, Hood's drawings and his maps are nothing more or less than metaphoric representations of a "reality," and thus represent what Jess Edwards has referred to as the "noisily rhetorical art" of map-making (1), which often represents "a falsely essentialist view of the world which negates or suppresses alternative views which might endanger the privileged position of its Western perceiver" (Huggan 16).

The Dene are nonplussed about this kind of topography, although their way of organizing space is no less a matter of metaphor, even if the metaphors are different—at least when compared to Hood's descriptions of the unexplored territories. For Greenstockings's mother Birdseye, for example, map-making is primarily a matter of *marking* territory. The narrator invokes Saussurean linguistics in one of Birdseye's dreams, in which she aptly describes the belief in the universal signifier of These English: "Sometime, somewhere, they have decided to believe this simplicity of the mark, and they will live their lives straight to the end believing that" (147). Birdseye's dream, however, does not touch on the arrival of These English, editing their arrival out of the story, a fact observed and commented on by Greenstockings: "as if by not speaking it into the story, it never can happen again. Even though everyone fears in silence that it will" (150). An insightful instance of mapping in the cultural style of These English occurs when Greenstockings's father, Keskarrah, who is frequently referred to as the "old mapmaker" (43, 45, 55, and so on), shares his topographical knowledge with the explorers: "He will dare to draw, with his finger on the ground between them, a small picture of the land," for he can "name a few places what they are" (20). As in a mirror, the order of the process in white and Dene "map-making" is reversed but otherwise similar. While Keskarrah knows places through their stories, it is the story in Dene culture (as depicted in the novel) and not the place itself, which takes prominence. At the same time, the Dene's storied way of organizing space occasionally infiltrates explorer discourse, for instance, when the names assigned to the land metonymically invoke stories. After the dangers of a rebellion are averted, These English name the place "Dissension Lake"; a successful hunt renders a "Sight unseen . . . Hunter Lake" (54). Generally, however, Greenstockings is struck by the absence of stories from explorer culture. Thus, their names are so short, "just one short word to name them. As if they had no stories in them" (39). For reasons to be specified below, it is worth noting that she says *as if*, preferring simile to metaphor.

Throughout the novel, Greenstockings and Hood are of special interest for an investigation of conceptual metaphor since they often expressly muse on representational questions. Hood is shown as principally invested in the positivist enterprise of mapping—but only up to a point. After all, his memories constitute an alternative narrative to his detailed, empirical observations, which he accordingly "will arrange and edit . . . properly, as always, so they will make *proper* and decent, *acceptable* sense" (247, emphases added). In fact, Hood consciously *mis*represents the bleak Arctic landscape in search of European aesthetics, a frame for mirroring the other culture: "he must be careful. But a tall tree on either side—that was still a possible frame, if he drew them foreground enough." For Hood, the aesthetic "improvement" on nature appears to be an innocuous activity. Earlier on he was "Scribbling in trees where none could exist; doing it now where they did seemed mere repetition" (62). Although the Dene are generally careful regarding mimetic processes, Greenstockings is willing to involve herself in the mirroring process. Allowing Hood to draw her, Greenstockings transgresses a cultural borderline since she believes that drawing reflects reality as transparently as does beholding one's mirror-image in a pool of water: "It's . . . really no different from looking in water, water makes pictures of us, all the time, you know it does." Her mother quickly deconstructs this notion, reminding her daughter that in "water often you have to see deeper than you want to. But the way These English make a picture . . . shows more . . . and less . . . " (38). Nevertheless, Greenstockings is fascinated by Hood's drawings of the landscape and of her.

Hood's drawings in fact propel the romance between Greenstockings and himself, and several critics describe the moment in chapter seven, in which the two of them are closest together and which "revolves around an existing drawing of the heroine Greenstockings" (Kaltemback 78-79), as the "literal and figurative centre of the novel" (Hoeppner 148). The relationship of Greenstockings and Hood represents the most genuine attempt at cross-cultural understanding in the novel, and related in the central chapter, marks the point in which self and reflection are closest to the mirror's glass.[6] Whereas the mirroring of chapters is rather abstract, the love scene explicitly foregrounds a non-verbal mirroring of cultures, in which, as Hoeppner suggests, the two lovers discover the strangeness of the other: "In this union of flesh, Greenstockings and Hood discover each other and they discover the strangeness of the 'other'" (148). I would emphasize, however, that the non-verbal mirroring at this point gives preference to cultural similarity given that the courtship of the two seems to follow generic,western gender roles, for example, when Greenstockings "cooks her favourite food for Hood" and later removes lice from his hair (157). I believe that the non-verbal mirroring replicates minutely the problematic epistemology of conceptual metaphor in its drive to similarity, its propensity for construing domains in terms of identity. Hood literally shapes "his" Greenstockings through the act of mirroring: He "laughs to see her laugh, to make her laugh again, to lengthen the sound of her singing voice. Not understanding a syllable of any word she has ever spoken. And not wanting to" (157-58). He further insists that he "does not want to understand any word she ever speaks. None. The freedom of watching, of listening with incomprehension, fills him with staggering happiness" (158). Greenstockings mirrors the sentiment: "she will tell him anything, whatever has always been unspeakable, his incomprehension gives her freedom" (159). Despite the fact that they both do not really want to comprehend what the other is saying, both would like to be understood, however. Witness Hood's laughable attempt to describe a horse: "I can walk to Bury in two hours, get off the eight-horse coach in Manchester and be—that's silly, you've never seen a horse!—a kind of . . . ridable caribou, without antlers!—but heavier, more like a movable tree than a caribou!" (159). The dish Greenstockings later prepares for him tastes "like haggis" (simile again). The mirroring continues with Greenstockings teaching him how to survive in the wilderness; he teaches her to eat with a spoon, which for Greenstockings becomes his name because of the phonetic similarity—"oo oo oo," as in Hood; her name is, in turn, metonymic since she is called Greenstockings on account of the stockings she receives from Hood (for which see also Omhovere 86; Hoeppner 148).

As the mirroring of cultures becomes more intense, several faultlines emerge, which shatter the mirror image that reflects Hood to/as Greenstockings and vice versa: "He leans closer to Greenstockings, his words such sibilant sound, while they both stare intently into the fire, both bent forwards but aware only (she thinks, he thinks) of each other side by side, the leaping fire that draws them together without touching" (160). The passage anticipates the surrender of the mirror. The mirroring is seemingly perfect, save for certain inconsistencies in the articulation; for example, would not an actual mirror reflect "she thinks" as "thinks he"? Such inconsistencies are more obvious in the general mirroring indicated above (of first chapter with thirteenth, of second chapter with twelfth, etc.), where the reflection concerns isolated aspects and never the complete picture, eventually testifying to the autonomy of the domains resistant to metaphorizing. When Hood's pencil finally drops, the mirroring of cultures stops for him—although one critic maintains that he "learns to listen with his body" initiating a "communion of bodies" (Hoeppner 148). Considering that Hood dies in the end because he does not listen to his body poses a problem for such interpretations. Rather, I think, what is at stake is the destruction of the mirror which is the only lens through which the other culture appears to make sense; without cultural mirroring, Dene culture would remain intangible. What Hood thus surrenders at the end is the process of understanding itself. This emerges in his remark upon the "austerity of ice, unnecessary to number or explain or record—or struggle to mirror somehow in a lined notebook" (159). A little later, Greenstockings gives up the mirror, too: "Her brown hands bright as glass rise together around his face and pull him over, his head down in her lap" (174, emphasis added). Nota bene, her hands are described by means of simile rather than metaphor. The "death of the mirror" here becomes the death of cultural representation. Without metaphor, cultures cannot be represented. With metaphors, cultures can be mapped, but this novel engages head-on with the complexities of such mapping by the "mirroring" of chapters and the emphasis of simile over metaphor. The narrator's (or perhaps Wiebe's) preference for metonymy over metaphor opens up the investigation of metaphoric mapping into the realm of conceptual allegory.

————————— • —————————

To talk of metonymies with reference to the many similes used in *A Discovery of Strangers* may be misleading in that the term is applied differently than in rhetorical theory—or conceptual metaphor theory, for that matter. In CMT, tropes such as metonymy, synecdoche, allegory, and so on, are more or less categorized as a subgroup of metaphor, whereby metonymy is understood as a mapping within one domain rather than across domains (Lakoff and Johnson, *Metaphors* 35-40; Lakoff, *Women* 77-90; Kövecses 143-62). In the few CMT studies that explicate the relationship between metaphor and metonymy in greater detail, metonymy emerges as describing a very different mapping process, however. To grasp the different conceptual mode of metonymy, one is well advised to revisit the work of Roman Jakobson, who believed that poetics and linguistics were mutually dependent discursive modes ("What Is Poetry"). In Jakobson's famous distinction between metaphor and metonymy, the latter denotes *contiguity* rather than *continuity*; his theory of the metaphoric and metonymic poles, the syntagmatic and paradigmatic axis respectively, probably requires little by way of explanation given its prominent treatment in the scholarly (and fictional) works of David Lodge ("Two Aspects"; see Lodge esp. 74). While Jakobson's theories, particularly for linguists, may seem outdated, the different mapping processes at work in metaphor and metonymy can be well illustrated within Jakobson's theoretical framework,[7] and thus point up again how studies in cognitive linguistics are forward-oriented to the extent that the history of the discipline itself is only rarely considered. Admittedly, CMT acknowledges that the relationship between metaphor and metonymy is problematic. Cameron and Low, for instance, believe that "One direction for future applied linguistics research ... needs to be the development of empirical techniques for disentangling metonymy from metaphor, and for coping analytically with complex situations where the two cannot easily be separated" (83); Jakobson himself had cautioned his audience with regard to the exclusiveness of the terms *metaphor* and *metonymy*: "In poetry, where similarity is superinduced upon contiguity, any metonymy is slightly metaphoric and any metaphor has a metonymic tint" ("Linguistics and Poetics" 42). Jakobson's view of the relationship between metaphor and metonymy is instructive for CMT insofar as it demonstrates that metonymy does not represent a mapping process within one domain, but rather a mapping process capable of main-

taining domains, as René Dirven has shown. He argues that Jakobson's definition of metonymy (in terms of contiguity rather than continuity) illustrates
that metonymic mappings, unlike their metaphoric counterparts, retain the
two involved domains:

> in metonymy the two domains both remain intact, but they
> are to be seen in line, whereas in metaphor only one do-
> main ... is kept and the other domain ... disappears ... by
> mapping elements of the ... source domain onto the tar-
> get domain, the source domain itself ceases to exist. This is
> completely different in metonymy. Therefore, contiguity in
> metonymy can be defined as the existence, side by side, of
> two domains. ...("Metonymy and Metaphor" [1993] 14)[8]

As has been noted above, the narrator's descriptions of both Greenstockings's and Hood's perceptions of each other (and each other's cultures) overwhelmingly draw on simile rather than metaphor. This phenomenon appears
to be exclusive to those characters who are genuinely interested in comprehending otherness; often, the use of metaphor serves to underline a different
stance towards the conception of otherness. While Hood's way of mirroring
culture is "metonymic," underscoring his attempted discovery of "strangeness," his "rival" Back, who is less interested in understanding the other (and
more interested in exploiting the other), generally refers to Greenstockings
(and Dene culture) metaphorically.[9] An illustrative example of the different
conceptualization of Greenstockings in the minds of Back and Hood can be
seen in their ways of describing her. At some point, both men compare her to
a Madonna. Back describes her metaphorically as "a leather Madonna lifting
water"; Hood says about her face that it "floats golden in the firelight, serene
as a madonna" (56, 175)—using a simile and rendering his Madonna a little
less stereotypically, perhaps, by virtue of lower case letters. In rhetorical theory and conceptual metaphor theory, metonymy and simile are usually seen as
different tropes. Conceptually, I believe, though, simile and metonymy represent similar, if not identical mapping processes; after all, as Cameron and Low
emphasize, "the existence of the similarity marker (e.g. *like, as if,* or *as*) flags
the fact that a direct identification is *not* being made" (83), which implies that
the source domain involved in the mapping process does not disappear, as it
does in conceptual metaphors. *A Discovery of Strangers*, then, represents the
processes of cross-cultural communication and understanding by means of
two mapping processes that work in radically different ways. That provided,
the novel becomes less of a *megametaphor*—a metaphorizing of one culture
in terms of another that is consistent throughout the novel. I would rather see

in Wiebe's differentiation an exploration of the epistemological problems of mapping processes as such, whereby the trope capable of maintaining both metaphoric and metonymic mappings is conceptual allegory. The novel, I believe, offers conceptual allegory as a viable alternative to conceptual metaphor due to its potential to encompass both mono-directional and bi-directional mappings in which it is possible, but not necessary, that the source domain disappears.

Etymologically, allegory is defined as saying one thing and meaning another (Fletcher, *Allegory* 2), as representing one thing by means of another—a process that is *prima facie* no different from metaphorical mapping (Lanham 4; Lausberg 441-42).[10] Recent work in rhetoric has increasingly resurrected the complexity and ambiguity (Laird; Miller) associated with the trope of *other-speak* already in classical rhetorical manuals, most prominently in Quintilian's definition of *allegory* as riddle and contradiction (8.6.52, 8.6.57). For readers of Wiebe's novel, allegory literally becomes *other-speak* in that it reinforces the quintessential otherness of literature (LITERATURE IS OTHER, as stated by Holland), which, for Wiebe, becomes the quintessential otherness of all cultures as well as the otherness within seemingly homogeneous culture. As a conceptual tool, allegory may represent mapping processes not altogether different from conceptual metaphor or metonymy; however, it is epistemologically expandable, as emerges from Michael Sinding's work on allegory. In his "Assembling Spaces: The Conceptual Structure of Allegory," Sinding attests to the fact that "while CMT had something to say about other rhetorical figures that are one-way mappings . . . it foundered on more complex ones." Emphasizing that allegory is "a kind of blending, a complex conceptual operation akin to metaphor" (504, 505), he subsequently illustrates that blending can express hidden meanings directly and veil other meanings at the same time. For Sinding, allegory is much more than simple parallelism or a "clean" mapping of one domain onto another. In contrast to metaphor, he perceives allegory as a scene: "To turn a sentence into an allegory, we must imagine entailments as participants in a rich scene, with a fictional existence. To do this, we must blend mapping elements and structure with the generic structure of a coherent scene, which we abstract from the space of everyday experience" (510). He concludes that:

> Allegory's global secondary reference constitutes an extended metaphor, or other-speech. This metaphor is also "extended" by numerous sub-metaphors, including personifications. But positing bi-level "correspondence" is doubly intractable: some details defy allegorization and some dis-

course makes allegorization superfluous. BT's [blending theory's] model of a networked but autonomous central blend space guided by a main topic accommodates this and other recalcitrant issues. That the topic *can* be the target of the dominant metaphor explains the persistent sense that allegory "is" an extended metaphor. That the blend can be linked to many spaces answers the fact that allegories are not *just* source-target "correspondences," but indeed integrate material from theory, culture, inner and outer experience, and more. (516-17)

My discussion of Wiebe's novel and its metaphorizing or metonymizing of other cultures represents precisely the complexities inherent in the multifarious mapping processes Sinding finds at work in what I would call conceptual allegory. The novel recognizes the necessity of metaphoric mappings, even if they ultimately foster a decidedly ill-advised sense of identity, where source and target domains overlap punctually. Simultaneously, *A Discovery of Strangers* highlights those mapping processes which I characterized as inherently metonymic, which map items from one domain onto another without the disappearance of the source domain—a mapping process that maintains domains as separate, enabling the discovery of otherness without the former eliminating the latter. The inclusion of Dene mythology attempts to preserve Mühlhäusler's "alternative metaphorical systems," the "impeding loss" of which may include "a large number of alternative (lateral from our perspective) ways of interpreting the world and ways of solving some of the political, scientific and ecological problems found in it." The promotion of "genuine interdisciplinary perspectives," Mühlhäusler concludes, is necessary to avoid misrepresentation (287). That Wiebe engages in the process of allegorizing both 1820s explorer culture and Dene mythology has been seen as an essentialist act;[11] and yet, without this act, cultural communication, in the light of cognitive theory, seems unlikely to occur. The important guidance offered to other such attempts lies in the carefully-crafted conceptual allegory emphasizing difference *and not* identity.

——————— • ———————

In the foregoing, I hope to have shown that Rudy Wiebe's A Discovery of Strangers provides an instructive example of how literary texts can be used in English literature classrooms in order to investigate the wider implications of conceptual mapping processes increasingly employed in teaching vocabulary and idioms in second and foreign language acquisition scenarios—processes that, as conceptual metaphor theory has it, are indispensable also to understanding otherness, whether linguistic or cultural. The latter seems particularly timely given the recent complication of CMT in the disciplines of anthropology and cultural studies. As a philosophical argument about the Rule of Metaphor and its attendant problems of constructing identity where none exists, the novel invites readers to reflect upon cognitive theories of understanding. On the one hand, the novel illustrates the inevitability of conceiving otherness (be it within one's own culture or other cultures) in terms of one's own cultural background, that is, by means of conceptual metaphor. On the other hand, the novel questions the ideological underpinnings of conceptual metaphor by offering divergent ways of perceiving and constructing otherness qua metonymic mappings, in which cross-cultural communications and cross-cultural understanding may entail a high degree of ambivalence without ultimately rendering strangeness in terms of the familiar. The novel offers similarity (metonymy, strangeness) as the middle ground between the seeming transparency of metaphor (identity, familiarity) and the opacity of utter dissimilarity. Hence, Wiebe's novel discovers strangeness by means of conceptual allegory, imparting several domains or layers which readers can construct as partially identical, similar, or radically dissimilar. While the novel's proposition of conceptual allegory as an epistemological tool for conceiving otherness may not be unique to Wiebe's novel, A Discovery of Strangers does foreground issues of cultural representation by means of cognitive and conceptual models: whether this is likewise true of other prairie writers' conceptualizations of otherness remains yet to be discovered.

Notes

1. Lakoff and Johnson's emphasis on the epistemological role of metaphor is anticipated, if not already formulated, by Olney who maintains that "Metaphor is essentially a way of knowing. New sensory experiences—or their consequence, emotional experience—must be formulated in the mind before one can grasp and hold them, before one can understand them and add them to the contents of knowledge and the complex of the self. . . .This is the psychological basis of the metaphorizing process: to grasp the unknown through the known, or to let the known stand for the unknown and thereby fit that into an organized, patterned body of experiential knowledge. A metaphor, then, through which we stamp our own image on the face of nature, allows us to connect the known of ourselves to the unknown of the world, and, making available new relational patterns, it simultaneously organizes the self into a new and richer entity"

(31-32).

2. They are quick to add that "In general the major orientations up-down, in-out, central-peripheral, active-passive, etc., seem to cut across all cultures, but which concepts are oriented which way and which orientations are most important vary from culture to culture" (*Metaphors* 24).

3. For a comprehensive list of CMT approaches to literary discourse, see Cameron and Low.

4. Lenk believes that CMT may provide a podium for what she calls "interdisziplinäre Anglistik" [interdisciplinary English Studies] (esp. 66-67). While she demonstrates that CMT approaches to literature insightfully extend data for metaphor usage, these findings are, in her own words, limited to specific "facets." The extent to which literary texts may contribute to an understanding, even a critique of CMT, remains unaddressed, however.

5. Such a reading of a literary text extends metaphor—that is, the figural language which constitutes literary texts (Lakoff and Johnson, *Metaphors*)—beyond the text itself into the realm of a more general application of conceptual metaphor theory. Wiebe's novel is metaphoric in that, structurally corresponding to CMT, it maps one domain onto another domain with the purpose of understanding the one in terms of the other. My brief account of the novel substantiates that there are innumerable instances in which the one-to-one correspondences between the domains of Dene and white culture do not work. Thus, Wiebe's novel oscillates between Jakobson's metaphoric *and* metonymic poles.

6. In a sense, this marks a structural metaphor along the two complementary reading axes identified by Frye (and the conceptual metaphor LIFE IS A JOURNEY): "Following a narrative is a metaphorical journey, and the journey is metaphorically horizontal, going from here to there. Coming to the end, and trying to understand what we have read, introduces a vertical metaphor of looking up and down" (*Words with Power* 95).

7. In fact, Jakobson himself sees his project in far more extensive terms than as restricted to workings of language—the dichotomy evinced in the opposition of metaphor and metonymy he believes to be of consequence for "all verbal behavior and for human behavior in general," anticipating the cognitive ("Linguistics and Poetics" 256). Dirven rightly points out that this critical neglect is surprising and he consequently envisions the potential for Jakobson's theories within conceptual metaphor theories. Jakobson uses these categories for generic distinctions between poetry and prose: "Thus, for poetry, metaphor, and for prose, metonymy is the

line of least resistance and, consequently, the study of poetical tropes is directed chiefly toward metaphor. The actual bipolarity has been artificially replaced by an amputated, unipolar scheme" ("Two Aspects" 259). Moreover, "It is no mere chance that metonymic structures are less explored than the field of metaphor. Allow me to repeat my old observation that the study of poetic tropes has been directed mainly toward metaphor, and the so-called realistic literature, intimately tied to the metonymic principle, still defies interpretation, although the same linguistic methodology that poetics uses when analyzing the metaphorical style of romantic poetry is entirely applicable to the metonymical texture of realistic prose" ("Linguistics and Poetics" 47).

8. In a revised version of the paper, Dirven complicates this view. He adds that "in spite of these fundamental differences between metonymy and metaphor, and the contiguity-similarity dichotomy underlying them, we have as yet no explanation for the fact that both mapping processes, however different they may be, can lead to new figurative meanings" ("Metonymy and Metaphor" [2003] 91). Like Dirven, Antonio Barcelona ("Clarifying" 223-26) concedes that metonymy is a mapping process, stressing that the *metonymic mapping* is *asymmetrical* compared to the symmetrical metaphorical mapping. Much of this is anticipated by Northrop Frye's analyses of biblical reading practice, which unfold analogously to Jakobson's paradigmatic axis (metonymy) in opposition to the syntagmatic axis (metaphor): "The basis of expression . . . is moving from the metaphorical, with its sense of identity of life or power or energy between man and nature ('this is that'), to a relationship that is rather metonymic ('this is put for that'). Specifically, words are 'put for' thoughts, and are the outward expressions of an inner reality. . . . Thus metonymic language is, or tends to become, analogical language, a verbal imitation of a reality beyond itself that can be conveyed most directly by words" (*Great Code* 7-8).

9. Maria Frühwald observes that "Hood, who at least attempts to understand the foreign, 'natural' way of life of the Dene, dies in the end, and with him, it seems, dies the last attempt at decency on the part of the European colonizers" (141).

10. Beginning with the popular definition of allegory as extended metaphor, Boucher anticipates the metonymic structure of allegory as I see it: "Since both metonymy and metaphor are tropes that twist meaning and speakother, then allegory, or particular kinds of allegory, such as typology, may consist of continued metonymy" (130).

11. For discussions of Wiebe's problematic representation and appropriation of the indigene, see Tefs and Woodcock; for a short discussion of the debate also with regard to *A Discovery of Strangers*, see Frühwald 133-35. For more positive evaluations of Wiebe's representational strategies, cf. Beck 861-63 and Clunie.

Michael J. Gilmour

•

Going Back to the Prairies:
Neil Young's Heterotopia in the Post-9/11 World

> Just as poets and novelists describe, painters paint, and ge-
> ographers analyze landscapes, so many composers of or-
> chestral music represent landscapes (and waterscapes) that
> are real, imagined, or mythical and reveal an awareness of
> various physical and human processes and attachments to
> place.
>
> David B. Knight, *Landscapes in Music:*
> *Space, Place, and Time in the World's Great Music* (vii)

David B. Knight provides a fascinating exploration of ways "compos-
ers have represented, structured, and symbolized real, imagined, and
mythical landscapes in their tonal compositions" (210). Though his
book focuses on classical, orchestral music the general line of inquiry Knight
pursues presents an intriguing option for analysis of the lyrical, popular music
compositions of Neil Young. I offer here a modest proposal regarding Neil
Young's 2005 album *Prairie Wind*, suggesting that attention to the real and
imagined geographies found in these songs provide helpful clues for understanding this album as, in part, a response to the traumas of 9/11.

When thinking about the complexities of everyday life, there is a tendency in the human sciences to focus on historical/temporal and social/relational
elements. However, in recent decades theorists have gradually introduced a
third dimension to their reflections on individual and collective behaviour.
Such thinkers as Henri Lefebvre and Michel Foucault urge those seeking
knowledge of the human condition to consider spatiality along with historical
and social contexts. Building on their insights, Edward W. Soja observes "a
growing awareness of the simultaneity and interwoven complexity of the social, the historical, and the spatial, their inseparability and interdependence"
(3). Through such terms as space and spatiality, these theorists indicate more
than physical locations that can be identified on maps and include imagined
and symbolic locations as well. In Neil Young's *Prairie Wind* songs, we find the
artist responding to the traumas experienced in real space by turning to an
imagined one, a place offering solace and a venue for political commentary.

In what follows, I turn to Soja's *Thirdspace: Journeys to Los Angeles and Other Real-and-Imagined Places* for general methodological direction.

I acknowledge at the outset that an analysis of song lyrics fits uneasily in a collection of essays largely concerned with novelists and poets. Literary scholarship rarely takes notice of songwriters. The academic fascination with Bob Dylan—a songwriter even nominated for the Nobel Prize for Literature—is perhaps an exception that proves the rule.[1] There are many reasons for this tendency to distinguish song lyrics from serious poetic writing. There is the challenge of definition, for one thing. Poems intended for readers are different in kind from songs written for musical accompaniment. Furthermore, there is the inevitable tendency to distinguish accessible art forms intended for mass consumption from the complexities of sophisticated, text-based poetry.[2] Put bluntly, many view rock songs as mere lowbrow, mass entertainment without qualitative merit, even though this strict demarcation of what constitutes valuable art forms is diminishing. A number of scholars now recognize what Linda Hutcheon refers to as a "bridging of the gap between élite and popular art" as well as "postmodernism's attraction to popular art forms" (20). Without belabouring the point, this paper proceeds with the assumption that while Neil Young is not a poet in the traditional sense, his work is poetic nonetheless. Like all good poetry, his writing suggests new possibilities for imagining the world and the relationships experienced in it.

Though this is not the place to rehearse in any detail the story of the Canadian-born Neil Young's remarkable career, there is a key biographical note necessary for the argument that follows. Young has a childhood connection to the Canadian prairies, specifically Winnipeg, Manitoba. He was born in Toronto in 1945, raised in the small town of Omemee, Ontario, and at the age of twelve moved to Winnipeg with his mother. It was from Winnipeg that Young set out on a musical journey toward the east, one that took him first through Fort William (now Thunder Bay) en route to Toronto, and then south to superstardom in the United States. Apparently, his relatively short time on the prairies left an impression on the songwriter. According to William Echard, Young treats wilderness spaces specifically, and the earth generally, as "a life-source." Furthermore, he often writes about "the countryside—not wilderness but agricultural land—as his own personal refuge" (205). This is an important connection for the following argument. Echard does not discuss *Prairie Wind* specifically—presumably, he completed his book before its release—but his comment remains pertinent for this album nonetheless. The emphasis on agricultural space is obvious in *Prairie Wind*, and reading this geography in Young's song writing as a "refuge" is particularly fitting, as the following remarks attempt to demonstrate. Earlier examples of Young's interest in referencing prairie spaces appear in various song and album titles (e.g., *Harvest* [1972]; "Thrasher" [1979]; *Harvest Moon* [1992]). His interest in the Farm Aid benefit concerts might also stem from a sense of connection to the rural landscapes of his youth. However, it is in *Prairie Wind* that this geographical connection comes to the fore. Here, the Canadian prairie becomes a dominant leitmotif that the singer infuses with symbolic import.

It is interesting to observe that Neil Young renewed his relationship with the Canadian prairies, specifically Manitoba, around the time of *Prairie Wind*'s release. He agreed to perform at the Juno Awards, the Canadian equivalent of the Grammy Awards, on the condition that Winnipeg host the event (which the City did on April 3, 2005). As it turned out, Young was unable to attend due to a health crisis (an aneurysm) but eventually made good on his promise to visit the city, performing with David Crosby, Stephen Stills, and Graham Nash on July 14, 2006. On that occasion, the Province honoured Young with induction to The Order of Manitoba.

Young's apparent affection for this real space allows this geographical context to serve as a kind of lyrical refuge, specifically one helping the artist cope with the traumas of 9/11 and its aftermath.[3] In the songs of *Prairie Wind*, Young returns home to this geographical space, "his Canadian prairie home," to use the language of the song "One of These Days" (*Harvest Moon*, 1992). The prairies are a literal space that takes on symbolic value, a place where singer and audience can find solace and reorientation.

Michel Foucault introduced the idea of heterotopias to theoretical discussions about space and spatiality in a lecture given in 1967.[4] Foucault contrasts utopias—"sites with no real place" that present society itself in a perfected form but that do not exist—with what he calls "counter-sites," a kind of "effectively enacted utopia" by which all the real sites that can be found within a culture are simultaneously represented, contested, and inverted (24). These counter-sites, unlike utopias, do in fact exist, though their location is difficult to pinpoint. Foucault continues:

> Because these places are absolutely different from all the sites that they reflect and speak about, I shall call them, by way of contrast to utopias, heterotopias. I believe that between utopias and these quite other sites, these heterotopias, there might be a sort of mixed, joint experience, which would be the mirror. The mirror is, after all, a utopia, since it is a placeless place. In the mirror, I see myself there where I am not, in an unreal, virtual space that opens up behind

the surface; I am over there, there where I am not, a sort of shadow that gives my own visibility to myself, that enables me to see myself there where I am absent: such is the utopia of the mirror. But it is also a heterotopia in so far as the mirror does exist in reality, where it exerts a sort of counteraction on the position that I occupy. From the standpoint of the mirror I discover my absence from the place where I am since I see myself over there. Starting from this gaze that is, as it were, directed toward me, from the ground of this virtual space that is on the other side of the glass, I come back toward myself; I begin again to direct my eyes toward myself and to reconstitute myself there where I am. The mirror functions as a heterotopia in this respect: it makes this place that I occupy at the moment when I look at myself in the glass at once absolutely real, connected with all the space that surrounds it, and absolutely unreal, since in order to be perceived it has to pass through this virtual point which is over there. (24)

Foucault's interesting use of a mirror's image presents the possibility of places simultaneously "absolutely real" and "absolutely unreal," from which to gaze on one's self. Young's prairies, as found in the 2005 songs, accomplish this mirror effect. They are real, physical, named spaces but also idealized constructs that allow for a kind of reconstitution of self and society.

Subsequent dialogues with Foucault's ideas explore the concept of spatiality as a vehicle for both self-reflection and forms of resistance. David Harvey, for one, describes heterotopias as "spaces of liberty outside of social control" (230) and for Kevin Hetherington, they are "places of alternate ordering" (41). Foucault's distinction between utopias (which are unreal) and heterotopias (which are more real) is instructive for Soja as well, who finds in these other places a conceptualization "that resonates" with what he calls the geography of Thirdspace (157).

For the present, I am particularly interested in Foucault's idea of a mirror's reflection as actual space, "a heterotopia in so far as the mirror does exist in reality." Neil Young's *Prairie Wind* develops the kind of self-reflexive space Foucault describes, permitting Young to "reconstitute" himself through the idealization of prairie space. For Foucault, one possible function for heterotopias is to "create a space that is other, another real space, as perfect, as meticulous, as well arranged as ours is messy, ill constructed, and jumbled" (27). This is a heterotopia of compensation. Foucault illustrates this last point by describing the carefully organized seventeenth-century Puritan societies that regulated all aspects of day-to-day life. They were, in effect, "absolutely perfect other places." The world of Neil Young's *Prairie Wind* creates its own "other place," one that stands in sharp contrast to the chaotic, violent, urban landscapes of the post-9/11 world, with its warmongering and restless anxiety.

Before looking at *Prairie Wind*, a few remarks about Soja's understanding of space are in order, as it provides a useful theoretical framework for reflecting on Neil Young's album. For Soja, space is tripartite in nature. He identifies Firstspace epistemologies as those focused on the analytical deciphering of material or materialized spatiality (74). Firstspace spatiality incorporates absolute and relative locations "of things and activities, sites and situations," in short, "the concrete and mappable geographies of our lifeworlds," from emotional and behavioural spaces to the social practices of households, communities, and nations. Firstspace epistemologies "tend to privilege objectivity and materiality, and to aim toward a formal science of space" (75). Firstspace is materialized, socially produced, and empirical space, which together Soja refers to—following Lefebvre—as *perceived* space, the kind of space that is measurable and describable (66).

Secondspace epistemologies, by contrast, often emerge in response to the "excessive closure" and overstated objectivity of Firstspace analyses, "pitting the artist versus the scientist or engineer, the idealist versus the materialist, the subjective versus the objective interpretation" (78). By the term Secondspace, Soja indicates the artist "re-presenting the world in the image of their subjective imaginaries" and this is not without effect. The imagined geographies of Secondspace tend "to become the 'real' geography, with the image or representational coming to define and order the reality" (79). Secondspaces, according to Soja, are *conceived* spaces that contain the conceptualized world of planners and scientists and artists. Such spaces are subject to control; they are dominating spaces, representing power and ideology, control and surveillance (67).

Finally, by the term Thirdspace, Soja indicates a further way of conceptualizing the spatiality of human life, and one capable of fomenting change. Whereas Firstspace ways of thinking emphasize concrete, mappable spaces, and Secondspace analyses are concerned with re-imagining and re-presenting that spatiality, Thirdspaces arise from "the sympathetic deconstruction and heuristic reconstitution of Firstspace-Secondspace duality," leading to a reopening and rethinking of spatiality, and "a radical skepticism toward all established epistemologies, all traditional ways of confidently obtaining knowledge of the world" (81). Thirdspaces are *lived* spaces where one can evaluate and re-imagine real and imagined spaces as counterspaces. They are sites "of resistance to the dominant order arising precisely from their subordinate, peripheral or marginalized positioning" (68). Thirdspaces involve the breakdown and disordering of rigid dichotomies in an attempt to create "an alternative 'postmodern geography' of political choice and radical openness attuned to making practical sense of the contemporary world" (63).

For Soja, this thirding of space, as he calls it (i.e., the introduction of a third way of imagining human sociality and spatiality by moving beyond the dichotomy of real and imagined spaces, or First and Second Spaces), involves the combination of the real and imagined, and a privileging and implied preference for the third category. This last step, this privileging of the third category, is a "political choice, the impetus of an explicit political project, that gives special attention and particular contemporary relevance to the spaces of representation, to *lived space as a strategic location* from which to encompass, understand, and potentially transform all spaces simultaneously" (68; italics original). Soja's insistence that the exploration of Thirdspace stems from some form of "emancipatory *praxis*, the translation of knowledge into action in a conscious—and consciously spatial—effort to improve the world in some significant way" (22) is significant for this reading of the lyrics in *Prairie Wind*. Young's writing moves well beyond an interest in the mappable Canadian prairies, and his re-presentation and re-imagining of this particular geographical space involves the articulation of a new way of seeing the world.[5] He offers a critique of what he believes to be bad government decisions and invites listeners to look at the world differently, to change their values, to come to the prairies, as it were. This critique and invitation is a form of praxis accompanying a renewed vision of space. I illustrate what this praxis might look like in an interpretive paraphrase of lines from "When God Made Me" in the table below.

Prairie Wind evokes numerous prairie images, some general (e.g., farmers, wind, buffalos, trains on straight prairie railroads), others specific, recalling Young's days in Winnipeg during the late 1950s and early 1960s — "the Red River still flows through my hometown" ("It's A Dream"); "Goin' back to Cypress River [Manitoba], back to the old farmhouse" ("Prairie Wind"). In the concert DVD *Neil Young: Heart of Gold*, which features songs from *Prairie Wind*, Young prefaces "Four Strong Winds" by Canadian songwriter Ian Tyson with comments about Winnipeg "where I grew up" and "Falcon Lake," a popular holiday destination just east of the Manitoba capital. For Young, the prairies come to represent a return to a time of simplicity, innocence, and safety known in his childhood/youth and desperately missed in the post-9/11 world. Indeed, that tragedy, and the subsequent military responses to it are prominent in Young's most recent work. The heroic efforts of passengers on United Airlines Flight 93 to subdue hijackers are the inspiration behind "Let's Roll" (released on *Are You Passionate?* [2002]), and the later *Living With War* (May 2, 2006) and *Living With War—In The Beginning* (November 27, 2006) represent Young's more overt commentary on the United States' foreign policy since September 2001. Young's political views are relatively subtle in *Prairie Wind* when compared to *Living With War*, sounding a more introspective note, one concerned to find personal peace in troubled times. Still, it remains a politically engaged collection of songs. The album is both a reaction to the attacks that occurred on American soil in 2001 and the invasion of Iraq in the years following.

Prairie Wind opens with "The Painter," a song about a female character functioning, by all appearances, as Young's muse. She is able to bring order out of chaos, an idea suggested by her ability to harmonize colours picked from the air: green-to-green, red-to-red, yellow-to-yellow, and so on. The songwriter needs her because he fears he "might get lost" during his travels in turbulent days ("a long road ahead"). Where does she lead him? This muse-Painter takes the album's narrator back to the prairies, reintroducing colour and contentment to an otherwise troubled life. Following this opening song's invocation, the world he rediscovers in *Prairie Wind* includes music (guitars and piano in "The Old Guitar"[6] and "Far From Home"), family (mother, daddy, uncle, sisters), nostalgia (Elvis in "He Was The King"), and perhaps even simple faith ("the old church on the hill" in "No Wonder"). Significantly, the singer embraces this return to his roots, giving instructions to "bury me on the prairie / where the buffalo used to roam . . . cause then I won't be far from home" ("Far From Home"). This retreat to comforting prairie spaces is necessary because "that song from 9/11" keeps ringing in his head ("No Wonder").

The return to prairie life pictured in these songs develops various implied binaries such as urban/rural, pride/modesty, greed/generosity, and ostentatious wealth/simplicity. This is not the first time Young has addressed politics and social justice issues in his songs, of course.[7] His strategy for articulating his views on this particular album involves introducing the term "prairie" as a contrast to various other "places" where abuses originate, such as institutional religion ("When God Made Me") and centres of political power like the Senator's office mentioned in "No Wonder."

Throughout *Prairie Wind*, the Canadian landscape of Young's songs alternate between First, Second, and Thirdspaces. There are unambiguous geographical markers—proper names—that recall concrete, real-world Firstspaces:

The Red River still flows through my hometown ("It's A Dream")

> Goin' back to Cypress River ("Prairie Wind")
>
> Walkin' Down the Trans-Canada Highway ("Far From Home")

However, the prairie-scape of this album, with its recurring references to clichéd signs of the North American plains—buffalo, wheat, wind, old churches—is mostly, and logically, an artistic Secondspace, a re-imagining and re-presenting of distant memories. So completely reworked is the prairie space of this album that the singer openly acknowledges his revisionist tendencies. For instance, he is aware of a place on the prairie "where evil and goodness play" but he deliberately ignores potential corruption of this space. "Daddy told me all about it," he recalls, "but I never heard a word he said" ("Prairie Wind"). Young is constructing, here and throughout *Prairie Wind*, what amounts to a virtually Edenic, prelapsarian world, one distinct from the corrupted urban landscapes he wants to escape.

This implied accusation of moral lapse, and the tropes of a fall and loss of paradise are familiar in popular music. Bob Dylan's "Gates of Eden" is a clear example of the integration of the Genesis garden imagery in songwriting, and Neil Young himself, with David Crosby, Stephen Stills, and Graham Nash turned Joni Mitchell's song "Woodstock," from her 1970 album *Ladies of the Canyon*, into an enormous hit. The latter includes the words, "Caught in the devil's bargain / . . . we've got to get ourselves / Back to the garden." Kelton Cobb points out that "Rock and roll, before it splintered into a multitude of niches in the 1980s, was heavy with the theme of lost paradise," citing among other examples, this line from Mitchell's song (211). Cobb also remarks on Young's 1979 song "Thrasher" (with Crazy Horse, *Rust Never Sleeps*), suggesting it echoes the longing to recover lost dreams in a way that recalls the plight of those expelled from the garden (211-12). This song strikes a "very Augustinian formula of confessing the many temptations and earthly pleasures that detour one who is yearning for something that is ultimately more satisfying" (212). Cobbs's remarks are helpful in that they demonstrate that statements about morality are somewhat commonplace in popular music generally, and found in Neil Young's work specifically. Furthermore, Young and some of his contemporaries operate with the spatiality of the Genesis garden/wilderness binary as a vehicle to articulate a kind of moral perspective. A morality is at issue when Neil Young invites us—those listening to *Prairie Wind*—to go to the prairies:

> I try to tell the people but they never hear a word I say
>
> They say there's nothin' out there but wheatfields anyway
>
> ("Prairie Wind")

What he is calling for is a kind of return to garden innocence.

As noted earlier, Soja argues that Thirdspaces involve "a radical skepticism toward all established epistemologies, all traditional ways of confidently obtaining knowledge of the world" (81). Despite the pastoral, musically gentle, and peaceful mood of *Prairie Wind*, Young's songs incorporate an understated yet sharp polemic against the United States Government's responses to the 9/11 disaster. I focus specifically for the following remarks on his song "No Wonder."

The songwriter seems unable to shake the memories of the 2001 attacks on the United States and the subsequent military reactions. He walks through a pasture, attempting to move "away from the pain" but at the same time "America the Beautiful (That song from 9/11) / Keeps ringin' in [his] head." Young does not actually sing the words "America the Beautiful" on either the *Prairie Wind* recording or the *Neil Young: Heart of Gold* DVD performance of the song, though it appears in the lyrics provided with the CD. If Young has in mind a specific performance of "America the Beautiful," it may be the stunning rendition by mezzo-soprano Denyce Grave during the prayer and remembrance service honouring victims of the 9/11 tragedy on September 14, 2001 at the Washington National Cathedral. This allusion clearly locates the song in a moment of grief and mourning. Young follows this line with another musical inspiration, this time one focusing on the violence following the 9/11 disaster. The phrase "I'm hearin' Willie singin' on the radio again" undoubtedly refers to Willie Nelson's antiwar song "Whatever Happened to Peace On Earth," written in protest against the United States' invasion of Iraq and first performed on January 3, 2004.[8] The lyrics to this song articulate a very clear perspective and political opinion regarding the Iraq invasion:

> How much oil is one human life worth
>
> . . . .
>
> We believe everything that they tell us
> They're gonna kill us
> So we gotta kill them first
> But I remember a commandment
> Thou shall not kill
>
> . . . .
>
> . . . don't confuse caring for weakness
> You can't put that label on me
> The truth is my weapon of mass protection
> And I believe truth sets you free[9]

Obviously, these lines allude to the questionable intelligence cited as justification for the Iraq invasion.

Young then introduces a third reference to contemporary popular culture, one that resonates with Nelson's criticisms of the post-9/11 American foreign policy: "I'll always remember something Chris Rock said." Comedian Chris Rock is one of the entertainment world's harsh critics of George W. Bush's presidency. Young may well be referring here to comments made by Rock when hosting the 77th Academy Awards ceremonies on February 27, 2005, during which he offered this criticism of the United States President.

> Bush did some things you could never get away with at your job, man. . . . Just imagine you worked at the Gap. You're $70 trillion behind on your register and then you start a war with Banana Republic 'cause you say they got toxic tank tops over there. You have the war, people are dying, a thousand Gap employees are dead, bleeding all over the khakis, you finally take over Banana Republic, and you find out they never made tank tops in the first place.[10]

Since Young released *Prairie Wind* on September 27, 2005, it is possible this is the "something Chris Rock said."

Young would add to this chorus of criticism about the flimsy evidence underlying the Iraq invasion in the album following *Prairie Wind*. In *Living With War* (2006), he wastes no time on subtlety. The song "Let's Impeach the President," opens with the words,

> Let's impeach the President for lying
> And misleading our country into war
> Abusing all the power that we gave him
> And shipping all our money out the door

This anti-Bush rant is not limited to this particular song. Young's website[11] even includes (at the time of writing) a clock indicating the days, hours, minutes, and seconds "Remaining For [The] Presidency." Young's recent work generally, and the *Prairie Wind* songs in particular, clearly present a political opinion. Said differently, these songs create a Thirdspace.

Neil Young is only one of many artists reacting to the horrors of 9/11 and the disastrous war in Iraq in the years following. While in *Prairie Wind* he urges listeners to "Ring Ring / The fallen soldier bells," many other musicians also use their lyrics to articulate their political opinions and anger at the destructive consequences of war. One recent example is Ozzy Osbourne's *Black Rain* (2007) which, though musically quite different from *Prairie Wind*, is politically sympathetic[12] and, like *Prairie Wind*, couched in spatial imagery. Osbourne's opposition to the British and American presence in Iraq is quite obvious: "What is the price of a bullet? / Another hole in the head / A flag draped over a coffin / Another soldier is dead / . . . Why are the children all marching / into the desert to die? / . . . War killing sons and daughters" ("Black Rain"). The recurring allusions to real/Firstspace tragedies (war in Iraq) stand alongside imagined spaces of liberation and peace. In one song he invites a lover to "lay your world on me" which implies he speaks from a different space, and in another he sings from a "no man's land" which he will not leave ("Not Going Away"). Osbourne's album illustrates Soja's spatial ideas rather well: *Black Rain* describes a real Firstspace (the actual war in Iraq) within Secondspace imaginative writing, to accomplish an ideological response to British and American foreign policy (Thirdspace, as the context of decon struction and critique, a venue to articulate his pacifism). Again, Thirdspaces are, as James W. Flanagan puts it in his summary of Soja's concept, spaces of "politics and ideology, where real and imagined are intertwined" (243).

Prairie Wind closes with the evocative "When God Made Me," a song com prised of various interrogatives followed with the title phrase. Here too we find the use of spatial terminology when the singer asks in the opening lines,

> Was he thinkin' about my country
> Or the color of my skin?
> Was he thinkin' 'bout my religion
> And the way I worshipped him?
> Did he create just me in his image
> Or every living thing?
>
> When God made me
> When God made me

This remarkable song questions the assumption that God aligns himself with any particular political, racial, or credal group, thus opening what we might consider a Thirdspace where deconstruction of Secondspace assumptions is possible and new valuation and praxis encouraged.

Young accomplishes this with gestures of solidarity and disruption of tra ditional binaries, ultimately moving beyond mere words to needed action: speak, see, and give compassion to "my fellow man." An interpretative para phrase of lines in "When God Made Me" allows us to see the Secondspace assumptions Young is questioning in this song as he looks at them from his Thirdspace perspective (see Table 1, page 218).

As noted earlier, Foucault uses the metaphor of a mirror's image to indi cate the simultaneity of "real" and "unreal" places as locations from which to gaze on self. Neil Young's *Prairie Wind* provides such a real/unreal location. The geography in these songs is both a real, physical, named space and an idealized construct allowing for a new way of imagining self and society. The prairies of these songs are heterotopias, by which Foucault, again, indicates space "that is other, another real space, as perfect, as meticulous, as well arranged as ours is messy, ill constructed, and jumbled" (27). In this idealized and symbolic prairie space, Young and his listeners escape turmoil. This is not a complete retreat. The symbolic prairie Neil Young creates in *Prairie Wind* is a Thirdspace, one reflecting his refusal and criticism of violent Secondspace ideologies. Exploration of Thirdspace, according to Soja, stems from some form of "emancipatory *praxis*, the translation of knowledge into action in a conscious—and consciously spatial—effort to improve the world in some significant way" (22). The compassion of "When God Made Me" articulates one possible alternative to the violence of both 9/11 and the military actions that followed that terrible event.

Notes

1. This is not to deny there is a lively, academic literature analyzing popular music. The difference between the scholarly energy directed at popular music compared to text-based literature is one of quantity, not quality. For theoretical considerations about the analysis of popular music widely, see Frith. For remarks about the unique position of the scholar-fan, see Echard, who attempts in his book about Neil Young "to make at least a small part of that implicit theory [used by academics] more explicit, but not to altogether abandon the position of the practically engaged fan" (3).

2. For helpful remarks regarding the separation of "low" and "high" art forms, and typical characteristics of each category, see Sheinbaum 23-25.

3. Young's wife Peggy suggests that the album is also a response to a health scare her husband faced around the time of recording (remarks made on the *Neil Young: Heart of Gold* DVD). In comments made during the concerts included in this DVD, Neil Young also mentions that his daughter moved out of the family home ("empty nest") around this time, and that his father recently passed away (the DVD is dedicated to his "Daddy"). Such candid, personal remarks open up the possibility that the writing and/or performances of the *Prairie Wind* songs involve attempts to find solace in his art.

4. This lecture did not appear in print until October 1984, posthumously published as "Des Espaces Autres" in the journal *Architecture-Mouvement-Continuité*. I cite Jay Miskowiec's English translation in this paper.

5. Young occasionally mentions his home country in his songs, as in the

reference to a nameless town in "north Ontario" in "Helpless" (*Deja Vu*, 1970) and the line about "going back to Canada" in "Journey Through The Past" (*Time Fades Away*, 1973) but generally his work is not particularly Canadian in content. Echard observes that "despite his early years as a Canadian and occasional passing reference to Canadian places, Canadian identity has never been a central theme in Young's work" (15).

6. Young's song about his sentimental attachment to an old musical instrument is consistent with his preference for vintage musical equipment. Echard, drawing on Paul Théberge, suggests old instruments provide a way of "sonically encoding nostalgia" (Echard 79; cf. 51-52). Young prefaces his performance of "This Old Guitar" on *Neil Young: Heart of Gold* by noting that the guitar he is playing is one that belonged to Hank Williams. There is also a picture of that guitar on the *Prairie Wind* liner notes.

7. Young is not rigid in his political positions. For instance, his apparent anti-Bush/anti-right/anti-Republican views of recent years contrast with his strong support for the Republican Ronald Reagan during the early 1980s. For discussion on this matter, see Echard 34, 40, 68.

8. Neil Young and Willie Nelson have known each other since the mid-1980s and together they developed the Farm Aid benefit concerts (see McDonough 600-02).

9. Taken from the official Willie Nelson website (http://www.willienelson.com). Nelson wrote these lines on Christmas Day, 2003.

10. Taken from *USA Today* (http://www.usatoday.com/life/movies/movieawards/oscars/2005-02-28-rock-rants_x.htm).

11. http://www.neilyoung.com

12. I say sympathetic, though I suspect Osbourne is a pacifist, whereas Young is not. Young is passionately opposed to the war in Iraq but not all military interventions, and therefore open to just-war scenarios. I base these remarks on the lyrics to Osbourne's *Black Rain* and comments made by Neil Young on *The Colbert Report* in an interview that first aired August 17, 2006 on The Comedy Network. In that interview, Young argues that the United States' military should focus its efforts on the search for terrorists, "especially terrorist leaders," and signals approval for the initial invasion of Afghanistan. The war against the Taliban, he argues, was "a real war" like World War II, with "a reason" for fighting.

Table 1

The Assumptions of Secondspace: Exclusiveness Questioned	The Possibility of Thirdspace: Inclusiveness Implied
the greater value of my country	the equal value of all countries
the greater value of my skin colour	the equal value of all skin colours
the greater value of my religion and the way I worship God	the equal value of all religions and all the ways people worship God
I alone am made in God's image	all are made in God's image
God is concerned for believers only	God is concerned for all, regardless of faith
God's plan includes wars fought in his name	God's plan does not include wars fought in his name
there is only one way to be close to God	there are many ways to be close to God
God gives the gift of love so we can choose [who to love]	God gives the gift of love so we will show love to all
God gives the gift of voice so some can silence me [when I see injustices?]	God gives the gift of voice and I should not keep silence [when I see injustices?]
God gives the gift of sight, not knowing what [despair and need?] I will see	God gives the gift of sight, knowing what [despair and need?] I will see
God gives me the gift of compassion but I am not obligated to help others	God gives me the gift of compassion and I am obligated to help others

Elspeth Tulloch

•

Screening the Outsider In/Out in NFB Adaptations of Western Canadian Literature

Although live-action film adaptations constitute a small body of the films produced wholly by the National Film Board of Canada (NFB), a significant number of those made in English explore the outsider's experience as originally portrayed in prairie literature, whether the short story or radio play. Given that there was little opportunity for making live-action drama at the NFB (as it opted to focus mainly on documentaries and to a lesser extent on animation), a pattern in the content selected for the even fewer live-action dramas made as adaptations is arguably significant. As Gary R. Bortolotti and Linda Hutcheon maintain, the interest in reiterating—through adaptation—a core narrative idea is a measure of its persistence and thus its success (450). Although the NFB's adaptations of the outsider's story are not based either on the same source text or on an identical core narrative but on different texts that provide varying perspectives on a common, often hurtful, and sometimes damaging social reality, these adaptations nevertheless serve as a barometer of the NFB's recurrent, if shifting, engagement with that reality.[1]

In these cases, rural and small town prairie life offers the NFB a pared-down world for exploring contexts for rejection and alienation in ways that may not always be historically accurate in their specific renderings but that nevertheless serve as powerful tropes for the situations of various types of outsider groups in broader Canadian society. My concern here is to examine the degree to which the outsider is integrated into the social narrative in four NFB adaptations of Western Canadian texts, two from the mid-twentieth century and two from the latter part, in an attempt to delineate patterns over time. I asked myself whether and how social diversity had been accentuated in these adaptations; whether and how the insider/outsider dichotomy had been sharpened, and to what end? In this line of questioning, difference between source text and film becomes an indicator of the political concern of the adapters, as Linda Hutcheon suggests in her recent *A Theory of Adaptation* (107).[2]

These questions are particularly relevant to pose regarding NFB adaptations, which have been largely unstudied (Dickinson 10, 11), as it has been argued that the NFB is "a site where the state's material practice of ideology is located" (Gittings 20).[3] In making programming choices, at least at the broader level, the NFB takes into consideration the federal government's engagement in various policy concerns. Recent scholarship has been putting more emphasis on examining links between government policy, cultural institutions, and cultural production, both in film (Dorland, Druick) and literature (Kamboureli and Miki). In this vein, Smaro Kamboureli affirms that it is a given that "there is a tight relationship—structural, ideological, and material—between cultural production and the representation of nation, between institutions producing and disseminating literature . . . and the apparatus of the state" (39). However, questions remain. How exactly is this relationship manifested in particular instances? How can it be delineated and, indeed, is it always as clearly evident or as tightly present as Kamboureli claims, especially ideologically? In examining NFB documentaries, Zoë Druick has argued that it is possible "to approach these films as engagements with state policy objectives, rather than as crude mouthpieces for them" (12). As the following close comparative readings show, while the NFB's selection and reworking of these literary texts are not audacious and while the adaptations can be read as reflecting general government interests in certain issues, neither are the film versions always and simply a pat and predictable rehashing of government discourse.[4]

Building on Himani Bannerji's interpretation of the politics of multiculturalism in Canada, Eva Mackey suggests that the undisputed insiders in Canadian society are of English or French extraction, with other inhabitants considered insiders only for the purposes of building and projecting a more holistic Canadian identity, one that embraces First Nations people and so-called multicultural immigrants (Bannerji 103-128, Mackey 14). National cultural institutions, such as the NFB, play a role in disseminating and shaping or attempting to shape these attitudes. While race, on which Bannerji is focused, is a significant factor in the ostracism of racialized others, cultural, ethnic, and language difference remain traits that members of the dominant culture may focus on to exclude newcomers. As Richard Dyer has observed, "some white people are whiter than others" (51).

This concern with the cruel differentiation between people of European origin is the focus of *Fires of Envy*, a half-hour film directed by Don Haldane and scripted by W. O. Mitchell for the *Perspective* series, which the NFB produced for the CBC in the late 1950s. Comprised mainly of documentaries or docudramas rather than adaptations, this series focused on wide-ranging issues of the day, including immigration (Clandfield 24; Evans 50-51). This particular episode, which was shot in 1956 and aired on CBC television on February 17, 1957, was adapted from W. O. Mitchell's radio play "Going to a Fire;" as such it had been twice broadcast on Mitchell's popular *Jake and the Kid* program on the CBC radio, first on January 13, 1952 and then again, with only minor changes, on January 25, 1953.[5] The various versions were thus developed during a renewed period of massive immigration; between 1946 and 1962 over two million immigrants would come to Canada, almost as many as during the large waves of the early part of the twentieth century (Kelley and Trebilcock 313). In particular, almost 100,000 displaced persons and refugees entered between April 1947 and March 1950, mainly from Eastern Europe (Burnet 41).

Although other Mitchell scripts from the radio series deal with forms of racial or social intolerance, Alan Yates, who has studied the series in detail, deems this particular episode to be the most compelling (110, 112). He is not alone in his assessment. For example, immediately following the airing of the script's first radio broadcast, the Executive Director of the Canadian Citizenship Council, John P. Kidd, wrote to congratulate the series' producer for a program that "packed a real punch."[6] Stating that it "beautifully and aptly portrayed some of the problems of some of our immigrants," he held out the hope that it would have "a positive effect on attitudes and actions of a number of people."[7] Arthur Irwin, then Commissioner of the NFB, took an active interest in the radio script, initiating the assessment process to determine whether, as he hoped, it could be turned into an NFB film.[8] Indeed, the script was one of Mitchell's personal favourites, the reason for his including it in story form in his later best-selling collection *According to Jake and the Kid* (1989).[9]

The film version may be situated within the broader context of the NFB documentary films treating issues of citizenship and immigration that Druick has identified in her research on the relationship between government policy and NFB productions (100-125). These issues came to the fore in the 1950s as Canada had finally legally assumed its power to create Canadian citizens in 1946, with the adoption of the first Canadian Citizenship Act. Concerned with the integration of large numbers of immigrants, including the many displaced persons following the Second World War, the government set up the Department of Citizenship and Immigration in 1950.[10] This publicly integrationist thrust follows a period when Canada, as a state, had harboured insecurities about Central European immigrants (Dowler 329-330) and communists. The latter fear was fed by the Gouzenko spy affair of 1945-46, which would unjustly taint the reputation of the NFB's founder, John Grierson. In the late 1940s, opposition Members of Parliament would charge the NFB with "harbour[ing] communist spies" (Evans 7), individuals that Film Commissioner Irwin was mandated with identifying upon his appointment in 1950, a task he did not relish (Evans 12-15). These Cold War anxieties would continue to shape immigration policy, putting Eastern Europeans low on a hierarchy of acceptability, quietly subjecting those with communist pasts to security controls (Whitaker 304). With this film adaptation, the NFB is attempting to present these less favoured immigrants, with whose possible political affinities the NFB is perceived to have had sympathies, in a more positive light.[11] The film's narrative is also picking up on another undercurrent of social opinion, anticipating the vision of "One Canada" and unhyphenated Canadianism that will help sweep John Diefenbaker to a landside victory in the 1958 federal election.[12]

Examining concepts of assimilation and citizenship as they become distorted by the local populace, the film, like the earlier radio play and the later short story, serves both as a cautionary tale about the tragic consequences of exclusion and a sermon on the basic equality of different European ethnicities. It recounts the growing jealousy of the small, fictional, town of Crocus, Saskatchewan towards Steve Kiziw, an immigrant farmer who is vaguely designated in all versions as "Central European" and who is enjoying unrivalled success, especially in acquiring land, while other farmers struggle. The community's escalating ill will is linked to the perceived inability of Kiziw and his wife to assimilate to the satisfaction of the locals, who are either of English descent or who have English loyalties and who support the preeminence of the English language and local customs. Against this rising tide of envious animosity stands the narrator-protagonist, who serves as a moral conscience. At the beginning of all versions he proudly proclaims that his community boasts "a mixture of people" from across Central and Eastern Europe and then, when describing the town's female elites, exposes the fallacy of English purity by gently poking fun at Aunt Lil's sense of being "pure English right down from William the Conqueror." However, this set up of a single Central European couple within a sea of English descendants and anglophiles is more emblematic of the situation of groups of post-war immigrants in larger English-speaking Canadian society than a realistic portrayal of a typical small Saskatchewan town of the 1950s, suggesting not only that Crocus is a "country of the imagination" (McLay 347), but that the particular plot conflict was created to address issues of more general import to Ontario, where, between 1948 and 1961, some 50 per cent of all immigrants were received compared to 17 per cent in the Prairies, a percentage that declined to 12 by 1961 (Kelley and Trebilcock 313).[13]

The film adaptation follows the radio play relatively closely (in particular the dialogue of the second broadcast, which made small additions to the first script). However, there are several significant alterations, revealing a shift in the way ethnicity and anti-immigrant feeling is broached, suggesting in turn a slightly different political slant. The most striking change is in the narrator-protagonist, with the substitution of the radio program's principal character Jake, an uneducated farmhand, for the well-spoken, small-town newspaper editor, Chet Lambert.[14] A secondary character in ten other *Jake and the Kid* radio plays, Lambert does not appear in the original "Going to a Fire" episode. Jake, whose language is decidedly colloquial, is completely cut from the film version, suggesting the discomfort among the adapters (most likely the director and/or producer) with an unrefined male lead carrying an important civic message and serving as a role model for the young boy (the Kid in the radio play, Gordie in the film), whose morals he nurtures. This change in narrator is perhaps in response to the fact that some of the "criticisms [of the radio series] were leveled at the portrayal of prairie townsfolk as 'country hicks'" (Yates 322).[15] However, hickishness, it seems, is acceptable in less important characters. Boorish secondary male characters with faulty English are retained in the film version and the language of a relatively correct speaker in the radio script, the barber Repeat (renamed Harvey Hoshal in the film), is mispronounced by the film actor. Although his dialogue in the film script is not written in mild vernacular, while it is for the other men just as it was in the radio play, the barber distorts words in the film, substituting, for instance, "ferners" for "foreigners." Either the actor or the director felt that sounding linguistically ignorant was warranted in the portrayal of this disseminator of local bigotry and xenophobic anxiety.

These modifications have several effects on the film adaptation. First, they simplify the characterization of the local male characters, associating ethnic discrimination with mere lack of education, since in the film all the local men except the more eloquent editor speak incorrectly and are decidedly narrow-minded and exclusionary. As a corollary to that simplification, Jake's erasure denies recognizing the hired hand's underlying acumen and sense of decency. Not only did Mitchell evidently perceive him as a character whose "colourful language," as Mitchell termed it, was worthy of a storyteller's role in both the radio plays and the later story versions over which he seemed to have more control, but he saw the hired hand as an everyman embodying the world, representing on the grand scale those working men, who, as Mitchell explains, came "from Russia, Poland, Hungary, the British Isles, the Scandinavian countries" (*According to Jake and the Kid* xi, ix). On some level Jake as the landless worker displays at least a symbolic, and arguably a real, affinity with the immigrant outsider, for whom Jake pleads more compassionate understanding.[16]

The cleaning up of the narrator-protagonist's colloquial speech in the film also, paradoxically, helps demarcate the difference between Kiziw as embodiment of other and the more abstract notion of linguistic purity that the locals espouse but for the most part are unable to exemplify. Of all the male characters, Lambert's speech most obviously contrasts with Kiziw's heavy accent, frequent mispronunciations, and broken syntax. Kiziw's compromised language abilities are a sore point with the townspeople and receive slightly more negative commentary in both the second version of the radio play and the film than in the first radio script, with the barber adding to his litany of language-related beefs his belief that after so many years in Canada Kiziw should be a better speaker. Complaints are also made about his wife's inability to speak English, a fact reinforced through her silence on screen. This somewhat increased attention to the language question, which is not equally notable in the later story version, suggests a heightened concern with the perceived inability of immigrants to assimilate. This narrative concern is ironic since, according to Howard Palmer, "the 1950s and 1960s were marked . . . by a greater acceptance of immigrants than in the prewar period (Palmer 315). The narrative seems to be hearkening back anachronistically to an earlier period when anti-Eastern European sentiment manifested itself in Saskatchewan in particular (Palmer 300-306). As such, both the source text and its adaptation seem to be reworking the past to address something that is more akin to a fear that the new post-war immigrants would not integrate (the official word at the time) than to a serious widespread social reality, at least as experienced to the dramatic degree portrayed in the film.[17]

Other strategies are also used to stress the Kiziw family's difference in the film version by taking advantage of its capacity for visual representation. Kiziw is shown to be physically more imposing than the other men; he is swarthy, dark haired, and dark moustached. The film script foresees casting Mrs. Kiziw as a woman with a "lined . . . Slavic . . . definitely European face with tenting cheekbones" (Mitchell film script 1), since she has no dialogue and there is no other way to distinguish her from the other women. These directions are followed. Her kerchief, also called for in the film script, differentiates her from the fashionably hatted townswomen. Worn at the end of the film only, it marks her as more of an outsider than ever when the narrative comes to a close. The Kiziws' only son is racialized with dark hair, a heart-shaped head, and almond-shaped eyes, in keeping with the film script's directions that "the face of young Steve [be] instantly recognizable as belonging to the same race as his mother" (Mitchell film script 20). He contrasts sharply with Gordie, the young boy to whom the narrator is teaching values of tolerance. This lad is fair-haired and narrow-headed, and his naturally large eyes frequently round yet wider when he excitedly shares information on the Kiziws' son with the narrator, emphasizing Gordie's physical difference with young Steve. Except for a brief reference to Mr. Kiziw's moustache in the radio play as a possible reason for his shunning, none of these traits is mentioned in the radio script. Careful casting was evidently done to help the film accentuate the Kiziws' physical dissimilarity, underscoring ethnicity as the reason for their social exclusion, expanding considerably on the radio play's dark hints of physical aversion. In scripting the film with greater attention to ethnic and racialized difference, Mitchell was recognizing a bias of the period, as expressed, for instance, in the controversy over using a stylized pioneer woman in a kerchief on the commemorative stamp designed for Saskatchewan's Golden Jubilee in 1955. It was deemed to present someone of "a distinct 'racial origin' rather than . . . [a] 'typical' Canadian . . . or a 'symbolic . . . woman'" and was thus replaced by a woman in a bonnet (Opp 218).

As previously mentioned, both the radio plays and the film raise the issue of assimilation, which relates to a fear of those who seem too different to blend in. A long barbershop scene between the barber and the narrator is devoted in both texts to the barber's near monologue on the Kiziws' failure to do just that. This whole scene takes place in front of a mirror, never mentioned in the source text, but an obvious prop, given the setting. The adapters use it to reflect—quite literally—the barber's implicit call for immigrants to replicate English identity and behaviour (i.e., to be like him, the barber, just as he is reflected in the mirror). This scene suggests that the people of the district want outsiders to engage in these acts of replication exactly, without question, problem, or even assistance—as easily as looking into a mirror.

The envious townsmen's refusal to assist in that on-going integration process is emphasized in the film by repeatedly setting Kiziw up as an outsider trying to enter communal space. His growing ostracism is further underlined in the film by delaying to varying degrees the moment at which he enters the scenes in which he is shown getting the cold shoulder from the local townsmen (in the beer parlour, pool hall, and curling rink scenes in the radio play and in the beer parlour, pool hall, and blacksmith scenes in the film). In each of the three film scenes, Kiziw enters the particular building from an outside door once the scene involving the local men is underway. In only the first cold shoulder scene in the radio script is his entrance delayed. After his jovial attempts at joining in his neighbours' talk or activities are rebuffed in the film in the latter two scenes, Kiziw leaves, realizing he is unwanted, thus underscoring his increasing outsider status. In these cases, the radio script merely concludes the scenes by ending the dialogue between Kiziw and another male character upon the latter's rejection, which makes Kiziw's forcing out seem less pronounced than in the film. The filmmaker evidently seeks to exploit filmic forms of mise-en-scène to take the radio play's concerns a step further in the build-up to the film's closing political statement.

The tensions between insiders and outsiders come to a head in the final, dramatic scene, in which Kiziw's large brick house, emblem of his prosperity, is engulfed in flames following the mysterious explosion of his oil furnace. Brandishing an axe, Kiziw refuses his neighbours' aid, their tardy offer of an ineffectual bucket brigade too little, too late. Having drawn, throughout the film, the ethnic lines of the English vs the non-English more heavily than in the radio play, the film renders all the more powerful in its political didacticism Kiziw's final impassioned, accented speech, in which cruel epithets for Central and Eastern Europeans are bitterly juxtaposed for rhetorical effect against comically deformed official descriptors of the British:

> You take hunky grain. You take hunyack vegetable. An' you take dorty foreigner money too! But we ain't like you. Oh no. Differnt Kiziw—his wife—his kid. Not British. Who the hall British—who they by God! . . .Why they so spacial— Angle-oh-Saxon! Jus' human bein'—me too. I got muscle— human muscle—I got human heart—same British! I work. Hard. Golden rule. Use Golden rule . . . . Terrible! So terrible [this disaster] I don't wish to happen even you. Even you! (Mitchell 1952, 22).

This sharpening of the ethnic divide also heightens the sermonic effect of the narrator's final voice-over comments, retained from the source text, about Kiziw having made his point about ethnic equality that fateful night, even if it was a little late for some of the local denizens.

That said, while the film accentuates Kiziw's difference, it simultaneously attenuates the most egregious stereotyping of Eastern and Central Europeans found in the radio version. Comments about "ignerant farmers . . . harness[ing] up their woman . . . to haul the garden plow" are eliminated, while others, such as "[they] beat their wimmen an' live like pigs," are deemphasized by reassigning them to less comprehensible background dialogue among extras. Thus, while highlighting the need for more acceptance, and greater effort to integrate and embrace the other, the NFB version takes a less jaundiced view of the host community, making its members' behaviour more palatable to a general audience. Evidently the NFB was only going to go so far in its exposure of bigotry, balancing out the civic role it held for itself in disseminating social messages against a civilizing one in the portrayal of Canadian-born citizens. This toning down exemplifies what Robert Stam calls "aesthetic mainstreaming" in which an "[a]daptation is seen as a kind of purge. In the name of mass-audience legibility [or acceptability], the novel is 'cleansed' [or in this case partially cleansed] of moral ambiguity" (43).

The focus on the notion of what constitutes an insider and an outsider outlined earlier is restricted to identities based on culture, language, race, and ethnicity, those factors considered significant to the efforts of nation building. They elide other factors influencing community building at the local level, such as the degree of social integration, sex, marital status, class,[18] vocation or lack thereof, sexual orientation, and mental and physical health or ability, that can quickly undo the designation of insider for even those generally considered insiders. The subsequent films address one or several of these factors, in conjunction with issues of ethnicity or immigration, either in a primary or a secondary role.

In 1963, the NFB turned to another recognized prairie writer, Sinclair Ross, best known for his novel *As for Me and My House* (1941) to again address the outsider theme, this time through his coming-of-age story "Cornet at Night,"[19] a text garnering steady interest at the time. First published in the *Queen's Quarterly* in 1939 and reprinted in the *Country Guide and Nor'west Farmer* in 1942, it had then been anthologized in McClelland and Stewart's collection *Saskatchewan Harvest*, in honour of the province's Golden Jubilee, in 1955, and adapted for CBC radio in 1958. After the CBC had decided against pursuing its option to adapt the story for television, the NFB picked it up, assigning Stanley Jackson to script and direct it.[20] Billing it in a publicity sheet of the period as "an idyll of boyhood on a prairie homestead," the NFB embraced the idea of depicting a young boy's encounter with an itinerant musician as seemingly "the peak of good fortune" (NFB 1963 publicity sheet "Cornet at Night").

This film can be read "in terms of the Diefenbaker government's 'save rural Canada' platform" (Waugh citing his student Scott Preston fn5, 546). The import of this observation should not be underestimated given the high priority that the Diefenbaker government gave agriculture; indeed, it was so great that it left a "pool of support" for the Conservatives in the prairies for the next thirty years (Kyba and Green-Finlay 66-67). That said, the agrarian setting also becomes a perfect nostalgic pretext for subtly exploring socially circumscribed desire through the insider/outsider dialectic and subtly seeding hope for future change on a more hidden front.

The source text and the adaptation mark the youth Philip Coleman as an outsider to an unnamed prairie community, not only through his literal outsider status (he is new in town) but also through his vocation (that of trombone player) and his lack of physical stamina for farm work (due to past illness, slight build, and soft, slender hands). The latter physical traits, in particular, serve as pretexts for the young man's rapid dismissal from the Edenic farm to which the young, infatuated protagonist, Tom Dickson, brings Philip, while his vocation along with his effeminacy serve as stereotypical tropes for his possible homosexuality. In selecting Philip as the new hired man, Tom defies his brusquely masculine father's orders to find someone suitable for stooking, i.e., "someone big and husky" (Ross 195).

Thomas Waugh observes that the adaptation is "defanged" (107). Arguably this is true, as the young boy's passion for the older teenage boy's musicianship is toned down, even deleted,[21] which in turn mutes the undercurrent of an emerging homoerotic crush, more evident in the source text. However, a comparative reading of several of the insider/outsider tropes in the source text and the film suggests a naturalization of difference, particularly in the film. Indeed, in the film, unlike in the story, the subtle integration of ethnic difference within the social narrative reflects part of that process. Moreover, ambiguous narrative and parental responses to the new feelings the outsider leaves in his wake suggest that the older boy's "expulsion . . . from paradise" by the father that Waugh observes as the violent end to the film narrative (107) is perhaps not as entirely permanent in the adaptation as he claims, at least not in paternal memory.

Unlike in the story, the attenuation of ethnic difference together with the incorporation of ethnic difference that is still notable into the documentation of daily life act as muted signals that other forms of difference can be minimized and perhaps one day even accepted. In the story, when the farm boy, Tom, goes to town in search of a stooker, he feels like, as he says, an "alien" (198), an outsider thrust into community life. This sense of alienation is echoed in his description of the town's Chinese restaurant, where he eventually meets Philip. In his words, it is "exotic" (199), its stale cigarette smoke "oriental" (199), and the Chinese waiter "indolent" (198). Not only is the foreignness of the restaurant not evident in the film, but the Chinese waiter is also shown in a more positive light, courteously and efficiently serving Tom. The film thus shifts representations and impressions of difference from allusions to the strange and self-indulgent to those of the helpful, if, to a more contemporary reading, the problematically homogenous.

Moreover, as Haldane does in *Fires of Envy*, the director, Jackson, makes use of mirror images, but this time using real reflections of the ethnic other to begin tracing the eventual erasure of the initial insider/outsider rapport between the main characters, Tom and Philip. The restaurant scene opens with the Chinese-Canadian waiter facing the mirror and the young Tom reflected in the background. The Caucasian boy is thus paired with an Asian man, revealing, yes, the man's position of servitude, but also documenting something of the typical or everyday of the time period. Masculine pairing is, in a sense, briefly, normalized, if troublingly within a hierarchy of race and age. Once the waiter moves out of frame, the boy alone is reflected in the mirror. Philip, whom Tom has not yet acknowledged by a look and who is sitting in frame to his left, is too far to one side to appear in the rectangular mirror. At this point, Philip is thus set apart as an outsider to Tom's own frame of reference—to his contained little world. However, once the two boys begin to get to know one another, they begin to be framed unambiguously together: in the restaurant, in the cart going to the farm, but perhaps most significantly in a window of the farm's bunkhouse. For a moment the fragility of glass—now a window, not a mirror—can contain them both.

This shot occurs during a film sequence that brings the parents outside, into nature and communion with Philip's music. These shots are developed from the barest mention in the story of the father's chores and the parents' appreciation of Philip's music. As this sequence builds in the film, Philip plays his cornet inside the outsider's bunkhouse, and the father, who is milking in the barn, is drawn outside. He peers voyeuristically into the bunkhouse through a four-paned window in the door. Philip and Tom are in shot, Philip to the left of the dividing windowpane frame, the enraptured Tom across the room, to the right of it. Figuratively, they are contained in rigidly separated boxes under the father's eye. (In the story the boys sit on the same bed, elbows almost touching; the father does not spy.) As Philip's cornet continues its haunting melody, however, we see a series of interior shots of Tom listening and Philip playing, of the father sitting and the mother standing outside to listen, and of idyllic nature. Gradually, Philip's music—the music emanating from the outsider's bunkhouse—is literally and metaphorically naturalized, as it is coupled with or giving voice to the beauty of nature, which had first been documented in the opening of the sequence. During this sequence, after a shot of the father seated, turning his head to listen but not peering in the window, we see a shot similar to what we saw earlier under the father's watchful eye, of Philip playing in the bunkhouse and Tom listening, but now without any dividing window frame and devoid of paternal oversight. The two boys are thus momentarily a part of the same world about which the father is appreciatively aware but respectfully outside. The idea of companionship, which Tom alludes to feeling with Philip in this scene in the source story, is thus suggested in the film but now within a context of parental appreciation of what can emanate from that company. Drawn to the music, the parents have been brought into an outsider's space and have discovered it resonating with an almost physical beauty that speaks to and augments their own reality. Here the text plays on the stereotype of prairie dwellers who have never been exposed to art, showing them nonetheless sensitive to it when the opportunity arises. By figurative extension, it also suggests a latent opening up to a socially circumscribed desire.

The close of the film gradually builds up to a more conciliatory position for the father. The next afternoon, after Philip fails at stooking and the father tells Tom that the young musician did not work out and will soon be leaving, the father's tone is different than the previous day, when he was angry about Tom's choice of a hired hand. He now speaks "quietly," as in Ross's story (Ross 211). However, the filmmaker then develops the father's sympathetic recognition of his son's disappointment more than in the story by cutting this brief scene on a reaction shot showing the father's silent commiseration. Continuing in this vein, the film goes on to alter slightly the adult Tom's final comments, suggesting the father's compassion later in life, something not conveyed in the story. The voice-over of an adult Tom closes by saying that his father had "understood something . . . wonder[ing in years to come] what [had] happened to the fellow who'd been brought to stook." Granted, the father does not come to the more profound realization that the adult Tom, the story's narrator, infers that his mother may have gained about the ephemeral magic of passion and music and, by implication, a first crush. However, the father at least seems to have developed some sort of sympathetic curiosity for this outsider who moved the father (literally and figuratively) from his mundane, relentless, spirit-numbing chores into the outside world. This subtle change in the narrator's commentary intimates the promise of a future sense of shared humanity among representatives of traditional masculinity for those outside its bounds.

Given that the film predates by six years legal amendments affecting homosexuality and by many more significant changes in societal attitudes, this admittedly timid gesturing towards a more accepting future time is significant. It introduces the tremor of narrative tension between paternal rejection and paternal conciliation, indicating that while the son's mild rebellion in bringing the wrong man home fails for now, later years may bring a different response. The father's change of heart may also suggest that he has his own history of latent desires, especially when the adaptation is read in light of Keath Fraser's biographical reading of Ross's *As For Me and My House.* Through this lens, the camera eye's recording of the father's earlier voyeuristic gaze could be interpreted in a more troubling way, even so far as becoming a stand-in for the source author's own gaze, exemplifying the "solipsistic fiction" of unrequited yearning that Fraser exposes (65).

Although *Fires of Envy* and *Cornet at Night* hold out some tentative hope for a change to more open attitudes, at least at some later date when lessons derived from encounters with difference have been learned by those who initially rejected the outsider, the next two adaptations of prairie fiction, *Tudor King* and *The Pedlar*, made in the late twentieth century, ultimately do not. Their scriptwriter and director, Allan Kroeker, chooses source texts that are much bleaker than the earlier source narratives and subtly renders them, at least in part, in even darker tones. The irony that they are reworked with a focus on the outsider-immigrant during a period when the federal government is promoting concepts of multiculturalism (Mackey 63-70) reveals the extent to which concerns with exclusion were, for the filmmaker, trumping official discourse. This suggests a sensitivity to the backlash against policies of multiculturalism and, most significantly, the possible attendant difficulties of that reaction for the outsider. While the adaptation of *Cornet at Night* had fashioned its source text to use representations of ethnicity to recuperate, if problematically, the emotional layers of homosociality, *Tudor King* reshapes its precursor text to examine, even more harshly, the relationship between the immigrant's isolation and madness, and *The Pedlar* reframes its source narrative to expose the complex links between despised forms of ethnicity and the vagrant class.

The permanency of the outsider position is suggested in the 10½-minute short film *Tudor King*, made in 1979. This first attempt at adaptation of Canadian fiction by the then relatively new NFB Prairie Studio is based on Rudy Wiebe's short story of the same name that was published not long before in Wiebe's 1974 collection *Where is the Voice Coming From?* Set on the prairies during the Second World War, it tells of a young farm boy's encounter with a deluded, secluded older bachelor who believes that he is the rightful heir to the English throne. The film version emphasizes Mr. Tudor's English roots by according him a mild English accent, something not mentioned in the source story, thus creating for him a more complicated partial insider/fully outsider position as both Englishman and immigrant. Ultimately, however, the film both accentuates and blurs the separation of insiders and outsiders through the use of space, drawing ambiguous lines between the antithetical states of mind of the immigrant man (mad) and the local boy (sane).

Specifically, the adaptation removes allusions to liminal space so that no shots show the boy entering or leaving Mr. Tudor's house. The film simply cuts between a sequence of shots outside the house, then a sequence suddenly inside, and then another suddenly outside, thereby clearly demarking insider and outsider space.[22] As a result, in the film, spatial symbolism is not used as it is in the story to suggest the boy's growing curiosity about Mr. Tudor (shown when with his friends in the summer he "inch[es] up to the cabin where the old man lived," entering the "door that squeaked open" [Wiebe 20]) nor his concern over Mr. Tudor's welfare (shown when in the winter he churns his way to the man's snow-buried door, penetrating the black interior). Removing these brief physical displacements from outside to inside excises the suggestion of the boy's inherently human interest in Mr. Tudor, his desire to probe this other's world, to get to know this strange and ragged old man.

Both the story and the film treat the notion of insider/outsider ironically, making the mad Englishman in his house the physical insider and the sane boy outside the house the physical outsider. However, the film changes both Mr. Tudor's companion and the ending, which removes the possibility of viewing the mad insider sympathetically. To explain: in the story Mr. Tudor has a sickly dog that he unsuccessfully attempts to save from the sub-zero cold during a five-day blizzard. Although both man and dog appear to be frozen to death when the boy and his brother find them, man curled around dog, in the snow-buried cabin at the end of story, the evidence of Mr. Tudor's valiant attempt to save another living creature teaches the boy something about "the fleeting stuff of human majesty" (25). No longer does Mr. Tudor's delusion about being the next king of England stand out as his characterizing feature but rather the greatness of the mad man's basic humanity. The majesty of an imaginary king becomes the nobility of a real man. In the film, by contrast, no one dies of cold nor even faces any imminent possibility of dying from it. The boy's wandering about in the obviously sub-zero weather at the beginning of the film does not seem to imperil but merely set him in a natural, if challenging, environment. There is no blizzard, let alone an unusually long one, leaving no opportunity for the mad man to show such heroic love of another, either human or animal.

In the film, the old man remains a deluded erstwhile immigrant, his madness rather than his vulnerability figuratively emphasized by showing him holed up in a ramshackle attic rather than dwelling in a "sagging" and eventually snow-encased cabin (20). That in his crazed seclusion he may share a capacity for humanity is only barely suggested when he has his helpmate, non-existent in the story, offer the boy some thin turnip soup, a complete narrative fabrication. This helpmate is a younger, equally deluded man, who gruffly cares for Mr. Tudor. Claiming to be the king's servant, his relationship to Mr. Tudor remains ambiguous. Is he a son? A male companion? Is their madness real or is it feigned to protect a forbidden relationship? Nothing is clear. However, this helpmate seems even more sinister than Mr. Tudor, spying on and then nabbing the boy from behind as he wanders curiously among the weatherworn farm buildings at the beginning of the film. The image of this menacing, dark-haired, dark-bearded, burly younger man, bundled in a dingy white parka, reminiscent of the iconic sheepskin coat, plays negatively on the pejorative stereotype of the "settler 'in a sheepskin coat'" (Palmer 311),[23] and as such sets this character up in even greater contrast than the older man with the innocent, more neutrally clad, blond boy. The Englishman's association with this outsider bearing vague Eastern-European traits thus further, albeit ambiguously, undoes the Englishman's tenuous insider status. While British-ness may ostensibly evoke insider status in much of Canada, in some regions of the prairies where bloc settlements flourished, people of Eastern and Cen-tral European extraction dominated demographically, although they were not always well accepted by the wider population. Thus, with the addition of the second mad man, the figure of the immigrant outsider, crazed by isolation, ironically doubles in the film, and, as such, is accorded no hope of receiving new compassionate understanding from even the most innocent and open member of the surrounding community—the curious, young school boy.

The most extensive exploration of the outsider theme is broached in *The Pedlar*, a 55-minute film adapted from W. D. Valgardson's short story "A Place of One's Own," made by the NFB in 1982 and aired on the CBC on June 4, 1983. Closely following the source narrative, which was originally published in Valgardson's short story collection *Red Dust* in 1978, the film recounts, in a minimalist way, the story of an itinerant merchant who lives and works from a homemade caravan, peddling salvaged goods to struggling farmers in the Interlake District of Manitoba, while saving his money and seeking a wife with whom to settle down. As does the short story, the film focuses on the pedlar's attempt to integrate into the community through his encounter with the hard-luck Fedorchuks, a father, mother, and unmarried pregnant teen-age daughter named Angela, who are eking out a living on an impoverished farm. Numerous changes in detail, however, both accentuate and attenuate the pedlar's difference from the family and their wider community, altering the significance of his difference and rendering it more ambiguous, complex, and, troubling.

As in *Fires of Envy*, the pedlar's ethnic difference is, at first glace, amplified in the film version, notably with a more swarthy appearance (a point to which I will return), but not, as in the earlier film, in contrast to a community of English descendants. Rather, he circulates among people of Ukrainian ancestry, with whom, ironically, it would seem he could more easily integrate than Kiziw by virtue of an apparently shared linguistic and cultural heritage. Whether, in fact, the pedlar in the film does share a common ethnic heritage is ambiguous, however, and even if he did, whether it would facilitate his integration is a question the adaptation subtly raises. Most notably, he speaks Ukrainian several times in the film, something he never does in the story. However, this linguistic ability does not appear to enhance his connection with the locals, as only once in the film, while he is hawking his wares, does a minor character briefly engage him in this language. The father, Harry Fedorchuck, to whom the pedlar speaks a few words of Ukrainian several times, seems more perplexed than able to understand, only fleetingly and awkwardly joining in with the pedlar's toast at Angela's and the pedlar's wedding meal. Given that the community is most likely several generations removed from Ukraine and largely assimilated linguistically, the original mother tongue becomes more of a marker of difference than a unifier in the adaptation.

Indeed, the pedlar's more apparent and fluent knowledge of Ukrainian suggests in the film that he is of a different generation of immigrants than those in the community. Given that the film is set in 1961 according to Kroeker's script (Kroeker i),[24] the pedlar may be part of the third phase of Ukrainian immigrants, displaced people who came immediately after the Second World War, whereas those in the community, evidently well-rooted in the region, are likely descended from the first wave who came around the turn of the twentieth century, when the area was first settled (Kaye and Swyripa 48, 52). Such an arrival time for the pedlar would have given him ample time to perfect his English to the excellent level seen in the film. Given some of the tensions experienced between the earlier and later waves of Ukrainian immigrants (Luciuk 121-122), the difference in linguistic ability in the film points to a possible new subtext, absent from the story—that of latent intergenerational and intra-ethnic misunderstanding caused by diverse migration histories. This carries wider significance than the narrative's Manitoba crucible, linking it to realities experienced in broader Canadian society, something Kroeker was evidently seeking to do, according to the film's preparatory documents (Arnason 6). The short story, in contrast, is far more ambiguous about the pedlar's origins, with little to suggest whether he is even an immigrant or not; all we know for certain is that he showed up in Eddyville three years previously. In an interview, Valgardson muses that the pedlar may have been involved in the Winnipeg Strike of 1919 (Valgardson interview, 5-6), expanding upon the locals' suggestion in the story that he may have been "involved in unsavoury politics" (Valgardson "Place," 53). This hint allows that the pedlar could be a European worker immigrant, as many, including Ukrainians, played a "prominent part" in the strike (Burnet 33), but in no way confirms that he is, in fact, an immigrant.

Besides speaking Ukrainian in the film, the pedlar, in both the film and the story, can fiddle Ukrainian folk music (anglicized as *kolamayka* in the story but more commonly written *kolomyika*) and does so well enough to attract other local players to join in. However, in neither source nor film narrative is it clear why, where, or from whom he learned to do so. Is it a marker of a genuine cultural heritage or of one that he has adopted and is using to construct a new identity? The answer is elusive, since, in spite of this evidence of cultural affinity, the pedlar chooses the outsider's existence, underscoring the notion that a little common cultural currency (whether through learning as an aficionado or learning from folk peers) is not enough for easy integration.

Here, around the figuration of the outsider's life, the source and film texts diverge. Near the opening of the source story, we learn that in the critical eyes of the Fedorchuk parents, the pedlar lives "no better than a gypsy" (Valgardson "Place," 53), one of the quintessential symbols of the outlander. As the source narrative explains, this man with no name left his work as a day labourer for this nomadic lifestyle after refusing, sometime prior to the story's opening, to show his torso-covering tattoos to a gang of local hooligans, who had heard tell of them. Having his shirt torn to shreds and his tattoos brutally exposed leaves him wary of the locals, "avoid[ing] crowds and towns, sticking to back roads, selling his goods at farms and camps," leaving any communal events "if any notice was taken of him" (54). As David Arnason points out in his interview with Kroeker done in preparation for the film, the tattoos in the story symbolize the wounded body and soul;[25] they become both the reason for and the expression of the pedlar's exclusion.

The film heightens the pedlar's outsider status by suggesting (among other things) that he may in fact be a real gypsy. In the eyes of some in the community, this would explain his multitude of tattoos, an explanation not alluded to in the source story. These tattoos, which are briefly mentioned several times in the source text but never fully described, are copiously displayed in two film scenes. With his repeated magic tricks for enticing buyers and his acts of showmanship, he plays the gypsy in the film in ways neither shown nor alluded to in the source text, expanding considerably on more generic gypsy-like traits he had in the story: his energetic love of music and his no-madism.[26] Indeed, in the context of linking the pedlar to gypsies, a voice-over of one of the local men at the beginning of the film overtly points out that the pedlar gained entry into farmsteads by finagling, intimating more supposed gypsy behaviour. Although he goes through the same steps to gain access in the story, devoid of any such commentary by community members or the implicit narrator, they seem less disingenuous, more open to interpretation, less linked to a nomad's sly calculation.

The pedlar's olive skin, black hair, and large black moustache, which in the film replaces the wavy reddish-brown beard he sports in the story, round out his vaguely gypsy-like features, building on a racialized view of gypsies (Mayall 125-126). Indeed, paradoxically, the pedlar in the film assumes the colouring of the Fedorchuk father, who, in the story, is described as "swarthy" (Valgardson "Place," 49) but who, in the film, is of a slightly ruddy complexion, more like the other locals than the pedlar. The film's emphasis not only on the pedlar's possible ethnic difference from the local people (which is intimated in the story but through opposite colouring) but also on his putative kinship in the eyes of at least one local with one of the traditionally most reviled of outsider ethnic groups, only underscores the difficulty facing him in being accepted. His off-white characteristics thus relate the film thematically to the period's burgeoning concerns with the plight of so-called visible minorities.[27]

This subtext of rejection based on difference is articulated in both source- and film texts in the dismay at the pedlar's tattoos expressed by the pregnant Angela, married off by her father to the smitten pedlar through a financial transaction likened in the story to selling cattle.[28] The more ethnically related basis, or at least partial basis, for her initial dismay is heightened in the film not only through the more extensive and visual attention given the tattoos that are linked, albeit questionably, to gypsy origins, but also later through a comment, non-existent in the story, that underscores the pedlar's physical difference with mother and child. It occurs at the end of the film when a shop-keeper coos that both Angela's and her child's eyes are blue, just like the baby's father, oblivious to the darker eyes of the pedlar, who is holding the baby and whom she mistakes for the father.[29] The accentuation of the pedlar's difference makes his desire to settle down and belong even more understandable in the film and simultaneously somewhat more perplexing if one takes literally the film's dubious suggestion of his gypsy identity, given that nomadism is one of the, albeit contested, traits of gypsies (Mayall 252-275).

The ambiguity of the man's gypsy identity is further suggested by his clothing, only nominally like Eastern European gypsies.[30] His caravan is also very plain and angular, denuded of any decor traditionally or stereotypically gypsy in ornamentation or colour. Indeed, as many of the pedlar's traits that suggest the gypsy, as many do not, including the facts that he wanders alone, is prepared to marry a non-gypsy, and is willing to adopt her static life-style (Salo 1979, 81-83, 93-94). The viewer cannot verify his ability to speak a form of the Gypsy language. If he is a gypsy, he seems to be the last of his people, divested of all ties with his community, which would explain his strong desire to integrate.

Although there is evidence of gypsies on the prairies, both anecdotal and anthropological,[31] the discrepancies in the pedlar's representation suggest that the film is manipulating the gypsy image for other reasons. As David Mayall explains, "[Gypsies] are and have been whoever people wanted them to be" (276). In this case, the gypsy becomes a trope for the construction and performance of identity—for the instability of identity. Indeed, when considering the popular stereotype of gypsy nomadism, the pedlar's gypsy image becomes an ironic attempt to create an identity that would enable integration. This trope becomes doubly ironic when considered in light of Michael Stewart's work on Hungarian gypsies. Stewart argues that in homogenizing environments, gypsies actually seek to cultivate their difference (9), which, when applied to the significance of both the pedlar's quest and his dress, puts him in the double bind of wanting to belong and wanting to stand out.

In exploiting the image of the gypsy, the film also adds heartrending irony to the ending by breaking one of the stereotyped conventions found in tales of wicked gypsies. In so doing, it emphasizes all the more the inherent goodness of the outsider. In keeping the original ending in which Angela leaves her former peddling husband with no forewarning, her infant in tow and wedding money in hand, the film reverses the convention of the pilfering, baby-snatching gypsy. Indeed, by creating scenes from their brief marriage, scenes that receive no mention in the story, the film increases the viewer's pity for him once his wife deserts him. These new scenes all intimate his desire to nurture love, since the trope of tender, loving creation underlies them all; he is shown proudly photographing his wife and step-daughter, buying them fabric, and painting a home-made rocking horse, always with a kindly, gentle air. In creating these scenes on the pedlar's generous bestowing of love, Kroeker may be attempting to develop the pedlar's Christ-like qualities, an association that Valgardson, himself, expanded upon in his interview with Kroeker (Valgardson interview, 3). If so, this may have been done to compensate for the excision of other overt links in the film, including his name bearing J. C. initials, revealed only late in the story, his beard, and the fact that he is a carpenter.

Nonetheless, as sincere as the pedlar may have been, he cannot integrate himself and the ostracized Angela into the community by buying her as a wife. Unlike in the other films, the outsider is not shown to be the simple victim of a closed community but rather the dupe of his own, ultimately self-interested, miscalculation. His is an unrequited love, which once forced on the unwilling recipient, can only be rejected. Forsaken by his only link to the community, he leaves the sedentary life and the now abandoned nest he created for his new family and returns to the road, two tattoos of daisies, symbols of unfaithfulness (Ferber 50), etched about his ears. The film ends as it began, with the pedlar confined to his caravan, held outside the farm fences, notably the Fedorchuks', whose gate is firmly shut. In developing this last scene, only hinted at in the story, and in linking it to the film's beginning through its visual content, the adaptation visually emphasizes a bitter fatalism: once an outsider, always an outsider. Thus the film's recuperation of the outlander within a more positive frame of reference than in the story through the brief depiction of the marriage is only more poignantly dashed, suggesting an even greater pessimism for the outsider's future within the community.

These four adaptations thus show a shift from either exhortative hope or naïve optimism about the outsider's eventual integration to a harsh pessimism about full and continued acceptance. Three of the four films accentuate ethnic difference, at least two of them ahistorically, suggesting the adapters' felt need to draw attention through fictional means to the alienation of the so-called other in an effort to raise audience empathy and provoke reflection. Ironically, over the period studied the art of cinematic adaptation becomes increasingly an act for expressing the hardship, if not impossibility, of social adaptation, and not a trope for a successful "screening in." As a set, these works thus largely underscore the challenges of heterogeneity, offering no pat solutions. The adaptations serve, therefore, not as mere vehicles for propagating official rhetoric or policy stances but for exploring issues of both nationally harmonizing and institutionally self-interested import (*Fires of Envy*), for expressing latent hopes and repressed desires (*Cornet at Night*), or for exposing the bitter realities of incomplete integration (*Fires of Envy, Tudor King, The Pedlar*). Within the staid constraints of a state institution, small teams of filmmakers at the NFB were able to probe more deeply or more equivocally into controversial aspects of various outsiders' experience under the subtle guise of genteel adaptation.

Notes

I wish to thank my graduate students Cristina Artenie, Jason Brunwald, and Anna Kavazovic, for their insightful observations on these films during various seminars and in later discussions. I also wish to acknowledge the helpful archival assistance of Apollonia Steele and Marlys Chevrefils of the University of Calgary Archives and Special Collections, André D'Ulisse of the National Film Board Archives, and Barbara and Ormond Mitchell of Trent University.

1. I have chosen to maintain the term "source" to qualify the text that is the object of the adaptation, Gary R. Bortolotti's and Linda Hutcheon's recent reservations notwithstanding. I disagree with their assertion that this modifier is part and parcel of fidelity criticism and as a result suggests "the denigration of adaptations" (445). I am using it as a descriptor for the precursor text. The term "adapted text," which Hutcheon adopts in her *A Theory of Adaptation* (xiii), is confusing in its ambiguity, suggesting both the object and the product of the adaptation.

2. Of course other factors can contribute to the need for making changes, especially when adapting from one medium to another. However, I will be focusing on those alterations that seem to fit a larger pattern of reworking underlying thematic concerns and that are not exclusively related to the demands of the new medium. Some of the changes that I will discuss may have been enhanced by exploiting the unique capacities of film but none can be related only to the need to conform to its unique demands. For more on how one can distinguish between what can be transferred from one narrative medium to another and what requires actual adaptation through the use of cinematic equivalences (when they exist), see Brian McFarlane's *Novel to Film: An Introduction to the Theory of Adaptation* (13).

3. See Christopher E. Gittings for more on his application of Louis Althusser's influential concept of the "ideological state apparatus" to the NFB (20, 73). It is to be recalled that the 1950 Film Act stated that NFB was to make films "in the national interest" (Evans 17).

4. Erica Sheen has observed the profitable and continued use of close readings for studies of adaptations. I concur with her observation that this approach need not suggest "that the literary text is superior to its adaptation" (11). I would add that the attention to detail afforded by this approach allows for a more complete and nuanced understanding of the resulting adaptation and would argue that it is not necessarily implicitly or explicitly judgmental, as Bortolotti and Hutcheon assert (445).

5. *Jake and the Kid* series commanded audiences of over 500,000 (Yates 9).

6. Letter from John P. Kidd to "The Producer, Jake and the Kid," January 14, 1952. The W. O. Mitchell Fonds, University of Calgary Library, Special Collections, Accession Number 19.7.10.14.6.

7. Ibid.

8. Letter from W. Arthur Irwin in reply to Peter Francis, producer of the CBC's *Jake and the Kid* radio series, February 22, 1952, who had submitted the script. The W. O. Mitchell Fonds, University of Calgary Library, Special Collections, Accession Number 19.11.4.3.

9. Letter from Ormond Mitchell to Elspeth Tulloch, December 18, 2006.

10. See Richard Day for more on the direction of new Department of Citizenship and Immigration (165-171).

11. Dowler is referring to the period around the Second World War, in particular. For an earlier period of films about Eastern Europeans, see Gittings for his application of Fatimah Tobing Rony's concept of "ethnographic cinema" to his analysis of the negative representation of Ukrainians in films made in Saskatchewan in the early 1920s (33, 38-46).

12. Both born and raised in multiethnic Saskatchewan, W. O. Mitchell and John Diefenbaker (prime minister from 1957-1963) share a common context for understanding multiethnic equality. For more on Diefenbaker's notion of the unhyphenated Canadian and its relationship to his prairie upbringing, see Sigurdson.

13. According to clues in the second radio play and the film, the Kiziws would most likely have arrived in Canada sometime in the 1930s. However, "large-scale immigration in the [prairie] region was virtually over by 1931" (Burnet 53). Indeed, comparatively few immigrants from anywhere entered Canada during the thirties, further underscoring the somewhat atypical quality of the Kiziws' particular situation, if read against history. Moreover, ethnic animosity directed at Central and Eastern Europeans found on the prairies in the early twentieth century into the 1920s had greatly subsided with the impact of the Second World War and the absorption of immigrant populations (Whitcomb 22-23, Thompson 116-122, 138-141). Finally, the demographic shift that post-war immigrants, such as new, incoming Ukrainians, caused on the prairies was negligible compared to Ontario, given the pre-existing makeup of the prairie population (Stebelsky 154).

14. In its only other foray into a Jake and the Kid adaptation, *Political Dynamite*, the NFB retained the Jake character.

15. See Catherine McLay (334) for more on the criticism of caricaturing

prairie people, which may be why the show was not popular on the prairies, unlike elsewhere. See also Sandy Stewart 135-6.

16. See McLay for more discussion on Jake's appeal as a frontier hero (334).

17. See Day for the discussion of the move to replace the term "assimilation" with "integration" (171). In that the film seeks to promote the acceptance of Central and Eastern European immigrants whom, on a much wider scale, the federal government was admitting as refugees between 1947 and 1953 in a effort to support democracy (Kelley and Trebilock 313), it is also possible to read the adaptation as part of the "[f]ilms produced at the NFB . . . [as] weapons . . . to fight communism" (Druick 112). Although, the film's anachronistic quality makes it difficult to make anything more than loose associations with this effort, it provides an ironic twist to the NFB's possible motivations for making the adaptation, given that the institution, itself, had been alleged to employ people with communist leanings.

18. Bannerji does go on to say that class is one of the key exclusionary factors facing immigrants of colour (121-2, 125).

19. For comments on the early assessment of Ross, see, for example, Edward McCourt's *The Canadian West in Fiction*.

20. Thomas Waugh points out that the NFB did an earlier but unacknowledged adaptation of Ross's story with Gundrun Parker's *A Musician in the Family* (1953) (102), further revealing the growing interest in the short story.

21. For example, the scene of the runaway horse is cut.

22. These jarring cuts may be a result of the film being a training film.

23. The Minister of Interior Clifton Sifton's vigorous immigration policies brought nearly three million people to Canada between 1896 and 1914, including over 120,000 Ukrainians, deemed undesirable in the eyes of some, between 1892 and 1914 (Lehr 31). In the wake of a hostile public reaction, political "opponents . . . launched venomous tirades against 'Sifton's sheepskins'" (Kaye 44).

24. A conversation that Kroeker had with critic David Arnason in preparation for the film set it in the 1950s (Arnason 8). Given the father's mention of TV, this seems more likely than the early to mid 1940s, which Valgardson, himself, suggests in a similar preparatory conversation for the film (Valgardson interview 5). Valgardson felt it needed to be early enough that one could still expect to see the occasional wagon on the road. Arnason felt the pedlar could be read as an anachronism – a man outside of time.

25. Interview with David Arnason by Allan Kroeker, June 2, 1980, p. 4, 5, NFB archival file, *The Pedlar* 36114.

26. The only reference to magic tricks in the story is metaphoric, in the context of the Fedorchuk's distrust of the stranger, alluded to, for instance, when Sophie, Angela Fedorchuk's mother, watches the pedlar "so closely she might have been afraid he would, through some magical sleight of hand, steal the pump before their eyes" (Valgardson 52). This distrust, reminiscent of feelings expressed towards gypsies in Europe, exemplifies more universally the wariness of rooted communities towards vagrants or migrants. See David Mayall for more on the reaction of sedentary communities to nomadic people (252-275); see Jean-Pierre Liegeois (138-141) for more on stereotypes of gypsies.

27. For example, during the early 1980s there was growing public concern with the employment opportunities of so-called visible minorities, an issue that resulted, after considerable study, in two important reports in 1984: *Equality Now!* tabled by the Special Parliamentary Committee on the Participation of Visible Minorities in Canadian Society and *Equality in Employment: A Royal Commission Report* by Commissioner Judge Rosalie Abella. Between 1982 and 1983 the NFB also made several films dealing variously with racial or ethnic discrimination, Ukrainian history, and even dance historically associated with gypsies, suggesting that the film *The Pedlar* was responding synergistically to a cross-section of interests circulating within the NFB and among federal government officials.

28. Her mother also expresses dismay at the tattoos in the story (61).

29. The pedlar's exact eye colour remains uncertain, again underscoring the enigmatic quality of his identity. Several early close-ups suggest they are brown but close-ups near the end suggest they are an indeterminate, lighter colour, not identical, however, to Angela's.

30. See the photos of men from Serbia in Tomasevic and Djuric (135) and from Romania in Houliat (131). These are quite unlike the ragged, tunic-clad gypsies iconized on the cover of David Crowe's *A History of the Gypsies of Eastern Europe and Russia*.

31. For example, Eastern European gypsies are reported to have gone to western Canada in the early twentieth century in "the wake of other east Europeans" and to "[have got] on better [than elsewhere in Canada] because they spoke Slavic languages" (Salo 1999, 643). These earlier arrivals may be too early to explain the pedlar's presence.

Alison Calder

•

Why Shoot The Gopher?
Reading the Politics of a Prairie Icon

How do you grow a prairie town?

> The gopher was the model.
> Stand up straight:
> telephone poles
> grain elevators
> church steeples.
> Vanish suddenly: the
> gopher was the model.
>
> Robert Kroetsch, *Seed Catalogue*

In late winter of 2002, the Saskatoon Branch of the Saskatchewan Wildlife Federation announced that it was initiating the Ken Turcot Memorial Gopher Derby. It seemed a simple idea: interested sharpshooters would pay a $20 entry fee, then shoot as many gophers as they could between April 1 and June 23. The hunters with the largest number of kills (tabulated daily on a website) would win cash prizes. Proof of the kills would be the gopher tails, frozen and bundled in packs of ten and delivered to the Wildlife Federation Office for tabulation. The plan caused immediate controversy, as hunters and farmers squared off against biologists and environmentalists. "We're in the 21st century, surely, not the 14th," wrote one reader of the Saskatoon *StarPhoenix*, who opposed what he termed a "mass murder derby" carried out by "executioners." He asked: "why does the SWF—which has ample opportunity for good programs—want to taint itself with such an event? What must the rest of the world think of this province? It's time to challenge head-on the kill-it-for-fun culture of backwater Saskatchewan" (Steck). Another reader, responding to this "pathetic" letter with "disgust" wrote:

> I suppose this brainwashed do-gooder would prefer to sell
> his cows and livestock and let the gophers have his pasture
> and fields. When I was a kid, we got two cents a gopher tail
> for killing them by any means possible. . . .I am from back-
> water Saskatchewan and proud of it. I have shot thousands
> of gophers and taught my kids to handle firearms safely to

kill skunks, coyotes, gophers, magpies and any other farm
predators. (Morgan)

The heated rhetoric of these letters may seem excessive—surely a gopher is
just a gopher.[1] But the extreme terms of this ongoing debate can be understood if, as I argue, the argument is not in fact primarily about gophers, but is
rather about those fundamentally western concerns: land and power.

Gophers pop up repeatedly in prairie literature and popular culture, but
they have received no critical attention. Although most criticism of prairie
writing focuses on the prairie environment, animals (indigenous or otherwise) are rarely included in that consideration.[2] Gophers may be so common on the prairie and in literature that their presence is taken for granted
by critics; alternatively, models of prairie writing that concentrate on battles
between human and landscape may ignore the seemingly trivial presence of
small animals. But examining representations of the gopher not only reveals
local colour—the gopher as scenery—but also reveals fundamental conflicts
within the prairie: rural versus urban, cultivation versus conservation, prairie
dweller versus tourist, even indigenous culture versus settler/colonizer culture. At the heart of these conflicts, I suggest, are questions of power: whose
land is the prairie, and whose interests should be protected? Who is seen to
have the right to prairie space? Conflicts centring on gophers are thus analogous to "site fights" like those over placement of garbage dumps and pig
farms, where neighbourly concerns about smelly air are deeply rooted in conflicts over whether a specific place is a working landscape or a recreational
one (Novek).

W. O. Mitchell's classic novel *Who Has Seen the Wind* provides an example of a gopher used as a symbol that crystallizes regional tensions. Brian,
the novel's young protagonist, struggles throughout the book to understand
the prairie's "awful" power (125). He is aided in this understanding by the
Young Ben, an unkempt child of nature who comes to symbolize the wild
nature of the prairie itself. A crucial scene occurs when Brian goes gopher
hunting with his brother Bobbie and his friends Fat and Art. When Art picks
up a stunned gopher, snaps its tail off, and throws the maimed animal onto
the dirt to die, the Young Ben, who has been hiding nearby, seizes the gopher
and mercifully kills it before attacking the bewildered Art. Brian is "filled with
a sense of the justness, the rightness, the completeness of what the Young Ben
had done—what he himself would like to have done" (124). Environmental
concerns are a major theme in Mitchell's novel. His inclusion of the gopher-
hunting scene is not only an invocation of local colour, but is also a statement
of the fundamental conflict within the region between conservation and ap-

propriation. Art wants to kill the gopher for financial gain, in the form of the agriculturally-motivated bounty offered for the gopher tail, while Brian rejects that project in favour of a more ecological sensibility, a choice later echoed in his decision to go to school to be a "dirt doctor" and learn about ecologically sustainable agricultural practices. Mitchell's gopher scene thus poses basic questions about whose land the prairie is, and about the extent of human responsibility to the creatures who live there.

Representations of the gopher invoke particular regional discourses; it is, in fact, a highly contested icon that represents any number of issues fundamental to prairie culture. Its status varies dramatically depending on the place from which it is viewed. To a farmer, a gopher is a pest, a menace to be eradicated. Document after document refers to "the gopher plague" and "the gopher menace," and suggests ways for gophers to be exterminated. To the city dweller, a gopher may be a cute diversion, an animal to be protected, fed, and visited at the zoo or nature preserve, as at Winnipeg's Oak Hammock Marsh or Saskatoon's Forestry Farm Zoo. To an environmentalist, the gopher is an essential part of the prairie ecosystem, while to a developer (of a golf course, for example) the gopher represents an obstacle that must be eradicated or controlled.[3] Gopher is a traditional food for some First Nations peoples, and gophers figure in some First Nations traditional stories.[4] Gopher fur was also used for clothing.[5] While gophers no doubt frustrated early First Nations agricultural projects, they also retained a certain use-value to other cultures. The gopher's status as exclusively a pest or "farm predator" is a relatively recent development.

—————————— • ——————————

> Gophers are the stupid heroes of springtime. They sight right
> up the barrel into a boy's eyes as if to say, *Go ahead, blow*
> *my guts into crowfood, son,* and the boy does, and waits for
> the black rain of crows to come. Later he drowns them out
> with pails of snowmelt, watches them deke crazy from the
> sunblazed fingers of his five-pronged spear. Once one cut
> between his legs, made him pitchfork himself through the
> rubberboot. Foot nailed to the ground, tetanus shot pend-
> ing. Jumping Jesus. For that he postmauled five gophers,
> waited for the crows to rain down. Best is taking them alive.
> Bindertwining them to a flat board, sailing it into the dug-
> out. Water roaring out of the snow like metamorphosis is
> pain and you never hear them sing when the dugout takes

them down like frightened leprechauns.

Rick Hillis, "Captain Gopher"

The gopher features prominently in prairie popular culture in two separate and simultaneous paradigms. The first model is gopher as demonic other.
Subsequent to fur trading, the Canadian prairie was originally conceived of
by settlers as agricultural space: the value of the place lay in its ability to produce crops.[6] Homesteaders were expected to farm, and small towns and cities
developed principally to support the agricultural industry. Agriculture was
seen as the means to progress: it was the *raison d'être* for the Canadian west.
In agricultural ideology animals are valued for their usefulness. As one veteri-
narian states, "Survival is just as hard for the farmer as it is for the animal. So
you're on equal footing. I mean, the animal has to pay its way, because you're
paying your way too. Nothing's free in this world" (qtd. in Sabloff 95-96). In
an agriculturally-based economy, gophers are villains, not only not paying
their way, but also actively destroying the farmer's livelihood. They eat crops
and their burrows may damage farm machinery and livestock. Because their
life cycle runs counter to the needs of agriculture, they have assumed the status of pest: that category of animals, like skunks, coyotes, and magpies that
it is deemed acceptable to exterminate.[7] Wallace Stegner's description of his
youthful gopher-hunting activities in *Wolf Willow* provides a clear illustration
of agricultural values:

> We lived an idyll of miniature savagery, small humans
> against rodents. . . .We were as untroubled by all our slaugh-
> ter as early plainsmen were by their slaughter of buffalo. In
> the name of the wheat we absolved ourselves of cruelty and
> callousness. Our justification came at the end of that first
> summer when my father, who was just six feet tall, walked
> into the field one afternoon and disappeared. . . .From a
> field of less than thirty acres he took more than twelve hun-
> dred bushels of Number One Northern. (275-76)

Stegner's words connect the economics of agriculture to the negative valuation of the gopher. Acceptance of a program like the Saskatoon Wildlife Federation's Gopher Derby requires a naturalization of the gopher's pest status:
no other definitions can be accepted, or the justification for the derby fails.
However, it is important to remember that the category "pest," like the category "pet," is no more natural than the designation "weed." Each label depends
on the needs and/or desires of the population doing the naming.[8]

While the gopher has only been considered a pest since the arrival of
agriculture on the prairies, it has occupied an extreme position from the be-

ginnings of the casting of the prairie as an agriculturally-intensive space. The Secretary of the Wolseley Agricultural Society wrote to his Member of Parliament in 1888 that "no greater or more serious drawback exists in the part of the country at present than the Gopher plague" (Bray). A farmer in Broadview, writing the same year, called gophers "an evil that individual farmers would be unable to contend successfully against—and the trouble would have to be grappled with as a public foe—even Municipalities scattered here and there as they are in the Territories cannot effectively combat the evil" (Thorburn). The descriptions of gophers as "a plague" and "evil" recalls descriptions of biblical scourges. Farmers' pleas for assistance led to several government-sponsored attempts to extirpate them, including federal programs to supply gopher traps at cost to farmers in the Territories in the 1890s, and to well-known bounty programs that later rewarded gopher hunters with one or two cents per tail. These attempts at eradication proved unsuccessful, and commercial gopher poisons were rapidly developed. Advertisements for these products often focused on the economic loss caused by gopher damage, representing gophers as thieves robbing farmers of what was rightfully theirs. "How long do you work for the Gophers each day?" asked a 1916 advertisement for Sure-Deth. Two advertisements for Mickelson's Kill-Em-Quick Gopher Poison in 1911 and 1912 spelled out the answer, asserting that "Every year the gophers rob you of 3 to 5 bushels of grain per acre" and asking "Will the gophers, squirrels, pocket gophers, field mice and prairie dogs steal $100 worth of your grain every 40 acres *again*?" (italics in original). Implicit in this representation is the belief that the prairies belong to the farmer; it is the gophers, not the settlers, who are invaders.

The rhetoric describing gophers as "evil" and as a "plague" found in the 1888 documents is reproduced almost exactly in newspaper headlines from the summer of 2001. Newspapers across Saskatchewan carried articles like the one in the Saskatoon *StarPhoenix* on August 1. Headlined "Prairie Enemy No. 1" and subtitled "Farmers step up war with plundering gophers in the face of crop loss," this article represents gophers as the biggest threat facing prairie farmers: they are "plundering" creatures who steal what they have no right to (McNairn). The description of the farmer-gopher relation as a war is another common rhetorical feature, as seen in the July 28, 2001 *StarPhoenix* article "Group Declares War on Population Explosion of Gophers," which describes the battle as "basically an invasion of gophers on a lot of farm land" (Parker). Barbara Kelcey has pointed out the military rhetoric used in anti-gopher campaigns during the First World War ("Keep the submarines out of the wheat fields" was one such slogan). In an American context, a 1941 advertisement for Bell System reads similarly, representing a threatening-looking gopher as enemy of the nation. "Ask a Gopher About Defense," the ad reads, then describes the company's special precautions taken to prevent gophers from chewing through buried telephone cables. "A small thing, but just one of the many things the Bell System is doing these days to prevent interruption in telephone service. For the telephone is a vital link in the whole program of National Defense." If, as the advertisement states, "Long Distance helps unite the nation," then the gopher clearly emerges as a disruptive and fragmentary force, capable of damaging America's "program of National Defense." This war, however, is not waged between two equal opponents: the gopher is seen to have the continual advantage because of its perceived superior numbers, and it is believed to have an infinite capacity to reproduce.[9] Consider the rhetoric of this 1927 article in the *Zealandia News*, titled "Gopher Destruction": "'A gopher in time saves nine.' Now is the zero hour to renew hostilities with the enemy. If nothing is done to destroy gophers until after seeding the opportune moment will be past. The enemy will be vastly increased in numbers."

The construction of the gopher-human relation as a war affects the perception and treatment of the animal. Annabelle Sabloff argues that the relation between humans and the natural world is deeply conflicted because of what she calls "a *poverty of discourse* related to nature" (11). She suggests that human-animal relations, which often appear strange, are governed by metaphors that have become deeply ingrained and so accepted as true, where the "as if" relation of the simile is replaced by "is." The result, she writes, is that

> people have come to think and speak of one thing as if it were *literally* the other, and act accordingly. In the West, for example, animals bred for scientific manipulation are often spoken about and treated literally as if they were non-sentient disposable laboratory materials or mini-factories. . . .To think of an animal as kin, for instance, elicits . . . much the same feelings and associated behaviours toward the animal as exist between a human parent and its young. (23)

To think of the gopher as an enemy with whom one is at war is then to promote a human-gopher relation that supports this metaphor. The gopher becomes an animal apart from other animals, a "menace" that it is good and right to exterminate, while attempts to defend it appear misguided and unpatriotic. It is also possible to draw clear battle lines. The rhetoric of war admits no confusion; one is either for the gophers or for the farmers, and there can be no compromise, as the "executioners" face off against the "brainwashed do-gooders." Couching the human-gopher relation in the language of war precludes any solution based on compromise.

As newspaper headlines from 2001 show, such military language is not limited to wartime, and the representation of the human-gopher relation in terms of a war is not without effect. In this rhetoric, the gopher is not just a pest. Instead, it is "the enemy," assigned a malevolent agency that demands a brutal response, as seen in Saskatchewan farmer Alan Powers's response to gopher infestations: "I've been shooting and my boys have been shooting and I'm not going to hazard to guess how many thousands of rounds we have used. We have shot gophers until the hills literally stunk" (qtd. in McNairn). The gopher thus appears as one of the few animals which it is seen as good and proper to exterminate, "by whatever means possible," as the Saskatchewan gopher derby supporter wrote—drowning, gassing, bludgeoning, shooting, running over them on the highway, and so on. That the gopher is not considered to be entirely in the same category as other animals is seen in a recent article containing an interview with the president of the Regina Humane Society, which took place "while his dogs were off hunting local ground squirrels" (White). Here, gophers occupy a different space than regular animals: even the president of the Humane Society condones killing them. This is not to minimize the difficulties that gophers cause farmers. One prairie community even declared a state of emergency in 2001, prompted by a gopher population so large that it devoured all green shoots and made the land hazardous for livestock to walk on. When the local Emergency Measures Organization objected to the use of the phrase "state of emergency," the administrator of the rural municipality spoke out in frustration: "They said we can't use those words but what the hell are we going to call it? State of gophers? . . .They can call it a disaster in the south when there's too much water but this is hurting us just the same" ("Town Declares Gopher Emergency").

It is possible to read the desire to eradicate the gopher as a symptom of a more general political dissatisfaction. Debate sprang up in 2001 around Saskatchewan's attempts to choose an animal to symbolize the province. The suggestion of a gopher met with scorn from at least one reader of the *Western Producer* who, self-consciously positioning himself as a "Westerner," wrote: "I'll bet my Winchester .22 that the NDP government had a hand in naming the gopher as the official representative of the animal kingdom for our great plains environment" (Hamon). Here the letter writer links gophers to the provincial government, another target of farmers' frustrations because of its perceived lack of support for agricultural communities. Prairie dwellers have also allied gophers with another traditional western Canadian enemy, the federal government, as in a satiric newspaper column titled "What Would Happen if

Gophers Took over the Government?" Writing about government-imposed restrictions on poison use, the columnist remarks that "the geniuses in Ottawa now want to drag away in handcuffs a farmer who shoots the pestiferous rodents with grandpa's unregistered .22 rifle. It's as if gophers have somehow seized control of the federal government and twisted it to their own diabolical ends. They seem to be going for world domination" (Macpherson). There is, however, a serious theme here, which sounds repeatedly in farmers' discussions about gopher damage they face: that "the geniuses in Ottawa" don't understand, that restrictions on strychnine use are put in place by a bunch of bureaucrats in suits who don't know or care anything about the life of a working farmer in the west. This east-west tension translates at an intra-regional level into an urban-rural split, with urban people standing in for the big-city fatcats and rural people being cast as gun-waving hicks. A strong strain of individualism, simultaneously mocked and reinforced by such self-conscious "backwater" positioning runs through anti-gopher rhetoric, as farmers argue that laws made by distant legislators are meaningless, and openly flout anti-strychnine regulations (McNairn).

Examining representations of the gopher also reveals the importance of examining the differences among communities on the prairies. People in cities do not have the same relation to wildlife as those in agricultural communities because the land base is treated fundamentally differently. Gophers are permitted to live in city parks and roadsides because they are cute and diverting; when they are exterminated, it is most likely to be because they interfere with housing or commercial development or with leisure activities like golf or baseball (their holes make ball diamonds dangerous to play on). In cities, people can more easily be conservationists: because city dwellers don't have to *use* the land in the same way that farmers do, they have an essentially different relation to the environment. This difference is not manifested only in attitudes to gophers, of course: virtually every battle over treatment of animals or preservation of land eventually is also expressed as a conflict between "city people" (environmentalists) and "country people" (those who live on and work the land).[10] As Michael Woods argues in a British context, "the hunting debate cannot be separated from the contesting of rurality, with representations of animals featuring prominently in many constructs of the rural" (182). These contestations centre on questions of identity, where shooting gophers is seen as a crucial part of "true" prairie identity. This identity is frequently framed in terms of heritage, as in the gopher derby supporter's recollection of teaching his "kids to handle firearms safely to kill skunks, coyotes, gophers, magpies and any other farm predators," or in the remarks of another pro-derby writer:

"Parents and kids will once again spend time together out shootin' gophers. Ask any hunter and he will tell you of the many fond memories he has of being out with dad, learning to shoot safely in a field of gophers" (Litwin). Challenging the gopher's status as pest is then seen not only as opposition to the shooting of gophers, but also is seen as an attack on the farm family and rural values in general.[11]

———————————— • ————————————

> Gophers, no doubt, become a serious menace, when in great numbers and do extensive harm to prairie and meadow land, yet, on the other hand, they may be a source of attraction to tourists, especially those from the East, who visit our Parks.
>
> Memo from Mr. Taylor to Mr. Harkin,
> Department of the Interior,
> re: Destruction of Gophers in Jasper National Park, 1932

The above memo highlights the second dominant model of the gopher in prairie popular culture: the tourist icon or plucky mascot, frequently celebrated for the same tenacity that causes farmers to despair. Considerations of tourism again lead to questions of ownership and identity, as tourists are seen to occupy a space only temporarily, while locals ostensibly know a place differently and occupy it in ways the tourist does not. The ways in which prairie communities choose to mobilize the gopher as a tourist attraction are interesting in that they may reveal a community's assumptions about what the gopher is and where it belongs. On the prairies, I suggest, we see images of the gopher used to attract two audiences: an urban audience from within the region, and a general audience of travellers from other regions. One instance of the gopher being mobilized to attract urban audiences occurs at the City of Winnipeg's Assiniboine Park Zoo. Where one might expect to see a lion or a flamingo on the cover of the brochure advertising the Assiniboine Park Zoo, the cover photograph is instead of two prairie dogs. The photograph, an extreme close-up, offers nothing to distinguish the prairie dogs, a non-native species, from the very similar but much smaller native gophers. The brochure seems intended for an urban population separated from "nature"; there would be no point in paying to go to the zoo if one could just look out of the window and see a gopher, as many rural people can do. Such an advertisement invites Winnipeg dwellers to be tourists in their own landscape, going to the zoo to see the "real" prairie from which they are ostensibly estranged.[12] The brochure appeals to prospective visitors by playing on the cuteness factor of the prairie dogs and by encouraging an anthropomorphic response in the viewer: the prairie dogs appear to be cuddling, or having a conversation. It is difficult to imagine these benign creatures as anyone's number one enemy. Inside the zoo, the ways in which animals are contextualized or framed is brought into sharp focus. The prairie dogs, a crowd favourite, are in their specific exhibit, labelled and contained. All around their enclosure, however, "wild" gophers run at large, tunnelling into the bison paddock and crossing fences with impunity. Here the "pest" and the "valuable zoo animal" exist side-by-side, both protected by their place within the zoo's borders. These analogous animals fill the same ecological and cultural niches, but are defined radically differently within the boundaries of the zoo. In her study of domestic tourism and art, Lucy Lippard writes that "every place is both local and foreign. The same place is the site of two very different experiences" (4). The juxtaposition of the prairie dog as zoo animal and the gopher as "wild" animal highlights the simultaneity of the local and the foreign; each animal is coded differently through its relation to the zoo, but each can also be understood simultaneously as exotic and local. The arbitrariness and contingency of these definitions is emphasized by the responses of zoo visitors, many of whom seem equally entranced with both the prairie dogs and the gophers.

Other instances of gopher tourism are aimed at tourists from outside the region. The use of the gopher can be in name only, as in Winnipeg's Prairie Dog Central, a tourist train that takes passengers on a brief sightseeing tour of the prairie. More thorough manifestations of gopher tourism include the construction of giant roadside gophers, as in Eston, Saskatchewan, which also hosts annual gopher races (see "Welcome to Eston"). Another gopher tourism event is the annual Gopher Drop in Cupar, Saskatchewan, which works on the same principle as charity plastic duck races. Participants purchase hand-sewn facsimile gophers, which are then taken up in a hot air balloon and dropped, along with some hand-sewn facsimile gopher holes. The gophers that land closest to the holes win prizes ("Gopher Drop"). One of the more fascinating manifestations is the Gopher Hole Museum and Gift Shop, in Torrington, Alberta. A website provides an introduction to the museum: "The Museum is a whimsical portrayal of daily life in the tiny, tranquil village of Torrington, Alberta. There are 31 displays housing 54 mounted gophers. Each display depicts a different theme: hockey, hairdressing, farming, etc. Each character is dressed in suitable attire to complement the artists' picturesque backgrounds" ("World Famous"). The museum's website offers gopher t-shirts, gopher songs, gopher teaspoons, and even natural mounted and novelty mounted gophers. "Are you looking for the perfect gift for that special person who has everything?" asks the website.

For $130 one can order a stuffed and mounted gopher dressed in the costume of one's choice (the site suggests dressing the gopher as a clown, a farmer, or a golfer). Also available are stuffed gophalopes, regional variations on the more widely-known jackalopes (mythical animals created by attaching antlers to a taxidermied jackrabbit).[13] Dioramas include such scenes as a gopher pastor preaching while a gopher angel hovers overhead, a gopher beautician styling a bewigged gopher wearing makeup, and a gopher RCMP officer complete with miniature police dog (presumably a replica). One exhibit even alludes to the controversy surrounding the museum's use of gophers. Two gophers, one wearing love beads and sporting long hair and a beard and the other clothed in a top hat and suit jacket, engage in a tug-of-war over the body of a third gopher, beneath a sign indicating "Torrington Village Office." A dialogue balloon emanating from the mouth of the gopher in the hat says "This one is needed for the museum," while in the foreground two signs read "Save the Gopher" and "G.A.G.S. Gophers Against Getting Stuffed." People for the Ethical Treatment of Animals has campaigned against the Gopher Hole Museum, but seems to have succeeded only in publicizing it.

On the surface, it would seem that rural communities' mobilization of the gopher as a tourist attraction flies in the face of logic: since the gopher is the farmer's enemy, one would suspect that it would be a small town's last choice as an attraction. However, it seems possible that use of the gopher as tourist icon is an extension of the ideology of agriculture rather than a counter to it. If agriculture as it is practiced on the Canadian prairies is about use-value (leading to the production of capital), then the transformation of the gopher into a tourist icon makes sense. As one volunteer at the Torrington Museum says, "the gophers are a tremendous problem for the farmers here. We have to kill them. Is it so bad to put them on display afterwards?" ("Torrington"). These rural communities are, in a way, putting these gophers to work, as they generate capital through their entrance into a commodity system. But the celebration of the gopher as represented in tourist kitsch does not lead to a corresponding increased valuation of the animal itself. Gopher tourism can be seen as representing a kind of rural wish-fulfilment: the crop-eating animal is eradicated, to be replaced by a useful simulacrum. These transformed gophers do not represent human-animal cooperation, but instead literally showcase human domination over nature, as the gophers are stripped of their animal qualities and reshaped as small, furry humans. The museum demonstrates a complex relation between humans and the natural world: the gopher as pest is eradicated, to be transformed through an anthropomorphic relation into a kind of pet (as shown in the costumes and dialogue attributed to the taxidermy displays). One wonders whether the gopher-tourism icon would remain popular if extermination campaigns like the Saskatoon Wildlife Federation's Gopher Derby were successful in ridding the prairie of gophers. My own suspicions are that the draw of gopher tourism is independent of the existence of the real animal, much as the existence of Mickey Mouse has not rendered mousetraps obsolete.

Related to the use of the gopher as tourist icon is the gopher as prairie mascot. Some instances of the gopher as mascot are simply predicated on the homonymic qualities of "gopher" and "go for," as in a Saskatoon Public Library reading contest that exhorts children to "gopher it!" and awards them certificates of achievement illustrated with gophers.[14] One of the best examples of the gopher as prairie mascot is Gainer the Gopher, the mascot of the Canadian Football League's Saskatchewan Roughriders. Gainer is a giant gopher clad in a shirt collar and striped tie, whose job is to incite the crowd. After every Roughrider touchdown, Gainer climbs into the Gainermobile, which is a white car with a simulated gopher hole in the roof, sticks his head out of the hole, and is driven around the field, waving to the fans. While Gainer receives much support from some people ("Gainer's Gang," his fan club for children, is popular, and stuffed toys made in his image sell well), he is not a hit with everyone. One frustrated fan urged the club to "do something exciting," writing, "Is there anything more mundane than a bloody gopher? What's he going to do, bite an ankle now and then? When a good thing happens, the least the bugger could do is dig a hole or something. . . . Punt that darn gopher. Hardly a soul in the province likes the little buggers. They're vermin, one step above rats and mice, and no one likes them much either" (Mcleod). If, as newspapers report, the gopher is "prairie enemy #1," why would it be chosen as a mascot for a prairie football team?[15] Part of the answer may be that while gophers may be agricultural pests, they are also indigenous wildlife, found only in the North American Great Plains. They are highly adaptable, living well in both country and city, and are thus familiar to urban and rural dwellers alike. They also have an underdog quality to them that fits well into ideas of western alienation. In addition, they are easy to endow with anthropomorphic qualities (Disney has a Gopher character, for example); even the manufacturers of gopher poison are unable to resist representing them as cartoon-like characters with human qualities. One 1921 advertisement for Gophercide, for example, shows two gophers, one of whom wears a dress, going on a date, only to consume poisoned grain the farmer has set out for them. In the final frame, a third gopher, wearing glasses and smoking a pipe, sits cross-legged in a library chair, reading the obituaries and lamenting the unusually high number of gopher deaths.

The gopher may also serve as a politically-inflected regional mascot. Its underdog qualities are highlighted in *Gopher Freedom* (1975), an anti-American comic book published in Saskatoon by the Trans-Prairie Gopher Freedom League Propaganda Press. The comic, responding to the events of the Vietnam War as well as to the 1973 world oil crisis, details the resistance of gophers to American attempts to exploit Canada's natural resources, particularly oil and fresh water. An American General remarks to his military colleagues, "Boys, these hyar gophers've been a burr in the side of American industry—an impediment to our manifest destiny" (4). After the gophers repulse an invading army of American soldiers, the Americans develop Operation Clone, designed to "show that the gopher is no match for good ol' American know-how and technology" (18). The American soldier-clones are mechanical rodents, "part mole—for underground vision: part black-footed ferret—for pure gopher hatred: part American boy—so it'll do anything we tell it to" (17). These menacing automata are ultimately defeated by the simple gophers, who celebrate their victory by having a lakeside bonfire and kissing each other goodnight. The comic's resistance to American imperialism is also made clear through faux advertisements, like the one for a cloned American ("In a few weeks he'll be ready to secure the chairmanship of any board of directors or an influential position at any of your cultural programming academies"), and games ("Make a shadow gopher 'n scare your Uncle Sam!"). Here the gopher functions as a vehicle for political protest by standing in for Saskatchewan's population as a figure of resistance able to defeat an imperial power through superior intelligence and general moral goodness.

——————— • ———————

> The gopher on his hind legs
>   is taut with holiness and fright.
>   Miniature and beardless,
> he could be stoned or flooded out,
> burnt alive in stubble fields,
> martyr to children for a penny a tail.
> . . .
> Little earth-otter, little dusty Lazarus,
> he vanishes, he rises. He won't tell us
> what he's seen.
>   Lorna Crozier, "A Prophet In His Own Country"

In studying the debate over fox hunting in Britain, Michael Woods found that the controversy incorporated "issues of morality, civil liberties, economics, rural-urban conflict, class, conservation and animal welfare" (182). Examination of the conflicted representations of the gopher in Canadian prairie popular culture reveals that this debate is just as complex. The gopher is not only a small, brown rodent indigenous to the Canadian prairie; it is also a highly contested regional icon that is mobilized in a number of simultaneous and contradictory ways to indicate prairie identity and ownership. In his long poem *Seed Catalogue*, Robert Kroetsch asks *"How do you build a prairie town?"* and answers that "the gopher was the model." I suggest that the gopher is, in fact, a model for prairie communities, in that its representations contain many of the dominant tensions within the region, particularly those over heritage, regional identity, and relation to the environment. Reading the gopher, then, means reading geography, politics, history, and culture, and understanding that like the prairie itself the gopher can mean many things simultaneously. Controversy over the gopher is in important ways symptomatic of the ever-present debates within the region over power as manifested in land ownership and the control of prairie space. These conflicting representations point to the vast space that remains to be crossed in any attempt to reconcile tensions over land use within the prairie region or to forge ties between different and differently embattled prairie constituencies.

Notes

I would like to acknowledge the support of the University of Manitoba University Research Grants Program for financial support during the research for this paper. I also thank my research assistant Tavia Hafso, and my informal research team, Bob Calder and Lorin Calder. This essay appeared in a slightly different form in *The American Review of Canadian Studies*.

1. Gophers and prairie dogs are different species, though they are similar animals and occupy similar cultural niches. Prairie dogs (*Cynomys ludovicianis*), common on the American great plains, are larger than what Canadians call gophers. Gophers, to Americans, usually mean pocket gophers (*Geomys bursarius*), which are a distinct species of burrowing rodent with large cheek pouches. What Canadians call gophers are really ground squirrels, of which there are two principal kinds on the Canadian prairies: thirteen-lined ground squirrels (*Spermophilus tridecemlineatus*), which are striped, and Richardson's ground squirrels

(*Spermophilus richardsonii*), which are not striped. In the Canadian vernacular, however, they are commonly referred to as gophers, and it is this vernacular sense that I mean when I use the label "gopher." The Canadian category "gopher" may also include pocket gophers and occasionally even moles; fundamentally, it is a blanket term for small, furry rodents.

2.   The three most recent books on Canadian prairie writing, Laurie Ricou's *Vertical Man/Horizontal World*, Dick Harrison's *Unnamed Country*, and Deborah Keahey's *Making It Home*, do not mention gophers. They are also absent from two comparative studies of Canadian and American prairie fiction, Robert Thacker's *The Great Prairie Fact and Literary Imagination* and Diane Dufva Quantic's *The Nature of the Place*. Only one study explicitly addresses human-animal relations in an agricultural milieu. Barney Nelson's *The Wild and the Domestic: Animal Representation, Ecocriticism, and Western American Literature* concentrates on representations of ranching and argues that ideas of "pure" wildness have been privileged over "domesticated" nature. Nelson suggests that humans rank animals on a sliding scale of value and that the category of "animal" must be recognized as culturally constructed. These ideas are helpful in developing a framework for considering attitudes to animals in a farming context.

3.   Gophers and golfers have a strange relationship, which I have termed "The *Caddyshack* Syndrome" after the film starring Bill Murray as a caddy desperate to eradicate a persistent gopher from his golf course. Symptoms of the syndrome include an increasing number of consumer items featuring gophers, which are aimed at golfers: gopher/golfer Christmas ornaments, gopher-shaped golf club covers, mugs labelled "the 19th hole" which reveal a gopher when emptied, and the like. This connection is fostered by two things: the similarity between the words gopher and golfer, which allow for many punning commercial items to be produced; and the similarities between the agendas of gopher and golfer, as one wishes to dig holes at random over a piece of land and the other wishes to allow holes only in certain places. Each seeks to use the land for similar but non-compatible ends.

4.   See references to eating gophers in Louise Halfe's books of poetry *Blue Marrow* and *Bear Bones and Feathers*, for example. See Yellowman and Barry Carlson for some instances of prairie dogs in Native American stories. European settlers also ate prairie dogs and gophers, as suggested by the title "*And Prairie Dogs Weren't Kosher": Jewish Women in the Upper Midwest Since 1855*, a history by American Linda Mack Schloff.

Interested parties may consult Glen Bunbury's on-line instructions on cooking gophers.

5. See John Gray's article for an account of a mummified human body discovered wearing a gopher-skin cloak.

6. As R. Douglas Francis points out, this image of the Canadian prairie as agricultural heartland preceded its settlement. Settlers came to the land with preconceived expectations that were not always met by the harsh prairie climate and its cyclical patterns of drought, grasshopper infestation, and gophers.

7. This list of pests points to the need to combine agriculture with ecology, rather than simply trying to remake the prairies in an agricultural image. Coyotes are natural predators of gophers; since farmers have so radically depleted the coyote population, gopher populations have soared, as have the attendant problems for farmers.

8. In connection with this point, see Richard Yarwood and Nick Evans's examination of how humans have not only socially constructed farm animals through categories like pest and pet, but also how "farm animals have, quite literally, been constructed by people to fit into particular rural spaces" (99). See also Alec Brownlow's discussion of the status of wolves in the Adirondacks, which documents a "radical change in the symbolic space of the wolf in America," as it moves from loathsome varmint to symbol of wildness and liberty (144).

9. The belief that animals are infinitely reproducible has a long tradition in western philosophical thought; see Akira Lippit's *Electric Animal* for an overview.

10. For discussions of urban/rural relations in connection with environmentalism and conservation, see *Contested Natures* by Kenneth Macnaughten and John Urry, *Creating the Countryside* edited by E. Melanie Dupuis and Peter Vandergeest, and "'Are You an Environmentalist or Do You Work For a Living': Work and Nature" by Richard White. See also Sharon Butala's account of the resistance she and her husband encountered in setting up Old Man on His Back Heritage and Nature Preserve in *Wild Stone Heart*.

11. The columnist's ironic erasure of the final 'g' in "shooting" is suggestive. People from the prairies are keenly aware of the stereotypes imposed on them from outside the region; here, the columnist deliberately plays the role of yokel, perhaps to defend himself from the charge of genuine yokelism.

12. Recent work in urban ecocriticism has pointed out that constructing

urban centres as entirely estranged from the natural world promotes a false relationship between the urban and the wild. George Melnyk argues that prairie cities contain many wild places, while critical essays in *The Nature of Cities* underscore the importance of "remind[ing] city dwellers of [their] placement within urban ecosystems and the importance of this fact for understanding urban life and culture" (Bennett and Teague 4).

13. For more on jackalopes, see Karel Ann Marling's study of roadside attractions, *The Colossus of Roads*.

14. This punning on "gopher" and "go for" is taken one step further in the case of Scooter, the Muppet character created by Jim Henson, who is a gopher working as a "go-for" for Kermit the Frog.

15. Gainer is not the only gopher mascot. University of Minnesota sports teams are called the Golden Gophers, and their mascot is a large gopher named Goldie. Minnesota is known as "The Gopher State."

Debra Dudek

•

"Prairie as Flat as the Sea": Realizing Robert Kroetsch's "Spending the Morning on the Beach"

> The Southern Cross signals the upset world. Even
> westward is lost in east. We are not where we were.
> Robert Kroetsch, "Spending the Morning on the Beach: Fiji"

I approach Robert Kroetsch's *Seed Catalogue* warily, wondering how I might teach this book to students studying Canadian literature with me in Australia. Wondering, pedagogically, what should be different, if anything. The book falls open, and my world shifts. There, at the cracked spine of my book, the final lines of "Seed Catalogue" meet "Spending the Morning on the Beach." Why had I never realized that the beach existed next to the prairie? What was it about my then only-prairie sensibility that did not allow me to see the beach until I, too, could feel the "salt on [my] skin . . . in the fluids of [my] body" (34)? The poet's persona flies towards the Southern Cross and the world is both upset and even. As the epigraph to this chapter states, "westward is lost in east. We are not where we were" (33). I hold this sense of dislocation, of disruption both poetic and corporeal, as the basis for my pedagogy. And this story about how I realized "Spending the Morning on the Beach" will be a starting point for me when I speak to my students about Canadian prairie literature, about how being dislocated or located elsewhere might realize a text anew.

Before I move towards offering responses to these questions, I want to provide some context for this chapter. My interest in this topic—on transnational perspectives and theories and specifically in Australian and Canadian literatures as interactive fields of study—overtly began four years ago when I was awarded a fellowship from the International Council of Canadian Studies to go to the University of Wollongong to team-teach an already-prepared comparative Canadian-Australian literature course. When I took up that four-month teaching position in Wollongong, I had quite a strong background in Postcolonial Studies but my focus was primarily on reading (multicultural and Aboriginal) Canadian literature through postcolonial and feminist theories, so I had not extended my research and teaching into the study of another so-called "national" literature.

Since that time, I have concentrated my research and teaching primarily on multicultural Australian children's literature because I was working as a Research Fellow at Deakin University in Melbourne on an Australian Research Council-funded grant called "Building Cultural Citizenship: Multiculturalism and Children's Literature." In other words, my academic career in Canada was underpinned by a study of multicultural Canadian literature and my academic career in Australia has been informed by studies of multicultural Australian texts. In July 2007, I commenced a full-time continuing position back at the University of Wollongong where I am now coordinating the subjects in Australian literature and Canadian literature, and in July 2008, I will be teaching *An Introduction to Canadian Literature* in Australia, for my first time. This subject, then, is another one of the starting points for this paper. My essay circulates around the question, "How will *I* teach Canadian prairie literature to students at the University of Wollongong?" One of my purposes is to extend the specificity of this question into a broader theorization of how one might approach Canadian prairie literature from abroad and how this approach might inform reading practices in Canada.

I acknowledge that there is perhaps nothing special about teaching a body of literature that is written, published, and primarily read from a space that another set of readers has little or no other imaginative access to, except via the literature these readers hold in their hands. Many Australian and Canadian university students might not be able to imagine regions of Africa or India, for instance, and there are many subjects in these universities organized around African and Indian literatures. Furthermore, there is already quite a large body of work that focuses on comparative Canadian-Australian studies across a range of disciplines, many of which are represented within ACSANZ (the Association for Canadian Studies in Australia and New Zealand), which also has a journal, *Australasian Canadian Studies*, which publishes comparative and intercultural topics that look to and from both Canada and Australia.

Additionally, writers such as Aritha van Herk and Miriam Lo have written about Canada in Australia, and other writers, such as Robert Kroetsch, have published poems about Australia in Canada. Indeed, the more I read, the more I realize connections between these two places. In Miriam Lo's article, "Towards a Particular Hybridity: A Beginning," for example, Lo begins to articulate her theory of hybridity from some of her own creative writing, which she published first in the Alberta journal *absinthe* and then reprints and revisits in the Australian *Westerly* article. Perhaps even more relevant—at least for the purposes of this paper—is the realization with which I opened this paper:

that one of my copies of Kroetsch's *Seed Catalogue*, the copy that I obtained when I first studied this poem as an undergraduate student taking a Canadian literature course, is divided into two sections: I "Seed Catalogue" and II "Spending the Morning on the Beach." The latter consists of "ten related lyrics" set in the Antipodes, and specifically Fiji, Australia, and New Zealand.

Realizing that *Seed Catalogue* includes "Spending the Morning on the Beach," that the prairie and the beach occupy the same space, I began thinking about how I might analyze *Seed Catalogue* as a hybrid text and about how I might put into practice an "intentional hybridity," a term that Australian critic Jacqueline Lo borrows from Bakhtin, in order to argue for this type of "hybridity as a deliberate strategy to effect an ironic double-consciousness which destabilises orthodox world views. Intentional hybridity is both a textual effect—that is, a form of aesthetic praxis which works by internal dialogisation—*and* a reading strategy informed by a self-reflexive doubleness" ("Beyond Happy Hybridity" 161). Canadian critic and poet Fred Wah also discusses the importance of hybridity in his essay "Half-Bred Poetics," in which he states that the "hybrid writer must (one might suspect, necessarily) develop instruments of disturbance, dislocation, and displacement" (73). While Wah is speaking specifically about the hybrid writer, I take his point to extend also to the critic and reader. If we put these two aspects of hybridity together, then, we have an intentional hybridity based on a self-reflexive doubleness that employs tools such as "disturbance, dislocation, and displacement."

This displacement, this potentially new approach in Canadian prairie literature, disturbs and dislocates precisely because it is being read from an Antipodean perspective. But to theorize this idea even further, I would like to look briefly at what an Antipodean gaze offers specifically, which another dislocated gaze might not. Peter Beilharz in his article "Australia: the Unhappy Country, or, a Tale of Two Nations" (2005) argues that the "Antipodes, having the feet elsewhere from the centres of metropolitan civilization, suggests that identity results from the relationship *between* places and cultures rather than emerging from place, or ground . . . that the image of the Antipodes . . . suggests movement rather than fixity" (74, italics mine). David Pearson, reading an earlier text by Beilharz, claims that "to be Antipodean . . . is to imagine one's identity and the places one belongs to, in transnational ways. . . .As Beilharz (1997: 187) stresses, 'the Antipodes is not a place so much as it is a *relation*, one not of our own choosing but one which also enables us'" (89, emphasis mine). This notion of the Antipodes being a "relation not of our own choosing" speaks strongly to me about my own sense of being positioned in the Antipodes and looking north to a prairie that I cannot see but to which I shall always relate. Pedagogically, it is important for me to embody this Antipodean space, this hybrid space of relationality and dialogism, so as not to fix students' ways of reading prairie literature along my own sense of what it is like to live on a "real" Canadian prairie.

When I first began thinking about and researching this paper, I went to Aritha van Herk's essay, "Prairie as Flat as . . .", which is collected in *A Frozen Tongue* published by Dangeroo Press in Australia, searching for how prairie academics have already written and theorized from and/or about the prairie from the space that is Australia because, as I already stated, one of my starting points for this paper is the question, "Does reading and teaching Canadian Prairie Literature in Australia—and in Wollongong in particular—produce a different kind of reading experience than one that might occur when reading this literature in the context/place from which it was produced?" And if so (and my intuition is that it does), then why is this Antipodean approach important? How does it deepen one's understanding of this body of literature? Furthermore, how do I position myself when I lecture on and facilitate seminars about Canadian prairie literature?

In her essay, van Herk argues that the prairie is "greater than, deeper than, more than simply a flattened sea. It now has irony, and voice, and multiplicity, its own becoming, beyond the one simple metaphor of man" (137). This idea of the prairie *as flat as* and *more than* the sea produces a working metaphor that fruitfully embodies both the visual comparison between prairie and sea as well as the metaphoric dynamism of a landscape and seascape that are neither flat nor static. I bring this comparison to the foreground of my discussion because I want to employ this metaphor as one that works *transnationally*—and between Canada and Australia in particular—as a way of realizing the depth and vitality of a landscape-based body of writing from a place where readers may have no access to the physical and political contexts upon which the literature is based.

I have emphasized the word *transnationally* in order to call attention to this notion of the *trans*. In January 2008, I travelled back to Canada because I received a grant from the International Council for Canadian Studies in order to gather resources and to speak to colleagues in Winnipeg, Guelph, Windsor, and Vancouver about teaching a Canadian literature subject in Australia. In Vancouver, I met with Fred Wah for coffee and conversation. I talked with him about how I might negotiate this looking both ways—from Australia to Canada and back—and he reminded me about the *trans*. In *Faking It*, Wah writes, "'Transing' has become an important compound in my poetics of writing actions that have to do with translation, transcreation, transposition, i.e., senses of crossing, and shifting" (2). Wah's emphasis on shifting and cross-ing—on transing—connects fruitfully with Beilharz's notion of the Antipodes as that which suggests movement and relationships between places and with my pedagogical methodology of looking both ways across the cracked spine of my copy of *Seed Catalogue* as a starting point for an Antipodean approach to reading Canadian prairie literature.

Before I move to a closer reading of Kroetsch's text, however, I want to contextualize my argument. To my knowledge, there has not been a focus upon *reading* and *teaching* Canadian prairie literature specifically from an Australian perspective, and it is this perspective—both the physical notion of perspective that signifies viewpoint and the adjectival notion that speci-fies pedagogical focus—that punctuates my argument. Over twenty years ago, Aritha van Herk published an article in the Australian journal *Kunapipi* (published out of the University of Wollongong) titled "Women Writers and the Prairie: Spies in an Indifferent Landscape" about the Canadian prairie, and about women writers and the prairie specifically. In this essay, van Herk writes,

> In landscape . . . the crucial point is the vantage from which
> the viewer sees the world. One must look at landscape from
> within landscape. What one sees is determined by position;
> the scene varies accordingly. There's a hell of a difference
> between the landscape a person sees standing on a hill and
> what that same person sees from the bottom of a coulee a
> few hundred feet away. Position dictates point of view and
> position's influence has been neglected. (139)

In this passage, van Herk contests a view of the prairie as a flat, masculine space from the perspective of a woman on the prairie who sees the land's un-dulations. I would like to borrow this argument about perspective, however, to speak about the prairie from the perspective of the landscape of Austra-lia, for the literature from both of these spaces—Australia and the Canadian prairie—has been defined and has defied the construction of their identity as grounded in landscape, and critics from both of these spaces have contested this grounding as the best or most useful way in which to analyze and realize their respective literatures.

I presented a short version of this chapter to an Australian interdisciplin-ary audience on 29 November 2007 at Monash University in Melbourne at *The Intercultural Workshop: Theoretical Approaches, Interdisciplinary Perspec-tives*. For the purposes of that workshop, I thought it useful to situate how Canadian prairie literature is placed within the larger field of Canadian literature. While for the implied audience of my essay in this collection, this gesture may not be as important as it was when I spoke to an Australian non-literary studies audience, what I found helpful about this workshop was the feedback about and interest in the notion of prairie literature as a regional literature that has been read as a body of literature that speaks back to dominant narratives about Canada.

While the concept of regionalism may no longer be in circulation as much as it once was as a theoretical lens through which to view Canadian literature, I believe some aspects of it translate well across more contemporary categories such as transnationalism and globalization. Indeed, as Marjorie Pryse argues in "Writing Out of the Gap: Regionalism, Resistance, and Relational Reading," "regionalism represents an impulse to keep alive alternative visions of national and global development" (22-23). It is this impulse for alternative visions that I want to put under pressure here, for perhaps one of the useful outcomes of reading regionalism in Canada from Australia is to turn that reading back on itself and to look at the regional aspects of Australian literature. For now, however, I want to keep my Antipodean view gazing at the Canadian prairies, for there is also a danger in this move, a danger that once again (and still), regional literature might become not about the literature itself, but about what that literature says about the centre, or in this case, about another globally marginalized literature from the Antipodes.

One of the reasons I want to maintain my Antipodean gaze is because much of this study of Canadian prairie literature has been firmly entrenched in the prairie itself. Generally, prairie writers hail from the prairie, their texts are published by prairie publishers, taught in courses at prairie universities, and consumed by prairie readers. As Alison Calder argues in "Reassessing Prairie Realism," if prairie texts *are* taught in Canadian literature courses, then they are likely to be taught in a "regional" module of the subject and they are usually texts that deal with prairie realism (52). This placement is likely to be exactly the move that I myself will make when I teach the upcoming introduction to Canadian literature course at Wollongong, but I want to ensure that this marginal literature is not again marginalized by its placement in the subject.

Similarly, I want to ensure that I do not reinscribe this body of literature with the geographical determinism that informs much Canadian prairie writing, under the heading of "prairie realism." As Calder argues,

> Criticism of prairie realism is predicated on a belief in the primacy of the land. Geographic determinism is evident even in the critical label: this is, after all, *prairie* realism.

> This label provides more than just geographic demarcation,
> however, in that assumption of geographic authority car-
> ries illusions of immutability and homogeneity. . . . the ac-
> tions of the characters, and indeed the construction of the
> characters themselves, is seen as a result of environmental
> determinism. (56)

Much of this writing from the margins has been characterized as a realist fiction that represents the struggles of man—and I use "man" intentionally—against the landscape, and this characterization still influences perceptions of prairie writing.

Here, however, for me, is one of the conundrums of teaching Canadian prairie literature in Australia: I realize that the landscape and the weather *are* primary differences that characterize life on the prairie and the writing that emerges from those lives. Or at least that is how I see it from my current per-spective as a prairie woman living by the beach and as a prairie woman who wants to write or speak her body in that landscape to her students in Austra-lia. I realize that I want to tell them about how icicles form on the edges of my eyelashes on a cold Winnipeg day, if my scarf is covering my face against the "RealFeel"[1] index that puts the temperature at −31C. About how my nostrils stick together if I walk outside on a similar day without a scarf. About how a summer day can be as hot as a winter day is cold and the sky as blue at both these extremes.

But perhaps I should leave such words to the creative writers, to the texts themselves, for the dangerous slip that Calder warns against is apt: that slip from prairie realism as fiction to prairie realism as reality, as a form of mime-sis that holds truth-value (58-59), the consequence of which is a static, barren literature that represents a static, barren landscape: "prairie realism and the real prairies are contained: prairie realist works are slotted into the 'regional text' place with all its attendant evaluative baggage, and the real prairies are continually defined as a sparsely populated, inarticulate, sterile region, whose lack of power and/or wealth is no one's fault but its own" (59-60). What I wonder, then, is whether or not this perception still holds when the view is not from within national or even regional boundaries of Canada. Will my Antipodean gaze still fix the prairie in this stagnant way?

The last fifteen years of literary criticism about Canadian prairie litera-ture has worked towards debunking and unsettling static metaphors and recurring descriptions about prairie dwellers and the prairie landscape and climate, which often rely upon precisely this geographical determinism, and extending it to include discussions about regionality from a transnational or *meso-regional* perspective, to use Pearson's terminology (Pearson 89). What happens, for instance, when this embodied knowledge is informed primarily by similes of sameness—for example, that a description of the prairie reads like the landscape of South Australia or like the sheep stations in Northern NSW—or by an impossible imagining? And what role do *I* play as a "transing" critic and teacher, born and raised on the prairie but now living and working in Australia? While I may not be able to respond beyond a guess at how to answer the first question, I can be conscious about the role that I myself play in the selection of texts I choose for the course and about how these texts are analyzed in the classroom.

Let me now turn to an analysis of Kroetsch's *Seed Catalogue*. As I mentioned earlier, it is the spine of my book, this space that joins the prairie and the beach via the sea, across which I shall move. I have subtitled this chapter "Realizing Kroetsch's 'Spending the Morning on the Beach'" in order to call attention to a process of realization, a process that Kroetsch's poem brings to the foreground. The verbal noun "realizing" occurs in nine out of the ten "related lyrics," with the verb "realize" occurring in the tenth. This emphasis on the "ing" form of the verb "realize" denotes a continuous action or existence of making something real, or giving reality to, or perhaps more aptly, "to make real as an object of thought" (*OED*). While I do not intend to make claims about some notion of "the real," I do want to emphasize the process by which a poem, in this case, becomes an object of thought, becomes an object about which one might think. Thus, reality becomes about process, about relationality, about positioning, about locating oneself and about reading the details of that location. Or to relate these ideas back to my argument: it was not until I relocated to Australia that "Spending the Morning on the Beach" became an object of my thought.

Before the "ten related lyrics" begin, there is the following epigraph from *Burning Water* by George Bowering, which utilizes an image of the sea as an in-between space that also unites seemingly distant places and people: "We all live in the same world's sea. We cannot tell a story that leaves us outside, and when I say we, I include you. But in order to include you, I feel that I cannot spend these pages saying *I* to a second person. Therefore let us say *he*, and stand together looking at them" (31). On a first reading, I felt alienated by this privileging of a *he* persona, and I perceived this move as once again performing that masculinist gesture by which women are alienated from the prairie and from other similarly-coded landscapes. And, indeed, my subsequent readings do not altogether dislodge my initial response.

I am, however, compelled by the opening "we" that connects me in rhyme to the "same world's sea." Furthermore, this epigraph contains echoes of an excerpt from Miriam Lo's poetry, which she quotes in "Towards a Particular Hybridity": "I wanted to write about how each place exists in the space of the same heartbeat, about how it boggles the mind that two different worlds can exist in the same space of time and not only two but countless, countless, others living moving churning flowing, foreign familiar friendly frightening in the one space of breath" (12). This "churning flowing" and "frightening" space calls to mind the very sea about which Bowering and Kroetsch write, and about the specific sea by which I walk each morning, and in which I frequently fling myself.

It is the two sentences that follow the epigraph, however, that suggest to me a more personalized tenor of the poems that both follow and precede: "I can no longer keep a journal. My life erases everything I write" (31). We may read this "I" back into "Seed Catalogue" as the poet's struggle to answer the repeated question: *How do you grow a poet?* (15, 16, 17, 20). In the ten poems that follow these epigraphs, the poet's persona no longer exists in the first person, with one exception, which I shall analyze later. Instead, the poet becomes *he*, he who stands together with himself and his friends to look at the sea and themselves in it, as poetry and the poem repeatedly eludes and torments and taunts him in this Antipodean space, which questions and disrupts the seasons of west.

The poet begins his journey in Fiji, and the opening line of the poem of the same name, begins the repetition of the poet's realization, all of which I shall quote here, in order to outline the trajectory of the poet's travels and to summarize the repetition and process of his realizations:

Realizing the poem for him has lost its expectancy, he
heads directly for Fiji. (33).

Realizing he's no longer obliged by the ache in his body to
write poems, he watches the grasstrees burning free of their
dead leaves. ("Brisbane" 34)

Realizing the poem is the tormentor of his sleep, he
strangles it by his refusal, in the hot sunlight, to close his
eyes. ("Noosa Heads 1" 35)

Realizing *poetry* is a mousetrap on the tongue, he calls
ashore for water. ("Noosa Heads 2" 36)

Realizing the poem. Talking the poem onto the page or writing the poem onto the tongue. Realizing he cannot foil his own inertia, he steals a pomegranate. ("Geelong, Victoria" 37)

Realizing that light, not dark, is the poet's affliction, he gives himself the Governor General's Award For Not Writing Poetry for the year 1999. ("Sydney" 38)

Realizing he is done with poetry, he goes to a museum to see a reconstruction of an extinct New Zealand bird . . . ("Wellington, New Zealand" 40)

Realizing that poetry is a hospital for the sane, he watches the Maoris building their replica village. ("Rotorua" 41)

You didn't read the sign, did you? the old woman says, at once patient and yet a bit testy.
It looks that way, he tells her. I realize that. ("North of Auckland, Parry Kauri Park" 42)

Realizing the poem is a cruising shark, he curls his toes in the mud. ("The Hibiscus Coast" 43)

Each of these passages, except the second last, about which I shall write short-ly, contains the same sentence structure. In each instance, the poet, the third-person *he*, apprehends the poem or poetry as an object of his thought from which he is separated. He exists in an independent clause performing an ac-tion that is not the act of writing poetry.

This poet's sense of loss, of no longer feeling compelled to write poetry, permeates the poems, so that even as the poems are emerging on the page, there is the sense that the poet himself is absent or lost, as he makes obvious in the first poem: "Somewhere in his recent flying is a lost day. Words are / like that. Once upon a time he was a gardener of the / possible fruition" (33). This concept of the poet as gardener moves the reader back across the sea and into the prairie west where home exists, where the poet speaks about himself in the first person, where poetry is a planting, and the seed catalogue and the garden, metaphors of growth, bloom poetry. Rather than being the gardener, being the one who is responsible for the planting, in Fiji he "drinks the juice of passion fruit, / he eats papaya and a thin slice of fresh pineapple" (33), none of which he has planted, none of which grow on the prairie.

Such recurring images of fruit and landscape remind the reader about the metaphor of gardening that structures "Seed Catalogue" and connects growth to the seasons, to a cycle in which April and May signify spring, and January unwaveringly represents the middle of winter. Indeed, "Seed Catalogue" opens in the spring or at the end of winter, and the phrase "Only the January snow. Only the summer sun" (5, 28) opens and closes the series of poems. When prairie readers move across the book's spine into the Antipodes, they may be dislocated by the line, "It is early winter, a morning in May" ("Noosa Heads 2" 36). Suddenly, the seasons are no longer stable entities, the life and death cycle no longer in synchronicity. This destabilization of the rhythms of the landscape reveals that the cycle of planting, the possibility of poetry, does not simply transplant regardless of location.

The one moment that strays from the repetition of the poet's realizations occurs when the poet moves away from the beach north of Auckland into Parry Kauri Park. Here he encounters an old woman, who asks him if he has read a sign that says the park is closed: "You didn't read the sign, did you? the old woman says" (42). This moment is the only time in the poem when the poet is addressed as "you," when he is in dialogue with another person, when he is addressed in the second person. It is significant that the woman's accusation becomes a question only through her reversal of "You didn't" to "did you?" This moment of accusation and address, of interaction, moves the poet away from the specificity and alienation of the beach and into a site of universality. He becomes the "I," the subject who realizes, the subject who is brought into being by an old woman, much like the whispering voice of the mother figure in "Seed Catalogue."

To spend the morning on the beach, then, is to contemplate the sea, to be separate from yet connected to that seemingly flat yet always moving space, which may serve as a simile for the prairie. It is to contemplate poetry from a third-person perspective, from a place where metaphors of new life, of growth represented as spring, no longer function. Calder ends "Reassessing Prairie Realism"—and I shall conclude this essay—with a reminder to myself and to other academics to take seriously and to be careful about how we place ourselves and the texts we teach in order not to reinscribe the prairies as an uninhabitable region in decline. Calder argues, "At a time when we are being told that place and referentiality no longer matter, that there is no national literature, and that we are living in a world without boundaries, those of us who call the have-not political regions home are becoming aware that placing ourselves, and our literatures, is more important than ever" (60). I want to take up Calder's challenge here, a challenge that still applies ten years after its published articulation—and to recall Miriam Lo's words that I quoted earlier—to place myself as an academic and a teacher for whom the prairies and the sea exist in the same heartbeat, the same breath. What I propose then, is an Antipodean reading practice that transcribes a relational, undulating wave between Canada and Australia, between Winnipeg and Wollongong, between the sea as the prairie and the prairie as the sea in order to realize anew the texts in which we emerge ourselves.

Notes

1. AccuWeather.com has patented the phrase RealFeel Temperature® which "lets you know what the weather actually feels like" (see http://www. accuweather.com/). The *Winnipeg Free Press* publishes this RealFeel Temperature® in its daily winter weather report.

Tina Trigg and Philip Mingay

•

Mapping Our Mental Geography:
Regionalism as Pedagogical Strategy

L iterature survey courses, by definition, require a broad sweep of material with few pauses for detailed study; they presume both breadth and accuracy in their concision. Yet to avoid unsettling or even bewildering fragmentation, they are dependent on careful structuring and selection—perhaps more so than are courses with narrower literary or historical range. Thus, facing the daunting task of encapsulating Canadian literature from its inception to the present in a single academic term while also fulfilling the Christian directive of a small private prairie university, Tina Trigg and Philip Mingay were keenly aware of the need for a single unifying factor in their senior literature survey course. There needed to be some thread holding together this selection of Canadian literature and culture for students—as well providing a sense of cohesion for the instructor—but what to choose? Among the myriad of pedagogical decisions, this question of focal point would dramatically direct the content as well as the mode of delivery.

Identifying a successful focal point around which to spin out the material involved assessing the particularity of this course and the Christian directive of the institution. English 389, the Canadian Literature course titled "Mapping Our Mental Geography" plays a key role at The King's University College in Edmonton, Alberta. In addition to being a literature survey course, with the particular demands this entails, during the time that Tina and Philip taught the course as devised (in 2005 and 2007, respectively), this class was the sole Canadian literature offering in the Department of English. As such, this single course had increasingly heavy expectations from students, the institution, and instructors. At King's University, "Mapping Our Mental Geography" is also a means for students to fulfil a required Canadian component of various other programs (including a popular primary Education after-degree) and, consequently, it is always widely subscribed.

As instructors, we were necessarily cognizant that unlike students in many other senior English courses, these students come from various disciplines. We were equally aware that in keeping with the general trend of small prairie universities, these students derive predominantly from the vicinity.

This point of contact, combined with the course title of "Mapping Our Mental Geography," suggested the relevance of regionalism as a helpful inroad and unifying factor. We independently arrived at the decision to focus not only on regionalism but specifically on prairie regionalism to structure our Canadian survey course. This noteworthy coalescence is that which the following seeks to explore. This chapter assesses how two instructors with disparate pedagogical strategies independently approached this literature course from the basis of regionalism. In particular, we examine the viability of prairie regionalism as a pedagogical tool in a senior Canadian literature survey course at a private faith-based university, including student and instructor assessments of the outcome. It should be noted that King's University emphasizes small classroom environments with a focus on class discussion. In addition to the generic course evaluations at its conclusion, we solicited student feedback through informal surveys and conversations throughout and subsequent to the course; we know these students well, and teach them throughout their degrees. With this in mind, the paper is divided by year of offering and framed in three major parts: terms of discussion, course models, and reflections.

•

Terms of Discussion: Tina

To introduce the concept of regionalism, I began with the broader notion of nationalism, querying students about their impressions of what it means to be a Canadian. We discussed accurate, erroneous, serious, and comical stereotypes of Canadians. Beyond the legal definition of citizen, students quickly recognized the complexity of this identity marker—particularly in our multicultural community. Most of the students were Canadian-born but had strong ethnic links to their cultural heritage, as do I, which led neatly to a discussion of Homi Bhabha's notions of hybridity and unhomeliness. I linked Canadian regions with our various cultural backgrounds, and we contemplated the value of interstices as contact zones rather than differentiating boundaries. By considering the "in-between spaces" as viable locations for negotiating identity beyond traditional fixed boundaries, students quickly realized the significance of power structures among social groups. Hence, we were able to discuss postcolonial concerns and to consider briefly Laura Moss's provocative question, "Is Canada postcolonial?" Students came to an awareness that geographical location is only a fraction of what constitutes regional identity and that even this seemingly stable marker is fractious and debatable. Finally, we turned our attention to the literary notion of regionalism and its ensuing complexities.

In 1943 E. K. Brown tolled the bell of regionalism as a coming wave of Canadian literature, characterizing it more like an inevitable plague. Brown predicted the imminent rise and fall of regionalism in the nation, famously declaring that "[i]n the end, however, regionalist art will fail because it stresses the peculiar at the expense, at least, if not to the exclusion, of the fundamental and universal" (21). This claim, of course, has proven unfounded as standard definitions of regionalism readily articulate. One undergraduate literary handbook, for example, defines regionalism as "[t]he literary representation of a specific locale that incorporates the particulars of geography, custom, history, folklore, and speech into the work. In regional narratives, the locale plays a crucial role in the presentation and progression of a story that could not be moved to another setting without artistic loss" (Kennedy 126). Even in such a generalized definition, specificity of place or persons is far from being considered a limiting factor to the literature. More scholarly assessments of regionalism generally begin with this connection of geographical locale to literary specificity and problematize the definition from there. Janice Fiamengo, for example, outlines "social, historical, economic, and cultural dynamics" and "relative poverty and political powerlessness" among the various debated elements of regionalism which create boundaries that are simultaneously hazy and overlapping (242). She further asserts that our contemporary focus on globalization has favourably positioned regional texts, while national narratives suffer from "a general waning of faith" (241).

In contrast to Brown's binary, then, regionalism is not a simple contrast to universalism; rather, regional literature is the particular made accessible through precise representation of geography, politics, history, and identity. In addition to all these features, regionalism arguably has a spiritual component which formed a significant part of our class discussions. In 1924 Archibald MacMechan, one of the pioneering professors of Canadian literature, contested that "[t]hrough its literature, the life, the soul of a people may be known" (17). This early link of literature to the soul is suggestive and, more recently, similar claims have been made of regionalism as "suggesting quasi-mystical explanations for the force of geography" (Fiamengo 242). In Sinclair Ross's work, among others, critics have identified the prairies as "the central subject both as an awesome physical fact and a site of metaphysical reflection" (249). Consequently, our class discussion of Ross focused on the link between spirituality and regionalism. Beginning with the Biblical allusion in the title *As For Me and My House*, we evaluated how closely Ross ties the representation of Christian faith to the regional aspects of the novel. Recognizing the titular origin in Joshua chapter 24, created an interesting background for consideration. This phrase appears in Joshua's farewell address, signifying an individual and communal renewal of covenant with God; the main urging of his address is against idolatry, which is linked to the presence of the Israelites in Canaan. Implicitly, then, both community and region can uphold or endanger one's faith position—a connection we sought to examine in various texts.

·

Course Models: Tina

My pedagogical strategy was to examine the historical development of Canadian literature and its correlation to other cultural change, including the role of spirituality or religion in society. The aim was for students to assess both how and how well the selected texts captured a regional and/or national "flavour"; through this assessment, students would be able to debate the relevance and significance of prairie literature to Canadian society (and to themselves). In addition to a number of shorter pieces (see syllabus below), my key text was Sinclair Ross's *As For Me and My House*.

Since the course necessitated period coverage, I arranged the material relatively chronologically with an eye to key trends and regional texts. Beyond the period considerations, the theme of regionalism was the major criterion for selection of texts. Rather than seeking to provide exposure to traditional canonical works in the course, I chose to cluster the text selection within two regions, spanning the coasts: the Maritimes (Alistair MacLeod, "As Birds Bring Forth the Sun"; David Adams Richards, From *Mercy Among the Children*; and Hugh MacLennan, From *Barometer Rising*) and the Prairies / West (including Sinclair Ross, *As For Me and My House*; E. J. Pratt, From *Towards the Last Spike*; Sheila Watson, From *The Double Hook*; Jane Urquhart, From *The Stone Carvers*; Guy Vanderhaeghe, "Man on Horseback"; and Aritha van Herk, From *Places Far from Ellesmere*). I employed texts such as Pratt's long poem celebrating the Canadian Pacific Railway to juxtapose notions of nationalism with regional concerns, basing the discussion on critiques of Pratt's homogeneous representation of history. W. H. New, for example, contends that *Towards the Last Spike* "appealed because it brought together the whole set of conventions that underlay the nationalism of the time . . . [in] a clearly anglophone, clearly European version of nation, and it was shortly to be challenged" (191). This challenge to Pratt's monolithism was represented in the course by F.R. Scott's pointed remarks in "All the Spikes But the Last." The Maritime texts were selected to offer a counterpoint to the prairie texts, highlighting both the distinctions and similarities between regional representations. I was especially interested in examining how place reconfigures both personal and national identity. In doing so, one of our reference points was Alistair MacLeod's snapshot theory of "getting words down on the page that convey what it is like to be living a certain kind of life in a certain place and at a certain time in history" (361). To probe how regionalism redefines "our mental geography" we utilized the chosen texts to question some of our assumptions about narrative, nation, and self.

Among the short texts on the syllabus, Guy Vanderhaeghe's "Man on Horseback" combines regionalism with issues of subjectivity and faith in a suggestive fashion. Vanderhaeghe in this story perceives his characters on two related levels which situate identity, if indirectly, in place. On the one hand, they are, as Vanderhaeghe himself has said, "overcome by feelings of powerlessness"—particularly male characters who struggle with traditional expectations "to be powerful, to take control of situations, and to shoulder sole responsibility" (qtd. in Hillis 24). The characters in "Man on Horseback" are most clearly challenged through the traditional expectations established by the regional setting of the story. On the other hand, Vanderhaeghe also argues that his characters are on a spiritual quest, where questions of the heroic lead directly to spiritual questions. Although Vanderhaeghe distances himself from a conventional Christian background, he cites Flannery O'Connor, Alice Munro, and Margaret Laurence as major influences and, more significantly, the Bible as his main intellectual influence (qtd. in Hillis 28). Thus, the external challenges test and reflect the internal mettle of his characters. In our class assessment, animated discussion revolved around issues of identity and subjectivity which Vanderhaeghe's story strongly located in place. These focal points included physical and moral courage, the constructed nature of history, the transitory nature of physical as opposed to spiritual life, and the dignity of human endurance. In particular, students were interested in the fictionalization of history, which led to discussions of Canadian history and regional history as imagined constructs; this discourse, then, led to discussions of the complexity of identity and place as formative of subjectivity. (Interestingly, another text with particular resonance for students in discussing place rather than relationship as formative of identity was an excerpt from Aritha van Herk's *Places Far From Ellesmere*, set here in Edmonton.)

To facilitate discussion at this point, I introduced two key critics: Linda Hutcheon and Benedict Anderson. Hutcheon's concept of "historiographic metafiction" outlines the self-conscious use of history in self-referential fiction as a means to subvert the illusions of fact and reality. The constructed nature of fact and fiction is overtly examined in a text that is itself fiction, thus suggesting that narrative can convey truths regardless of fact or fabrication. Further, Anderson's notions of "imagined communities" and "simultaneity" highlight the way nations are continuously constructed both synchronically and diachronically by individuals. Just as Derrida asserts that metanarrative is entirely illusory but is necessitated by the human psyche, so the autonomous existence of a nation or region is a necessary illusion. Some of the students found this blurring of fact, fiction, place, and identity unsettling—perhaps even dislocating. However, others reported finding that this tenuous characterization provided some relief, justifying their postmodern suspicion of neat categorization and discomfort with static identity—both individual and collective.

This same duality of response coloured our discussion of Sinclair Ross's *As For Me and My House*. Despite E. K. Brown's bleak prediction of the rise and fall of regionalism, he also offers a set of instructive remarks about regionalism's "admirable virtues." These include accuracy of fact and, more significantly, accuracy of tone (21). Ross's novel arguably fulfils the latter in a meaningful way; the tone is certainly not forcibly upbeat, nor are the characters or setting idealistically presented. Hence students claimed both to identify with the bleakness and to chafe against it. George Woodcock posits it as the best Canadian regional novel, avoiding "sentimental pseudo-history [and] amiable rusticity" (7). Similarly, Brown himself identifies *As For Me and My House* as "notable," "deeply sincere and tragic," a novel in which "the milieu imparts something of great importance to the day-to-day drama of human relationships" (292). In fact, Malcolm Ross contends that the best review of the novel was written by Brown (262). Clearly, *As For Me and My House* is a text where place is fundamental, yet ironically Ross creates the town of Horizon as a distinct prairie town without specifying provincial location; although it is often placed in Saskatchewan by critics, the novel nowhere names the province. As such, the text suggests the accessibility of regional texts rather than their exclusivity.

The many aspects of place are nonetheless crucial to the novel. As John Moss contends, "Ross so meticulously integrates landscape and personality that human events themselves assume cosmic proportion" (122). Our class discussions considered Ross's pivotal use of regional setting, including landscape (drought, wind, prairie fields, ravine), the parsonage (closed study door, garden, leaky roof, grayness), and demarcations of civilization (town of Horizon, Partridge Hill, the Ranch, railroad tracks, grain elevators). Consensus was that the detailed descriptions of location were integral to the delineation of character. The linkage of place with person and purpose is also echoed by Northrop Frye's famous fundamental question for Canadians: "where is here?" As Margaret Atwood explains in *Survival*, this reconfiguring of identity as inherently linked to place is vital for Canadians:"[f]or the members of a country or a culture, shared knowledge of their place, their here, is not a luxury but a necessity. Without that knowledge we will not survive" (19). If anything, Ross's novel is about survival—physical, emotional, intellectual, linguistic, relational, artistic, and spiritual.

Consequently, *As For Me and My House* seemed an ideal text for a more intense study of regionalism. It presented a testing ground to determine whether these prairie students would relate to a prairie text with greater immediacy and, if so, what this connection might suggest about regionalism's accessibility or exclusivity. As a point of comparison, we aligned the student response with general critical reception. Malcolm Ross outlines three consecutive branches of critical response to Sinclair Ross's work. Early critics focused on history and the novel's "representational accuracy" of the Depression era; subsequently, critics sought stability in characterization as a bastion against a crumbling world; more recently, postmodern critics have moved beyond the concerns of fragmented identity and, instead, have sought to examine reality as a construct created through the particularity of discourse in the text (176-77). In short, critical reception of Ross has followed the trend of critical theory towards post-structuralist concerns. Such proximation enabled us to consider how well regional literature resonates with the larger theoretical concerns and contemporary ideologies of a diverse audience. Indeed, Janice Fiamengo notes that the critical debate about what constitutes regionalism, while deeply contentious, has served the practical purpose of "shift[ing] attention to the way that regions are created in language" (245). Perhaps this is the most viable avenue of discussion in a postmodern classroom; without attempting to stabilize the term regionalism, one can enter into dialogue within the shifting interstices rather than focusing on the boundaries.

———————————— • ————————————

Reflections and Student Responses: Tina

In retrospect, the focus on regionalism was particularly apt, enabling me to spin out threads, unravel ideas, and acknowledge the intricate tangles that create the particular body of Canadian literature which this course examined. I concluded the course with some reflections on our journey "from there to here," reminding students that every course is a construct; just as the canon constructs the literature of a nation—however contentiously—so our text

Week	Subject of Discussion
1-2	**General introduction to Can Lit: What are we doing here?** **Early English-Language Publications** Frances Brooke, From *The History of Emily Montague* **Early Humour** Thomas Chandler Haliburton, "The Trotting Horse," "The Clockmaker" **Pioneer Memoirs** Catharine Parr Traill, From *The Backwoods of Canada* Susanna Moodie, From *Roughing it in the Bush*
3-4	**The Confederation Poets** Charles G. D. Roberts, "The Flight of the Geese," "The Skater" Archibald Lampman, "The Railway Station," "The City of the End of Things" **The Montreal Poets** F. R. Scott, "The Canadian Authors Meet," "Poetry" A. J. M. Smith, "The Lonely Land" **The Long Poem** E. J. Pratt, From *Towards the Last Spike* F. R. Scott, "All the Spikes But the Last"
5-6	**The Prairie Novel** Sinclair Ross, *As For Me and My House*
7	**The Modern Short Story** Morley Callaghan, "Watching and Waiting" **The Modern Novel** Hugh MacLennan, From *Barometer Rising*
8-9	**The Postmodern Novel** Margaret Atwood, *Oryx and Crake*
10-13	**Postmodern Literature** Sheila Watson, From *The Double Hook* Alice Munro, "The Progress of Love" Carol Shields, "Hazel" Alistair MacLeod, "As Birds Bring Forth the Sun" Thomas King, "A Coyote Columbus Story" Jane Urquhart, From *The Stone Carvers* David Adams Richards, From *Mercy Among the Children* Guy Vanderhaeghe, "Man on Horseback" Aritha van Herk, From *Places Far from Ellesmere* **Summary of Can Lit seen from there to here**

selections, focal points, and criticism also create a particularized reading of a nation. Within this model of "interpretive community," to borrow Stanley Fish's term, each student was a particular reader, contributing to the interpretation and the paradoxical creation of a representative national literature through this regional approach.

Summatively, we gathered our loose threads around five centering spools: place, structure, continuity, voice, and truth. Most prominently, we recognized that regionalism formed a solid, revealing framework for our discussions. Even for those texts which were not representative of prairie literature, the sense of place became increasingly dominant in our analyses—as critical as historical placement in our attempts to uncover the shape of this slice of Canadian literature. Through observation of regionalism's varying favour among critics and its pervasive pockets of presence within the nation's literature, students came to view their own sense of place with greater significance. The situatedness of the text called forth the situatedness of the reader as subject, and students began to question what it meant to be a prairie student reading prairie literature in a prairie university. In what ways was this subject position formative? Did it limit their access points to some material or, conversely, privilege their point of contact with the regional material?

Through course discussion, it became evident that students had an increasing awareness of the complexity that a course outline with its pre-selected texts blithely masks. That Canadian literature could be traced in cycles of popularity and of critical reaction allowed students a new awareness of the interplay between canonical structure and continuity. Moreover, they became aware of the absences that monolithism engenders and began to question some of the parameters of the Canadian canon. If MacMechan's pioneering critical claim that "[l]iterature . . . is the voice of a people" holds true (17), where are the pockets of resistance to hegemony? To what extent is geographical location a factor in fostering inclusiveness and agency? How homogeneous is Canada as a community or, conversely, is regional diversity reflected in our literature? Hence, the question of voice became central—both that of authorship and of readership. Conceptualizing the sterile notion of public inscription of text as a more nuanced articulation of private writing that is publicized retained the subjectivity of the author in the act of creation without privileging her/him to an authoritative role in the interpretive act. Similarly, we were careful to nuance our role as readers to include the particularity of reading in a small private faith-based institution. What does it mean to read this localized material in a university setting that relies on some basic shared tenets of belief in a metanarrative of God's creation, humanity's fall, and Christ's redemption of humanity?

Together, the assessments of authorship and readership highlighted the elusive and, at times, illusory notion of truth. Not only did students come to realize that the texts trouble the question of truth through their post-structuralist understanding of language, but also that the existence of this language as fiction (an inherently ironic context for evaluating truth) necessitates a self-conscious understanding of the constructedness of any truths we might imagine discovering in a text. Ultimately then, structuring the course around regionalism enabled students to recognize their situatedness and the particularity of all acts of reading—including a faith-based one. Regionalism proved itself to be neatly aligned with such a project, and student evaluations of the course revealed that the majority of them identified most closely with the prairie texts. That said, many found *As For Me and My House* to be a depressing novel both in its representation of faith and the church, and also in its seemingly stereotypical topography. The latter view, of course, is prominently held by literary critics as well, identifying Ross's novel as a significant example of prairie realism—though in largely laudatory terms. While King's University holds to vision and mission statements that call faculty to teach from a Biblical perspective about the integration of Christian faith in daily living, students are not required to subscribe personally to faith tenets and so include atheists, agnostics, and members of a variety of faith communities. Consequently, the most engaging avenues of discussion with these senior-level students proved to be about the oppressive lifelessness of faith as manifested in Ross's characters and of religion as manifested in the church. Not only were we able to debate the aesthetic value of Ross's juxtaposition of faith and artistry, but also to discuss the convincing accuracy of his depiction of a stale faith on individual and collective levels. While admitting the problematic nature of such human failings, many of these senior students were still ready to argue—at times vociferously—for the viability of Christian faith and its metanarrative of hope in a contemporary secular society often characterized by brokenness, dislocation, and despair.

In retrospect, the focus of prairie regionalism was crucial to the success of this survey course of Canadian literature. It enabled me to craft a manageable syllabus with effective centering points while also being transparent about its constructedness. This duality opened up telling discussions of canonicity, identity, truth, and subjectivity as malleable constructs, and simultaneously provided a rationale for the selection of authors and texts. Other than the limitations created by any selection of texts with its necessary exclusion of others, I cannot determine any negative repercussions from the regional framework of the course. Moreover, student response to the course, and to the prairie texts in particular, was highly favourable and suggested a desire for a course more strongly regional in its focus. In part, these responses played a role in the subsequent restructuring of the Canadian literature course into two chronological segments to be offered over consecutive academic terms beginning in Fall 2008.

———————————— • ————————————

Terms of Discussion: Philip

Any introduction to Canadian literature requires an introduction to its key themes and terms, so students will find their footing as they proceed to study the works themselves. Like many other scholars, Tina included, I have been taken by Benedict Anderson's notion of nationalism and the socially constructed "imagined community." It is particularly applicable to Canada and its desire to produce cultural and national cohesion; "regardless of the actual inequality and exploitation that may prevail in each, the nation is always conceived as a deep, horizontal comradeship" (7). Canada's colonial past is also very much a part of this politically deliberate identity, and many of my scholarly and pedagogical pursuits are engaged in this subject. However, contradictorily or not, I also believe in Declan Kiberd's assertion that "it is wise to recognize—despite current critical fashions—that certain masterpieces do float free of their enabling conditions to make their home in the world" (4). In other words, I never want to lose the possibility that texts are created from outright creative genius, and that authors repeatedly write in spite of, rather than because of, their "enabling conditions." Literature should, if only briefly, transcend the politics of its production if it is to delight, which ultimately is my main concern not just with this course, but any course.

However, this "delight" is affected by the stereotypes students bring to Canadian literature, and to prairie literature in particular. Reflecting this apprehension is the section "Prairie writing 1983-1996" in *The Oxford Companion to Canadian Literature*, which begins humorously, but glumly: "Strangely, the notion persists of 'prairie writing' as a kind of remote, fenced area best left to gophers and dust storms. One might almost imagine it hanging around the basement of Canadian literature" (963). Similarly, students are sceptical about the merits of prairie literature, for if a single semester is to introduce Canadian authors, then the students assume that the majority of these authors will be from eastern Canada. However, it is not so strange that students mistakenly equate the potency of the work of art with the supposed topographic "lack" of the prairies. Historically, Canadian artists have had an ambiguous relationship with the extensive and domineering British and European traditions of their various crafts, with their audience displaying similar doubts. People still suggest that "good" Canadian art does not necessarily come from the prairies, and "good" art in general does not come from Canada. As Walter Benjamin once noted, "the greater the decrease in the social significance of an art form, the sharper the distinction between criticism and enjoyment by the public. . . .The conventional is uncritically enjoyed, and the truly new is criticized with aversion" (234). Thus, teaching the ambiguities of creative inspiration to students who focus on setting and geography can be difficult. However, Canadian artists do, obviously, inhabit distinct, creative spaces of margin/centre binaries, and present counter-figures to customary configurations of nationhood, and to assumptions about taste.

To respond to such assumptions, and to balance the need to introduce students to essential literary theory and to cultivate the enjoyment of reading Canadian literature, I focus on introducing regionalism and nationalism, but through the visual arts so students recognize the weight of tradition that informs early Canadian literature. Students are asked the question that many Canadian artists (visual and other) have asked themselves: How do I render my world, my landscape, my home, with tools and techniques that are intended to depict somewhere else (somewhere better)? Are Canadian artists confined to mimicry? To illustrate this point, I juxtapose Canadian topographic painter James Cockburn's painting "Montmorency, Chutet" (1833) to English Romantic painter John Constable's "Salisbury Cathedral from the Bishop's Grounds" (1831), suggesting that Cockburn had to deconstruct his colonial world and begin to know his immediate, physical surroundings in order to paint his new landscape. Similarly, Alberta-born painter William Kurelek was influenced by 16th century Dutch painter Pieter Bruegel. The illustrations and themes from Kurelek's *A Prairie Boy's Summer* (1975) are remarkably similar to Bruegel's painting "Children's Games" (1650). The details of children playing, the various smaller stories within the images, the simple act of eating lunch, are unique yet familiar. Kurelek has captured the Depression on the prairies, leading the class to discuss the role of struggle, adversity, and spirituality not only in the act of creation, but in the depiction of worth in the everyday lives that the texts reveal throughout the course. This, to me, is the thrust of regionalism: artists immersed in their own patch of landscape, inventing and imagining new ways of seeing an emerging culture and country in a distinctive regional setting. And it is from this thematic and theoretical premise that I approached the course "Mapping Our Mental Geography."

This approach may appear backward, beginning with more complex theories of identity and creativity before more conventional ones. However, the implications of Homi Bhabha's concept of "mimicry" are helpful early in the course, for they reveal how various regions can be creatively imagined in similar fashions to "unsettle [colonialism's] central authority," yet retain the uniqueness of Canada's frequently disparate landscapes (88). Thus, when we arrived at Northrop Frye's "garrison mentality" and Margaret Atwood's "bush myth," we were able to discuss in detail the Canadian fascination with stories about ordinary people doing extraordinary things in a harsh, dangerous land, as Atwood has aptly pointed out, and although Frye and Atwood may not necessarily explain more recent fiction about our evolving cultural complexity, they are a significant part of regionalist theory's influence on Canadian canon formation.

Students are initially presented with an uncomplicated definition of "nation" from a popular online dictionary: "a people who share common customs, origins, history, and frequently language; a nationality; a relatively large group of people organized under a single, usually independent government; a country" (dictionary.com). We then dissect this definition, focusing on its homogenous intentions before revealing that "nation" cannot be understood in such unifying terms and that "imagined communities" might better serve our purposes. Students take a similar approach to the term "regionalism" and the inherent difficulties in "the theory or practice of emphasizing the regional characteristics of locale or setting" (dictionary.com). Keeping in mind George Woodcock's assertion that Canadian texts are always regional, students are encouraged to find exceptions to these "rules," and to invent other definitions that focus on the various issues of geography, politics, economics, and language that offered more entrances into our texts.

Further investigations into regionalism began with *The Bush Garden*, in which Frye outlines his "garrison mentality":

> Small and isolated communities surrounded with a physical or psychological "frontier," separated from one another and from their American and British cultural sources: communities that provide all that their members have in the way of distinctly human values, and that are compelled to feel a great respect for the law and order that holds them together, yet confronted with a huge, unthinking, menacing, and formidable physical setting—such communities are bound to develop what we may provisionally call a garrison mentality. (225)

Although Frye's view now appears rather romantic, I argue that this "garrison mentality" is the foundation of much Canadian literature and theory, and it initiated a creative shift to stop imitating a European tradition of art and artists in order to establish Canada's own traditions and artists. Kiberd believes that, in order to flourish, "the task [of the postcolonial artist] . . . is to show the interdependence of past and future in [an] attempt to restore history's openness" (292). Canadian literature's emphasis on regionalism seemingly implies a certain unity among regions, but creates two distinct issues: On one hand, I would argue that "home" and "community" are often unfixed, ambiguous spaces, nameable only out of the necessity to determine politically the writer's location. On the other hand, the prairie soil and its inhabitants are the tangible means by which the artist perceives the world and the place from which art is created. This is what Atwood hints at in *Survival*: "Nature is a monster, perhaps, only if you come to it with unreal expectations or fight its conditions rather than accepting them and learning to live with them. Snow isn't something you necessarily die in or hate. You can also make houses in it" (227). Artistic activity, like the prairie landscape, is not static, and Canadian artists find, even seek, creativity within homogenous, potentially repressive notions of nationhood.

———————— • ————————

Course Models: Philip

Designing a single semester course intended to cover the literary history of Canada was a daunting task, particularly in terms of text selection. Furthermore, one of the course's aims is to introduce prairie literature to mainly Canadian students who are from the prairies. I am pedagogically inclined to assume material that may be familiar to me is new to the students. Thus, mainly canonical texts from the Bennett and Brown *A New Anthology of Canadian Literature in English* were chosen because theoretical focus on regionalism and mimicry would make it possible to teach such varied literature in such a short time. Frank Davey points out in "Toward the Ends of Regionalism" that "there has been some movement away from regionalist understandings like 'west' or 'prairies' toward political ones based on provincial boundaries" (10). However, students need to know this regionalist literary history if they are to debate current trends for evaluating Canadian literature, particularly my key text, Margaret Laurence's *The Stone Angel*.

After the aforementioned comparison between European and Canadian visual art, the class discussed early Canadian explorer literature, focusing on John Franklin's *Narrative of a Journey*. In *Narrative*, the north is described in precise, documentary style, reflecting the early colonists' interests in topography and other military matters. The prose is cold, especially Franklin's description of how he "put an end to the life" of Michel Teroahauté, an Iroquois voyageur who supposedly threatened the survival of Franklin's group (63). After I introduced key passages from Atwood's *Survival*, the students were asked how Franklin's *Narrative* instigated persistent myths about Canada—the antagonistic relationship between a personified nature that was no longer simply topographic, and the people who survived it or perished in it. Students offered their own stories of confrontations with nature, and agreed that the prairies were just as "malevolent" as the Canadian arctic, but raised questions about the role of God in nature, and how nature could not simply be seen in topographic terms. Specifically, Franklin implies that Michel, as a representation of this untamed, frozen wilderness, is murderous because he is not a Christian, thus justifying Michel's execution. Discussion of Franklin's writing inevitably leads students to question the intentions and actions of Canadian explorers.

In the next sections of the course, which examined the memoirs and autobiographies of pioneers such as Catherine Parr Traill and Susanna Moodie, the Confederation Poets, and the practitioners of the long poem, students were now able to reflect on the way in which poets such as Charles Sangster saw nature as a location where "the Genius of Beauty truly dwells. / I worship Truth and Beauty in my soul"—a place where the spirit and consciousness meet (94-5). The lectures were informed by key thematic concerns that revealed not only the similarities between Canadian and English authors, but the relationship of the students to these authors: Could students imagine a world outside of the one in scripture? Is not the influence of tradition, and the creation of a literary canon, informed by the same concerns that we have now? Are not today's concerns about the environment, equality, spirituality, still rooted in the value and struggle of everyday life, and how do early Canadian writers such as Sangster reflect or mimic the concerns of the English Romantics? In *Strange Things*—Margaret Atwood's 1991 Clarendon lectures—Atwood concludes the series by noting that soon "the [Canadian] north will be neither female or male, neither fearful or health-giving, because it will be dead" (116). Can these ideas about the Canadian north apply to representations of the prairies? Farley Mowat characterized the north as a place that has no boundaries "except insofar as one exists in us as a state of mind" (217), encouraging us to see the north in all of Canada, including "winter blizzards on the western prairies [that] can match, in ferocity if not in intensity, the worst weather the north produces" (220). These are important concerns for ecologically-minded students attending a faith-based, interdisciplinary institution such as The King's University College, and ones not unlike questions asked by our biology and environmental studies departments. If, through a critical understanding of regionalism, we are able to "imagine the north" in the activity of the Alberta tar sands, for example, what do we do with these images? For Christians, these difficult questions that expose the complexities of Christian care are not unlike the myth of the north, and the Canadian canon is an ongoing conversation, critical inquiry, and creative openness to new ways of living in the world.

It is this conversation and intertextuality that provides the transition from memoirs and autobiographies, with their emphasis on the struggles of living in early Canada, to the distinctive combination of myth and realism in Laurence's *The Stone Angel*. Students are struck how in the novel the prairie landscape is deceptively simple, as are the people who inhabit it. Yet nothing is as it initially seems. They also begin to see the particular ways that early Canadian fiction authors "play" with form and content, moving on from and developing the cultured but sometimes ponderous memoir style of Traill and Moodie. Thus, the novel becomes an entry into current theories about the imaginative differences between "home" and "place," and the corresponding negotiation of identity that also arises later in the course in texts such as Alistair MacLeod's *No Great Mischief* and the film version of Mordecai Richler's *The Apprenticeship of Duddy Kravitz* (89). Specifically, Hagar Shipley in *The Stone Angel* is reluctant to sell her house and its contents in British Columbia because, as she says, "if I am not somehow contained in them and in this house, something of all change caught and fixed here, eternal enough for my purposes, then I do not know where I am to be found at all" (36). "Home" is an ambiguous place, both stable and unstable, necessary to determine Hagar's physical location, but accentuating the fact that it can only be a temporary condition. Hagar's world is shrinking (282), beginning with the farm in Manawaka and ending in the nursing home with its shrinking patients, revealing how it is memory, not realist depiction of landscape, that determines home and place. She is determined to make the cannery her new home because she briefly "believe[s] [that] you carry nothing with you—all is cancelled from before" (155). Metaphorically, this need to domesticate is rooted in Frye's garrison mentality, as Hagar strains to belong both to her family and the community of Manawaka; yet it is clear that this belonging is stifling.

Laurence's novel anticipates many of the questions that are asked by the end of the course. When Hagar's son, John, trades the Shipley pin for a pocket-knife, he is symbolically severing himself from his colonial past, yet he is never able to leave Manawaka and the Shipley farm. Students are asked, then, what are the criteria for belonging, be they regional or national, and what is the role of a seemingly realistic setting in this imagined Canada? An examination of Joy Kogawa's Obasan extends this question: Is the novel an example of prairie literature because it is set in Alberta, or is the setting negligible beside the overt themes of Canadian immigration and national security policies? Does our regional, fractured identity help or hinder our desire to confront social or environmental injustices, or is "the creation of new transcultural forms within the contact zone produced by colonization" a mark of Canadian art's distinctiveness (Ashcroft 118)? The excerpt from Fred Wah's *Diamond Grill* helped answer some of these questions, for it is a text that explicitly articulates many of the course's theories. Because of our diversity, and the instability of "Canadianness," Canadian authors, as Wah notes, "live in the hyphen" (834). In fact, Canadians embrace the hyphen, the margin, because it actually offers creative freedom that is not tied to genre. Theory and fiction become a place of play, not anxiety. Significantly, Wah exploits what Phillipe Lejeune in *On Autobiography* calls "the horizon of expectation," whereby an autobiographical text fails to live up to the expectations of its readers who refuse to see it as an "obvious practice of nonidentity" (15). Thus, the students now recognize the destabilizing effect genre has on notions of "centre" and "inspiration" and are able to carry these theories into the discussions about *No Great Mischief*, the excerpt from Michael Ondaatje's *In the Skin of a Lion*, and the film of *Duddy Kravitz*.

Finally, complementing our discussions were student presentations. Each student gave a 10-15 minute presentation about an aspect of Canadian culture or literature that he or she considered important but was not on the syllabus, and then tied the topic to that week's thematic or theoretical thread. As evident in the Schedule below, students chose a variety of topics and media, including several noted representatives of Canadian culture such as the television show *Corner Gas* and Rick Mercer's *Monday Report*. Those that presented distinctly prairie texts did so with the intention of showing the dynamism and elusive mystery of the prairies, to demonstrate that the prairie texts, like the seasons/weather/landscape/vegetation, are surprising to those who think of the prairies as literally and figuratively flat. There was a keenness not only to fill the empty spaces left by the syllabus, but also to demonstrate how other genres produced similar theoretical conclusions as the literature.

Week	Subject of Discussion
1	**Early Publications and Explorers** Brooke, *The History of Emily Montague* Franklin, *Narrative of a Journey*
2-3	**Settlers, Pioneers and the Bush Myth** Traill, *The Backwoods of Canada* Moodie, *Roughing it in the Bush* The Group of Seven Paints Canada Purdy, "Wilderness Gothic," "Lament for the Dorsets" Smith, "The Lonely Land"
4	**Confederation Poets** Roberts, "The Flight of the Geese," "The Skater" Lampman, "The Railway Station," "The City of the End of Things" **The Long Poem** Pratt, *Towards the Last Spike* Scott, "All the Spikes But the Last" Student Presentation: "Emily Carr" Student Presentation: "The Price of a Country"
5	**Regionalism and the Can Lit Explosion** *The Stone Angel* Student Presentation: "Canadian Beer"
6-7	*The Stone Angel* Vanderhaeghe, "Man on Horseback" Student Presentation: "The Mad Trapper" Student Presentation: "Canadian Bacon"
7-8	**Celebrities and Best Sellers** Cohen, "Suzanne" and "The Future" Atwood, "This is a Photograph of Me," "Disembarking at Quebec" Shields, "Hazel" Student Presentation: "Fiddle Music" Student Presentation: "The Sweater"
9	**The Immigrant Experience** Kogawa, *Obasan* Wah, *Diamond Grill* Student Presentation: "Rick Mercer" Student Presentation: "Hockey Night in Canada"

Week	Subject of Discussion
10	**Memory**
	Ondaatje, *In the Skin of a Lion*
	Mistry, "Swimming Lessons"
	Student Presentation: "L. M. Montgomery"
	Student Presentation: "Robert Munsch"
	Student Presentation: "Alice Munro"
11	**Native Literature**
	King, "A Coyote Columbus Story"
	Highway, *Kiss of the Fur Queen*
	Johnson, "Songs My Paddle Sings"
	Student Presentation: "Corner Gas"
	Student Presentation: "Paul Brandt"
12-13	**The Old and the New**
	MacLeod, *No Great Mischief*
	Student Presentation: "Degrassi"
13-14	*The Apprenticeship of Duddy Kravitz* (film)

•

Reflections and Student Responses: Philip

The student comments are from both course evaluations and a questionnaire that students completed after the course. I also solicited feedback throughout the semester. Students were asked a number of questions, including: What has changed in Canadian fiction since the beginning of the course? Did the earlier fiction have an implicit, concrete Christian worldview, and how has that changed by the final text? Also, did the concept of regionalism make the prairies more prominent in Canadian literature, and did a regionalist approach to the prairies give you a better understanding of the prairies in Canada as a nation? Some students admitted that when they first saw the course syllabus, they thought that the prairies were going to be under-represented, but that this opinion changed by the course's conclusion. They also remarked that their initial trepidation was marked by an uncertainty about exactly what was a Canadian author. However, out of the student presentations came an intriguing perspective on Canadian artists: they are often ambiguous in their origins and styles, they often imitate a British tradition of art and aesthetics, but they all consciously or unconsciously challenge this tradition by describing the features of the local culture and landscape. The few students who wondered why we were not studying W. O. Mitchell's *Who Has Seen the Wind* now wished to read it anew as a key novel in Canadian prairie representation. Alison Calder in "Reassessing Prairie Realism" claims that the postsecondary study of prairie literature is usually confined to "prairie realism" literature because "they are texts that the teachers themselves have been taught; inexpensive editions are relatively easy to find; and they are easy to peg into that blank space on the course syllabus marked 'regional text'" (55). In other words, Canadian prairie literature, as Calder also points out, is one of environmental determinism, in which the specifics of the landscape determine the region. This assessment is one of the reasons that I did not select Mitchell's novel. I wanted the students to understand that a prairie novel does not necessarily focus on landscape, and that they are complex, nuanced, and diverse in ways outside of obvious representations of landscape.

One of the drawbacks of using an anthology is that instead of prompting the student to read the remainder of the novel on his or her own, it might cause the student to see the excerpt as sufficient. This created some issues with texts such as *Obasan* because even though much of the novel takes place in southern Alberta, as one student remarked, the "narrator Naomi is there by force, and therefore the text was still about British Columbia, and not 'true prairie literature,'" despite the implications for Canada as a whole. Thus, I would venture that teaching only novel chapters, and not the novel in its entirety, highlighted issues that I had not anticipated. Although the students loved the texts, many of their themes and concerns were lost, and I found it difficult to lecture without the entire text in mind. For example, the first chapter of Tomson Highway's *Kiss of the Fur Queen* (1998) failed to provide the students with the appropriate introduction to Native Canadian issues. In turn, this put considerable "pressure" on the other texts to fulfill my pedagogical mandate, a point which a few astute students noted in their evaluations.

One could argue that in this respect *The Stone Angel* is no different from *Who Has Seen the Wind*. It is familiar and readily available. However, it is possible to teach the intricacies of canon production alongside the canonical text itself, which was my pedagogical strategy. Furthermore, intertextuality is key if the students are to recognize the multiple discourses that inform Canadian literature and culture, and *The Stone Angel* is influential in this respect. Some students remained unsure where Manitoba stood in a prairie and regional context, claiming "that it is still sort of the east." Instead, they focused on treatment of the aged that, in its own way, is a regionalist approach. Students commented on the way Hagar and the other elderly patients in the seniors' home, in their "world that has shrunk," reverted to former languages and dialects from other parts of Canada and beyond (Laurence 260).

In addition, the students were fascinated by the fact that the novel was once banned. As we watched a January 25, 1983 CBC news broadcast about Peterborough County's Citizens for Bible-Based Study, who claimed that the text is "anti-Christian blasphemy and degrading, dehumanizing filth," students both giggled and expressed embarrassment ("Laurence's Books Banned"). It never occurred to them that the novel was so contentious, and it led to a valuable discussion about faith, reading, and definitions of obscenity. Ironically, class discussion returned to regionalism and its frequent relationship with Christian identity. One student assumed that the prairies were inherently more conservative and Christian, and was surprised that the move to ban the novel came from Ontario.

Regionalism became most evident in the student presentations. Specifically, students wanted to examine how the prairies are presented in popular culture. One student, for example, believed that the "only two aspects of the course that dealt with the prairies alone were the student presentations on the popular television show *Corner Gas* and country singer Paul Brandt." This comment raised an interesting point. Specifically, students still expected and possibly needed a distinct setting or locale to meet their expectations about prairie literature. There was also a distinct sense of pride when students discussed a regional celebrity. One student was related to Albert Johnson, the "Mad Trapper of Rat River," who in a trapline conflict in the 1930s killed a police officer. The student's presentation eagerly sought to tell the story, be it predominantly fact or fiction, but nevertheless negotiated the relationship between realism and regionalism that I hoped students would understand by the end of the course.

Of particular note is the role that Alistair MacLeod's wonderful novel *No Great Mischief* played in cementing an understanding of regionalism, which, in turn, led many students to reflect upon the prairie fiction studied earlier. The students enjoy this novel because it is a distinctly "oral" narrative, a "never-ending circle [that] is also a braid or knot that binds life and death, past and future…the cycle not only binds, but links and returns one to nature's rhythms as well as to one's ancestry" (Jirgens 88). Identity in the novel is distinctly tied to both landscape and language, while intruders are seen as threats, even if they have share similar cultural and mythical backgrounds, such as Fern Picard, the leader of the Quebecois miners at Renco Development. The *clan Calum Ruadh* are isolated and protectionist, like the Shipley clan in *The Stone Angel*, unified by the Gaelic language and a historical obsession with General Wolfe. Yet, the *clan Calum Ruadh* is spread across the country—imaginatively fixed in Cape Breton, but unable, like other Canadians, to answer fully "the complicated question of exactly who they are" (MacLeod 197).

————————— • —————————

Final Remarks

If the prairie landscape is deceptively simple, so is the literature of the prairies. Explore a little and you will find diversity, complexity and drama, yet the prairies are "young" enough to be witty and self-conscious. One of Philip's students wryly suggested that current issues of prairie regionalism and identity began in 1987 when the Canadian Football League moved the Winnipeg Blue Bombers from the West Division to the East Division. Now no one knows were the east ends and the west begins. It is a humourous point that speaks with surprising directness to the task of defining the prairies. To tackle this, since Tina and Philip taught the course, they have made it into two courses: pre-1980 and post-1980. This will likely resolve many of the coverage concerns of the course. In particular, both professors were disappointed by the lack of Native Canadian content in their syllabi; an emphasis on canon has definite disadvantages, and we felt continually compelled to seek and add different voices.

Many students are reluctant to read literary theory, as they believe it detracts from their enjoyment of the text. This is true for not just this course, but for other literature courses. However, we both found that this matter is mitigated by the fact that there is little differentiation between the Canadian theoretical canon and the Canadian literary canon, as so many authors are also critics, and vice versa. There is entertaining literary theory, and complex theoretical fiction. Thus, a Canadian course that includes prairie literature can evolve according to student interests, and we can ensure that prairie stories have a vital presence in our Canadian literature courses.

Bibliography

Adorno, Theodor. *Minima Moralia: Reflections from Damaged Life*. Trans. E.F.N. Jephcott. London: New Left, 1974.

"Alcoa in Trinidad and Tobago." http://www.alcoa.com/trinidad_tobago/en/home. asp. 19 Dec. 2007.

"Alcoa Smelter in Trinidad—Environmental Dangers, Crime, Industrialization." No Smelters in T and T. http://www.nosmeltertnt.com/trinidad_master_plan.html. 19 Dec. 2007.

Anderson, Benedict. *Imagined Communities*. Rev. ed. London: Verso, 1991.

Appadurai, Arjun. "Global Ethnoscapes: Notes and Queries for a Transnational Anthropology." *Recapturing Anthropology: Working in the Present*. Ed. Richard G. Fox. Santa Fe: SAR, 1991. 191-210.

Arnason, David. Afterword. *Wild Geese*. By Martha Ostenso. Toronto: McClelland & Stewart, 1989. 303-309.

Arnason, David. "The Development of Prairie Realism." Diss. U of New Brunswick, 1980.

Arnason, David. Interview with Allan Kroeker. NFB document on "Capital." 2 June 1980.

Arnason, David, and Dennis Cooley. "Outcasting: A Conversation with Margaret Laurence about the World of Manawaka." *Border Crossings* 5.4 (1986): 32-34.

Arnason, David, and Mhari Mackintosh. *The Imagined City: A Literary History of Winnipeg*. Winnipeg: Turnstone, 2005.

Ashcroft, Brian, Gareth Griffiths and Helen Tiffin. *Post-Colonial Studies: The Key Concepts*. London: Routledge, 2003.

Atherton, Stan. *Martha Ostenso and Her Works*. Toronto: ECW, 1991.

Atwood, Margaret. "Face to Face." Woodcock, *A Place to Stand On* 20-27.

Atwood, Margaret. *Strange Things: The Malevolent North in Canadian Literature*. Oxford: Clarendon, 1995.

Atwood, Margaret. *Survival: A Thematic Guide to Canadian Literature*. Toronto: Anansi, 1972.

Bannerji, Himani. *The Dark Side of the Nation: Essays on Multiculturalism, Nationalism, and Gender*. Toronto: Canadian Scholar's Press, 2000.

Bannerji, Himani. "On the Dark Side of the Nation: Politics of Multiculturalism and the State of 'Canada.'" *Journal of Canadian Studies* 31.3 (Fall 1996): 103-28.

Banting, Pamela. "The Angel in the Glacier: Geography as Intertext in Thomas Wharton's Novel *Icefields.*" *Interdisciplinary Studies in Literature and the Environment* 7.2 (2000): 67-80.

Banting, Pamela. *Body Inc.: A Theory of Translation Poetics.* Winnipeg: Turnstone, 1995.

Banting, Pamela. "The Land Writes Back: Notes on Four Western Canadian Writers." *Literature of Nature: An International Sourcebook.* Ed. Patrick D. Murphy. Chicago: Dearborn, 1998. 140-46.

Barcelona, Antonio. "Clarifying and Applying the Notions of Metaphor and Metonymy within Cognitive Linguistics: An Update." *Metaphor and Metonymy in Comparison and Contrast.* Ed. René Dirven, R. Pörings. 2002. Berlin: de Gruyter, 2003. 207-77.

Barcelona, Antonio. "On the Systematic Contrastive Analysis of Conceptual Metaphors: Case Studies and Proposed Methodology." *Applied Cognitive Linguistics II: Language Pedagogy.* Ed. M. Pütz, M., S. Niemeyer, and R. Dirven. Berlin: de Gruyter, 2001. 117-46.

Baum, Rosalie Murphy. "Martha Ostenso's Wild Geese: More insight into the Naturalistic Sensibility." *Journal of Canadian Culture* 1.2 (1984): 117-35.

Beck, Ervin. "Postcolonial Complexity in the Writings of Rudy Wiebe." *Modern Fiction Studies* 47.4 (2001): 855-86.

Beilharz, Peter. "Australia: The Unhappy Country, or, a Tale of Two Nations." *Thesis Eleven* 82 (Aug. 2005): 73-87.

Bell System. Advertisement. *Life* 1941: 3.

Benjamin, Walter. "The Work of Art in the Age of Mechanical Reproduction." Trans. Harry Zohn. *Illuminations.* Ed. Hannah Arendt. New York: Schocken, 1968. 217-51.

Bennett, Michael, and David W. Teague, eds. *The Nature of Cities: Ecocriticism and Urban Environments.* Tucson: U of Arizona P, 1999.

Bennett, Russell, and Donna Brown, eds. *A New Anthology of Canadian Literature in English.* Toronto: Oxford UP, 2002.

Benson, Eugene, and William Toye, eds. *The Oxford Companion to Canadian Literature.* 2nd ed. Toronto: Oxford UP, 1997.

Bentley, D. M. R. "*As For Me* and Significant Form." *Canadian Notes and Queries* 48 (1994): 18-20.

Bentley, D. M. R. "Psychoanalytical Notes upon an Autobiographical Account of a Case of Paranoia (*Dementia Paranoides*): Mrs. Bentley in Sinclair Ross's *As for Me and My House.*" *University of Toronto Quarterly* 73.3 (Summer 2004): 862-85.

Berger, Carl. *The Sense of Power: Studies in the Ideas of Canadian Imperialism,*

1867-1914. Toronto: U of Toronto P, 1970.

Berland, Jody. "Nationalism and the Modernist Legacy: Dialogues with Innis." *Capital Culture: A Reader on Modernist Legacies, State Institutions and the Value(s) of Art*. Ed. Jody Berland and Shelley Hornstein. Montreal: McGill-Queen's UP, 2000. 14-38.

Berry, Wendell. "The Prejudice Against Country People." *The Progressive* (April 2002). FindArticles.com. 7 July 2008. http://findarticles.com/p/articles/mi_m1295/is_4_66/ai_84866884.

Berry, Wendell. "Writer and Region." *What are People For? Essays by Wendell Berry*. New York: North Point, 1990. 71-87.

Bertacco, Simona. *Out of Place: The Writings of Robert Kroetsch*. New York: Lang, 2002.

Bevan, Allan. Rev. of *The Diviners*, by Margaret Laurence. *The Dalhousie Review* 54 (1974): 360-63. Rpt in New, *Critical Views* 214-18.

Bhabha, Homi K. *The Location of Culture*. London: Routledge, 1994.

Bhabha, Homi. *The Location of Culture*, with a new preface by the author. London: Routledge, 2006.

Boers, Frank. "Metaphor Awareness and Vocabulary Retention." *Applied Linguistics* 21.4 (2000): 553-71.

Bortolotti, Gary R. and Linda Hutcheon. "On the Origin of Adaptations: Rethinking Fidelity Discourse and 'Success'—Biologically." *New Literary History* 38 (2007): 443-458.

Boucher, Holly Wallace. "Metonymy in Typology and Allegory, with a Consideration of Dante's *Comedy*." *Allegory, Myth, and Symbol*. Ed. Morton Bloomfield. Cambridge, Mass: Harvard UP, 1981. 129-45.

Boughton, Noelle. *Margaret Laurence: A Gift of Grace: A Spiritual Biography*. Toronto: Women's Press, 2006.

Bourdieu, Pierre. "The Field of Cultural Production." *The Field of Cultural Production*. New York: Columbia UP, 1993. 29-73.

Bourdieu, Pierre. "The Production of Belief." *The Field of Cultural Production*. New York: Columbia UP, 1993. 74-111.

Bowen, Gail. 2004. 28 July 2008. http://www.gailbowen.com.

Brand, Dionne. "Notes for Writing thru Race." *Bread Out of Stone*. Toronto: Vintage, 1998. 187-192.

Bray, S. Letter to W.D. Perley. 20 April 1888. National Archives, Ottawa, Canada. RG 17, Agriculture, vol. 574, docket 64993.

Brown, E. K. "The Problem of a Canadian Literature." 1943. *Responses and Evaluations: Essays on Canada*. Ed. David Staines. Toronto: McClelland & Stewart, 1977.

1-23.

Brownlow, Alec. "A Wolf in the Garden: Ideology and Change in the Adirondack Landscape." *Animal Spaces, Beastly Places: New Geographies of Human-Animal Relations.* London: Routledge, 2000. 141-58.

Bruce, Phyllis. Rev. of *The Diviners*, by Margaret Laurence. *The Canadian Forum* 54 (1974): 15-16.

Bunbury, Glen. "Gophers, a ready meal." 6 Sept. 2000. http://yukonweb.com/business/lost_moose/books/great/gophers.html.

Burke, Kenneth. *A Grammar of Motives.* 1945. Berkeley: U of California P, 1969.

Burnet, Jean R., and Howard Palmer. *"Coming Canadians": An Introduction to a History of Canada's Peoples.* Toronto: McClelland & Stewart, 1988.

Buss, Helen M. *Mother and Daughter Relationships in the Manawaka Works of Margaret Laurence.* Victoria: U of Victoria, 1985.

Buss, Helen M. "Who Are You, Mrs. Bentley? Feminist Re-vision and Sinclair Ross's *As for Me and My House.*" Stouck 190-209.

Butala, Sharon. "Field of Broken Dreams." *West* 2.6 (1990): 22-30.

Butala, Sharon. *Luna.* 1988. Toronto: HarperPerennial, 1999.

Butala, Sharon. *The Perfection of the Morning: An Apprenticeship in Nature.* Toronto: HarperCollins, 1994.

Butala, Sharon. *Wild Stone Heart: An Apprentice in the Fields.* Toronto: HarperPerennial, 2000.

Calder, Alison. "Coming Home, Going Away." *NeWest Review* 25.3 (2000): 6-7.

Calder, Alison, and Robert Wardhaugh, eds. *History, Literature, and the Writing of the Canadian Prairies.* Winnipeg: U of Manitoba P, 2005.

Calder, Alison. "Reassessing Prairie Realism." Riegel and Wyile 51-60.

Calder, Alison. "Who's from the Prairie? Some Prairie Self-Representations in Popular Culture." Wardhaugh 91-100.

Cameron, Barry A. Rev. of *The Diviners*, by Margaret Laurence. *Queen's Quarterly* 81 (1974): 639-40.

Cameron, Donald. "Margaret Laurence: The Black Celt Speaks of Freedom." *Conversations with Canadian Novelists.* Toronto: Macmillan, 1973. 96-115.

Cameron, Lynne, and Graham Low. "Metaphor." *Language Teaching* 32 (1999): 77-96.

Campbell, SueEllen. "The Land and Language of Desire: Where Deep Ecology and Post-Structuralism Meet." *The Ecocriticism Reader: Landmarks in Literary Ecology.* Ed. Cheryl Glotfelty and Harold Fromm. Athens: U of Georgia P, 1996. 124-36.

Carlson, Barry F. "Coyote and Gopher." *Coyote Stories*. Ed. William Bright. Chicago: U of Chicago P, 1978. 3-14.

Carpenter, David. *Writing Home: Selected Essays*. Saskatoon: Fifth House, 1994.

Casey, Allan. "The Place Where Words Stop." Interview with Sharon Butala. *Books in Canada* 21.4 (1992): 14-17.

Casid, Jill. *Sowing Empire: Landscape and Colonization*. Minneapolis: U of Minnesota P, 2005.

Chambers, Iain. "Citizenship, Language, and Modernity." *PMLA* 117.1 (2002): 24-31.

Chambers, Robert D. *Sinclair Ross and Ernest Buckler*. Montreal: McGill-Queen's UP, 1975.

Clandfield, David. *Canadian Film*. Toronto: Oxford UP, 1987.

Clunie, Barnaby W. "A Revolutionary Failure Resurrected: Dialogical Appropriation in Rudy Wiebe's *The Scorched-Wood People*." *University of Toronto Quarterly* 74.3 (2005): 845-65.

Cobb, Kelton. *The Blackwell Guide to Theology and Popular Culture*. Malden, MA: Blackwell, 2005.

Coldwell, Joan. "Margaret Laurence." *The Oxford Companion to Canadian Literature*. Ed. William Toye. Toronto: Oxford UP, 1983. 434-36.

Coleman, Daniel. *White Civility: The Literary Project of English Canada*. Toronto: U of Toronto P, 2006.

Comeau, Paul. *Margaret Laurence's Epic Imagination*. Edmonton: U of Alberta P, 2005.

Cooley, Dennis. *The Bentleys*. Edmonton: U of Alberta P, 2006.

Cooley, Dennis, ed. *RePlacing*. Downsview: ECW, 1980.

Cooley, Dennis. *The Vernacular Muse: The Eye and Ear in Contemporary Literature*. Winnipeg: Turnstone, 1987.

Coopsammy, Madeline. *Prairie Journey*. Toronto: Tsar, 2004.

Cornet At Night. Dir. and screenplay by Stanley Jackson. NFB, 1963.

Cowart, David. *Trailing Clouds: Immigrant Fiction in Contemporary America*. Ithaca: Cornell UP, 2006.

Cronon, William, ed. *Uncommon Ground: Rethinking the Human Place in Nature*. 1995. New York: Norton, 1996.

Cronon, William. "The Trouble with Wilderness; or, Getting Back to the Wrong Nature." Cronon 69-90.

Crowe, David M. *A History of the Gypsies of Eastern Europe and Russia*. New York: Griffin, 1996.

Crozier, Lorna. "A Prophet In His Own Country." *Apocrypha of Light*. Toronto: McClelland & Stewart, 2002. 13.

Cude, Wilfred. "Beyond Mrs. Bentley: A Study of *As for Me and My House*." Stouck 76-95.

Culler, Jonathan. *On Deconstruction: Theory and Criticism after Structuralism*. Ithaca, NY: Cornell UP, 1982.

Curran, Bev. "Against the Grain: The Canadian Desert." *Bulletin of Aichi Shukutoku University, Department of Creative Culture* 3 (2003): 1-12.

Dainotto, Roberto Maria. "'All the Regions Do Smilingly Revolt': The Literature of Place and Region." *Critical Inquiry* 22.3 (1996): 486-505.

Davey, Frank. "Toward the Ends of Regionalism." *Textual Studies in Canada* (Spring 1997): 1-17.

Davey, Frank. "A Young Boy's Eden: Notes on Recent 'Prairie' Poetry." *Reading Canadian Reading*. Winnipeg: Turnstone, 1988. 213-229.

Davies, Robertson. Interview with Adrienne Clarkson. *Adrienne Clarkson Presents*. CBC TV. 1992.

Day, Richard J. F. *Multiculturalism and the History of Canadian Diversity*. Toronto: U of Toronto P, 2000.

Deignan, Alice, Danuta Gabryś, and Agnieszka Solska. "Teaching English Metaphors Using Cross-Linguistic Awareness-Raising Activities." *ELT Journal* 51.4 (1997): 352-60.

Deleuze, Gilles, and Felix Guattari. *Anti-Oedipus: Capitalism and Schizophrenia*. Trans. R. Hurley et al. New York: Viking, 1977.

Deming, Alison H. and Lauret E. Savoy. "Introduction as Conversation." *The Colors of Nature: Culture, Identity, and the Natural World*. Ed. Alison H. Deming and Lauret E. Savoy. Minneapolis: Milkweed, 2002. 3-15.

DeVore, Lynn. "The Backgrounds of *Nightwood*: Robin, Felix, and Nora." *Journal of Modern Literature* 10 (1983), 71-90.

Dickinson, Peter. *Screening Gender, Framing Genre: Canadian Literature into Film*. Toronto: U of Toronto P, 2007.

Dirven, René. "Metonymy and Metaphor: Different Mental Strategies of Conceptualisation." *Leuvense Bijdragen* 82.1 (1993): 1-28.

Dirven, René. "Metonymy and Metaphor: Different Mental Strategies of Conceptualisation." *Metaphor and Metonymy in Comparison and Contrast*. 2002. Ed. René Dirven and Ralf Pörings. Berlin: de Gruyter, 2003. 75-111.

"Discover the City of Winnipeg's Assiniboine Park Zoo." Advertising Brochure. City of Winnipeg.

Divay, Gaby. "Fanny Essler's Poems: Felix Paul Greve's or Else von Freytag-Loringhoven's?" *Arachne: An Interdisciplinary Journal of Language and Literature* 1.2 (Nov. 1994): 165-197.

Divay, Gaby. "Felix Paul Greve / Frederick Philip Grove's Passage to America: The Discovery of the Author's Arrival in North America and its Implications." *New Worlds: Discovering and Constructing the Unknown in Anglophone Literature.* Festschrift Presented to Walter Pache on Occasion of His 60th Birthday. Ed. Martin Kuester, Gabriele Christ & Rudolf Beck. Munchen: Vogel, 2000. 111-132.

Djwa, Sandra. "False Gods and True Covenant: Thematic Continuity Between Margaret Laurence and Sinclair Ross." *Journal of Canadian Fiction* 1.4 (Fall 1972): 43-50.

Dorland, Michael, ed. *The Cultural Industries in Canada: Problems, Policies and Prospects.* Toronto: Lorimer, 1996.

Dorland, Michael. *So Close to the State/s: The Emergence of Canadian Feature Film Policy.* Toronto: U of Toronto P, 1998.

Dowler, Kevin. "The Cultural Industries Policy Apparatus." *The Cultural Industries in Canada: Problems, Policies and Prospects.* Ed. Michael Dorland. Toronto: Lorimer, 1996: 328-346.

Dragland, Stan. *Apocrypha: Further Journeys.* Edmonton: NeWest, 2003.

Druick, Zoë. *Projecting Canada: Government Policy and Documentary Film at the National Film Board.* Montreal: McGill-Queen's UP, 2007.

Dupriez, Bernard. *A Dictionary of Literary Devices.* Trans. A. Halsall. Hemel Hempstead: Harvester, 1991.

DuPuis, E. Melanie, and Peter Vandergeest, eds. *Creating the Countryside: The Politics of Rural and Environmental Discourse.* Philadelphia: Temple UP, 1996.

Dyck, E. F., ed. *Essays on Saskatchewan Writing.* Regina: SWG, 1986.

Dyer, Richard. *White.* New York: Routledge, 1997.

Echard, William. *Neil Young and the Poetics of Energy.* Indianapolis: Indiana UP, 2005.

Edwards, Jess. "How to Read an Early Modern Map: Between the Particular and the General, the Material and the Abstract, Words and Mathematics." *Early Modern Literary Studies* 9.1 (2003): 1-58. 4 June 2007 http://purl.oclc.org/emls/09-1/edwamps.html.

Eggleston, Wilfred. *The Frontier and Canadian Letters.* 1957. Toronto: McClelland & Stewart, 1977.

Elliott, Jean Leonard, and Augie Fleras. "Immigration and the Canadian Ethnic Mosaic." *Race and Ethnic Relations in Canada.* Ed. Peter S. Li. Toronto: Oxford UP, 1990. 51-76.

Elssler, Fanny. "Fanny Elsler (sic!). Lithograph (G. Leybold, 1840)." *Broom* 4.1 (Dec. 1922): [2].

Engel, Marian. "Steps to the Mythic: *The Diviners* and *A Bird in the House*." Woodcock, *A Place to Stand On*.

Engler, Bernd. "'Spiritual dislocations': Strategien der Neuverortung des Spirituellen in Rudy Wiebe's *A Discovery of Strangers*." *Spiritualität und Transzendenz in der modernen englischsprachigen Literatur*. Ed. Susanne Bach. Paderborn: Schöningh, 2001. 245-58.

Essler, Fanny. "Ein Porträt: drei Sonette." *Die Freistatt* 6: 840-841.

Essler, Fanny. "Gedichte." *Die Freistatt* 6: 700-701.

Essler, Fanny. "Gedichte." *Die Freistatt* 7: 185-186.

Evans, Gary. *In the National Interest: A Chronicle of the National Film Board of Canada from 1949-1989*. Toronto: U of Toronto P, 1991.

Fabre, Michel. "From *The Stone Angel* to *The Diviners*: An Interview with Margaret Laurence." Woodcock, *A Place to Stand On* 193-209.

Fabre, Michel. "Words and the World: *The Diviners* as an Exploration of the Book of Life." Woodcock, *A Place to Stand On* 247-69.

Fairbanks, Carol. *Prairie Women: Images in American and Canadian Fiction*. New Haven: Yale U P, 1986.

Ferber, Michael. *A Dictionary of Literary Symbols*. Cambridge: Cambridge UP, 2007.

Fiamengo, Janice. "Regionalism and Urbanism." Kröller 241-62.

Fiorentino, Jon Paul, and Robert Kroetsch. "Post-Prairie Poetics: A Dialogue." *Post-Prairie: An Anthology of New Poetry*. Vancouver: Talonbooks, 2005. 9-13.

Fiorentino, Jon Paul, and Robert Kroetsch, eds. Post-Prairie: *An Anthology of New Poetry*. Vancouver: Talonbooks, 2005.

Fires of Envy. Dir. Don Haldane. Screenplay by W. O. Mitchell. NFB, 1957.

Fish, Stanley. *Is There a Text in this Class?* Cambridge: Harvard UP, 1980.

Flanagan, James W. "Space." *Handbook of Postmodern Biblical Interpretation*. Ed. A. K. M. Adam. St. Louis: Chalice, 2000. 239-44.

Flaubert, Gustave. *Briefe an Zeit-und Zunftgenossen*. Autorisierte Übersetzung von F. Greve. Minden: Bruns, [1906?].

Flaubert, Gustave. *Briefe über seine Werke*. Ausgewählt, eingeleitet und mit Anmerkungen versehen von F. Greve. Ins Deutsche übertragen von E. Greve. (pref., Sept. 1904). Minden: Bruns, 1905.

Flaubert, Gustave. *Die Versuchung des heiligen Antonius*. Autorisierte Übersetzung von F. Greve. Minden: Bruns, 1904.

Flaubert, Gustave. *Madame Bovary*. Paris: Livre de Poche, 1961.

Flaubert, Gustave. *Reiseblätter: Briefe aus dem Orient. Über Feld und Strand*. Zusammengestellt von F. Greve. Ins Deutsche übertragen von E. Greve. (pref.: "Paris-Plage, Oktober1905." Minden: Bruns, 1905.

Fletcher, Angus. "'Positive Negation': Threshold, Sequence, and Personification in Coleridge." *New Perspectives on Coleridge and Wordsworth: Selected Papers from the English Institute*. Ed. Geoffrey Hartman. New York: Columbia UP, 1972. 133-64.

Fletcher, Angus. *Allegory: The Theory of a Symbolic Mode*. Ithaca, NY: Cornell UP, 1964.

Florby, Gunilla. *The Margin Speaks: A Study of Margaret Laurence and Robert Kroetsch from a Post-Colonial Point of View*. Lund, Sweden: Lund UP, 1997.

Foss, Krista. "Preserving a Piece of the Prairies: A Canadian Author is Glad She Gave her Saskatchewan Ranch over to Conservation." *Globe and Mail* 13 May 2002: n.p.

Foucault, Michel. "Of Other Spaces." Trans. Jay Miskowiec. *Diacritics* 16 (1986): 22-27.

Francis, R. Douglas. "Changing Images of the West." *The Prairie West: Historical Readings*. Ed. R. Douglas Francis and Howard Palmer. Edmonton: U of Alberta P, 1995. 717-739.

Frank, Sheldon. Rev. of *The Diviners*, by Margaret Laurence. *New Republic* 27 July 1974: 28.

Franklin, John. "From *Narrative of a Journey to the Shores of the Polar Seas in the Years, 1819, 20, 21, and 22*." Bennett and Brown 50-68.

Fraser, Keath. *As for Me and My Body: A Memoir of Sinclair Ross*. Toronto: ECW, 1997.

Freeman, Margaret H. "Cognitive Mapping in Literary Analysis." *Style* 36.3 (2002): 466-83.

Freud, Sigmund. *On Metapsychology: The Theory of Psychoanalysis: Beyond the Pleasure Principle, The Ego and the Id, and Other Works*. Ed. Angela Richards. *Penguin Freud Library*. Ed. James Strachey. Vol. 11. 1984. Harmondsworth: Penguin, 1991.

Freud, Sigmund. "The Uncanny." *Art and Literature: Jensen's Gradiva, Leonardo Da Vinci and Other Works*. Toronto: Penguin, 1985.

Freytag-Loringhoven, Else Baroness von. *Autobiography*. Typescript (205 p.). U of Maryland, College Park. [Also: U of Manitoba Archives, Winnipeg].

Freytag-Loringhoven, Else Baroness von. *Baroness Elsa*. Ed. Paul I. Hjartarson and Douglas O. Spettigue. [Ottawa]: Oberon, 1992.

Freytag-Loringhoven, Else Baroness von. "Circle." *Broom* 4.2 (Jan. 1923): 128.

Freytag-Loringhoven, Else Baroness von. "Schalk." Ms. poem. U of Maryland, College Park.

Freytag-Loringhoven, Else Baroness von. "Wolkzug." Ms. poem. U of Maryland, College Park.

Friesen, Gerald. *River Road: Essays on Manitoba and Prairie History.* Winnipeg: U of Manitoba P, 1996.

Frith, Simon. *Performing Rites: On the Value of Popular Music.* Cambridge, Mass: Harvard UP, 1996.

Fromm, Harold. "From Transcendence to Obsolescence: A Route Map." *The Ecocriticism Reader: Landmarks in Literary Ecology.* Ed. Cheryl Glotfelty and Harold Fromm. Athens: U of Georgia P, 1996. 30-39.

Frühwald, Maria. "A Discovery of Strange Things in Rudy Wiebe's *A Discovery of Strangers." New Worlds: Discovering and Constructing the Unknown in Anglophone Literature; Presented to Walter Pache on the Occasion of his 60th Birthday.* Ed. Martin Kuester, Gabriele Christ, and Rudolf Beck. Munich: Vögel, 2000. 133-47.

Frye, Northrop. *The Bush Garden: Essays on the Canadian Imagination.* Toronto: Anansi, 1971.

Frye, Northrop. *The Great Code: The Bible and Literature.* London: Routledge, 1982.

Frye, Northrop. *Words with Power: Being a Second Study of The Bible and Literature.* San Diego: Harcourt, 1990.

Fulford, Robert. "It's Fascinating Despite The Flaws." *The Toronto Star* 18 May 1974: H5.

Gammel, Irene. *Baroness Elsa: Gender, Dada, and Everyday Modernity: A Cultural Biography.* Cambridge, Mass: MIT, 2002.

George, Stefan. *Stefan George, Friedrich Gundolf: Briefwechsel.* Hrsg. Robert Boehringer mit Georg Peter Landmann. München: H. Küpper, 1962.

Gibson, Graeme. "Margaret Laurence." *Eleven Canadian Novelists.* Toronto: Anansi, 1973. 185-208.

Gide, André. "Conversation avec un allemand." Ed. Claude Martin. *Bulletin des amis d'André Gide* 32 (Oct. 1976): 23-39.

Gittings, Christopher E. *Canadian National Cinema.* London: Routledge, 2002.

Glassner, Barry. *The Culture of Fear: Why Americans Are Afraid of the Wrong Things.* New York: Basic, 1999.

Glotfelty, Cheryl, and Harold Fromm, eds. *The Ecocriticism Reader: Landmarks in Literary Ecology.* Athens: U of Georgia P, 1996.

Goethe, Johann Wolfgang von. *Goethe's Faust*. Ed. Calvin Thomas. Boston: Heath, 1892.

Goethe, Johann Wolfgang von. *Goethe's Poems*. Comp. and ed. Charles Harris. Boston: Heath, [1899].

Goethe, Johann Wolfgang von. "Gott, Gemüt und Welt." *Goethe's Poems*. 1899. 26-28.

Goldie, Terry. *Fear and Temptation: The Image of the Indigene in Canadian, Australian, and New Zealand Literatures*. Montreal: McGill-Queen's UP, 1989.

"Gopher Destruction." *Zealandia News* 21 April 1927.

"Gopher Drop." 20 Feb. 2001 http://members.tripod.lycos.com/townofcupar/gopherdrop/htm.

Gotlieb, Phyllis. Rev. of *The Diviners*, by Margaret Laurence. *The Tamarack Review* 63 (1974): 80-81.

Grace, Sherrill E. *Canada and the Idea of North*. Montreal: McGill-Queen's UP, 2001.

Gray, James H. *The Roar of the Twenties*. Toronto: Macmillan, 1975.

Gray, John. "Young Kwaday Dan Sinchi Was Trekking High Up On A Barren Glacier In His Gopher-Skin Cloak When Disaster Struck." *Globe and Mail* [Toronto] 4 Aug. 2001: F7.

Greve, Felix Paul. *Correspondence with S. George, Gide, Gundolf, Schmitz, and Wolfskehl*. Mss., Spettigue Collection, U of Manitoba Archives, Winnipeg.

Greve, Felix Paul. *Correspondence with the Insel Verlag*. Ms., Nationale Forschungs- und Gedenkstätten der klassischen deutschen Literatur, Weimar. (Also: U of Manitoba Archives, Winnipeg).

Greve, Felix Paul. "Erster Sturm." *Die Schaubühne* 3.6 (7 Feb. 1907): 154.

Greve, Felix Paul. *Fanny Eßler: ein Roman*. Stuttgart: Juncker, [1905].

Greve, Felix Paul. Letter to André Gide, Cologne, 7 June 1904. *Bulletin des amis d'André Gide* 32 (Oct. 1976): 37-38.

Greve, Felix Paul. Letter to André Gide, Wollerau, 17 Oct. 1904. *Bulletin des amis d'André Gide* 32 (Oct. 1976): 39-41.

Greve, Felix Paul. Letter to Franz Brümmer, 6 March 1907. Grove, *Letters* 538-541.

Greve, Felix Paul. *Maurermeister Ihles Haus*. Berlin: Schnabel, 1906.

Greve, Felix Paul. "Nachgelassene Werke von Friedrich Nietzsche, Bd. XI und XII." *Beilage zur Allgemeinen Zeitung* (München) 235 (1901): 6-7.

Greve, Felix Paul. *Wanderungen*. Berlin: Holten, Feb. 1902.

Grosskurth, Phyllis. "A Looser, More Complex, More Sexually Uninhibited Laurence: And Never An Atwood Victim." *The Globe and Mail* 4 May 1974: 35.

Grove, Frederick Philip. *Correspondence with A. L. Phelps*. U of Manitoba Archives, Winnipeg.

Grove, Frederick Philip. "Die Dünen fliegen auf...". Ms. poem. U of Manitoba Archives, Winnipeg.

Grove, Frederick Philip. "The Dying Year." Ts poem. U of Manitoba Archives, Winnipeg.

Grove, Frederick Philip. *In Search of Myself*. Toronto: Macmillan, 1946.

Grove, Frederick Philip. *It Needs to be Said*. 1929. Ottawa: Tecumseh, 1982.

Grove, Frederick Philip. *Jane Atkinson* (novel). Ts., U of Manitoba Archives, Winnipeg.

Grove, Frederick Philip. "Jean Jacques Rousseau als Erzieher." [von Fred Grove, Hauptlehrer an der Mittelschule zu Winkler, Manitoba]. *Der Nordwesten*, Nov. 25 to Dec. 16, 1914. M. Stobie Collection, U of Manitoba Archives, Winnipeg.

Grove, Frederick Philip. "Konrad, the Builder." Ms. poem. U of Manitoba Archives, Winnipeg.

Grove, Frederick Philip. *The Letters of Frederick Philip Grove*. Ed. Desmond Pacey. Toronto: U of Toronto P, 1976.

Grove, Frederick Philip. "The Life of Saint Nishivara." 60 ms. Aphorisms, U of Manitoba Archives, Winnipeg. Also, "Of Nishivara, the Saint" in Hjartarson 83-87.

Grove, Frederick Philip. *Over Prairie Trails*. Toronto: McClelland & Stewart, 1922.

Grove, Frederick Philip. *Poems/Gedichte*, by F. Grove/F. Greve und "Fanny Essler." Ed. Gaby Divay. Winnipeg: Wolf Verlag, 1993.

Grove, Frederick Philip. *A Search for America: The Odyssey of an Immigrant*. Ottawa: Graphic, 1927.

Grove, Frederick Philip. *Settlers of the Marsh*. 1925. Ed. Alison Calder. Ottawa: Tecumseh (Canadian Critical Editions), 2006.

Grove, Frederick Philip. *Settlers of the Marsh*. 1925. Toronto: McClelland & Stewart, 1966.

Grove, Frederick Philip. *The Turn of the Year*. Toronto: McClelland & Stewart, 1923.

Grove, Frederick Philip. *Two Generations: A Story of Present-Day Ontario*. Toronto: Ryerson, 1939.

Gruending, Dennis. Introduction. *The Middle of Nowhere: Rediscovering Saskatchewan*. Saskatoon: Fifth House, 1996. 1-5.

Gunnars, Kristjana, ed. *Crossing the River: Essays in Honour of Margaret Laurence.* Winnipeg: Turnstone, 1988.

Halfe, Louise. *Bear Bones and Feathers.* Regina: Coteau, 1994.

Halfe, Louise. *Blue Marrow.* Toronto: McClelland & Stewart, 1998.

Hall, D. J. "Clifford Sifton: Immigration and Settlement Policy, 1896-1905." *The Settlement of the West.* Ed. Howard Palmer. Calgary: U of Calgary P, 1977. 60-85.

Hammill, Faye. "The Sensations of the 1920s: Martha Ostenso's *Wild Geese* and Mazo de la Roche's *Jalna.*" *Studies in Canadian Literature* 28.2 (2003): 74-97.

Hamon, John J. Letter. *Western Producer* 3 Aug. 2000. http://www.producer.com/articels/20000803/opinion/letters.html.

Harrison, Dallas. "Where is (the) Horizon? Placing *As for Me and My House.*" *Essays on Canadian Writing* 61 (1997): 142-69.

Harrison, Dick, ed. *Crossing Frontiers: Papers in American and Canadian Western Literature.* Edmonton: U of Alberta P, 1979.

Harrison, Dick. *Unnamed Country: The Struggle for a Canadian Prairie Fiction.* Edmonton: U of Alberta P, 1977.

Harrison, Robert Pogue. *Gardens: An Essay on the Human Condition.* Chicago: U of Chicago P, 2008.

Harvey, David. *The Condition of Postmodernity: An Enquiry into the Origins of Cultural Change.* Cambridge, Mass: Blackwell, 1989.

Harvey, David. *Justice, Nature, and the Geography of Difference.* Malden, MA: Blackwell, 1996.

Heine, Heinrich. *Heine's Poems.* Ed. Carl Edgar Eggert. Boston: Ginn, [1906].

Helwig, David. "Gunn Myths." *Books in Canada* 3.4 (1974): 7.

Henighan, Stephen. *When Words Deny the World: The Reshaping of Canadian Writing.* Erin: Porcupine's Quill, 2002.

Hepburn, Allan. "Urban Kink: Canadian Fiction Shakes Off Its Rural Roots." *Quill and Quire* 66.4 (2000): 30-32.

Herriot, Trevor. *River in a Dry Land: A Prairie Passage.* Toronto: Stoddart, 2000.

Hesse, M. G. "The Endless Quest: Dreams and Aspirations in Martha Ostenso's *Wild Geese.*" *Journal of Popular Culture* 15.3 (1981): 47-52.

Hetherington, Kevin. *The Badlands of Modernity.* New York: Routledge, 1997.

Hillis, Doris. "Interview [with Guy Vanderhaeghe]." *Wascana Review* 19.1 (1984): 17-28.

Hillis, Doris. *Plainspeaking: Interviews with Saskatchewan Writers.* Regina: Coteau, 1988.

Hillis, Doris. *Voices and Visions: Interviews with Saskatchewan Writers*. Moose Jaw: Coteau, 1985.

Hillis, Rick. "Captain Gopher." *The Blue Machines of Night*. Regina: Coteau, 1988. 13.

Hind-Smith, Joan. *Three Voices: The Lives of Margaret Laurence, Gabrielle Roy, Frederick Philip Grove*. Toronto: Clarke, 1975.

Hinz, Evelyn J., ed. *Beyond Nationalism: The Canadian Literary Scene in Global Perspective*. Winnipeg: U of Manitoba, 1981.

Hjartarson, Paul. "Of Greve, Grove, and Other Strangers: the Autobiography of the Baroness Elsa von Freytag-Loringhoven." Hjartarson 269-284.

Hjartarson, Paul, ed. *A Stranger to My Time: Essays By and About Frederick Philip Grove*. Edmonton: NeWest, 1986.

Hoeppner, Kenneth. "The Spirit of the Arctic or Translating the Untranslatable in Rudy Wiebe's *A Discovery of Strangers*." *Echoing Silence: Essays on Arctic Literature*. Ed. John Moss. Ottawa: U of Ottawa P, 1997. 145-52.

Holden, Clive. "Trains of Winnipeg." *Trains of Winnipeg*. Montreal: DC Books. 50-51.

Holland, Norman N. *The Brain of Robert Frost: A Cognitive Approach to Literature*. New York: Routledge, 1988.

Houliat, Bernard. *Tsiganes en Roumanie*. Paris: Éditions du Rouergue, 1999.

Huggan, Graham. "Decolonizing the Map: Post-Colonialism, Post-Structuralism and the Cartographic Connection." *Ariel* 20.4 (1989): 115-31.

Hughes, Kenneth James, ed. *Contemporary Manitoba Writers: New Critical Studies*. Winnipeg: Turnstone, 1990.

Hunter, Catherine. "Two Thousand and Two." Fiorentino and Kroetsch. 82-84.

Hutcheon, Linda. *The Canadian Postmodern*. Toronto: Oxford UP, 1988.

Hutcheon, Linda. *A Poetics of Postmodernism: History, Theory, Fiction*. New York: Routledge, 1988.

Hutcheon, Linda. *A Theory of Adaptation*. New York: Routledge, 2006.

Hyland, Gary. "Home Street." *Love of Mirrors*. Regina: Coteau, 2008.

Jakobson, Roman. "Linguistics and Poetics." *Roman Jakobson: Selected Writings*. Ed. S. Rudy. Vol. 2. The Hague: Mouton, 1981. 18-51.

Jakobson, Roman. "Two Aspects of Language and Two Types of Aphasic Disturbances." *Roman Jakobson: Selected Writings*. Ed. S. Rudy. Vol. 2. The Hague: Mouton, 1981. 239-59.

Jakobson, Roman. "What Is Poetry?" Trans. M. Heim. *Roman Jakobson: Selected Writings*. Ed. S. Rudy. Vol. 3. The Hague: Mouton, 1981. 740-50.

James, William Closson. "'A Land Beyond Words': Rudy Wiebe's *A Discovery of Strangers*." *Mapping the Sacred: Religion, Geography, and Postcolonial Literatures*. Ed. Jamie S. Scott and Paul Simpson-Housley. Amsterdam: Rodopi, 2001. 71-89.

Jewinski, Ed, and Andrew Stubbs, eds. *The Politics of Art: Eli Mandel's Poetry and Criticism*. Atlanta, GA: Rodopi, 1992.

Jirgens, Karl E. "Lighthouse, Ring and Fountain: The Never-ending Circle in *No Great Mischief*." *Alistair MacLeod: Essays on his Works*. Ed. Irene Guildford. Toronto: Guernica, 2001.

Johnson, Brian. "Unsettled Landscapes: Uncanny Discourses of Love in Ostenso's *Wild Geese*." *Wascana Review* 34.2 (1999): 23-41.

Johnson, Randal. Introduction. *The Field of Cultural Production*. New York: Columbia UP, 1993. 1-25.

Jones, D.G. *Butterfly on Rock: A Study of Themes and Images in Canadian Literature*. Toronto: U of Toronto P, 1970.

Justice, Daniel Heath. "The Necessity of Nationhood: Affirming the Sovereignty of Indigenous Nation Literatures." *Moveable Margins: The Shifting Spaces of Canadian Literature*. Ed. Chelva Kananganayakam. Toronto: TSAR Publications, 2005. 143-160.

Kaltembach, Michele. "Explorations into History: Rudy Wiebe's *A Discovery of Strangers*." *Études Canadiennes / Canadian Studies* 44 (1998): 78-79.

Kamboureli, Smaro. "The Culture of Celebrity and National Pedagogy." *Home-work, Postcolonialism, Pedagogy, and Canadian Literature*. Ed. Cynthia Sugars. Ottawa: U of Ottawa P, 2004. 35-56.

Kamboureli, Smaro. "The Culture of Nature and the Logic of Modernity: Sharon Butala's *The Perfection of the Morning: An Apprenticeship in Nature*." *Revista Canaria de Estudios Ingleses* 43 (2001): 37-58.

Kamboureli, Smaro. *Scandalous Bodies: Diasporic Literature in English Canada*. Oxford: Oxford UP, 2000.

Kamboureli, Smaro, and Roy Miki, eds. *Trans. Can. Lit.: Resituating the Study of Canadian Literature*. Waterloo: Wilfred Laurier UP, 2007.

Kanaganayakam, Chelva. *Moveable Margins: The Shifting Spaces of Canadian Literature*. Toronto: TSAR, 2005.

Kattan, Naim. "L'ambitieux roman de M. Laurence." *Le Devoir* 27 July 1974: 13.

Kaye, Vladimir J. and Frances Swyripa. "Settlement and Colonization." *A Heritage in Transition: Essays in the History of Ukrainians in Canada*. Ed. Manoly R. Lupul. Toronto: McClelland & Stewart, 1982.

Keahey, Deborah. *Making It Home: Place in Canadian Prairie Literature*. Winnipeg: U of Manitoba P, 1998.

Keefer, Janice Kulyk. "'The Sacredness of Bridges': Writing Immigrant Experience." *Literary Pluralities*. Ed. Christl Verduyn. Peterborough: Broadview, 1998. 97-110.

Kelcey, Barbara. "The Great Gopher War." *The Beaver* June/July 1999: 16-21.

Kelley, Ninette and Michael Trebilcock. *The Making of the Mosaic: A History of Canadian Immigration Policy*. Toronto: U of Toronto P, 1998.

Kennedy, X.J, Dana Gioia, and Mark Bauerlein, eds. *Handbook of Literary Terms*. New York: Pearson, 2005.

Kertzer, Jonathan. *Worrying the Nation: Imagining a National Literature in English Canada*. Toronto: U of Toronto P, 1998.

Kiberd, Declan. *Inventing Ireland*. Cambridge: Harvard UP, 1995.

Killam, G. D. Introduction. *A Jest of God*. By Margaret Laurence. Toronto: McClelland & Stewart, 1974. np.

Kincaid, Jamaica. *A Small Place*. New York: Farrar, 1988.

King, James. *Jack: A Life with Writers*. Toronto: Knopf, 1999.

King, James. *The Life of Margaret Laurence*. Toronto: Knopf, 1997.

King, Thomas. *Green Grass, Running Water*. Toronto: HarperPerennial, 1993.

King, Thomas. *The Truth About Stories: A Native Narrative*. Toronto: Anansi, 2003.

Kippenberg, Anton. Letter to Else Greve, 21 Sept. 1909. Grove, *Letters* 548-552.

Klar, Barbara and Paul Wilson. Foreword. *Fast Forward: New Saskatchewan Poets*. Regina: Hagios, 2007. 7-8.

Klein, Melanie. "Infantile Anxiety Situations in a Work of Art and in the Creative Impulse." *International Journal of Psychoanalytic Studies* 10 (1929): 436-43.

Knight, David B. *Landscapes in Music: Space, Place, and Time in the World's Great Music*. Lanham, MD: Rowman, 2006.

Knönagel, Axel. *Nietzschean Philosophy in the Works of Frederick Philip Grove*. Frankfurt: Lang, 1990.

Kolbe, Jürgen. *Heller Zauber: Thomas Mann in München, 1884-1933*. Berlin: Siedler-Verlag, 1987.

Koster, Patricia. "Hagar 'The Egyptian': Allusions and Illusions in *The Stone Angel*." *Ariel* 16.3 (1985): 41-52.

Kövecses, Zoltán. *Metaphor: A Practical Introduction*. Oxford: Oxford UP, 2002.

Kövecses, Zoltán, and Peter Szabó. "Idioms: A View from Cognitive Semantics." *Applied Linguistics* 17.3 (1996): 326-55.

Kreisel, Henry. "The Prairie: A State of Mind." 1968. Dyck 171-180.

Kroeger, Arthur. *Hard Passage: A Mennonite Family's Long Journey from Russia to Canada*. Edmonton: U of Alberta P, 2007.

Kroeker, Allan, "The Pedlar." Screenplay (fourth draft). National Film Board of Canada, Prairie Region, Oct. 1981.

Kroetsch, Robert. Afterword. *As for Me and My House*. By Sinclair Ross. Toronto: McClelland & Stewart, 1989. 217-21.

Kroetsch, Robert. "The Cow in the Quicksand and How I(t) Got Out: Responding to Stegner's *Wolf Willow*." *A Likely Story* 65-86.

Kroetsch, Robert. "Don't Give Me No More of Your Lip; or, the Prairie Horizon as Allowed Mouth." Wardhaugh 209-215.

Kroetsch, Robert. *Essays. Open Letter*. Fifth Series, No. 4. 1983.

Kroetsch, Robert. "In Conversation with Rudy Wiebe at Canadian Mennonite University." 18 May 2007. *Prairie Fire* 29.3 (Fall 2008):4-13.

Kroetsch, Robert. Introduction. *Sundogs: Stories from Saskatchewan*. Moose Jaw: Coteau, 1980. i-iv.

Kroetsch, Robert. *A Likely Story: The Writing Life*. Red Deer, Alta: Red Deer CP, 1995.

Kroetsch, Robert. *The Lovely Treachery of Words: Essays Selected and New*. Toronto: Oxford UP, 1989.

Kroetsch, Robert. "The Moment of the Discovery of America Continues." *The Lovely Treachery of Words* 1-20.

Kroetsch, Robert. "No Name is my Name." *The Lovely Treachery of Words* 41-52.

Kroetsch, Robert. "Seed Catalogue." *Seed Catalogue*. Winnipeg: Turnstone, 1986. 1-28.

Kroetsch, Robert. "Spending the Morning on the Beach: Ten Related Lyrics." *Seed Catalogue*. Winnipeg: Turnstone, 1986. 29-43.

Kroetsch, Robert. "Stone Hammer Poem" and "After Paradise." *Completed Field Notes: The Long Poems of Robert Kroetsch*. Edmonton: U of Alberta P, 2000. 3-8, 245-259.

Kroetsch, Robert, and Reingard M. Nischik, eds. *Gaining Ground: European Critics on Canadian Literature*. Edmonton: NeWest, 1985.

Kroller, Eva-Marie, ed. *The Cambridge Companion to Canadian Literature*. Cambridge: Cambridge UP, 2004.

Kuester, Hildegard. *The Crafting of Chaos: Narrative Structure in Margaret Laurence's* The Stone Angel *and* The Diviners. Amsterdam: Rodopic, 1994.

Kurelek, William. *A Prairie Boy's Summer*. Toronto: Tundra, 1975.

Kyba, Patrick, and Wendy Green-Finlay. "John Diefenbaker as Prime Minister: The Record Re-examined." *The Diefenbaker Legacy: Canadian Politics, Law and Society Since 1957*. Ed. Donald C. Story and R. Bruce Shepard. Regina: CPRC, 1998. 57-69.

Kymlicka, Will. "Well done, Canada: Multiculturalism is Working." Rev. of *Unlikely Utopia: The Surprising Triumph of Canadian Pluralism*, by Michael Adams. *The Globe and Mail* [Toronto] 1 Dec. 2007: D22.

Laird, Andrew. "Figures of Allegory from Homer to Latin Epic." *Metaphor, Allegory, and the Classical Tradition: Ancient Thought and Modern Revisions*. Ed. G. R. Boys-Stones. Oxford: Oxford UP, 2003. 151-75.

"Lakeside Workers Vote on New Deal." http://www.cbc.ca/story/news/national/2005 /11/04/LakesideVote_051104.html. 14 Dec. 2006.

Lakoff, George. *Women, Fire and Dangerous Things: What Categories Reveal about the Mind*. Chicago: University UP, 1987.

Lakoff, George, and Mark Johnson. *Metaphors We Live By*. 1980. Chicago: U of Chicago P, 1981.

Lakoff, George, and Mark Turner. *More than Cool Reason: A Field Guide to Poetic Metaphor*. Chicago: U of Chicago P, 1989.

Lanham, Richard A. *A Handlist of Rhetorical Terms*. 2nd ed. Berkeley: U of California P, 1991.

"Laurence, (Jean) Margaret (Wemyss)." *Contemporary Literary Criticism*. Vol. 62. Ed. Roger Matuz. Detroit: Gale, 1991. 262-66.

Laurence, Margaret. *A Bird in the House*. Toronto: McClelland & Stewart, 1970.

Laurence, Margaret. *Dance on the Earth: A Memoir*. Toronto: McClelland & Stewart, 1989.

Laurence, Margaret. *The Diviners*. Toronto: McClelland & Stewart, 1974.

Laurence, Margaret. *The Fire-Dwellers*. Toronto: McClelland & Stewart, 1969.

Laurence, Margaret. "Gadgetry or Growing: Form and Voice in the Novel." Woodcock, *A Place to Stand On* 80-89.

Laurence, Margaret. "A Gourdful of Glory." *The Tomorrow-Tamer and Other Stories*. Toronto: McClelland & Stewart, 1963.

Laurence, Margaret. *Heart of a Stranger*. 1976. Ed. Nora Foster Stovel. Edmonton: U of Alberta P, 2003.

Laurence, Margaret. "Ivory Tower or Grass Roots?: The Novelist as Socio-Political Being." *A Political Art: Essays and Images in Honour of George Woodcock*. Ed. W. H. New. Vancouver: U of British Columbia P, 1978. 15-25.

Laurence, Margaret. *A Jest of God*. Toronto: McClelland & Stewart, 1966.

Laurence, Margaret. "Living Dangerously . . . by Mail." *Heart of a Stranger*. Ed. Nora Foster Stovel. Edmonton: U of Alberta P, 2003. 141-46.

Laurence, Margaret. *Long Drums and Cannons: Nigerian Dramatists and Novelists, 1952-66.* 1968. Ed. Nora Foster Stovel. Edmonton: U of Alberta P, 2001.

Laurence, Margaret. "A Place to Stand On." *Heart of a Stranger*. Ed. Nora Foster Stovel. Edmonton: U of Alberta P, 2003. 5-9.

Laurence, Margaret. "A Place to Stand On." Woodcock, *A Place to Stand On* 15-19.

Laurence, Margaret. *The Prophet's Camel Bell*. Toronto: McClelland & Stewart, c1963.

Laurence, Margaret. "Sources." *Mosaic* 3 (Spring 1970): 80-84.

Laurence, Margaret. *The Stone Angel*. 1964. Toronto: McClelland & Stewart, 1988.

Laurence, Margaret. "Ten Years' Sentences." *Canadian Literature* 41 (1969): 10-16. Rpt. in New, *Critical Views* 17-23.

Laurence, Margaret. "Ten Years' Sentences." Woodcock, *A Place to Stand On* 28-34.

Laurence, Margaret. *This Side Jordan*. Toronto: McClelland & Stewart, 1960.

Laurence, Margaret. "Time and the Narrative Voice." Rpt. in New, *Critical Views* 156-160.

Laurence, Margaret. "Time and the Narrative Voice." Woodcock, *A Place to Stand On* 155-59.

Laurence, Margaret. *The Tomorrow-Tamer and Other Stories*. Toronto: McClelland & Stewart, 1963.

Laurence, Margaret. *A Tree for Poverty*. Nairobi: Somaliland Protectorate / Eagle Press, 1954.

"Laurence's Books Banned." *The CBC Digital Archives Website*. Canadian Broadcasting Corporation. 7 Dec. 2003. 7 March 2008 http://archives.cbc.ca/ politics/rights_freedoms/clip/803/.

Lausberg, Heinrich. *Handbuch der literarischen Rhetorik: Eine Grundlegung der Literaturwissenschaft*. 2 vols. Munich: Hueber, 1960.

Lawrence, Robert G. "The Geography of Martha Ostenso's *Wild Geese*." *Journal of Canadian Fiction* 16 (1976): 108-14.

Lawson, Alan. "Postcolonial Theory and the 'Settler' Subject." *Unhomely States: Theorizing English-Canadian Postcolonialism*. Ed. Cynthia Sugars. Peterborough: Broadview, 2004. 151-64.

Le Carré, John. *The Constant Gardener*. London: Penguin, 2001.

Lecker, Robert. "The Canonization of Canadian Literature: An Inquiry into Value." *Making It Real: the Canonization of English-Canadian Literature*. Concord: Anansi, 1995. 25-48.

Lecker, Robert. *Robert Kroetsch*. Boston: Twayne, 1986.

Lehr, John C. "Peopling the Prairies with Ukrainians." *Canada's Ukrainians: Negotiating an Identity*. Ed. Lubomyr Luciuk and Stella Hryniuk. Toronto: U of Toronto P, 1991.

Lejeune, Phillipe. *On Autobiography*. Trans. Katherine Leary. Minneapolis: U. of Minnesota P, 1989.

Lenk, Uta. "Konzeptuelle Metaphern zu Sprache in literarischen Texten: Möglichkeiten einer interdisziplinären Anglistik." *AAA—Arbeiten aus Anglistik und Amerikanistik* 27.1 (2002): 51-68.

Lennox, John, and Ruth Panofsky, eds. *Selected Letters of Margaret Laurence and Adele Wiseman*. Toronto: U of Toronto P, 1997.

Lenoski, Daniel S. "Martha Ostenso's *Wild Geese*: The Language of Silence." *North Dakota Quarterly* 52.3 (1984): 279-96.

Lessing, Doris. Preface. *The Golden Notebook*. 1962. Toronto: Grafton, 1986.

Lever, Bernice. "Manawaka Magic." *Journal of Canadian Fiction* 3.3 (1974): 93-96.

Lever, Bernice. Rev. of *The Diviners*, by Margaret Laurence. *Canadian Author and Bookman* 50 (1974): 26.

Levy, Sophie. "'This Dark Echo Calls Him Home': Writing Father-Daughter Incest Narratives in Canadian Immigrant Fiction." *University of Toronto Quarterly* 71.4 (Fall 2002): 864-880.

Liegeois, Jean-Pierre. *Gypsies: An Illustrated History*. Trans. Tony Berrett. London: Al Saqi, 1986.

Life and Debt. Dir. Stephanie Black. Mongrel, 2001.

Lippit, Akira. *Electric Animal: Toward a Rhetoric of Wildlife*. Minneapolis: U of Minnesota, 2000.

Litwin, Lloyd. "Opponents Of Gopher Derby Are Such Pests." *StarPhoenix* [Saskatoon] 11 March 2002: C7.

Lo, Jacqueline. "Beyond Happy Hybridity: Performing Asian-Australian Identities." *Alter/Asians: Asian-Australian Identities in Art, Media and Popular Culture*. Annandale, NSW: Pluto, 2000. 152-68.

Lo, Miriam. "Towards a Particular Hybridity: A Beginning." *Westerly* 44.4 (Summer 1999): 9-20.

Lodge, David. *The Modes of Modern Writing: Metaphor, Metonymy, and the Typology of Modern Literature*. 1977. London: Arnold, 1979.

Lousley, Cheryl. "Home on the Prairie? A Feminist and Postcolonial Reading of Sharon Butala, Di Brandt, and Joy Kogawa." *Interdisciplinary Studies in Literature and the Environment* 8.2 (2001): 71-95.

Lousley, Cheryl. "'Hosanna Da, Our Home on Natives' Land': Environmental Justice and Democracy in Thomas King's *Green Grass, Running Water*." *Essays on Canadian Writing* 81 (2004): 17-44.

Lousley, Cheryl. "Writing the Rural Other: Sharon Butala Meets Trinh T. Minh-ha." Environmental Studies Association of Canada (ESAC) Conference. June 1999.

Luciuk, Lubomyr Y. "'This Should Never Be Spoken or Quoted Publicly': Canada's Ukrainians and Their Encounter with the DPs." *Canada's Ukrainians: Negotiating an Identity*. Ed. Lubomyr Luciuk and Stella Hryniuk. Toronto: U of Toronto P, 1991.

Lucking, David. *Ancestors and Gods: Margaret Laurence and the Dialectics of Identity*. Bern: Lang, 2002.

Mackey, Eva. *The House of Difference: Cultural Politics and National Identity in Canada*. Toronto: U of Toronto P, 2002.

MacLennan, C. H. G. "Metaphors and Prototypes in the Learning Teaching [sic] of Grammar and Vocabulary." *IRAL* 32.2 (1994): 97-110.

MacLennan, Hugh. *On Being a Maritime Writer*. Sackville: Mt. Allison UP, 1984.

MacLeod, Alistair. "'At the Moment': Notes on Fiction." *The Art of Short Fiction*. Brief ed. Ed. Gary Geddes. Don Mills, On: Longman, 1999. 361-62.

Macnaughton, Phil, and John Urry. *Contested Natures*. London: Sage, 1998.

Macpherson, Les. "What Would Happen If Gophers Took Over The Government?" *StarPhoenix* [Saskatoon] 4 Aug. 2001: A3.

MacSween, R. J. Rev. of *The Diviners*, by Margaret Laurence. *Antigonish Review* 18 (1974): 107-08.

Maddin, Guy, dir, and screenplay. *My Winnipeg*. Buffalo Gal Pictures / Maximum Films, 2007.

Maeser Lemieux, Angelika. "The Scots Presbyterian Legacy." Riegel, *Challenging Territory* 63-68.

Mandel, Eli. *Another Time*. Erin: Porcepic, 1977.

Mandel, Eli. "Strange Loops." *The Family Romance*. Winnipeg: Turnstone, 1986. 11-27.

Mandel, Eli. "Writing West: On the Road to Wood Mountain." Sproxton 39-54.

Mann, Thomas. *Die Buddenbrooks: Verfall einer Familie*. 1901. Frankfurt: Fischer, 1981.

Mann, Thomas. Letters to F. P. Grove from Princeton, 19 April 1939 & 5 June 1939. Spettigue Collection, U of Manitoba Archives, Winnipeg.

Mann, Viktor. *Wir waren fünf: Bildnis der Familie Mann.* Konstanz: Südverlag, 1949.

Marling, Karel Ann. *The Colossus of Roads: Myth and Symbol Along the American Highway.* Minneapolis: U of Minnesota P, 1984.

Massey, Doreen. "A Global Sense of Place." *Space, Place, and Gender.* Minneapolis: U of Minnesota P, 1994. 146-156.

Mayall, David. *Gypsy Identities, 1500-2000.* London, Routledge, 2004.

McCourt, Edward. *The Canadian West in Fiction.* 1949. Rev. ed. Toronto: Ryerson, 1970.

McDonald, Marci. "The Author: All The Hoopla Gets Her Frazzled." *The Toronto Star* 18 May 1974: H5.

McDonough, Jimmy. *Shakey: Neil Young's Biography.* Toronto: Random House, 2002.

McFarlane, Brian. *Novel to Film: An Introduction to the Theory of Adaptation.* Oxford: Clarendon, 1996.

McLay, Catherine. "Crocus, Saskatchewan: A Country of the Mind." *Journal of Popular Culture* 14.2 (Fall 1980): 333-349.

McLean, Ken. "Dividing *The Diviners.*" *New Perspectives on Margaret Laurence: Poetic Narrative, Multiculturalism, and Feminism.* Ed. Greta McCormick Coger. Westport: Greenwood, 1996. 97-111.

McLeod Sr., Don. Letter. *StarPhoenix* [Saskatoon] 16 Aug. 2001: B2.

McNairn, Kim. "Prairie Enemy No. 1." *StarPheonix* [Saskatoon] 1 Aug. 2001: A3.

Mehta, Brinda. *Diasporic (Dis)locations: Indo-Caribbean Women Writers Negotiate the Kala Pani.* Kingston, Jamaica: U of the West Indies P, 2004.

Melynk, George. "The Five City-States of the West." *Ring* 133-151.

Melnyk, George. *The Literary History of Alberta. Volume One: From Writing-on-Stone to World War Two.* Edmonton: U of Alberta P, 1998.

Melnyk, George. *The Literary History of Alberta. Volume Two: From the End of the War to the End of the Century.* Edmonton: U of Alberta P, 1999.

Melnyk, George. "The Urban Prairie: Between Jerusalem and Babylon." *New Moon at Batoche.* Banff: Banff Centre, 1999. 103-15.

Michael, Friedrich. "Verschollene der frühen Insel." *Börsenblatt für den deutschen Buchhandel* 28 (1972): A79-82.

Mickelson's Kill-Em-Quick Gopher Poison. Advertisement. *Grain Growers' Guide* 24 Jan. 1911: 17.

Mickelson's Kill-Em-Quick Gopher Poison. Advertisement. *Grain Growers' Guide* 17 Jan. 1912: 9.

Mickleburgh, Brita. Rev. of *The Diviners*, by Margaret Laurence. *The Fiddlehead* 104 (1975): 111-14.

Miller, J. Hillis. "The Two Allegories." *Allegory, Myth, and Symbol.* Ed. Morton Bloomfield. Cambridge, Mass: Harvard UP, 1981. 355-70.

Milton, John. *Paradise Lost* and *Paradise Regained.* Ed. Christopher Ricks. New York: Signet/Penguin, 2001.

Mitchell, Barbara and Ormond Mitchell. *The Life of W.O. Mitchell: The Years of Fame, 1948-1998.* Toronto: McClelland & Stewart, 2005.

Mitchell, Ken. Preface. *Horizon: Writings of the Canadian Prairie.* Toronto: Oxford, 1977. x-xi.

Mitchell, Ken. *Sinclair Ross: A Reader's Guide.* Moose Jaw: Coteau, 1981.

Mitchell, W. O. *According to Jake and the Kid.* 1989. Toronto: McClelland & Stewart, 1990.

Mitchell, W. O. "Going to a Fire." Early version of the film script for the film, eventually re-titled *Fires of Envy.* n.d. W.O. Mitchell Fonds U of Calgary Library Special Collections, Accession No. 679/00.10 57.10.

Mitchell, W. O. "Going to a Fire." Radio play in the series *Jake and the Kid.* Produced by Peter Francis. CBC. Jan. 13, 1952.

Mitchell, W. O. "Going to a Fire." Radio play in the series *Jake and the Kid.* Produced by Arthur Hiller. CBC. Jan. 25, 1953.

Mitchell, W. O. *Who Has Seen the Wind.* 1947. Toronto: Macmillan, 1993.

Mohanty, Chandra Talpade. *Feminism Without Borders: Decolonizing Theory, Practicing Solidarity.* Durham, NC: Duke UP, 2003.

Moi, Toril. "Appropriating Bourdieu: Feminist Theory and Pierre Bourdieu's Sociology of Culture." *New Literary History* 22 (1991): 1017-1049.

Morgan, Elwyn. Letter. *StarPhoenix* [Saskatoon] 4 Mar. 2002: A8.

Morley, Patricia. "Canada, Africa, Canada: Laurence's Unbroken Journey." *Journal of Canadian Fiction* 27 (1980): 81-91.

Morley, Patricia. *Margaret Laurence: The Long Journey Home.* Boston: Hall, 1981.

Moss, John. Introduction. *The Canadian Novel: Here and Now.* Toronto: N C, 1978. 7-15.

Moss, John. *Patterns of Isolation in English Canadian Fiction.* Toronto: McClelland & Stewart, 1974.

Moss, Laura, ed. *Is Canada Postcolonial?: Unsettling Canadian Literature.* Waterloo: Wilfrid Laurier UP, 2003.

Mowat, Farley. "The Nature of the North." *The Broadview Reader*. 3rd ed. Ed. Herbert Rosengarten and Jane Flick. Peterborough: Broadview, 1999. 215-221.

Mühlhäusler, Peter. "Metaphors Others Live By." *Language & Communication* 15.3 (1995): 281-88.

Mukherjee, Arun P. "Canadian Nationalism, Canadian Literature and Racial Minority Women." *The Other Woman: Women of Colour in Contemporary Canadian Literature*. Ed. Makeda Silvera. Toronto: Sister Vision, 1995. 421-444.

Muller, Gilbert H. *New Strangers in Paradise: The Immigrant Experience and Contemporary American Fiction*. Lexington: UP Kentucky, 1999.

Murray, Jeffrey S. "Sell, Sell, Sell" and "Printed Advertisements." *Moving Here, Staying Here: The Canadian Immigrant Experience*. Library and Archives Canada. 20 Oct. 2006. 16 July 2008. http://www.collectionscanada.gc.ca/immigrants.

Nancekivell, Sharon. "Margaret Laurence: Bibliography." *World Literature Written in English* 22.2 (1983): 263-84.

Naumann, Francis M. *Conversion to Modernism: The Early Work of Man Ray*. New Brunswick, N.J.: Rutgers UP / Montclair Art Museum, c2003.

Naumann, Francis M. *New York dada*. New York: Abrams, 1994.

Nelson, Barney. *The Wild and the Domestic: Animal Representation, Ecocriticism, and Western American Literature*. Reno: U of Nevada, 2000.

Neuman, Shirley, and Robert Wilson, eds. *Labyrinths of Voice: Conversations with Robert Kroestch*. Edmonton: NeWest, 1982.

New, W. H. *Articulating West: Essays on Purpose and Form in Modern Canadian Literature*. Toronto: New, 1972.

New, W. H., ed. *Critical Views on Canadian Writers: Margaret Laurence*. Toronto: Ryerson, 1977.

New, W. H. *A History of Canadian Literature*. 2nd ed. Montreal: McGill-Queen's UP, 2003.

New, W. H. Introduction. *Margaret Laurence*. Toronto: Ryerson, 1977. 1-11.

New, W. H. Introduction. *The Stone Angel*. By Margaret Laurence. Toronto: McClelland & Stewart, 1968. Rpt. in New, *Critical Views* 135-42.

New, W. H. *Land Sliding: Imagining Space, Presence, and Power in Canadian Writing*. Toronto: U of Toronto P, 1997.

New, W. H. "Tops and Tales: Mountain Anecdote and Mountain Metaphor." *Canadian Poetry* 55 (2004): 111-32.

Nicholson, Colin. *Critical Approaches to the Fiction of Margaret Laurence*. London: Macmillan, 1990.

Nikiforuk, Andrew. "Pandemonium: Global Trade and the New Free Market for Disease." University of Alberta International Week. Council Chambers, U of Alberta. 1 Feb. 2007.

Nixon, Rob. "Environmentalism and Postcolonialism." *Postcolonial Studies and Beyond*. Ed. Ania Loomba, et al. Durham: Duke UP, 2005. 233-251.

Northey, Margot. *The Haunted Wilderness: The Gothic and Grotesque in Canadian Fiction*. Toronto: U of Toronto P, 1976.

Novek, Joel. "Factory Farms on the Prairies: Stench, Site Fights and Rural Governance." The Prairies: Visited and Revisited Conference. University of Manitoba, Winnipeg. 21 Sept. 2001.

Olney, James. *Metaphors of Self: The Meaning of Autobiography*. Princeton, NJ: Princeton UP, 1972.

Omhovere, Claire. "The North in Rudy Wiebe's *A Discovery of Strangers*: A Land beyond Words." *Commonwealth Essays and Studies* 24.2 (2002): 79-91.

Omhovere, Claire. *Sensing Space: The Poetics of Geography in Contemporary English-Canadian Writing*. Canadian Studies (Brussels, Belgium). New York: Lang, 2007.

Opp, James. *Canadas of the Mind: The Making and Unmaking of Canadian Nationalisms in the Twentieth Century*. Ed. Norman Hillmer and Adam Chapnick. Montreal: McGill-Queen's UP, 2007.

Ostenso, Martha. *Wild Geese*. Toronto: McClelland & Stewart, 1989.

Pabby, D. K. *The Fiction of Margaret Laurence and Anita Desai: Discourse in Alienation*. New Delhi: Prestige, 2005.

Pacey, Desmond. *Frederick Philip Grove*. Toronto: Ryerson, 1945.

Pacey, Desmond. Introduction. Grove, *Letters* ix-xxvi.

Palmer, Howard. "Reluctant Hosts: Anglo-Canadian Views of Multiculturalism in the Twentieth Century." *Multiculturalism as State Policy*. Canadian Consultative Council of Multiculturalism. Ottawa: Department of Secretary of State for Canada, 1976. Rpt in *Immigration in Canada: Historical Perspectives*. Ed. Gerald Tulchinsky. Toronto: Longman, 1994. 297-333.

Parker, James. "Group Declares War On Population Explosion Of Gophers." *StarPhoenix* [Saskatoon], 23 July 2001: A3.

Pearson, David. "Reconnecting the Antipodes: A Reflective Note." *Thesis Eleven* 82 (Aug. 2005): 88-96.

Pell, Barbara. "The African and Canadian Heroines: From Bondage to Grace." Riegel, *Challenging Territory* 33-46.

Philip, [M.] Nourbese. "Taming Our Tomorrows." *Literary Pluralities*. Ed. Christl Verduyn. Peterborough: Broadview, 1998. 270-277.

Philip, M. Nourbese, et al. "Fortress in the Wilderness." *Borderlines* 45 (1997): 20-25.

Piercy, Marge. "Gritty places and strong women." *New York Times Book Review* 23 June 1974: 6. Rpt. in New, *Critical Views* 212-13.

Pilkington, Edward. *Beyond the Mother Country: West Indians and the Notting Hill White Riots.* London: Tauris, 1988.

Poovey, Mary. *The Proper Lady and the Woman Writer: Ideology as Style in the Works of Mary Wollstonecraft, Mary Shelley, and Jane Austen.* Chicago: U of Chicago P, 1884.

Porter, John. *The Vertical Mosaic: An Analysis of Social Class and Power in Canada.* 1965. Toronto: U of Toronto P: 1969.

Powe, B. W. *A Climate Charged.* Oakville: Mosaic, 1984.

Powers, Lyall. *Alien Heart: The Life and Work of Margaret Laurence.* Winnipeg: U of Manitoba P, 2003.

Probert, Kenneth G., ed. *Writing Saskatchewan: 20 Critical Essays.* Regina: CPRC, 1989.

Pryse, Marjorie. "Writing Out of the Gap: Regionalism, Resistance, and Relational Reading." Riegel and Wyile 19-34.

Quantic, Diane Dufva. *The Nature of the Place: A Study of Great Plains Fiction.* Lincoln: U of Nebraska P, 1995.

Quinn, Naomi. "The Cultural Basis of Metaphor." *Beyond Metaphor: The Theory of Tropes in Anthropology.* Ed. James W. Fernandez. Stanford, CA: Stanford UP, 1991. 56-93.

Quintilian. *Institutio oratoria.* Trans. H. E. Butler. 4 vols. Cambridge, Mass: Harvard UP, 1921.

Reimer, Douglas. *Surplus at the Border: Mennonite Writing in Canada.* Winnipeg: Turnstone, 2002.

Rich, Adrienne. "Notes toward a Politics of Location." 1984. *Blood, Bread, and Poetry: Selected Prose* 1979-1985. New York: Norton, 1986. 210-31.

Ricoeur, Paul. *The Rule of Metaphor: Multi-Disciplinary Studies of the Creation of Meaning in Language.* 1977. Trans. R. Czerny, K. McLaughlin, and J. Costello, Sr. London: Routledge, 1978.

Ricou, Laurence, ed. *Twelve Prairie Poets.* Ottawa: Oberon, 1976.

Ricou, Laurence. *Vertical Man/Horizontal World: Man and Landscape in Canadian Prairie Fiction.* Vancouver: U of British Columbia P, 1973.

Ricou, Laurie. "Other Edens." *Canadian Literature* 170/171 (2001). http://www.canlit.ca/reviews/archive/170_171/5553_ricou.html.

Riegel, Christian and Herb Wyile, eds. *A Sense of Place: Re-Evaluating Regionalism in Canadian And American Writing*. Edmonton: U of Alberta P, 1998.

Riegel, Christian, ed. *Challenging Territory: The Writing of Margaret Laurence*. Edmonton: U of Alberta P, 1997.

Riegel, Christian. *Writing Grief: Margaret Laurence and the Work of Mourning*. Winnipeg: U of Manitoba P, 2003.

Ring, Dan, ed. *The Urban Prairie*. Saskatoon: Mendel Art Gallery / Fifth House, 1993.

Riviere, Joan. "Womanliness as a Masquerade." *International Journal of Psycho-Analysis* 10 (1929): 303-13.

Robinson, Jill M. *Seas of Earth: An Annotated Bibliography of Saskatchewan Literature as it relates to the Environment*. Regina: CRPC, 1977.

Rooke, Constance. "Hagar's Old Age: *The Stone Angel* as *Vollendungsroman*." Gunnars 25-42.

Ross, Morton L. "Sinclair Ross and His Works." *Canadian Writers and their Works*. Ed. Robert Lecker, Jack David, and Ellen Quigley. Fiction ser. 4. Toronto: ECW, 1991. 257-98.

Ross, Sinclair. "Cornet at Night." *Saskatchewan Harvest*. Ed. Carlyle King. Toronto: McClelland & Stewart, 1955. 190-212.

Ross, Sinclair. *As for Me and My House*. 1941. Toronto: McClelland & Stewart, 1989.

Rudy Dorscht, Susan. *Women, Reading, Kroetsch: Telling the Difference*. Waterloo, ON: Wilfrid Laurier UP, 1991.

Russell, Andy. *The Life of a River*. Toronto: McClelland & Stewart, 1987.

Sabloff, Annabelle. *Reordering the Natural World: Humans and Animals in the City*. Toronto: U of Toronto P, 2001.

Salo, Matt T. "Gypsies/Rom." *Encyclopedia of Canada's Peoples*. Ed. Paul Robert Magocsi. Toronto: U of Toronto P, 1999. 642-648.

Salo, Matt T. "Gypsy Ethnicity: Implications of Native Categories and Interaction for Ethnic Classification." *Ethnicity* 6 (1979): 73-96.

Sangster, Charles. "From *The St. Lawrence to the Saguenay*." Bennett and Brown 125-29.

Saunders Doris, and Robin Hoople, ed. *Manitoba in Literature: An Issue on Literary Environment*. Winnipeg: U of Manitoba P, 1970.

Schaub, Danielle. *Reading Writers Reading: Canadian Authors' Reflections*. Edmonton: U of Alberta P, 2006.

Schloff, Linda Mack. *"And Prairie Dogs Weren't Kosher"*: Jewish Women in the Up-

per Midwest Since 1855. St. Paul: Minnesota Historical Society, 1996.

Schmitz, O. A. H. *Tagebücher*. (Typescript, 718 p). Deutsches Literaturarchiv, Marbach.

Schroeder, Andreas. *Dustship Glory*. Toronto: Doubleday, 1986.

Shakespeare, William. *Richard II*. Ed. Francis Dolan. London: Penguin, 2000.

Sheshandri, Vijay. *Beyond the Walls: Women in the Novels of Shashi Deshpande and Margaret Laurence*. New Delhi: Creative, 2003.

Senior, Olive. "Rejected Text for a Tourist Brochure." *Over the Roofs of the World*. Toronto: Insomniac, 2005. 53-54.

Sheen, Erica. "Introduction." *The Classic Novel: From Page to Screen*. Manchester: Manchester UP, 2000.

Sheinbaum, John J. "Progressive Rock and the Inversion of Musical Values." *Progressive Rock Reconsidered*. Ed. Kevin Holm-Hudson. New York: Routledge, 2002. 21-42.

Shepard, R. Bruce. *Deemed Unsuitable: Blacks from Oklahoma Move to the Canadian Prairies in Search of Equality in the Early 20th Century Only to Find Racism in their New Home*. Toronto: Umbrella, 1997.

Sigurdson, Richard. "John Diefenbaker's One Canada and the Legacy of Unhyphenated Canadianism. *The Diefenbaker Legacy: Canadian Politics, Law and Society Since 1957*. Ed. Donald C. Story and R. Bruce Shepard. Regina: CPRC, 1998. 71-86.

Simmel, Georg. "Introduction to 'The Stranger.'" *Sociological Theory in the Classical Era: Texts and Readings*. Ed. Laura Desfor Edles and Scott Appelrouth. London: Pine Forge, 2005. 275-279.

Sinding, Michael. "Assembling Spaces: The Conceptual Structure of Allegory." *Style* 36.3 (2002): 503-23.

Smith, A. J. M. "Wanted: Canadian Criticism." *The Making of Modern Poetry in Canada*. Ed. Louis Dudek and Michael Gnarowski. Toronto: Ryerson, 1967. 31-33.

Soja, Edward W. *Thirdspace: Journeys to Los Angeles and Other Real-and-Imagined Places*. Cambridge, Mass: Blackwell, 1996.

Sontag, Susan. *Illness as Metaphor*. 1977. Harmondsworth: Penguin, 1983.

Sparrow, Fiona. *Into Africa with Margaret Laurence*. Toronto: ECW, 1993.

Spettigue, Douglas O. "Felix, Elsa, André Gide and Others: Some Unpublished Letters of F. P. Greve." *Canadian Literature* 134 (Autumn 1992): 9-39.

Spettigue, Douglas O. *FPG: The European Years*. [Ottawa]: Oberon Press, 1973.

Spettigue, Douglas O., and Paul Hjartarson. Introduction. Freytag-Loringhoven,

Baroness Elsa 9-40.

Sproxton, Birk, ed. *Trace: Prairie Writers on Writing*. Winnipeg: Turnstone, 1986.

Staines, David. "Margaret Laurence." *Dictionary of Literary Biography*. Vol. 53. *Canadian Writers since 1960*. First Series. Ed. W. H. New. Detroit: Gale, 1986. 261-69.

Staines, David, ed. *Margaret Laurence: Critical Reflections*. Ottawa: U of Ottawa P, 2001.

Stam, Robert. "Introduction: The Theory and Practice of Adaptation." *Literature and Film: A Guide to the Theory and Practice of Film Adaptation*. Ed. Robert Stam and Alessandra Raengo. Oxford: Blackwell, 2005.

Stamp, Robert M., ed. *Writing the Terrain: Travelling Through Alberta With the Poets*. Calgary: U of Calgary P, 2005.

Stebelsky, Ihor. "The Resettlement of Ukrainian Refugees in Canada after the Second World War." *Canada's Ukrainians: Negotiating an Identity*. Ed. Lubomyr Luciuk and Stella Hryniuk. Toronto: U of Toronto P, 1991. 121-154.

Steck, Warren. Letter. *StarPhoenix* [Saskatoon] 28 Feb. 2002: A14.

Steele, Charles. *Taking Stock: The Calgary Conference on the Canadian Novel*. Downsview: ECW, 1982.

Stegner, Wallace. *Where the Bluebird Sings to the Lemonade Springs: Living and Writing in the West*. New York: Penguin, 1992.

Stegner, Wallace. *Wolf Willow: A History, a Story, and a Memory of the Last Plains Frontier*. 1962. New York: Penguin, 1990.

Stephens, Donald G., ed. *Writers of the Prairies*. Vancouver: U of British Columbia P, 1973.

Stewart, Michael. *The Time of the Gypsies*. Oxford: Westview, 1997.

Stewart, Sandy. *A Pictorial History of Radio in Canada*. Toronto: Gage, 1975.

Stobie, Margaret. *Frederick Philip Grove*. New York: Twayne, 1973.

Stockwell, Peter. *Cognitive Poetics: An Introduction*. London: Routledge, 2002.

Stouck, David. Rev. of *The Diviners*, by Margaret Laurence. *The West Coast Review* 10.1 (1975): 43-46.

Stouck, David, ed. *Sinclair Ross's* As for Me and My House: *Five Decades of Criticism*. Toronto: U of Toronto P, 1991.

Stovel, Nora Foster. *Divining Margaret Laurence: A Critical Study of Her Complete Writings*. Montreal: McGill-Queen's UP, 2008.

Stovel, Nora Foster. "'The Sleeping Giant': The Influence of Nigerian Literature on Margaret Laurence's Manawaka Fiction, as Illustrated by *Long Drums and Cannons: Nigerian Dramatists and Novelists*." *Postcolonial Subjects: Canadian and Australian Perspectives.* Ed Miroslawa Buchholtz. Torun: Copernicus UP, 2004. 81-98.

Stratton, Florence. "Cartographic Lessons: Susanna Moodie's *Roughing It in the Bush* and Thomas King's *Green Grass, Running Water.*" *Canadian Literature* 161.2 (1999): 82-102.

Stubbs, Andrew. *Myth, Origins, Magic: A Study of Form in Eli Mandel's Writing.* Winnipeg: Turnstone, 1993.

Sugars, Cynthia. "Introduction: Unhomely States." *Unhomely States: Theorizing English-Canadian Postcolonialism.* Ed. Cynthia Sugars. Peterborough: Broadview, 2004. xiii-xxv.

Sullivan, Rosemary. "An Interview with Margaret Laurence." Woodcock, *A Place to Stand On* 61-79.

Sure-Deth. Advertisement. *Grain Growers' Guide* 29 Mar. 1916: 37.

Swayze, Walter E. "Margaret Laurence: Novelist-as-Poet." *New Perspectives on Margaret Laurence: Poetic Narrative, Multiculturalism, and Feminism.* Ed. Greta M.K. McCormick Coger. Westport, CT: Greenwood Press, 1996. 3-16.

Swift, Jonathan. *Historical and Political Tracts, Irish.* London: Bell, 1905. *Prose Works,* v. 7. (Grove Library Collection, University of Manitoba Archives.)

Swift, Jonathan. *Prosaschriften.* Herausgegeben, eingeleitet und kommentiert von Felix Paul Greve. Berlin: Oesterheld, 1909-1910.

Symons, R. D. *Silton Seasons: From the Diary of a Countryman.* Toronto: Doubleday, 1975.

Tapping, Craig. "Margaret Laurence and Africa." *Gunnars* 65–80.

Taylor. Memo to Mr. Harkin. 17 June 1932. National Archives, Ottawa, Canada. RG84, Canadian Parks Service, ser. A-2-a, vol. 157, reel T-12914, file U263.

Tefs, Wayne A. "Rudy Wiebe: Mystery and Reality." *Mosaic* 11.4 (1978): 155-58.

Thacker, Robert. "Erasing the Forty-Ninth Parallel: Nationalism, Prairie Criticism, and the Case of Wallace Stegner." *Essays on Canadian Writing* 61 (1997): 179-202.

Thacker, Robert. *The Great Prairie Fact and Literary Imagination.* Albuquerque: U of New Mexico, 1989.

The Pedlar. Dir. and screenplay by Allan Kroeker. NFB, 1982.

Thomas, Audrey. "A Broken Wand?" *Canadian Literature* 62 (1974): 89-91.

Thomas, Clara. "'Martha Ostenso's Trial of Strength." *Writers of the Prairies.* Ed. Donald G. Stephens. Vancouver: U of British Columbia P, 1971. 39-50.

Thomas, Clara. "'Morning Yet on Creation Day': A Study of *This Side Jordan.*" Woodcock, *A Place to Stand On* 93-105.

Thomas, Clara. "Myth and Manitoba in *The Diviners*." *The Canadian Novel: Here and Now*. Ed. John Moss. Toronto: N C, 1978. 103-117.

Thomas, Clara. "'Planted Firmly In Some Soil:' Margaret Laurence and the Canadian Tradition in Fiction." Nicholson 1-15.

Thomas, Peter. *Robert Kroetsch*. Vancouver: Douglas, 1980.

Thompson, John Herd. *Forging the Prairie West*. Toronto: Oxford UP, 1998.

Thorburn, A. Letter to W.D. Perley. 23 April 1888. National Archives, Ottawa, Canada. RG17, Agriculture, vol. 574, docket 64993.

Tiefensee, Dianne. *"The Old Dualities": Deconstructing Robert Kroetsch and his Critics*. Montreal: McGill-Queen's UP, 1994.

Tiessen, Hildi Froese, and Peter Hinchcliffe, eds. *Acts of Concealment: Mennonite/s Writing in Canada*. Waterloo, ON: U of Waterloo P, 1992.

Tomaševič, Nebojša Bato and Rajko Djuric. *Gypsies of the World*. New York: Henry Holt, 1988.

"Torrington, Alberta's Claim to Notoriety!" 12 Sept. 2001 http://www.roadtripamerica.com/places/gopher.htm

"Town Declares Gopher Emergency." *Red Deer Advocate* 23 June 2001: 5.

Tudor King. Dir. and screenplay by Allan Kroeker. NFB, 1979.

Urquhart, Jane. Introduction. *The Penguin Book of Canadian Short Stories*. Toronto: Penguin, 2007. ix-xv.

Valgardson, W. D. "A Place of One's Own." *Red Dust*. Ottawa: Oberon, 1978. 48-72.

Valgardson, W. D. Interview with Allan Kroeker. NFB document on "A Place of One's Own." 28 May 1980.

Vanderhaeghe, Guy. "'Brand Name' vs. 'No-Name': A Half-Century of the Representation of Western Canadian Cities in Fiction." Ring 111-129.

Van Herk, Aritha. "Prairie as Flat as . . . ." *A Frozen Tongue*. Sydney: Dangaroo, 1992. 127-38.

Van Herk, Aritha. "Women Writers and the Prairie: Spies in an Indifferent Landscape." *A Frozen Tongue*. Sydney: Dangaroo, 1992. 139-51.

Von Maltzahn, Nicholas. "Guy Vanderhaeghe." *Profiles in Canadian Literature*. Ed. Jeffrey M. Heath. Vol. 8. Toronto: Dundurn, 1991. 139-146.

Wah, Fred. "From *Diamond Grill*." Bennett and Brown 829-42.

Wah, Fred. "Half-Bred Poetics." *Faking It: Poetics & Hybridity: Critical Writing 1984-1999*. Edmonton: NeWest, 2000. 71-96.

Wah, Fred. *Faking It: Poetics & Hybridity: Critical Writing 1984-1999*. Edmonton: NeWest, 2000.

Waiser, Bill. *Saskatchewan: A New History*. Calgary: Fifth, 2005.

Wardhaugh, Robert, ed. *Toward Defining the Prairies: Region, Culture, and History*. Winnipeg: U of Manitoba, 2001.

Warwick, Susan. "Margaret Laurence: An Annotated Bibliography." *The Annotated Bibliography of Canada's Major Authors*. Vol. 1. Ed. Robert Lecker and David Jack. Downsview: ECW, 1979. 47-101.

Waugh, Thomas. *The Romance of Transgression in Canada*. Montreal: McGill-Queen's UP, 2006.

Wayman, Tom. "Marty and Zieroth: Two Writers from Elsewhere." *A Country Not Considered: Canada, Culture, Work*. Toronto: Anansi, 1993. 36-76.

Weakerthans, The. "Confessions of a Futon-Revolutionist." *Fallow*. Lyric by John K. Samson. G7 Welcoming Committee Records, 1997.

Weakerthans, The. "Left and Leaving." *Left and Leaving*. Lyric by John K. Samson. G7 Welcoming Committee Records, 2000.

Weeks, Edward. Rev. of *The Diviners*, by Margaret Laurence. *Atlantic Monthly* June 1974: 108-109.

"Welcome to Eston." 7 Sept. 2000 <http://www3.sk.sympatico.ca/estonsk/>.

Whitaker, Reg. "Immigration Policy." *The Oxford Companion to Canadian History*. Ed. Gerald Hallowell. Toronto: Oxford UP, 2004. 303-305.

Whitaker, Reg. *Canadian Immigration Policy Since Confederation*. Ottawa: CHA, 1991.

Whitcomb, Ed. *A Short History of Saskatchewan*. Ottawa: Sea to Sea, 2005.

White, Ed. "Views From Both Sides Of The Fence." *Western Producer* 4 May 2000. 28 Aug. 2001 http://www.producer.com/articles/20000504/special_report/20000504huntfarm2_p.html.

White, Richard. "'Are You an Environmentalist or Do You Work for a Living?': Work and Nature." Cronon 171-85.

"Who is the Roughrider Mascot?" 7 Sept. 2000. http://www.ensu.ucalgary.ca/~terry/riders/faq/node13.html.

Wiebe, Rudy. *A Discovery of Strangers*. 1994. Toronto: Vintage, 1995.

Wiebe, Rudy. Introduction. *Stories from Western Canada*. Toronto: Macmillan, 1972. ix-xiv.

Wiebe, Rudy. "Tudor King." *Where is the Voice Coming From?* Toronto: McClelland & Stewart, 1974.

Wiens, Jason. "The Prairies as Cosmopolitan Space: Recent 'Prairie' Poetry." Wardhaugh151-64.

Wilde, Oscar. *Lehren und Sprüche für die reifere Jugend*. Deutsch von Felix Paul

Greve. München: In Commission, J. Littauer, Kunsthandlung, [1902].

Williams, Raymond. *The Country and the City*. New York: Oxford UP, 1973.

Wolfskehl, Karl und Hanna. *Briefwechsel mit Friedrich Gundolf*. 2. Aufl. Amsterdam: Castrum Peregrini, 1977.

Woodcock, George. *Introducing Margaret Laurence's* The Stone Angel: *A Reader's Guide*. Canadian Fiction Studies. Toronto: General, 1989.

Woodcock, George. Introduction. *The Canadian Novel in the Twentieth Century*. Toronto: McClelland & Stewart, 1975. vii-xi.

Woodcock, George. "The Meeting of Time and Space: Regionalism in Canadian Literature." *Northern Spring: The Flowering of Canadian Literature*. Vancouver: Douglas & McIntyre, 1987. 21-43.

Woodcock, George. "The Muse of Manawaka." *100 Great Canadians*. Edmonton: Hurtig, 1980. 157-59.

Woodcock, George. *Odysseus Ever Returning: Essays on Canadian Writers and Writings*. Toronto: McClelland & Stewart, 1970.

Woodcock, George, ed. *A Place to Stand On: Essays by and about Margaret Laurence*. Edmonton: NeWest, 1983.

Woodcock, George. "Prairie Writers and the Metis: Rudy Wiebe and Margaret Laurence." *Canadian Ethnic Studies* 14.1 (1982): 9-22.

Woodcock, George. Preface. *A Place to Stand On* 9-12.

Woods, Michael. "Fantastic Mr. Fox? Representing Animals in the Hunting Debate." *Animal Spaces, Beastly Places: New Geographies of Human-Animal Relations*. Ed. Chris Philo and Chris Wilbert. London: Routledge, 2000. 182-202.

Woodsworth, J. S. *Strangers Within Our Gates; or, Coming Canadians*. Toronto: Stephenson, 1909.

Wyile, Herb. *Speculative Fictions: Contemporary Canadian Novelists and the Writing of History*. Montreal: McGill-Queen's UP, 2002.

Wyile, Herb. *Speaking in the Past Tense: Canadian Novelists on Writing Historical Fiction*. Waterloo, Ont.: Wilfrid Laurier UP, 2007.

Xiques, Donez. *Margaret Laurence: The Making of a Writer*. Hamilton: Dundurn, 2005.

Yarwood, Richard, and Nick Evans. "Taking Stock of Farm Animals and Rurality." *Animal Spaces, Beastly Places: New Geographies of Human-Animal Relations*. Ed. Chris Philo and Chris Wilbert. London: Routledge, 2000. 98-114.

Yates, Alan. "W. O. Mitchell's *Jake and the Kid*: The Canadian Popular Radio Play as Art and Social Comment." Diss. McGill U, 1979.

Yellowman, with Barre Toelken and Tacheeni Scott. "Coyote and the Prairie Dogs." *A Coyote Reader*. Ed. William Bright. Berkeley: U of California P, 1993.

92-100.

Young, Neil. *Neil Young: Heart of Gold*. A Jonathan Demme Picture. Paramount, 2006.

Young, Neil. *Prairie Wind*. Reprise, 2005.

Zeman, Timothy. *An Annotated Bibliography of the Radio Drama of W.O. Mitchell in the Special Collections of the University of Calgary Libraries*. MA Thesis. U of Alberta, 1993.

Index